Ybor City

JUSTICE, POWER, AND POLITICS
Coeditors

Heather Ann Thompson
Rhonda Y. Williams

Editorial Advisory Board

Peniel E. Joseph
Daryl Maeda
Barbara Ransby
Vicki L. Ruiz
Marc Stein

The Justice, Power, and Politics series publishes new works in history that explore the myriad struggles for justice, battles for power, and shifts in politics that have shaped the United States over time. Through the lenses of justice, power, and politics, the series seeks to broaden scholarly debates about America's past as well as to inform public discussions about its future.

A complete list of books published in Justice, Power, and Politics is available at https://uncpress.org/series/justice-power-politics.

Ybor City

Crucible of the Latina South

Sarah McNamara

The University of North Carolina Press CHAPEL HILL

This book was published with the assistance of the Fred W. Morrison
Fund of the University of North Carolina Press.

Set in Merope Basic by Westchester Publishing Services
Manufactured in the United States of America

Library of Congress Cataloging-in-Publication Data
Names: McNamara, Sarah, 1987– author.
Title: Ybor City : crucible of the Latina South / Sarah McNamara.
Other titles: Justice, power, and politics.
Description: Chapel Hill : The University of North Carolina Press, [2023] | Series: Justice,
    power, and politics | Includes bibliographical references and index.
Identifiers: LCCN 2022036014 | ISBN 9781469668154 (cloth ; alk. paper) |
    ISBN 9781469668161 (pbk. ; alk. paper) | ISBN 9781469668178 (ebook)
Subjects: LCSH: Cubans—Florida—Tampa—History. | Cuban American women—Florida—
    Tampa—History. | Cuban Americans—Florida—Tampa—Social conditions. | Ethnic
    attitudes—Florida—Tampa—History. | Women cigar makers—Political activity—
    Florida—Tampa. | Anti-fascist movements—Florida—Tampa. | Cigar industry—
    Florida—Tampa—History. | Cubans—Political activity—Florida—Tampa. |
    Immigrants—Florida—Tampa—History. | Immigrants—Political activity—
    Florida—Tampa. | Ybor City (Tampa, Fla.)—History. | Ybor City (Tampa, Fla.)—
    Race relations—History. | Cuba—History—Autonomy and independence movements.
Classification: LCC F319.T2 M36 2023 | DDC 975.9/65004687291—dc23/eng/20220817
LC record available at https://lccn.loc.gov/2022036014

Cover illustration: Tobacco leaf © Oleksii Bernaz/Alamy Stock Vector.

Illustration opposite introduction: Woman rolling Cuban tobacco at the Cuesta Rey and
Company cigar factory, Ybor City, 1950. Burgert Brothers Collection, University of South
Florida Libraries–Tampa Special Collections, Tampa, Florida.

To my grandmother, Norma Alfonso, who taught me to remember.
To my grandfather, Gus Alfonso, who told me stories.
To my parents, Andi and Jim McNamara, who taught me to question.
To my sister, Katie McNamara, who learned with me.

Contents

Illustrations and Map

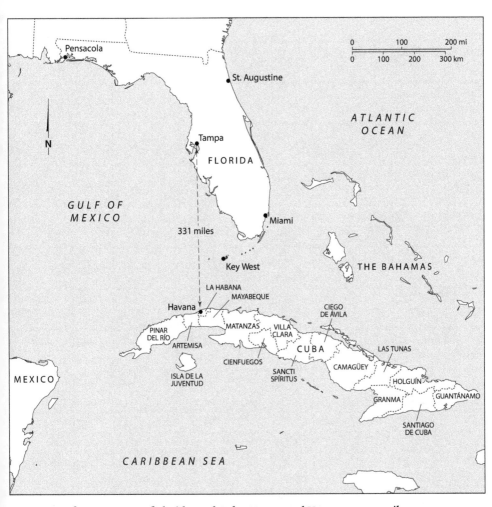

Map of Tampa, state of Florida, and Cuba. Tampa and Havana are 331 miles apart.

Ybor City

Searching

Amelia Alvarez was born in Cuba when the island was a Spanish colony. Yet by Amelia's ninth birthday, her home as she knew it no longer existed. The Cuban War for Independence, which U.S. imperial ambitions turned into the Cuban–Spanish–Puerto Rican–Filipino–American War, brought an end to Cuba's colonial status as well as Cubans' hopes for a truly independent island.[1] When Amelia turned sixteen, U.S. troops occupied Cuba for the second time in her life. That year, 1906, she boarded the steamship *Olivette* and sailed 110 miles from the Port of Havana to Key West. Soft winds from the Florida Straits wrapped around Amelia as she passed through immigration and rested for a night. The next morning, she climbed aboard the same boat and journeyed another 250 miles northward through the warm waves of the Gulf of Mexico. Once the ship docked, Amelia descended the gangway and walked into Tampa, Florida.[2]

At the turn of the twentieth century, Tampa brimmed with chaotic possibility. Sounds of Spanish and English hovered in the heavy, humid air as Amelia navigated the throngs of people who crowded the port. More than one hundred passengers charged forward with their luggage in hand, while stevedores unloaded bales of Cuban tobacco leaves from the ship's hold.[3] Thirty years earlier, this swampy town featured little more than an obscure military outpost and a settlement of sweaty Confederates. But by the time of Amelia's arrival, the Cuban cigar industry had changed nearly everything. Black and white immigrants, primarily from Cuba, along with others from Spain, Italy, and Puerto Rico, collided in Tampa as they searched for work in the city's new cigar factories. Once hired, cigar workers "stripped, sorted, and bunched [tobacco] leaves," then "rolled, banded, and boxed cigars."[4] The labor of these women and men transformed Tampa into the leading industrial center of the state, while their bodies, cultures, and politics created an international borderland in Jim Crow Florida.[5] On the dock, Amelia stayed near her family, for she had not come alone. Her sister and brother-in-law, their two children, and three aunts arrived together with fifty-six dollars between them. As the family of eight emerged from the bustling masses, they likely boarded a streetcar to carry them six miles down the road to their new home in a neighborhood called Ybor City.[6]

To Amelia, Ybor must have felt familiar and foreign at the same time. Red-brick buildings with Moorish arches lined the streets, while ornate wrought iron twisted across glass windows and framed outdoor patios. Architectural remnants of colonial Spain seemed to echo through the streets, but it was the politics of Cuban independence that lived in people's homes. Some of Amelia's neighbors told tales of when José Martí, the famed Cuban poet and revolutionary, organized and collaborated with cigar workers to bring an end to Spanish rule in Cuba. Although this fight ended in 1898, when Amelia was nine years old, the community she joined in Ybor remained unapologetically anticolonial, prolabor, and radically leftist in their self-proclaimed exile. From the perspective of Amelia's neighbors, Ybor City served as their sanctuary from the restrictive imperialist agendas and the oppressive, anti-labor, antidemocratic conservative forces that lingered in their homeland even after the Spanish relinquished claim over the island. The two-story Centro Obrero (Labor Temple) stood at the helm of this neighborhood and operated as the space where women and men organized unions, planned strike actions, and created a culture of labor on their own terms. Cigar factories defined the city landscape and separated Ybor's immigrants from Tampa's Anglo residents—a racialized border that likely seemed uniquely American.[7] De jure segregation generally did not exist in Cuba during Amelia's lifetime, but de facto segregation did and Amelia likely recognized the practice.[8] As a Cuban woman with white skin, however, being the subject of segregation would have been a new experience that made her acutely aware of her place within the South's racial hierarchy.[9]

Inside Ybor City, Amelia found acceptance. The things that Anglos believed made her seem different—her appearance, her labor, her politics, her traditions, and her language—were foundational elements that bonded this immigrant community. Despite living in a new country, Amelia never had a problem with communication because nearly everyone in Ybor spoke Spanish, and those who did not learned upon arrival.[10] Sicilian grocers transformed their markets into hybrid bodegas as they sold Spanish chorizo alongside Italian pickled vegetables and elevated, what is now known as, the Cuban sandwich. The local version of this delicacy stacked layers of mojo-marinated roasted pork, boiled ham, and hard salami on slices of Cuban bread dressed with a swipe of yellow mustard, a piece of Swiss cheese, and a sliver of crisp dill pickle.[11] According to community lore, the last three ingredients reflected the food traditions of Jewish merchants who came to Tampa in search of refuge from the escalation of anti-Semitism in Romania and Germany. Many of these families sold fabrics, clothing, shoes, and auto parts in dry goods stores, while others used their profits to purchase cigar factories of their own.[12]

Spanish-language newspapers thrived in Ybor and reported daily news from Havana, Madrid, Key West, and Tampa. This vibrant print culture not only kept Amelia and her neighbors informed of global affairs and local events but made Ybor City an integral hub within a cross-national network of leftist activism and intellectualism that reached from the Caribbean to the Americas and across the Atlantic Ocean. As Amelia walked through the streets of Ybor City, she may have brushed shoulders with women such as Luisa Capetillo and Luisa Moreno—Latina feminist labor organizers and leftist thinkers—as well as Eugene V. Debs and Elizabeth Gurley Flynn—leaders of the socialist and communist movements—all of whom visited, organized, or sought refuge from political persecution in Ybor City. Each Saturday, the Afro-Cuban rhythms of rumba and the melodies of danzón, once outlawed in Spanish-controlled Cuba, spilled out from the ballrooms of the *centros* (mutual aid societies) and filled the streets.[13] Yet as Amelia twirled across the dance floor of the Círculo Cubano (Cuban Club), she would have noticed that the Black Cuban women and men who worked beside her in the cigar factory were absent from this space. According to her neighbors, when the city of Tampa annexed Ybor City and made it part of Hillsborough County in 1887, Anglo political powerholders mandated that the centros segregate their membership and create a separate club for Afro-Cubans. La Sociedad de la Unión Martí-Maceo, the mutual aid society built by and for Black Cubans, emerged as a result of this moment.[14] The Ybor City of Amelia's youth was a place where multiracial, multiethnic Latina/o self-determination endured under the watchful eye of a reconstructed southern order.

After nearly two years of living and working in Ybor, and shortly after celebrating her seventeenth birthday, Amelia met and married a Spanish immigrant named Pedro Blanco.[15] The young couple moved down the street and rented a house near their families. When Amelia looked out her front door she would have seen rows of identical, whitewashed, shotgun houses that sat on narrow lots and flanked Ybor City's wide dirt roads. In many ways, Amelia's neighborhood was the turn-of-the-century version of a cheap housing development—a company town built for profit, not for comfort. In wintertime, families pasted old newspapers to the walls in hope of stopping cold air from seeping into the house. During summertime, the wooden planks expanded and softened from the inescapable humidity that penetrated the wood. Although the casitas were imperfect, people made do. These homes, flaws and all, were better than the lodgings most cigar workers could access in Cuba or in smaller cigar-working towns such as Key West. Amelia spent her days in the cigar factory and her nights gossiping on her front porch or gambling with other women in secret.[16] Each night after dinner, her husband joined the men of Ybor at one of the local cantinas, where the sounds of clinking dominoes cut through the smoke-filled room and the scent of whiskey clashed with the smell of sweet tobacco and the bellows of masculine laughter. I imagine that, in the absence of men, Amelia and her friends talked about everything from politics and children to money and memories of Cuba, Spain, and Italy.[17]

Amelia created a life in Ybor City, but she never fully let go of the island. She and Pedro had four children—Delia, Pedro, Margot, and Dalia—yet only the last three survived infancy.[18] Her sister, Concepción Camero, rented the house next door, until she and her three sons moved to Puerto Rico, where they stayed. Amelia visited her parents and siblings in Cuba roughly once a decade and always in July. At first, she traveled by water, retracing her original path to Tampa. By the 1940s, however, the steamships stopped sailing and Amelia flew Pan American Airways. Every time Amelia left Florida she used her Cuban passport because she never applied for U.S. citizenship. Perhaps U.S. citizenship seemed unnecessary, perhaps it seemed impossible to obtain, or perhaps Cuban citizenship was a part of herself she never wished to surrender. In 1952, at the age of sixty-three, Amelia passed away and was buried in Ybor City, Florida.[19]

I learned about Amelia when I was a teenager. My grandmother, Norma Alfonso, showed me an article she clipped from the *Tampa Tribune* in 1990, roughly twelve years earlier. "Sarah, come look at this," she yelled, calling me over to her rose-colored kitchen island. On the counter my grandma placed a white, two-inch, three-ringed binder I had seen many times before. Norma, who was born in Ybor City in 1931, saved anything and everything she found about the old neighborhood. Placemats from lunch counters, pamphlets from museums, excerpts from books, and articles from newspapers all found their way into her portable archive. As I took a seat in the kitchen, my grandmother slipped the pristine clipping from its acetate sleeve, extended her finger, and pointed at two women in a reprinted photograph. "This is Abuela Amelia," she said, "and here's her daughter, your aunt Margot." The black-and-white image captured a sea of women linked arm in arm marching through what I recognized as La Avenida Séptima (Seventh Avenue), the main thoroughfare of Ybor City. As I sat there gazing at the picture, Norma drew two arrows on the clipping and labeled the women in our family.

For as long as I can remember, my grandmother was on a one-woman mission to be sure my sister and I never forgot Ybor City. She drove us through the neighborhood, told us stories of our families, and kept traditions alive. Even before I saw the clipping, I knew Amelia was my grandmother's favorite grandparent. Like Norma, she hated the beach but loved to read. Amelia had a talent for cigar making, a passion for bingo playing, and infectious joie de vivre.[20] Those who knew her say she was loud and outspoken, a family trait that has survived generations. According to my grandfather, Gus Alfonso, Norma's husband, "Amelia was an activist who was always up to something" and the foil to his self-proclaimed respectable, rule-abiding family.[21] In reality, his father was a member and organizer of the Communist Party USA (CPUSA)—a truth he once revealed with a whisper and a look that made clear we would never revisit the subject. Despite the many stories Norma shared, she never told me the context of the image. Instead, I had to search for this answer on my own. In the process, I found that there was much more to Ybor City and the women in my family than my grandma was willing to explain. After all, sometimes it is the stories we hold back, rather than the ones we share, that reveal the essence of who we are.

My grandma passed away years before I discovered the truth behind the photo of Amelia. But when I did, it shifted my understanding of both the Ybor community and the women who lived there. The picture depicted the day in 1937, when Norma was five years old, when 5,000 Latinas from Ybor protested the rise of fascism in Spain and the United States' refusal to condemn it.[22] Amelia was part of this coalition of women who, during that decade, joined the ranks of Cuban and Spanish antifascists as they vocally opposed the Spanish Civil War abroad and Jim Crow at home, at least the ways Jim Crow applied to themselves and their community.[23] African Americans and Ybor Latinas/os did not create a cross-ethnic, interracial coalition for economic equality and civil rights during this period. In fact, such an effort never even began. What emerged instead was an environment where Latinas/os and Black Americans fought distinct battles that served what each community understood as their independent concerns. The activism of Amelia, and women like her, derived from an internationalist commitment to anti-imperialism, anticolonialism, and radical leftist politics inherited from their ancestors. Throughout her life, Amelia belonged to unions, attended meetings at the Ybor Labor Temple, and participated in strikes. Collective action came naturally to Amelia, but it would have felt foreign, perhaps even dangerous and un-American, to her granddaughter. Unlike the generations of people who fought to live in Ybor City, the survival of

Women in antifascist march, Seventh Avenue, Ybor City, May 1937. Handwriting is that of Norma Alfonso, author's grandmother. Author's collection.

Norma's generation depended on their transition out of the neighborhood—a process that required the remaking of their politics and the remaking of themselves.

Norma's Ybor City was different from the place that pulled Amelia to Florida's southern shores near the turn of the twentieth century. Cigars fell out of fashion in the 1930s, in part because they were a luxury few could afford in the midst of the Great Depression. The world, instead, developed a cheap cigarette addiction and replaced the slow draw of Ybor City's famed El Príncipe de Gales brand of cigars with the quick burn of North Carolina's Lucky Strikes.[24] This market shift devastated the industry that once made the city of Tampa a manufacturing powerhouse and pushed many Latinos, often the highest-paid cigar workers, into unemployment or underemployment. Desperate for work, many Latinas/os left the city and went to New York and Pennsylvania in search of work or assistance from the Works Progress

Administration (WPA). Much like African Americans in Tampa and throughout the South, Latinas/os, regardless of their citizenship status, had difficulty gaining access to relief work in this town. Powerholding Anglos in Tampa had the authority to determine who was and was not a member of the deserving poor, and they privileged native-born Anglos, like themselves, when it came to dolling out the limited spaces on WPA rosters. Norma's father—Amelia's only son, Pedro—was one of thousands of men who drifted in and out of cigar factories throughout the Depression. In 1930, at the age of twenty, Pedro held the esteemed, high-paying position of "hand roller," yet by 1936 he worked as an iceman and later as a delivery driver. Pedro's experience was typical of thousands of men in Ybor City. Those once trained as artisans never imagined they would be desperate enough to accept unskilled positions, but during the Depression they had no other choice. Like many men in Ybor during this era, Pedro vacillated between head of household and living with his wife's parents as an employed yet secondary contributor. As the heyday of the "clear Havana" handmade cigar industry dwindled, so too did men's pseudo monopoly on cigar making and steady wages.[25]

Amelia was a cigar maker in a large factory when my grandmother was young, a position that would have been difficult for her to hold ten years earlier. Both in Havana and in Ybor City, cigar making was highly skilled work, men's work, and few women occupied this professional space. Instead, women were among the many cigar workers (a term reserved to describe all laborers in the cigar industry) who performed other jobs within the factories. At the height of the industry, most women spent their days in factory basements as *despaldilladoras* (strippers), those who ripped the stem from the tobacco leaf and prepared the raw material for production, and made a low wage. A lucky few labored on the main floor as *buncheras* (bunchers), those who sat next to or stood behind a cigar maker and prepared filler for the center of the cigar, and brought home slightly higher weekly paychecks. Other women earned a pittance assembling cigar boxes or slipping bands on finished cigars. In an attempt to preserve what was left of the Cuban cigar industry, however, Ybor City manufacturers fired skilled Latino craftsmen and hired unskilled Latina workers to take their place on the main floor as cigar makers. Not only did this decision save the handful of factories that survived the aftershock of the Depression, but it gave women a place of value within the factory and transferred economic and political power from Latinos to Latinas within households, unions, and the Ybor community. The Ybor City of Norma's youth was a place where women wielded considerable authority.

While women such as Amelia marched through the streets of Ybor City and assumed positions of influence within cigar factories, children like Norma navigated a new world. My grandmother grew up surrounded by the ghost of what the Cuban cigar industry and Ybor City used to be—central to the economic survival of broader Tampa, a reality that once gave this immigrant community local power. Norma listened to her family members tell stories of great strikes and watched as her parents, grandparents, aunts, and uncles followed in the footsteps of their ancestors as they traveled in and out of leftist political circles in an attempt to regain what the Ybor community had lost. Despite the hours women and men of the immigrant and first U.S.-born generation spent in union halls, on strike, and in the streets during the Depression years, their advocacy failed to result in an increase of salary or the establishment of a living wage within the Cuban cigar industry of Ybor City. My grandma often reminded my sister and me that although she was a part of a family with working parents, grandparents, aunts, and uncles—all of whom shared resources—both she and her brother would slice the soles of their shoes and insert cardboard to extend their length and prolong their use because new clothing was a luxury the family could not afford. The memory of poverty and the stress of struggle was not something my grandmother cherished later in life, but she did praise the soup kitchens and community storehouses that opened in Ybor City as a result of the New Deal. Access to government subsidies kept the Blanco family fed and led to new culinary inventions within the Ybor community. *Platillo* (little plate)—an eclectic combination of cooked spaghetti, sliced Vienna sausages, *sofrito* (sautéed garlic, onion, and green pepper), and canned tomato sauce mixed together and topped with a fried egg—became a nostalgic favorite, as did sweet treats such as saltine crackers topped with cream cheese and guava paste. Like many children of my grandma's generation, such assistance endeared Franklin D. Roosevelt—as well as the U.S. government—to them throughout their lifetimes.

As Norma walked through Ybor City during the 1940s, the whitewashed, wooden casitas—now aged, sun bleached, and termite-ridden—seemed to reflect the state of her community. Ybor City, indeed, was still there, but the Cuban cigar industry and the future of the neighborhood seemed as precarious as the structures that provided shelter to its residents. As a result, Latina/o parents began to encourage formal education, rather than the monetary value of early wage work, to provide their children with a path toward broader occupational opportunities, even at the cost of the family's immediate economic needs. My grandmother, along with her peers, entered

Tampa's segregated public education system, where she learned that race determined which school one attended and the stereotypes connected to being a native Spanish speaker from Ybor City in an English-speaking, Anglo-dominated, southern society. Because Norma was a Latina with light skin, understood as non-Black in broader Tampa, she received her education inside institutions designed for Anglo students. In these places, Anglo teachers used corporal punishment to discourage the use of Spanish in their classrooms, while Anglo students invoked locally created racial epithets to refer to anyone from Ybor City regardless of their race or ethnicity. Such personal experiences—combined with the knowledge of anti-leftist, anti-Latina/o intimidation and violence perpetrated by Anglos against Latinas/os in the Ybor community—led to a personal and political remaking. The children of Norma's generation did not dream of a place at the cigar makers' benches; instead, they hoped to join the cheerleading squad, participate on the school baseball team, and be seen as people who were equal and accepted by Anglo society and able to access a future that entailed a steady salary and a pathway out of poverty for themselves and their extended families. Along the way, everyone made choices as they decided who they would be in a new world.[26]

The arrival of World War II and the rise of performative patriotism during the 1950s created a space for this young generation to illustrate that they too were American and to redefine what it meant to be from Ybor City. Young Latinos served in the military and attended college or pursued vocational education with assistance from the G.I. Bill. Young Latinas sought scholarships to subsidize their pathway into academe or attended affordable trade schools to broaden their professional prospects. Meanwhile, Latinas with partners who earned a steady wage often became homemakers or did part-time work as they managed family finances, joined civic organizations, and cared for their children, extended families, and aging relatives. This shift in work, education, and identity established a new relationship between Latinas/os from Ybor and the city of Tampa, as young tampeñas/os (Tampa-born Latinas/os) settled beyond the boundaries of Ybor City, labored alongside Anglos, became a powerful voting bloc, and secured a different life for themselves and their families. Yet as this period of change swept through Ybor City and Tampa, so too did the era of urban renewal. While Latina/o leaders from Ybor City advocated for the city of Tampa to invest in the old neighborhood for posterity and tourism, Tampa politicians, city planners, and urban renewal officials sent bulldozers and wrecking balls into what remained of the old neighborhood. Norma's family home was among the hundreds of casitas Tampa tore down to make way for Interstate 4. Likewise, the city approved the razing of thousands of other houses in Ybor for supposed neighborhood improvements, which never came. The result of this destruction gave way to a sense of *latinidad* (Latina/o-ness) that lived on through memory, culture, and tradition rather than within Ybor itself.

Ybor City: Crucible of the Latina South examines the transformation of three generations of Latinas/os—one immigrant and the others U.S.-born—who struggled, worked, and dreamed in Ybor City and Tampa, Florida. It centers on the years between the movement of the Cuban cigar industry from the island to Florida in the 1860s and the rise of urban renewal's wrecking ball in the 1960s, to tell the story of how people, places, and politics become who and what they are. From the turn of the century through the 1930s, women, along with men, immigrated to Ybor, where they made cigars, raised families, and created community as they battled for just employment, supported Cuban independence, organized against fascism, and wrestled with Jim Crow. After World War II, however, their children and grandchildren negotiated a very different world. This changing social and political landscape pushed the younger generation to redefine who they were in order to survive. In the racial milieu of the South, U.S.-born Latinas and Latinos disavowed radical, leftist politics and defined themselves against Blackness to transform their image from foreign subversives to acceptable U.S. citizens. The result of this shift was the creation of a new ethnic, non-Black identity as well as proximity to Anglo society and the gain of political power.

This study explores the South as an international, multiracial borderland and argues that in this space gender played a central role in the (re)making of race, community, region, and nation. These stories, many of which center on Latinas, expand our limited understanding of women's leadership in the early movements for social and economic justice. By demonstrating how Latina/o identities and community solidarities evolved, this book illustrates the ways Latinas developed and directed political strategy to achieve economic security and political representation for themselves and their community. At times, these tactics were vehemently anti-imperialist and anti-racist, but, at others, they aligned with ideas of white supremacy as some Latinas/os bent to the pressure of Jim Crow as they sought entry into Anglo society and mainstream politics. Furthermore, this book examines the city as a space of transnational collisions. In Ybor City and Tampa, political networks and cultural identities connected the United States, Cuba, Puerto Rico, Central and South America, and Europe. Over three generations, these cross-border exchanges critically influenced the physical shape of Ybor and

Tampa as well as the political and social consciousness of the people within these places. By scrutinizing the South through the lens of gender, this story of Ybor City illustrates how Latinas and Latinos navigated the real and imagined borders that emerged, and shifted, between people and communities across space and time.

A crucial part of this story is an intimate examination of the fractures and fissures within radical leftist politics. Many histories of Latinas/os in the United States explore the rise of civil rights coalitions, power politics, and cultural nationalism, while others center on the fortitude of progressive community building. These analyses follow the efforts to reform local and national politics through collective action as women and men fought to create a sense of Latina/o-centric self-determination. Furthermore, much research celebrates the fight to dismantle racism and demolish colonialism within the United States and beyond its borders, which oftentimes centers on the might of interracial coalition building.[27] Such narratives do indeed inspire and, no doubt, constitute part of why nearly all scholarship on Ybor City privileges the immigrant generation and the force of their grassroots labor and political movements. While this book includes such moments, it also examines the personal divisions that existed and expanded within the community over time and shows that there is no clean, bilateral lens of good versus evil or oppression versus liberation.[28]

Latinas and Latinos in Ybor City, like Amelia, were not perfect radical leftist soldiers. They carried ideological contradictions, especially about race, which influenced generational political patterns. For example, in Ybor City it may have been relatively simple for someone to convince a person to join the CPUSA because of the benefit they believed the party could bring them and their community. To those who lived in Ybor, leftist politics were neither controversial nor revolutionary. In fact, many members of Ybor City declared themselves political exiles who sought shelter from the oppression of the Spanish colonial government in Cuba and saw the Ybor neighborhood as a place where they could choose their political path freely. Yet despite this penchant for leftist radicalism, it would have been difficult, if not seemingly impossible, to convince the same person to embrace portions of the CPUSA's agenda that required they march for those beyond their cultural network. The historian Natalia Molina explains that "we understand each new 'other' in relation to groups with which we are already familiar," even when that group is not physically present.[29] If we return to the women pictured marching in my grandmother's clipping, this process becomes quite clear. Latinas and Latinos in Ybor City imagined a more intimate sense of political and social kinship among themselves, Cubans on the island, and Spaniards in western Europe than they did between themselves and African Americans who lived nearby and worked in sewing rooms or in low-wage jobs within and close to Ybor City. When it came to an international struggle against fascism, many of Ybor's women and men were willing to fight a political regime they could not see. Yet when it came to the question of segregation along the U.S. color line in their own backyard, most were not willing to organize on the basis of a shared racially oppressive experience. In fact, many denied one existed and some thought African Americans had no authority to live in Ybor City.

As in other southern states, law in Florida solidified the enduring power of anti-Blackness with the establishment of segregation in the midst of Reconstruction.[30] What law did not achieve, however, social practice enforced. One of the many problems with this system was that people like Amelia did not fit neatly into the dichotomous racial landscape southern states curated. Phenotypically, Amelia's skin was white, her hair was dark, and her facial features reflected those of southern Europe. While Amelia could read, write, and speak Spanish, she never learned to read, write, or speak English. Each time Amelia crossed over from Cuba, the U.S. immigration official on duty noted her nationality and her race. Ten times they noted her nationality as Cuban, nine times they noted her race as Cuban, and one time they noted her race as Spanish.[31] These classifications were not mistakes but part of a process that racialized ethnicity upon entry and relegated Amelia, and those like her, to a non-white yet non-Black space in the United States.

The city of Tampa never established a formal, de jure system of segregation that included Latinas/os. By all accounts, under Florida law, the people of Ybor were white as long as their skin was not Black.[32] Yet at the local level, Tampa Anglos used de facto measures such as social isolation, vigilante violence, and economic exclusion to enforce difference on the basis of race and ethnicity. Signs that read "No Blacks, Dogs, or Latins Allowed" hung outside of public spaces such as Sulphur Springs, a community swimming and recreation area, while restaurant owners and theater proprietors in Tampa routinely refused service to residents of Ybor City, be their skin Black or white.[33] Anglo leaders in Tampa created the White Municipal Party and the white primary system to exclude Black women and men from voting, which also excluded from the ballot any political candidate who did not support the rule of local Anglo politicians and their white supremacist policies, including the socialists and communists Latinas/os endorsed. Those from Ybor who did not live according to these principles were vulnerable to the threat of beatings and lynchings from members of the Ku Klux Klan, the citizens' committee, or the Tampa Police Department, much as their African American neighbors were.[34] On the surface, this shared experience seems like it could have been fertile ground to establish a coalition of people of color. But that never came to fruition. Instead, Latinas/os from Ybor adapted to their surroundings and found safety by indicating that they, too, were not Black. For Latinas/os with light complexions, this tactic was not simply a result of their experiences in Florida but also reflective of racial ideologies they brought with them from Cuba and elsewhere. With time, and predominantly in the post–World War II era, Black Latinas/os who called Ybor City home began to travel in and between Tampa's African American community, and some entered civil rights circles as they joined organizations such as the National Association for the Advancement of Colored People to advocate for equality in the city.

This story of Ybor City encourages readers to rethink what it means to be of Cuban descent, live in Florida, survive in the South, and advocate for visibility and representation within the United States. Such a charge requires that people consider Latinas/os of Cuban descent as more than a singular, monolithic, conservative, political stereotype. The history of Latinas/os in Ybor City exists in the shadow of the history of Latinas/os in Miami. Although both of these communities trace their roots back to the island of Cuba, the circumstances of their migration, the development of their politics, and the creation of their communities are distinct despite the existence of a shared national heritage. For example, the Naviera coffee company—a century-old coffee mill in Ybor City that makes espresso for *café con leche* (coffee with boiled milk) and demitasse—produces different blends of coffee to satisfy the tastes of the Tampa and Miami markets. The original blend—developed for the residents of Ybor—is strong, yet it is cut with chicory, a preference that emerged with time as laboring cigar workers added the root to their espresso to stretch resources and make their grounds last longer. The Miami blend, in contrast, consists of pure, dark-roasted beans intended to mirror the taste of espresso from the island. In short, being of Cuban descent and from Ybor City or Tampa is different from being of Cuban descent and from Miami or South Florida (the present-day term used to describe Miami-Dade and Broward Counties, West Palm Beach and Palm Beach, and the Florida Keys). The distinctions between the two communities is not merely political but also cultural and evident in something as simple as coffee preference.[35]

The women and men who came to Ybor City began their migration roughly seventy years before the end of the Cuban Revolution in 1959—the moment that began the process of turning Miami into Havana USA and making the state of Florida synonymous with Cubans, Cold War politics, and anti-communism. This timeline is important. The people who went to Ybor City, decades prior, were part of the first wave of Cuban migration to Florida. They were working class, politically leftist, and multiracial and had a sense of self that conflicted with the predominantly white, pro-capitalist, middle-class and upper-class people who fled Cuba in the immediate wake of Fidel Castro's rise to power. In fact, many Ybor residents of the immigrant generation would have considered themselves as living in exile as a result of the ideas and politics of those who arrived in Miami between the late 1950s and early 1960s. During the 1950s, some of the women and men from Ybor City joined and supported the local 26th of July Movement club (the organization that supported Castro and the Cuban Revolution) and the Fair Play for Cuba Committee (the organization that advocated for the interests of the new Cuban government in the United States). Most Latinas/os from Ybor, however, were tepidly supportive observers who hoped the revolution would improve their ancestral homeland, but they were not passionate enough about this war to donate their money or dedicate their time to the cause. Few of the U.S.-born generation from Ybor City, which came of age during World War II, defined their lives in support of or in opposition to the new Cuban government because the Cuban Revolution was not their primary political focus of the era. These women and men, instead, concerned themselves with gaining political power in Florida and were successful in developing a Latina/o Democratic Party contingent.

Since Nick Nuccio—an Ybor City native—became mayor of Tampa in 1956, the city has elected only one Republican to lead Tampa. Such a voting pattern remains consistent with the election of congresspeople from Tampa—only two Republicans have been elected since the creation of Florida's 14th district in 1973. Although Tampa and Hillsborough County can swing in presidential elections, a Republican candidate has not received a majority vote in Tampa since 2008. According to the 2020 census, the area recognized as Tampa—which includes all suburbs within Hillsborough County—is the third-largest metropolitan region in Florida, behind Jacksonville and Miami, and includes roughly 1.5 million people, of whom 56 percent are non-Anglo, including 30 percent who self-identify as Latina/o or Hispanic. In this place—the third most populous state in the nation—that controls twenty-nine electoral votes and frequently determines the outcome of national elections, it is essential to understand how people become who they are. Rather than thinking of Florida as a place defined by one Latina/o community, this book urges readers to consider the state as a place with multiple Latina/o communities, many of which have different political ideologies, traditions, and concepts of self.[36]

In the pages that follow, as well as those that preceded, I have made the decision to use the term *Latina/o* rather than *Latin*, the term most commonly associated with the people of Ybor City. I do this for two reasons. First, when the women and men of Ybor City began to think of themselves as a collective community during the early twentieth century, they referred to themselves as "latinos" and to Ybor City as "la colonia latina" or "el pueblo latino" in local publications. Such terminology emerged as people began to imagine themselves as from Ybor City, which happened as they worked there, married there, and fought to survive there. These references and these words are prevalent throughout the community's Spanish-language newspapers. The term *Latin* was what Anglos called these women and men; however, even that was not consistent. Between the 1880s and the 1960s, the Tampa Anglo press used words such as *Latin American, Latin, Spanish-speaking people,* and *Cuban* to refer to those from Ybor, regardless of their ethnicity or nationality.[37] *Latina/o* invokes the historic term used by this community as the idea of being from Ybor began to emerge within the shared consciousness of the residents from this neighborhood.

Second, I use *Latina/o* to position this story within the context of Latina/o history itself. Too often, Ybor City, and even Florida, is seen as an exception—a place where latinidad is everywhere and has always existed and is therefore unnecessary for inclusion in broader and more expansive understandings of Latinas/os within the South and the nation. This assumption not only relegates the history of Latinas/os in Ybor City, and throughout Florida, to the margins, but it disconnects these women and men from the historical experiences of immigration and reactionism that they and their community navigated. In reality, the history of Latinas/os in Florida is severely understudied and misunderstood. This phenomenon affects the way historians examine Ybor City and Florida as well as how people from Ybor think of themselves in relation to new immigrant groups within the state, the region, and the nation. As one of the first people I interviewed from Ybor City told me, "*Latina/o* is a word used to describe people who have recently arrived," but "*Latin* is who you are once you've been here longer." Words and language often reflect popular narratives and have the power and the ability to create connections across communities as well as the power and the ability to rupture the acknowledgment of common experiences between people across space and time. What the women and men of Ybor City underwent from the turn of the century through the 1960s, and that the interviewee could not see or did not wish to see, is similar to what many Latina/o migrants and immigrants in the U.S. South experience today—fierce rejection from native-born, white residents of the places where new arrivals seek to establish community as well as threats to personal security and efforts of survival from state policies. Recognizing that this history is part of a bigger regional and national story allows historians, scholars, and members of the Ybor City community to consider what it means to be Latina/o in the U.S. South and Latina/o in the United States.[38]

This book includes four thematic, chronologically aligned chapters that analyze the gendered dimensions of survival, activism, and redefinition as distinct phases.[39] Chapter 1, "Building," situates the state of Florida, and the city of Tampa, as an international borderland where people and ideas competed for authority over this place as well as their independent sovereignty since the sixteenth century. It likewise follows the movement of the Cuban cigar industry from the island to Florida during the 1860s and examines the establishment and early history of Ybor City through the turn of the twentieth century. Chapter 2, "Resisting," chronicles the culture of labor unionism and leftist political ideologies that governed Latinas/os' understanding of self and guided them as they battled oppression from cigar manufacturers, vigilantes, and the city of Tampa. The focus of this chapter is the 1930s, the period during which the power of the Cuban cigar industry began to decline, but also the same era during which Latinas rose as powerful political advocates for themselves and their communities as these women fought against, what they understood was, fascism abroad and fascism at home. Chapter 3, "Surviving," explores the years from 1939 through 1946, during which the rise of national anti-radicalism collided with restrictive immigration policies that forced Latinas/os to navigate a society that barred them from access to social services as a result of a locally constructed stigma of latinidad. This chapter analyzes the ways women and men of both the immigrant and U.S.-born generations fought against these racial and ethnic stereotypes through new forms of advocacy that pushed them beyond the borders of Ybor City and, for many, left avenues to perform what ethnic Americanism meant to them in the midst of World War II. Chapter 4, "Remaking," follows Ybor City Latinas and Latinos as they remade their public image, remade their politics, and remade their community once the Cuban cigar industry fell into a state of disrepair. The lessons from this chapter illustrate how people from this community navigated latinidad against great challenges as they worked to survive and endure outside the place that gave meaning to what it meant to be from and of Ybor. Through a blend of oral histories and newspaper accounts, local and federal government documents, union and community institutional records, and *testimonios* and artifacts, this book tells the history of Florida's first sustained Latina/o community and shows how Ybor City became the crucible of the Latina South.

CHAPTER ONE

Building

> We made not only what Tampa is today,
> but the whole state of Florida. . . .
> We gave it life and placed it on the map of the United States.
> This state owes everything to us.
> —ENRIQUE PENDAS, Federal Writers' Project, 1936

A tall oak tree once stood outside the Tampa courthouse. When the bay breeze blew across the Hillsborough River and flowed into downtown, the Spanish moss that draped over the oak's long limbs swayed back and forth. Unlike the sapling palms that flanked the square, the oak tree was sturdy and older than the city itself. Over its lifetime the tree survived hurricanes, floods, and wars. It provided shade to Tocobagan and Seminole peoples and witnessed Spain, Britain, the Confederacy, and the United States compete to colonize the soil that nourished its roots. For centuries its leaves sprouted in the spring, unfurled in the summer, and fell in the winter. At one time the oak was one of many, but now it stood alone as a testament to what this land once was—a constant reminder that a new authority supplanted its dominion.[1]

It was the first Monday of September 1899. Three thousand people from Ybor City assembled along the streets of downtown Tampa to see the Labor Day parade. That day, the sun hung high and beat down with unrelenting might. The crowds of people who lined the sidewalks must have felt sweat drip down their backs, percolate on their brows, and slide across their necks as the heat of the season swelled around them. A lucky few found refuge from the sun's blinding brightness underneath the canopy of that old oak tree. As the sounds of a marching band grew louder and louder, anticipation turned to excitement. For the women, men, and children who stood in the streets that Labor Day, this event was more than a celebration of work; it was a claim to the space their labor and their politics built.[2]

Like most people who shaped Florida, those who created modern Tampa came from somewhere else. Beginning in 1886, Cuban and Spanish cigar workers followed the cigar industry from Havana to Tampa amid the resurgence of anticolonial movements in Cuba. At first these women and men arrived as exiles in search of safety from political persecution. After independence, they came as immigrants in search of a steady wage. Together these newcomers lived and labored in Ybor City—the industrial suburb on the eastern outskirts of Tampa and the stateside home of the Cuban cigar industry. By day, cigar workers labored in factories where they transformed Cuban tobacco into consumable works of art. By night, they met in cantinas, union halls, and living rooms to champion the ideals of Cuban independence and define labor equality on their own terms. To anyone downtown that Labor Day in 1899, it would have been impossible to deny that these women and men had revolutionized this place. Cigar factories now sat on the lands where cattle once grazed, and a city of immigrants emerged in a place where slavery once thrived. Tampa was no longer the "sleepy, shabby, southern town" it had been thirteen years earlier. It was the industrial center of Florida and an international hub of labor activism.[3]

A journalist from the *Tampa Morning Tribune* stood among the crowd as he watched these workers and their families flood, what he believed to be, his side of town. Courthouse Square, the ultimate rallying point of the Labor Day parade, epitomized the center of city power. It was inside this courthouse where laws were made and trials were held by the same Anglo elites who executed vigilante violence to exert their will. People talked and memory endured of when a judge left his courtroom to tie the "hangman's knot" around the neck of a mob victim. On that day, strange fruit hung from the limbs of the old oak tree while the circuit court remained in session a few steps away. To men like this in a place like this, little was more important than control—the control of race, the control of labor, the control of politics, and the control of capital. Yet as the journalist stared at the scene before him, he knew control was not so simple. These women and men were powerful, and they knew it.[4]

A procession of 1,000 Cuban cigar workers, led by the First Florida Regimental Band, crested into downtown Tampa at noon that Labor Day. There were cigar workers on wheels, on foot, and in carriages. Families cheered from the sidelines as "fifty men and boys on bicycles" wove through the parade to the beat of "popular march music" played by "two colored brass bands." Fliers that praised organized labor and the eight-hour day sprinkled from the sky as the sounds of Spanish hung suspended in the air. According to the *Tribune*, the most shocking element of the day was the pièce de résistance of the event. The "Queen of Labor, a very dark brunette" encircled by "Cuban girls arrayed in bright colors," rode on a float with a slogan that read "Labor Knows No Color, Creed, or Class." When the reporter relayed the prominence of the "dusky belle" to his readers, he proposed that the central tableau "would have been much more effective and met more approval

Hillsborough County courthouse, 1899. State Archives of Florida, Florida Memory.

from the discerning public had the attendants been colored and the queen white."[5]

From the perspective of the Anglo journalist, it was difficult to interpret all he saw. People, who he believed did not belong in this space, marched proudly through the streets as though they owned the city. In the moment, nobody tried to stop them. After the event, nobody retaliated against them. Together these women and men celebrated politics he did not support and bent the ideas of gender and womanhood that upheld his version of southern respectability. When the journalist sat down to write his article, he struggled to explain the "dusky belle" with the "very dark" hair. While it is likely this woman was Afro-Cuban, representing the centrality of interracial labor organizing to cigar workers at the turn of the century, it is also possible that she was not. Regardless of who she was, the journalist concluded that the most important fact about her was that she was not white, as he understood whiteness.[6] According to him, a more comfortable display of southern values, white beauty accompanied by Black servitude, would have made native-born Anglo-Tampans more sympathetic to the message of the day. What the *Tribune* journalist could not see was that this event was not a plea for approval but a declaration of authority and a statement of autonomy.

The Labor Day parade opens a door into the world cigar workers built. Women and men who left their homelands, crossed the Florida Strait, and sailed up the Gulf coast of this southernmost state ruptured the rules that long determined life in this place. Jim Crow—the rigid racial system of de jure and de facto segregation—faltered when these immigrants arrived, because the economy of this one-industry town depended on their labor and their presence. It was impossible to produce Cuban cigars without Cuban tobacco and Cuban cigar workers. If Tampa were to maintain its status as the industrial center of Florida and the "Cigar Capital of the World," the city had to entice these workers and the industry to stay—a fact known to Anglo, native-born elites and foreign-born Cuban cigar workers alike. It was this reality that allowed the women and men of Ybor City to march through the streets. Tampa was, after all, part theirs—a city that did not exist in isolation but whose economy, population, and politics were part of a network that reached across borders.

Tampa was a borderland—a space with "multiple claims to final authority" where nothing was static and everything was in flux.[7] As this chapter details, between 1886 and 1929, this place underwent dramatic transformation. It developed industry, became part of a cross-border economy, and emerged as a southern city with a population that was predominantly foreign-born and non-Anglo. Such change was not comfortable and required that Cuban cigar workers and native-born Anglos traverse uncharted territory as they redefined the city as well as their places within it. Women and men who came here from abroad participated in this process as they created families, committed themselves to international political movements, and established a collective sense of self. Together they negotiated class, gender, race, and politics as they turned their corner of this space, Ybor City, into one that reflected their values, their principles, and their labors. In the process, these Cuban cigar workers made Florida Latina/o.[8]

The Shifting Foundations of a Southern Borderland

Florida sits in the popular imagination as a place where latinidad has always existed. While there are reasons for this association, the history of Florida reveals a more complex story.

In 1565, the Spanish arrived on the northeast coast of Florida and established a military outpost they called St. Augustine.[9] The land on which these men built their garrison was, by no means, vacant but home to roughly 200,000 Timucua peoples who lived in thirty-five distinct chiefdoms. For hundreds of years the Timucua fished the Atlantic Ocean, planted seeds to farm crops, foraged the peninsula's piney forests, and hunted wild game as they created trade networks and negotiated political alliances between their chiefdoms and those of other Native peoples.[10] The Spaniards who founded St. Augustine were not the first Europeans to encroach on Timucua lands. Between 1520 and 1540 the expeditions of Lucas Vásquez de Ayllón, Pánfilo de Narváez, and Hernando de Soto journeyed through this space, and in 1562 the French claimed these lands as part of their new Huguenot colony that reached from South Carolina to Florida.[11] While the Timucua were weary of the Spanish, some chiefdoms recognized that the imperial ambitions of these newcomers could work in their favor and established a military alliance to expel the French from these lands. This campaign was successful.[12] As of October 1565, the Spanish declared themselves to be the only European authority in Florida, and henceforth St. Augustine became the first, permanent European settlement in North America.[13] For the remainder of the sixteenth century the relationship between the Timucua and the Spanish remained "tenuous and sporadic." While Spanish claim to Florida certainly changed the contours of this borderland, the Crown never wielded absolute control over the peninsula. Florida was, first and foremost, Native land.[14]

By the seventeenth century, St. Augustine was central to Spanish imperial claims. This "seaside presidio" served as the sole coast guard station for "600 miles of strategic sea lane" and acted as a tactical barrier between Spain's prized Caribbean colonies and the expanding reach of the British and French empires.[15] In many ways, the Spanish Crown invested in Florida as it did in California. It established a mission system, attempted to evangelize and convert Indigenous peoples to Catholicism, permitted African slavery, and tried to encourage *peninsulares* (colonists born in Spain) and high-ranking members of the colonial, Spanish elite to make Florida their home. But unlike colonial spaces on the West Coast and in the Southwest, this version of Florida did not endure.[16]

Spaniards who came to this place tended to be transient merchants, interested migrants, and soldiers on assignment. Few people intended to emigrate, and neither the ecology, the weather, nor the political landscape enticed many to reconsider. This sweltering, mosquito-laden, hurricane-prone place seemed to encourage the cultivation of disease and the wind-induced destruction of infrastructure and yielded few crops or opportunities for personal or imperial economic growth.[17] Spaniards struggled to navigate relationships with Indigenous peoples who fiercely defended their lands, their territories, and their authority over this place.[18] As a result, Spanish

Florida never developed a consistent, stable local economy rooted in agriculture and the local fabrication of products. It became, instead, a place through which things passed, both goods and people.[19] Though the Spanish permitted slavery, many enslaved women and men, whether they arrived from West Africa or were freedom seekers from neighboring southern states, were able to find refuge and liberty within Native nations.[20] By the early eighteenth century, the experience of the Spanish in Florida seemed to reflect what Luís de Velasco, the second viceroy of New Spain, pondered more than a hundred years earlier. La Florida was "too low and sandy, her countryside too poor in resources, her harbors too barred and shallow" and the Indigenous peoples who populated it too powerful "to permit practical settlement."[21] The lack of consistent colonial community, scant Spanish population, and formidable neighboring Native nations made Spanish Florida vulnerable to competing imperial claims. During the eighteenth century, the peninsula passed between Spanish and British hands twice. Then in 1821—seven months before Spain relinquished claim over Mexico—the Crown yielded Florida to the newest imperial power on the North American continent, the United States.[22]

The presence of the Spanish in Florida was by no means inconsequential. "More than three centuries of sunrises and sunsets lay between the first and final appearances of the Spanish flag" over the peninsula—"it will be the twenty-second century before the same can be said of the United States."[23] An understanding of this history, as well as the broader experience of Spanish colonialism in the North American borderlands, challenges the assumption that the United States emerged solely from an Anglo-Protestant legacy. The Spanish established St. Augustine "four decades before the founding of Jamestown," and the expansive territories of the Spanish Crown reached from coast to coast and across through dozens of Native nations.[24] This history is significant, even if obscured by contemporary master narratives. Such a story, however, is not simple. This tale does not necessarily supplant the history of British colonialism with a Spanish heritage. Instead, it illustrates the importance of recognizing the varied experiences of peoples and empires within the vast North American borderland that later included the U.S. nation-state.[25]

The history of the Spanish in Florida does not follow the pattern of California, Texas, Arizona, or New Mexico—all present-day U.S. states with a history of Spanish colonialism and high Latina/o populations. In the latter locations, a sense of being California/o, Tejana/o, or Hispana/o—all local iterations of latinidad grounded in colonial racial hierarchies, imperial claims to space, cultural exchange with Indigenous peoples, a sense of community, and political distinction — lives on to this day.[26] The same cannot be said of Florida. A sense of being Floridana/o was not a legacy the Spanish left behind when they relinquished authority over this region because it was not a place where many members of the Spanish empire chose to live or chose to stay. Florida was, as the historian Amy Turner Bushnell explains, the "hollow peninsula" with two colonial population hubs, St. Augustine on the eastern Atlantic coast and Apalachee (near present-day Pensacola) on the western Gulf coast.[27] These settlements were important defense centers and trade posts, but they were not thriving imperial metropoles that encouraged a lasting sense of place or a distinct sense of self that future generations inherited or persists today. People who saw themselves as Spanish subjects, and did not wish to live under U.S. control, went to Cuba, Texas, or Mexico before La Florida, the Spanish colony, became Florida, the U.S. territory.[28]

Florida began the process of becoming a southern state the moment the last Spanish soldier left St. Augustine on July 10, 1821.[29] The period that followed was not one of accommodation but one of reinvention. Florida did not become some political or ideological middle ground where Spanish customs and ideas fused with those of the incoming U.S. territorial government and readily accepted Indigenous authority and sovereignty.[30] Instead, new laws and customs overtook the old as the rigidity of U.S. policies replaced the fluidity of the Spanish borderlands. As the United States declared Florida a territory, the young nation solidified its claim over the southeastern region, which strengthened its might as an imperial force — conquering spaces across the North American continent and instituting government structures that reinforced its power.

Acquisition of Florida was driven by more than imagined import of U.S. control over the North American continent. Among the primary reasons the United States wished to possess and populate the continent's southernmost peninsula was to "eliminate the [Florida] province as a destination for [freedom-seeking enslaved peoples] and to remove the Seminole presence from the northern region of the colony."[31] White southerners, regardless of whether or not they were enslavers, invested in a white supremacist racial hierarchy that defined the right to citizenship, belonging, and freedom on the basis of skin color. Chattel slavery, upheld by a complex legal code instituted by individual states as well as the federal government, sought to control Black women and men, while the federal government refused the recognition of Indigenous sovereignty and barred these peoples from access to citizenship.[32] Wealthy plantation owners, middle-class merchants, and poor laborers invested in this system because it gave them status and granted them political and economic control.[33]

Spanish policies toward Africans, enslaved and free, as well as Indigenous peoples differed from those of the United States. The historian Jane Landers explains that in Spanish Florida enslaved women and men had the right to petition the court when maltreated, legally negotiate and sue for manumission, participate in trade and marketplace commerce, and take part in religious life. In theory, if not often in practice, these regulations provided limited protections to the many enslaved peoples who labored across the Spanish empire.[34] This reality in no way overrides the fact that these women and men remained unfree, and subject to abuse, and that Spaniards operated sizable plantations that depended on "labor forces [of] between 50 to 200" enslaved peoples throughout the colonial period.[35] Still, this legislation did provide some pathways to freedom for a small subset of the enslaved African population of Spanish Florida. Freedwomen and freedmen lived in St. Augustine and in autonomous communities. Such spaces did not exist in obscurity—they were recognized, and at times established, by the Spanish colonial government. During the eighteenth century, the governor of Florida supported the founding of one such place, Gracia Real de Santa Teresa de Mose—a township of freedpersons and a sanctuary for African and African American peoples who made daring escapes from lives of enslavement in the Carolinas and Georgia.[36] Sometimes Indigenous people joined these communities alongside enslaved persons.[37] Yet it was not simply the dominion of the Spanish that provided avenues for freedom-seeking immigrants and migrants to assert their liberty. Under the authority of the Seminoles, Black women and men—both bonded and free—could seek refuge and autonomy among their peoples. The Seminoles forced the Spanish to abide by their territorial boundaries, which resulted in the Crown's recognition of this Indigenous nation's claim to all lands south of Gainesville as well as the majority of non-coastal spaces in the northern region of the peninsula. When subjects of the Spanish Crown transgressed these lines, Seminoles enforced their territorial control by razing plantations, farms, and villages that abutted or trespassed on their lands.[38]

It was the white citizens of Georgia, those who lived near the Florida border, who found these practices most alarming. To them, Florida was a place where the women and men they enslaved sought illegal refuge and where mixed-race Indigenous peoples claimed land white people believed should be theirs. With the memory of the Haitian Revolution fresh in the minds of white southerners throughout the region, the fact that the Spanish Crown traded arms and munition with both free people of color and Seminole peoples bred additional anxieties among white women and men across the U.S. South. Florida, they believed, was a borderland and a wilderness that required harnessing.[39]

New laws instituted by the territorial government contributed to the remaking of Florida. Under U.S. authority, chattel slavery as well as the legislative measures that protected the institution, applied to the entire peninsula.[40] As a result, white plantation owners and wealthy white southerners migrated to Florida to expand the reach of their personal empires. These newcomers took solace in the legal protection of their investments, both landed and embodied, as they purchased acreage they believed to be unclaimed. Florida's free people of color were not safe in this new environment.[41] At first the territorial government castigated free Black women and men for fomenting discontent among enslaved peoples. Local press accused these people of being futile scalawags and "hopeless, degraded, wretched, and forbidden outcasts," whose status and presence undermined the biracial order that defined life and liberty in Florida.[42] "Discriminatory laws against free [B]lack [people]," which included "harsh punishments for minor offenses" as well as restrictive measures "aimed at eliminating emancipation and free [B]lack status," emerged in this space. In response, many free Black women and men left Florida during the early territorial years. Those who lived in or near Pensacola—on the western side of the peninsula—boarded vessels sailing to Mexico, while those who lived in or near St. Augustine—on the eastern side of the peninsula—went to Cuba and others to Haiti.[43] Although many plantation owners chose to stay, perhaps even finding new laws advantageous, some left. One such person, Zephaniah Kingsley Jr., manumitted fifty enslaved women and men "from his Florida plantations and moved them to Haiti under indentured labor contracts." Kingsley, who had mixed-race children he recognized, found himself in the precarious position of negotiating their liberty and that of their mother under this new government as he sought to preserve his property and his wealth.[44]

In addition to the considerable attention territorial authorities paid to instituting a clear division between Blackness and whiteness, they likewise sought to lay legal claim to lands they wished to control throughout the peninsula. The U.S. government's brutal Indian removal policies thrust the Seminoles into the Long Seminole War with the Florida territorial militia and the U.S. Army between 1817 and 1858. As a result of either "death in combat or deportation to Indian Territory," the Seminole population fell from roughly 5,000 people to fewer than 200.[45] In the midst of this chaos, the territorial government of Florida passed the Armed Occupation Act (AOA), which "permitted a head of family or single man capable of armed defense to claim 60 acres of land south of Gainesville and north of the Peace river."[46] An estimated 1,200 white men received 200,000 acres of Native lands under this provision, and the population of Florida increased by more than 6,000 residents, both enslaved and free.[47] From the perspective of those who governed this place, the AOA signaled success. The policy drew white people and enslaved persons to Florida and populated the southern region of the peninsula. It also continued the coordinated effort of dispossessing Seminoles of their lands and eliminating Seminoles from Florida.[48] Despite the onslaught of imperial violence within this borderland, staunch Seminole resistance ensured the survival of their community and enabled a portion of their nation to remain in their original homelands. Today the Seminole nation thrives and continues to be a political and economic force in Florida.[49]

By the 1840s, the population of territorial Florida looked similar to that of other southern states. The white settlers, often referred to as homesteaders, occupied every rung of the socioeconomic ladder. Some were lawyers, judges, and generals. Others were merchants, tradespeople, and laborers. Many were wealthy plantation owners who wished to expand their personal empires by usurping Native lands in North Florida and enslaving Black women and men to work them. All new arrivals were immigrants. Some of their neighbors, and fellow plantation owners, were once Spanish subjects who preferred to adjust to life under a new government than to surrender or sell their properties—both the land they claimed was theirs and the people they believed they owned.[50] Perhaps the most famous, or nostalgically notorious, group of people who came to the Florida Territory were those known as the "crackers." These people were poor, white farmers who relocated to Florida with their livestock and their families in pursuit of cheap and fertile land. The crackers were "highly individualistic and mobile, fiercely dedicated to popular democracy, generally possessing antipathy toward Native Americans and African Americans, and quick to anger."[51] As the population of white people grew, so too did the population of enslaved African Americans. For example, in 1830, 47 percent of the population in northern Florida—the area including Duval, St. Johns, and Nassau Counties—were enslaved Black people. Thirty years later, Alachua County, Middle Florida, and the northern Gulf coast region revealed a similar pattern. In Leon County, the district including present-day Tallahassee, 74 percent of the 12,243 residents who occupied these lands were Black and enslaved persons.[52] Together these women and men—Black, white, enslaved, and free—shaped an economy fueled by logging, cotton, cattle, and housing development. As these people felled yellow pine trees and cleared the lands essential for agriculture, "wagon caravans of [white] settlers and their [Black] slaves rolled" through North Florida "with tools and supplies needed to build homes."[53] This place that had once been a backwater yet a strategically positioned borderland from the perspective of the Spanish, the British, and U.S. southerners, now had enough obedient subjects and sufficient importance to become a state, according to the U.S. government.

The transition of Florida from territory to state happened amid the growing abolition movement and mounting tensions surrounding the imbalance of free states and slave states. Leaders of the Florida Territory lobbied southern politicians in Washington, D.C., and advocated that admission of Florida into the United States was both essential and urgent. These men made the case that because it seemed likely that Iowa would enter the Union as a free state within the next year, it was essential to admit Florida as a slave state to avoid leaving white southerners in the representative minority. Florida, they argued, had the ability to maintain the national balance of power. This tactic proved to be successful. Congress introduced a bill in January 1845 that proposed statehood for both Florida and Iowa—a solution intended to appease "slaveholding" southerners and "non-slaveholding" northerners.[54] Following approval by both houses of Congress, President John Tyler signed the bill on March 3, 1845. That day, Florida became the twenty-seventh state of the United States of America.[55]

Following acceptance into the Union, Florida politicians kept their promise and maintained the alignment of the state's principles and positions with those of its fellow southern neighbors. Despite pockets of Whig and Republican supporters, political leaders in the state capital, Tallahassee, as well as the majority of white men registered to vote aligned with the Democratic Party and supported positions of "states' rights" and calls for secession.[56] As the historian Daniel L. Schafer explains, both "states' rights" and "'Southern rights' . . . meant the implicit and unrestricted right to own [enslaved persons]." Likewise, the "defense of property rights came to mean protection of slave property from abolitionists."[57] Although many twenty-first-century Floridians insist that the state's decision to secede and join the Confederacy had nothing to do with slavery, "political leaders in Florida during the late antebellum years would have unapologetically and strenuously disagreed."[58] For example, John G. McGehee—an enslaver, Florida plantation owner, and member of the Florida political elite who assisted in the drafting of the state's constitution—stood and addressed the Florida legislature in 1861 to pronounce: "Of course, slavery is the element of all value, and [the] destruction of [slavery] destroys all that is property. [The Republican Party], now soon to take possession of the powers of government, is sectional, irresponsible to us, and, driven on by an infuriated, fanatical madness that defies all opposition, must inevitably destroy every vestige of right growing out of property in slaves."[59] These principles were central to the social, political, and economic fabric of Florida.

Abraham Lincoln did not appear on the Florida ballot in the election of November 1860, the political contest that made the Civil War inevitable in the eyes of many white southerners.[60] Despite the majority of Floridians' refusal to support Lincoln, who some mocked as "an obscure . . . man without experience in public affairs," he became the sixteenth president of the United States.[61] In response, demands for secession echoed from the northern panhandle to the southern swamplands as proslavery demonstrations erupted in cities such as Jacksonville and Tallahassee.[62] By January 1861, just two months shy of the sixteenth anniversary of Floridian statehood, delegates at the state's Constitutional Convention voted to secede from the United States. Representatives from Florida then traveled to a convention in Montgomery, Alabama, where they joined white men from Mississippi, South Carolina, Georgia, Louisiana, and, of course, the hosting state. Together this group of enslavers and white men founded the Confederate States of America and elected Jefferson Davis as their president.[63]

Florida entered the Civil War, along with its Confederate comrades, in April 1861. However, most Floridians' experiences during the war differed sharply from those of their compatriots in states such as Virginia, Tennessee, and Georgia. While residents of these states endured a high concentration of battles and incursions, which left their lands and families war-torn and economically depressed, Floridians experienced comparatively minor physical destruction and fighting in their homelands. Florida emerged from the Civil War relatively unscathed. There were three primary battles in the state, one of which devastated Jacksonville's infrastructure and damaged its port. Yet all things considered, the Sunshine State was by no means the center of the action or a high priority for either the United States or the Confederacy. Despite this reality, white Floridians did not seem to lack enthusiasm for the Stars and Bars. According to the historian Robert A. Taylor, between 14,000 and 15,000 men, out of the 140,000 people who lived in Florida, or just over 10 percent of the total population, joined the Confederate army by choice or by conscription. This was the highest proportion of Confederate volunteers from any southern state.[64] A minority of these men, however, protected the peninsula they called home. Instead, they served in the Army of Northern Virginia and the Army of Tennessee as they defended their principles in fields as famous as Gettysburg.[65]

In addition to the troops Florida supplied the Confederate army, the state provided over 50,000 heads of cattle to the war effort as well as thousands of pounds of salt necessary to cure the meat and tan the leather yielded from the slaughter of these animals. Although lauded as the "granary of the Confederacy" and the "garden farm" of the South, Florida never managed to provide enough food to prevent hunger among the Confederate ranks.[66] This was not simply a question of production but a problem with shipment. U.S. Army blockades that surrounded the state's major ports made it difficult to move goods. Deft and capital-driven smugglers navigated these murky waters as best they could, while plantation owners and small farmers tried to calculate whether their sacrifice was worth the resulting damage to their economic well-being.[67] As the defeat of the Confederacy began to seem inevitable, emboldened U.S. troops increasingly waded through Florida's swamps and onto the mainland to encourage enslaved men to join their ranks. While many did, the majority remained on the peninsula. On April 9, 1865, after four years of war, the Confederacy surrendered to the U.S. Army, and by May 20, 1865, federal troops rode into Tallahassee and raised the flag of the United States over Florida's capitol. Years later, Black women and men celebrated this day as Emancipation Day.

The same anti-Black sentiments and desires that led to the Civil War—the prevention of Black Americans from accessing the rights and privileges of citizenship—continued to structure postwar politics in Florida.[68] John Darling of Tampa, one of the delegates who supported secession, reflected on his position with unwavering conviction years later. Darling explained that secession was, and in his eyes remained, "a rightful and proper remedy to break down the policy of Negro emancipation believed to be intended by the Republican Administration." John Sanderson, the Vermont-born Confederate congressman, enslaver, and plantation owner from Duval County, noted that his actions represented the principles of the "states interested in the institution of slavery." Sanderson stood steadfast in his position that the goal of secession and the purpose of the war was to "secure permanent guarantees for the interests and institutions of the South."[69] Initial attempts to reconstruct Florida echoed the politics of men like this.

After readmission of Florida into the United States, politicians of this southernmost state forged a new government and wrote a new constitution.

As required by federal authority, this revamped doctrine declared slavery and secession illegal and recognized all acts and laws passed by the United States since 1861.[70] Thus, in 1865, the Florida legislature, composed solely of white men, assembled a committee to review all existing state laws and make recommendations for modification. The outcome of this statutory evaluation was that the Florida legislature was to maintain as many elements of "the benign, but much abused and misunderstood, institution of slavery" as were possible.[71] In response, the state legislature passed laws that denied African Americans the right to provide testimony against white people and approved a litany of legal measures that "clearly discriminated between white and [B]lack citizens, even to the extent of substituting corporal punishment for fines." While historians have highlighted that such provisions were particularly problematic when it came to the issue of labor disputes with employers, it is essential to note that these restrictions likewise inhibited the ability of Black women and men to seek recourse for any offense ranging from sexual assault to battery to theft to murder to the denial of civil rights. If a white person were the individual who committed the injustice, the Black citizens of Florida had no avenue to right such wrongs. This legal loophole satisfied the recommendation of the legislative committee and gave birth to Florida's Black Codes.[72]

Florida was far from the only member of the former Confederacy that attempted to reestablish the antebellum order through law. Most states throughout the southern region incorporated similar provisions into their revised constitutions. The U.S. Congress—which refused to approve the foundational documents of southern states that included discriminatory provisions, thereby precluding southern politicians from representation in Washington, D.C.—responded by passing the Civil Rights Act, expanding the power of the Freedmen's Bureau, and rejecting state constitutions that violated the Thirteenth Amendment of the U.S. Constitution (the amendment that abolished slavery). The Florida legislature had no choice other than to accept the rejection of its 1865 constitution and acquiesce to military occupation during Congressional Reconstruction.[73] Divisions and demoralization within the Democratic Party coupled with the rise in Black votership contributed to the election of Black Republicans to Congress at the state and national levels. These men continued to shape the U.S. Constitution through the passage of the Fourteenth and Fifteenth Amendments, which granted birthright citizenship and equal citizenship rights to all people born in the United States and extended the vote to Black men. While such monumental change illustrated the importance of federal regulation to those who supported a more equitable nation, this shift represented a threat to those who endorsed whiteness as an ideology of supremacy.[74]

Black men who exercised their right to vote and helped elect Black politicians and white allies to represent them trusted that the people they sent to Tallahassee and Washington would continue to advocate for equality and serve as examples of Black citizenry. The Republican Party, however, was not united. The might of Radical Republicans—the faction of the party that once supported abolition and now advocated, in part, for racial equality—was a perpetual minority in Florida. Most Republicans in the state were part of the more moderate faction concerned with postbellum economic development above all else. Although African Americans hoped the Black men they elected would help shape a more inclusive Florida, these men met forceful resistance, and the majority of their white Republican colleagues "never [gave] 'Negro rights' more than secondary consideration." The historian Jerrell H. Shofner explains that "Black voters contributed more to the Republican Party than they ever received from it," as the focus of Reconstruction turned increasingly toward economic stability exclusively rather than the reinvention of a state that created space for fair and equal labor as well as profitable sustainability for all.[75]

Regardless of the formal positions of the Republican Party, the inclusion of African Americans into the political structure of the state and nation invoked reactionary brutality. The Ku Klux Klan (KKK) and the Young Men's Democratic Club employed violence and terror to dissuade Black men from participating in elections throughout the Sunshine State.[76] Sounds of gunshots echoed through polling places, while self-proclaimed "Conservative" plantation owners and merchants refused "credit and land rentals to freedmen who continued to vote the Republican ticket."[77] The historian Paul Ortiz notes that African American women and men organized against such violence. Black women guarded voting places to ensure that Black men could vote and even linked arms to create a human barrier to thwart vigilante attempts to lynch Black men who challenged white authority. Such action came with great personal risk.[78] Representatives of the Freedmen's Bureau, stationed in Florida to counteract white hostility and noncompliance with the constitutional provisions that granted racial equality, encountered mounting resistance in the early 1870s from enraged white mobs and vengeful white sheriffs, neither of whom concerned themselves with the letter of the law but dedicated themselves to white supremacy.[79]

When federal troops ceased occupation of southern states in 1877, thereby bringing Reconstruction to an end, much of the work federal officials had done to create a more equal union was rendered null and void.[80] Florida was no exception. Conservative Democrats reestablished control over state politics, wrote another constitution, and passed laws such as the poll tax to extinguish the participation of Black men in the electoral process. Within one election cycle, Black voter turnout plummeted from 62 percent to 11 percent in the state of Florida.[81] In the years that followed, additional barriers, such as multiple voting boxes and the regulation of separate public physical spaces, codified the color line.[82] City ordinances as well as statewide provisions that prohibited idleness and vagrancy stripped Black citizens of the right to quit a job or even the right to leisure in public. Such laws pushed Black men and women into a prison pipeline system, which allowed the state to gain revenue from brutal, forced convict labor while owners of large-scale farms and upstart factories increased their profits by hiring unfree workers through the state. It was in this version of Florida that massacres of Black women and men who dared to vote or exert their autonomy occurred in Ocoee, Rosewood, and Perry.[83] By the end of the nineteenth century, Florida politicians had constructed a Jim Crow state and a rigid conservative order in a place that once had free Black communities and concepts of racial fluidity in the expanse of the Spanish borderlands.

While racial oppression was a, if not the, central component of the political and social structures that controlled labor and economic growth in this state, this fact seems to have mattered little to the women and men who came here in search of paradise and opportunity in the late nineteenth century. Many of the people who traveled southward were once ardent abolitionists and dutiful soldiers in the U.S. Army. Yet like the white southerners who grew tired of the presence of federal troops, the white Northerners who felt satisfied with the reunification of the United States and the legal end to slavery were indifferent toward racial inequality and white supremacy in the broader nation that continued after the Civil War. Harriet Beecher Stowe, the author of *Uncle Tom's Cabin* and the person Lincoln allegedly called "the little woman who wrote the book who made this great war," was perhaps the most famous of all the abolitionist snowbirds who traveled to Florida to escape the harsh northern winters.[84] Stowe's winter home located in Mandarin, an area within Jacksonville on Timucuan lands, became the place where she came to write and relax. Stowe, however, repeatedly landed in political turmoil among those of her former activist circles when she attempted to defend the discriminatory politics of her adopted state.[85] Despite Stowe's dedication to the cause of abolition in the antebellum period, her belief in the ills of slavery did not preclude her from deeming Black people as inferior to white people. Much like those who vacationed and invested in Florida, Stowe looked the other way when it came to the emergence of post-bellum racial inequality, Jim Crow, and racial violence.[86]

The historian Julio Capó Jr. explains that it was in this atmosphere that "Floridians aggressively marketed their state as a health resort, whose unmatched tropical climate made it an ideal place for people in the Midwest and Northeast to live in or visit." Advertisements, travel books, and newspapers boasted the healing powers of the state's natural landscape as an escape from the stress of urban life.[87] When it came to the creation of a tourist industry, one of Florida's problems—its low population—turned out to be an asset. Those who came to Florida for relaxation or adventure reveled in its supposed wildness. Among the most popular activities for tourists were paddle steam-boat tours down the St. Johns, Ocklawaha, and Suwannee Rivers as well as trips to see the crystal-clear waters of Silver Springs. Florida wildlife, from majestic cranes to Cretaceous alligators, mesmerized those who visited this place and captured the imaginations of people who wished they could. This escapist fantasy emerged through a rebranding of Florida as an untouched land by city boosters and boards of tourism. Central to this narrative was the denial that this place was Native land. Brightly colored marketing materials that celebrated Florida's lush and romantic landscape sought to obscure the reality that Florida was never vacant or unclaimed and that even as recent as twenty years before the rise of the state's tourist economy, Seminole peoples battled the U.S. government over the invasion and claim of their lands by white U.S. citizens.[88] Cities and towns in the northern region of the state that promoted such romantic narratives were able to attract the most visitors and investors. Northern Florida became a place where wealthy businessmen, industrialists, and politicians brought their families to get away from the cold and to be seen by people who they believed mattered.[89]

People such as Henry Flagler, one of John D. Rockefeller's partners in Standard Oil, invested in the myth of a curative, empty Florida and came to Jacksonville in the 1870s in hopes that the state's climate would alleviate his wife Mary of her chronic illness. During the time Flagler and his wife spent in Florida, they visited various towns in the northeastern region of the state, such as St. Augustine. Flagler, however, found the former Spanish colonial capitol depressing. To him, it seemed more like a ruin—a place with potential that was never truly realized. In 1881, two years after Mary's death, Henry Flagler returned to Florida with a new wife and a new plan. Flagler invested in the expansion of the railroad in Florida as well as in the construction of

Postcard, paddleboat on the St. Johns River, ca. 1910. State Archives of Florida, Florida Memory.

high-end destination hotels. Among his most famous projects was the construction of the Hotel Ponce de León in St. Augustine.[90] This resort mimicked Spanish architectural styles with its red terracotta tiled roof, Moorish arches, and open-air patios. A visit to the hotel, a fortress in its own right, felt as though one were inside an ornate *castillo* (castle) during Spain's golden age. Flagler built other hotels in St. Augustine as well as in Palm Beach and acquired additional resorts in Jacksonville. Countless investors followed in Flagler's footsteps.[91]

It is this version of Florida that lives most prominently in our collective imaginations. If you close your eyes and think of the state, you may envision a place where Spanish colonial architecture seems as natural as the palm trees that hover near the skyline and cast shadows along white sand beaches. Spanish heritage feels so endemic to this place that the landscape reflects its essence. Florida lives in popular memory as an exotic escape rather than what it is, a southern state. In this sense it seems inevitable that this gateway to the Caribbean became the home to Cuban exiles, Puerto Rican citizens, and Central and South American immigrants. But such an association is driven by current politics and historical myths rather than reality.[92]

Latina/o peoples indeed moved between borders over time, but there was not a natural place for them in this space by the late nineteenth and early twentieth centuries. While Spanish colonialism poured the foundation on which Florida sits, it was U.S. imperial policies and southern racial politics that fortified the structure of this state. Florida, in many ways, relishes in its perceived exceptionalism. Politicians, city boosters, boards of tourism, and everyday Floridians invested in the construction of such a myth in the wake of the Civil War and continue to do so to this day. After all, if this place has a history so singular, then things must be different there. The focus on the state's uniqueness makes it possible for some to believe that Native peoples were not treated *so* badly here, that slavery was not *so* common here, that Floridians were not *so* dedicated to the Confederacy here, and that racism was, and is, not *as* bad here. A narrative like this, however, requires much forgetting. Florida was not, and is not, so different, and Tampa is no exception.

When Cuban cigar workers walked into Tampa in 1886, they arrived in a place where local history mirrored that of the broader state. Hernando de Soto, the conquistador who sailed to the peninsula in search of gold and the mythical fountain of youth, landed near Tampa in 1534. Yet as with so many other places throughout the peninsula, the Spanish decided this was not a location where they wished to stay.[93] In some ways, little had changed by 1880. Tampa remained hot, humid, sandy, pestilent, malaria-ridden, and isolated, with only 720 people willing to call this place home. This southern town seemed as though it had hardly evolved since its 1824 founding as Fort Brooke, the military garrison that occupied this space during the Long Seminole War.[94] Most people who lived in Tampa by the 1880s had arrived roughly forty years earlier, following the passage of the AOA. Crackers, small-scale farmers, and hopeful homesteaders, many of whom brought with them the Black women and men they enslaved, saw opportunity in Tampa as well as the surrounding prairies throughout Hillsborough County. As these white men laid claim to Native lands they believed they had the right to own, they established a local economy grounded in cattle and salt production and fueled by forced, Black labor.[95] Enslaved women and men worked the fields and accounted for one-third of the town's population.[96]

As the call for secession traveled from Tallahassee to Tampa in 1860, the white people who lived here "marched lockstep with the Confederacy."[97] During the Civil War, local white militiamen acted as blockade runners to move goods and foodstuffs between Tampa and the larger South. This activity resulted in two incursions, the Battle of Tampa and the Battle of Fort

Brooke, during which the town experienced shelling.[98] While this physical destruction was minor when compared to the burning of Atlanta, such action left an emotional and economic scar on the city. White, native-born Tampans grew resentful of the presence of federal troops in their home during Reconstruction and invested in the lore of the Lost Cause rather than efforts that sought to incorporate Black women and men into society as free and equal citizens. The white people of Tampa held "chivalric festivals" that reinvented the antebellum era as one where violence did not exist and where African Americans worshipped their white enslavers for the supposed gift of benevolent paternalism. As the historians Gary R. Mormino and George E. Pozzetta explain, "this retreat to a halcyon past could not ignore the realities of [economic] depression, yellow fever, and poverty" that plagued Tampa throughout the postbellum period.[99]

By the late nineteenth century, the politics of Tampa reflected those of the broader state. Southern Democrats defended one-party rule through the enforcement of laws that disfranchised Black citizens and established a white primary system. Likewise, the town's active KKK, supported by white political elites and empowered by local law enforcement, ruled by fear when regulation failed to make clear who had the right to be powerful in this town.[100] The political landscape of Tampa did not deter men such as Henry Plant, the New York industrialist and neighbor to Flagler, from bringing the entrepreneurial spirit of the Gilded Age to this corner of the Sunshine State. Although Plant and his family preferred to enjoy their Floridian retreats in the company of other wealthy Northerners in search of escape along the state's upper Atlantic coast near Jacksonville, he recognized the opportunity for profit in scantly populated Tampa.[101] During the 1880s, Plant extended his railroad system to this Gulf coast town, created a deepwater port, and built a steamship line that connected Tampa to Havana. While it was the Plant railways and the Plant waterways that moved Cuban tobacco, Cuban cigar workers, and Cuban cigars from the island, throughout the United States, as well as around the world, it was the arrival of this industry and these people that created an international borderland within the reach of a reconstructed southern order and paved the path toward building Latina/o Florida.[102]

The Rise of the Cuban Cigar Industry

During the 1860s, a Cuban cigar manufacturer, who would one day redefine the city of Tampa, came to Florida in exile. Vicente Martínez Ybor—the Spanish-born Cuban cigar factory owner—fled Havana and went to Key West in 1869, one year after the start of the Ten Years' War.[103] This armed, colonial struggle was the first of three wars for Cuban independence from Spain during the late nineteenth century. Martínez Ybor, like many members of the upper and professional classes, was a separatist who supported and funded Cuban independence because he believed Spanish taxes on his business and his income were too high.[104] When Spanish officials learned of his treasonous activities, they ordered his arrest. In response, Martínez Ybor turned to his powerful colleagues for help. Vicente Galarza, a fellow cigar manufacturer, offered sanctuary to Martínez Ybor, while others attempted to exert their influence over the colonial administration. Their campaign was unsuccessful. With the assistance of friends and family, Martínez Ybor assembled as much capital as possible, slipped into a carriage, and boarded a schooner that waited for him at a dock in Havana. This vessel clandestinely carried him ninety miles across the Florida Strait and left him in Key West. Once Spanish officials learned that Martínez Ybor escaped their grasp, they allegedly pillaged his home and destroyed the property he left behind as a warning to other separatists.[105]

Perhaps to the chagrin of Spanish colonial officials, Martínez Ybor reestablished his Cuban cigar empire on the other side of the Florida Strait. At first, his business was modest. Martínez Ybor rented a few small buildings near the docks of Key West and hired Cuban cigar workers to produce his famed El Príncipe de Gales brand of cigars. To maintain the quality of his product, however, Martínez Ybor could not use domestically grown U.S. tobacco due to its caustic flavor and harsh smoke. In order to provide consumers with the high-quality cigars they expected from his brand, he had to import Cuban tobacco from the Vuelta Abajo region in the Piñar del Río Province of the island.[106] To achieve this feat while in political exile, Martínez Ybor trusted Ignacio Casteñada, his son-in-law, to act as his liaison in Cuba. Casteñada brokered relationships with Cuban tobacco plantation owners and arranged for the transportation of raw tobacco from the western fields of Cuba to the port of Havana, across Caribbean waters, and onto the southernmost shores of Florida.[107] Access to the labor of skilled Cuban cigar workers was never a problem for Martínez Ybor. Although Key West had a modest Cuban cigar community as early as the 1830s, an estimated 100,000 Cubans had left the island since the eruption of the Ten Years' War in 1868. The elite fled to Europe and Latin America, while the business, professional, and intellectual classes went to New York, Philadelphia, and Boston; the working class sought refuge in the southeastern United States, and cigar workers went, predominantly, to Key West.[108] According to census reports, approximately 1,100 Cubans lived in Key West in 1870, and each week it seemed as though more and more people arrived. By 1873, Cubans constituted the majority of the population in this growing city.[109] It was these women and men whom Martínez Ybor employed. Cuban cigar workers, many of them ardent separatists and leftist radicals, saw the burgeoning Key West cigar industry as an opportunity to earn a steady wage through their craft as they advocated and organized for Cuban independence without the threat of assassination by Spanish authorities.[110] These people believed that an independent Cuba could bring liberation to the island through fair pay and improved living conditions, as well as the right to political self-determination. The cigar factory floor was a refuge and a revolutionary space.[111]

Over the course of the next ten years, both Martínez Ybor and his industrial enterprise thrived. In many ways, exile achieved what Martínez Ybor once hoped the separatist cause could—an increase in revenue. Stateside production evaded Spanish taxes and bypassed U.S. tariffs on imported manufactured goods.[112] In short, in the Florida Keys, taxes were lower and profits were higher. Furthermore, the proximity of Key West to Cuba precluded Martínez Ybor from many of the challenges his Cuban cigar manufacturing colleagues in New York, Philadelphia, and Chicago experienced. Because the climate of Key West mimicked that of Cuba, Martínez Ybor did not have to absorb the expense of purchasing and installing expensive humidors. The warm, moist air of the Keys prevented raw tobacco and finished cigars from dehydrating and becoming unusable. Key West was a natural humidor. Likewise, the access to a steady stream of skilled, Cuban cigar workers meant that there was rarely a labor shortage or a problem finding workers with the skills needed to transform Cuban tobacco into Cuban cigars. Other cigar manufacturers took note of the many benefits of this place and relocated their enterprises or opened branch factories in the southernmost point of the Sunshine State. As a result, Key West became the center of Cuban cigar production in the United States.[113]

Cuban cigar workers who worked in the Florida-based cigar industry turned this place into the southern center of Cuban independence movement making. Cuban cigar workers founded revolutionary clubs, created Spanish-language pro-independence newspapers, and fundraised for the ongoing fight for a free Cuba. Some even circulated between the island and Florida to participate in the armed struggle in their homeland.[114] The signing of the Pact of Zanjón, which brought the Ten Years' War to a conclusion in 1878, was met with protest in Key West, for Spain remained the colonial overlord of the island. As a result, Cuban cigar workers in Key West joined the efforts of Cuban expatriates and intellectuals in New York in the continued effort to organize for *Cuba libre* (free Cuba). As revolutionary currents swelled in Key West, it became difficult for manufacturers such as Martínez Ybor to maintain production and profit. Inside cigar factories, trade unionism was fused with separatist politics and threatened the stability of the Cuban cigar industry with the strength of hurricane-force winds. By 1884, the combination of frequent strikes and work stoppages in protest of politics on the island encouraged Martínez Ybor to consider the relocation of his factories and his business.[115]

Martínez Ybor initially considered Pensacola and Galveston as potential sites for the relocation of his enterprise. Both cities, from his perspective, had decisive advantages. Pensacola, located on the northwestern coast of Florida, and Galveston, positioned along the eastern coast of Texas, were portside towns with railway access nestled in the borderlands of the Gulf South. These cities, like Key West, connected the U.S. southern states to the Caribbean as well as Central and South America. Although the weather of neither city was as warm as the Keys, their climates seemed humid and temperate enough to preserve precious Cuban tobacco and fabricated Cuban cigars. Yet most important to Martínez Ybor was that the location of each city provided distance between leftist cigar workers, on whom production depended, and revolutionary labor and political organizing forces in Cuba. Martínez Ybor envisioned the next home of his cigar enterprise to be a place where he could build a company town that fostered the control of labor and permitted the expanse of his capitalist dreams.[116]

Before Martínez Ybor booked his trip to tour Pensacola and Galveston, he had a chance encounter with two friends who changed his mind and the future of Tampa. Bernardino Gargol and Gavino Gutiérrez lived in New York City, where they owned and operated successful import businesses. Gutiérrez, a Spaniard and trained civil engineer, imported and distributed liquor, while Gargol, a Cuban, imported and distributed guava jelly and guava paste. The two men decided to stop in Key West and visit with Martínez Ybor before returning northward. That night, Martínez Ybor welcomed Gargol and Gutiérrez to dine with him and Ignacio Haya, a friend and fellow Cuban cigar manufacturer also visiting from New York City. As the four men sat together, Gargol and Gutiérrez shared that they came to Florida because they heard of a town called Tampa, located on the state's west coast, where guava fruit allegedly grew in abundance. Gargol, who wished to move the production of his goods from Cuba to the United States, hoped the rumors of a guava-filled paradise were true—unfortunately for him, they were not. Despite this fact, both Gargol and Gutiérrez reported that they believed Tampa had great potential as a port town and site of economic investment. Martínez Ybor and Haya, who both wished to relocate their Cuban cigar factories, booked tickets to visit this Gulf coast town to assess its potential as a site for their enterprises.[117]

On their first trip to Tampa, Martínez Ybor and Haya were pleased by what they found. Land was cheap and plentiful in this scarcely populated place, and the climate was warm, humid, and ideal for the preservation of Cuban tobacco and Cuban cigars. Just over 331 miles separated Tampa and Havana. From the perspective of Martínez Ybor, this distance seemed short enough to facilitate the efficient shipment of tobacco but far enough to sever the connection of the cross-border labor unionism and political activism that thrived in Key West. A new railroad—the work of the investor and railway tycoon Henry Plant—made Tampa easily accessible by land and water, a strategic advantage that had the potential to make the transportation of goods and people easier than it was in Key West.[118] Martínez Ybor and Haya reported what they found in Tampa to their respective business partners, Eduardo Manrara and Serafín Sánchez, both of whom responded positively and supported investment.[119]

In September 1885, Martínez Ybor and Haya made their second trip to Tampa to meet with the local Board of Trade and purchase land. While Haya and Sánchez wished to buy a single plot to build a factory, Martínez Ybor and Manrara wanted to acquire enough acreage to build a company town. After the two men traveled throughout Hillsborough County and surveyed the area, Martínez Ybor selected a forty-acre parcel of land on the eastern outskirts of Tampa. John T. Lesley, a member of the Tampa Board of Trade, owned this land and offered to sell it for $9,000. Martínez Ybor, who knew Lesley purchased the land for $5,000 a few months earlier, refused the offer and threatened to examine other towns for potential investment. The Board of Trade quickly assembled on October 5, 1885, to reach a compromise with Lesley and secure the promise of industrial investment in Tampa. In the end, Martínez Ybor consented to pay Lesley $9,000 for his land, and the Board of Trade agreed to reimburse Martínez Ybor $4,000.[120] This solution satisfied all parties, and the Board of Trade proudly proclaimed that an "arrangement had been consummated to secure the factory of Ybor and Co."[121]

Martínez Ybor hired Gutiérrez to plan and oversee the construction of his cigar factory and the creation of his company town.[122] Both Gutiérrez and Martínez Ybor found inspiration for Ybor City in the work of the industrialist George M. Pullman as well as various southern mill towns designed to maximize the control manufacturers held over their work-force.[123] The plans for Ybor City included grid-patterned streets, brick fac-tories with open courtyards, decorative wrought iron that laced across balconies, and simple shotgun lodgings for worker housing.[124] From its in-ception, Ybor City was intended to be a place where people would live to work but choose to stay.

Perhaps one of the primary challenges of this project was the engineering necessary to harness the landscape. The northernmost region of the Mar-tínez Ybor property boasted soft, sandy terrain covered in spiky palmettos, while the eastern and western areas were dense, pine-laden forests. In the southern portion of these lands lay swamps and marshes.[125] Gutiérrez and Martínez Ybor hired local workers to clear the trees, pull the palmet-tos, and drain and fill the swamps. Yet even after this space seemed prepared for construction, the wildlife remained. Alligators meandered through the barren plot, while mosquitoes and other insects filled the air. Fernando Lemos, one of the first residents of Ybor City, remembered that at times people walked "about with goggles to keep the gnats from [their] eyes." José García, another early Ybor immigrant, recalled this place as a "wilderness."[126] Although managing the local flora and fauna was a perpetual struggle, con-struction of the community was well underway by early 1886. An article in the *Tampa Guardian*, a local newspaper, remarked on the progress of this venture with awe and excitement: "If a person would visit this place every day there would be something new to see, some new evidence of the sub-stantial growth and development. . . . A person cannot fail to be impressed until the idea that the enterprise is backed by immense capital and at the same time is being directed by master minds."[127]

As the ambition of Martínez Ybor and Haya grew, so too did the territory of Ybor City. Haya and Sánchez purchased ten acres adjacent to Ybor City's original forty acres, while Martínez Ybor and Manrara bought an additional seventy acres of land. By the fall of 1886, this company town reached across 111 acres of Hillsborough County.[128]

Although the construction of Ybor City was a work in progress, Cuban ci-gar production was underway by the summer of 1886. The first cigar enter-prise to open its doors in Ybor City was the Sánchez y Haya factory, owned by Ignacio Haya and Serafín Sánchez, followed by the V. M. Ybor & Co. fac-tory, owned by Vicente Martínez Ybor and Eduardo Manrara.[129] One mil-lion handmade Cuban cigars rolled by skilled Cuban *tabaqueras/os* (cigar makers) left this Gulf coast, portside town in the first year of production. As

Martínez Ybor and Haya expanded their vision of what Ybor City could be, they worked to convince other manufacturers from Cuba, Key West, and New York to relocate their enterprises or open a branch factory in this up-start town. The entrepreneurial duo proposed a "free ten-year lease on land and a new factory built to [the] specifications" of interested parties and po-tential investors. In exchange, those who accepted this offer agreed to pro-duce "a quota of cigars and furnish a fixed number of workers who would rent or buy houses" from Martínez Ybor or Haya, respectively. While industrial expansion was the primary goal of Ybor City, the benefactors of this town viewed company housing as essential to the creation of a place where they could exert greater control over the workforce and diversify their investment portfolios through profits garnered from rent, mortgages, and cash home sales. Their plan was a success. By 1900, Tampa was home to 129 Cuban cigar factories that produced 20 million cigars. This feat required the import of 1,180 tons of Cuban tobacco that workers "transformed into 10 million [dollars] worth of cigar exports." That same year, the internal revenue of Tampa accounted for two-thirds of the total revenue in the state of Florida, and the duties collected in this city "approached 1 million [dollars] a year, tenth highest in the nation."[130] Tampa grew from a village of 720 in 1880 to a city of 15,839 by 1900. As a result of Ybor City, Tampa surpassed Key West as the center of Cuban cigar production in the state as well as by its popula-tion of Cuban residents and Florida-born Latinas/os.[131]

The majority of immigrant workers who made such growth possible la-bored in the massive cigar factories that defined the Tampa skyline at the turn of the century. While the first factories were made of wood, builders transi-tioned to redbrick, fire-proof structures over time. These three-story build-ings were approximately fifty feet across and positioned in an east-to-west orientation to enhance air circulation and protect the structures from dam-age wrought by the occasional hurricane.[132] Inside the factories, manufactur-ers separated workers into six distinct departments—"the preparing, the stripping, [the sorting,] the manufacturing, the packing, and the shipping."[133] The production of cigars in Ybor City followed the Spanish hand process, which was a delicate, difficult business that required organization and skill.

Cuban cigar production began on the bottom floor of the factory in the "casing room." Here, workers unbanded and loosened the bundles of tightly packed Cuban tobacco leaves, and then *mojadores* (moisteners) dipped the leaves into buckets of water to restore their pliability and hung them to cure.[134] Next, the supple tobacco leaves were transferred to *despaldilladoras* (strippers), who ripped the stems from the center of the plants. This job,

Sánchez y Haya cigar factory, Ybor City, 1928. Burgert Brothers Collection, University of South Florida Libraries—Tampa Special Collections, Tampa, Florida.

performed predominantly by women, was among the lowest-paid positions in the factory.[135] As these women worked, they separated tobacco into two categories, filler and wrapper. Filler—the visually unappealing leaves, typically rendered from tobacco plants grown in the sun—went to the blending and storing department, where workers "mixed tobacco . . . for the purpose of giving different tastes or flavors to cigars."[136] Each cigar factory had its own proprietary filler blend, which gave each cigar brand its distinct essence. The remaining leaves known as wrapper—the visually appealing leaves rendered from tobacco plants typically grown in the shade and fit for the exterior of the cigar—went to the *rezagadores* (selectors), who sorted the leaves according to shape and size. This position, highly skilled and composed entirely of men, required that a person train for "at least three and a half years as a[n] apprentice." For their skill, these men earned a salary that averaged $27.50 a week, an impressive sum for the turn of the century. As the *rezagadores* inspected each leaf, they scrutinized "the prominence of the side veins, the texture, 'oily' or 'dry' wrappers, and [searched for] any discoloration which would disqualify an otherwise perfect [specimen]." Once these men determined which wrappers passed inspection, they separated the leaves "into pads of twenty five" and "hand[ed] them to the cigar makers."[137]

Cigar making took place on the second floor of the factory. Until the 1930s the majority of tabaqueras/os were men. It took the average person "twelve to eighteen months to acquire [the technique]" necessary to make a Cuban cigar using the Spanish hand method.[138] Cigar manufactures paid cigar makers according to a piecework system rather than by a set salary. In Ybor City, the average tabaquera/o made $12.50 a week. This sum, however, could be higher or lower depending on how quickly one could work and the type of cigar one rolled.[139] Cheap cigars, which typically sold for five cents, earned a cigar maker less money than the production of high-quality cigars, which typically sold for fifty cents or more. To construct a cigar, a tabaquera/o required "a special board, [typically made of apple wood], about fifteen-by-eighteen inches [in length], upon which to roll [their] cigars"; a *chaveta* (small knife) to smooth and trim the wrapper; a gauge to measure the length and size of the cigar; and "a sanitary cup of gum" to mold the head of the finished product.[140] First, cigar makers trimmed the wrapper leaf using their *chaveta* and created the "bunch" by scrunching filler leaves in their hand. Factory owners who wished to increase productivity employed *buncheras/os* (bunch makers), who sat next to, or stood behind, the tabaqueras/os and made the filler bunches either by hand or with a mold for the cigar makers.[141] Next, the tabaqueras/os oriented the leaf so the tip was "always toward the 'burn' of the cigar and the side veins [pointed] upward and toward the left" of the product.[142] Then the cigar makers spread and stretched the wrapper on the board, placed the bunch on the wrapper leaf, and rolled the tobacco until the filler and wrapper became one. To finish the cigar, the tabaqueras/os dipped their finger in the gum, applied a dab of it to the head of the cigar, and then molded the finished product.

The final step in cigar production was the process of picking and packing. Pickers, also known as *escogedores*, apprenticed for four years to hone their craft. These workers were typically men, who earned an average salary of $27.00 a week. Pickers and packers labored in pairs—one picker and one packer per team. The job of the *escogedor* was to separate cigars according to color. While this job may seem simple according to the description, in practice it required that a person have the ability to discern between 150 different shades of Cuban tobacco leaves. Once the picker identified fifty cigars of the same shade, the packer examined and arranged the cigars into the box according to shade so all the cigars appeared to be the same color. In the banding department, "girls [took] each cigar from the box, band[ed] it and replace[d] it in identically the same position as when [the cigar box] left the hands of the packer." Finally, an inspector (at times the original packer) examined and sealed the cigar box, then sent it along to be shipped around the world.[143]

Ybor City, and by extension Tampa, garnered international acclaim for the quality of the cigars produced in this place. The *hecho a mano* (handmade), clear Havana cigars—those made purely of Cuban tobacco—earned this place the reputation as the world's "Cigar City." The success of Ybor City and the demand for Cuban cigars ignited the entrepreneurial spirit among others in Tampa. Hugh MacFarlane, a Scottish-born lawyer and investor, replicated the vision of Martínez Ybor when he purchased "several hundred acres of cypress wetlands, drained the swamp," and established West Tampa near Ybor City.[144] This community boasted bungalow housing for workers and welcomed cigar manufacturers eager to expand their enterprises southward. West Tampa was a success. Likewise, some Cuban cigar workers, in Ybor City and West Tampa, took matters into their own hands and established small-scale production sites known as buckeyes, or *chinchales*, in modest rented dwellings or in their own houses. "How I love the wit of cigarmakers!" remarked Jose Yglesias, a writer and poet from Ybor City. "That word *chinchal* . . . it comes from the Spanish word for bedbugs which is *chinches* and so chinchal is a place where bedbugs gather and as you can imagine [neither bedbugs nor cigar makers in these small businesses] . . . need[ed] much space."[145] Those who worked in these homespun enterprises did the labor themselves—the prepping, the stripping, the sorting, the rolling, and the packing—and many evolved into local brands that gained fame of their own.

By the twentieth century, nearly everything in Tampa revolved around Ybor City and the Cuban cigar industry. In fact, Tampa could not exist without it. The success of this company town spurred the creation of a secondary economy of supportive businesses. Cedar mills created box factories that employed women and men to construct cigar boxes, while artists established lithographic firms to design and print cigar labels and cigar bands. Martínez Ybor established the Florida Brewing Company to quench the thirst of cigar workers, and for a period its beer became the most popular in Florida and Cuba.[146] Restaurants, cafés, and theaters opened their doors to serve and entertain the women and men of Ybor as well as the native-born Anglo-Tampans brave enough to venture into "little Havana."[147] Development companies flocked to Tampa ready to assist in the construction of the next cigar factory or the expansion of the company towns. While West

Tampa managed to remain an independent municipality until 1925, the city of Tampa forcibly incorporated Ybor City in 1887 under the guise of needing to extend "law and order" and enforce "proper sanitary regulation" in Ybor City.[148] In reality, Tampa leaders wanted access to a widened tax base to expand the city's infrastructure by paving roads and sidewalks, extending the trolley and public transportation system, and installing an electrical grid.[149] Ybor City, and the labor of Cuban cigar workers, made Tampa a modern city.

The Landscape of Ybor City

While Vicente Martínez Ybor envisioned his self-named company town as a place of control, it became a community of immigrant power. The distance between Tampa and Havana neither severed the connection Cuban cigar workers had with their homeland nor diminished the passion they held for Cuban independence or the leftist ideals that motivated their migration. Those who came to Ybor City solidified Tampa's place as a borderland that connected the Jim Crow South to the fields of Vuelta Abajo and linked the community to leftist political movements across the globe. Ybor City became a city within a city—a place with a culture, a politic, and an authority of its own built and defended by the people who lived there.

The foundation of Ybor City was, and remains, its Cuban population. Cuban immigration outpaced that of all other foreign-born residents between 1886 and 1930, the years during which the rate of immigration to Tampa was at its height. Four years after the founding of Ybor City, the census reported that 2,424 foreign-born Cubans lived alongside 233 foreign-born Spaniards and 56 foreign-born Italians. Ten years later, 3,533 foreign-born Cubans lived in Ybor City with 963 foreign-born Spaniards and 1,315 foreign-born Italians. Women and men from Cuba, Spain, and Italy continued to come to Ybor City until 1930, when the rate of immigration slowed as a result of economic turmoil. On the eve of the Great Depression an estimated 5,112 foreign-born Cubans, 457 foreign-born Spaniards, and 2,817 foreign-born Italians lived in Ybor City alongside U.S.-born Ybor community members, altogether numbering more than 20,000 people.[150]

Cubans, both Black and white, immigrated to Ybor City from Havana as well as Bejucal, San Antonio de los Baños, Santiago de las Vegas, and Cárdenas. A small number hailed from Piñar del Río, the westernmost province of the island. The Spaniards who lived in Ybor City originated from the regions of Asturias and Galicia, both located in the northern part of the country, while a handful came from the Canary Islands. Many of the Spaniards who immigrated to Ybor lived and worked in Cuba prior to their migration to Florida, and some had families on the island. Most Italians came from the *comune* (municipality) of Santo Stefano Quisquina in Sicily. Few of these women and men, however, migrated to Ybor City directly but learned about the southern community through friends, family, and immigrant networks in New Orleans and New York. The majority of Italians arrived in Ybor after 1900. A combination of hope for economic opportunity, escape from political persecution, and family reunification motivated the migration of the Cubans, Spaniards, and Italians to this Gulf coast town.[151]

Most people who came to work in Ybor City put down roots and called this place home. Over time they married, had children, and encouraged their extended families to join them stateside. By 1920, the population of Ybor City was self-sustaining and included parents and children with Spanish surnames who were Florida-born (at times both parents and children were U.S.-born even as early as 1900). Cubans, Spaniards, and Italians intermarried and, in the process, created a culture that was uniquely Ybor. Jose Yglesias—an Ybor community member who sought to understand his own Latina/o identity through his writing—once explained: "A typical Ybor City Tampan of my generation [born in the 1920s] has, like me, a mother of Cuban parentage and a father from Galicia, uncles from Asturias and Cuba, and at least one cousin or sister married to a Sicilian." As a young man who came of age in the 1930s and 1940s, Yglesias identified as Cuban in recognition of who he was and as an indicator of his leftist politics. Yglesias was aware, however, that he could have chosen to identify as Spanish. To him, the rejection of his Spanish ancestry meant a rejection of Spain's imperialist past as well as its fascist and antidemocratic present. Over time, Yglesias conjugated his identity not as something that was purely Cuban but as something that was a product of being born in the United States of mixed parentage and growing up in a community that was multiethnic. One reflection of this experience was Yglesias's choice to exclude accent marks from the spelling of his name. As Yglesias, and so many others from Ybor City have described, being from Ybor had distinct meaning. It was an identity with a Cuban foundation that included Spanish and Italian influences and a blended experience that required navigating the South as a person whose first language was Spanish (at times even for Italians) and was read as non-white by Anglos in Tampa. To Yglesias, it was the combination of being from Ybor and the backlash to his perceived difference and non-Americanness that made him a tampeño (Latino born in Ybor or Tampa) and his community Latina/o.[152]

Inside Ybor City, women and men lived in boardinghouses or casitas. Boardinghouses looked like modest two-story homes and attracted bachelors who rented single rooms. While most boarders wanted cheap housing, some opted for higher rent, which included meals. The casitas, built to attract families, were shotgun-style structures made of wide wooden planks and elevated by brick risers to protect houses from the elements and facilitate air circulation. Each home sat on a narrow lot surrounded by a white picket fence. In the small backyard was a shared outdoor privy for none of these workers' homes had electricity or indoor plumbing. During the initial years of the community, cigar workers had the option to rent or purchase their home. The cost of a casita ranged from $750 to $1,000, depending on the size and location.[153] Both Martínez Ybor and Haya offered interest-free mortgages as they developed Ybor City. This practice encouraged home ownership and community investment from early immigrant cigar workers and neighborhood residents.

As more and more people arrived, Ybor City became an immigrant suburb. By 1900, the majority of houses had been purchased, and the opportunity to own property was not an option in later years. Most people, therefore, rented their casitas and had landlords, some of whom were cigar workers themselves. Within the neighborhood, Italians lived near one another on the eastern outskirts of the community in houses with larger lots that facilitated the farming of vegetables and the raising of livestock. Cubans and Spaniards, however, determined where they put down roots based on cost. The most expensive homes were those near Seventh Avenue, the main thoroughfare of the neighborhood, while the cheapest houses were those on the western outskirts of Ybor City near the Scrub, an African American community. Black Cubans—who often earned the lowest wages in the cigar factories and performed low-wage, non-cigar work in Ybor—frequently lived in the western region of Ybor City, but nearly none lived in the African American neighborhood during Ybor's early years. A combination of language, ethnic, political, and cultural differences maintained divisions between Afro-Cubans and African Americans until the 1940s. The boundaries that existed within Ybor City, however, were neither exclusive nor restrictive—people could live wherever they could afford to rent within this neighborhood. Those who migrated with their families often lived in multigenerational homes or rented casitas next to or near one another, while those who migrated alone built family from the connections they established in Ybor.[154]

At the center of Ybor City was Seventh Avenue. Along this street were cafés, bars, and restaurants as well as ten-cent stores, pharmacies, and clinics with Spanish-speaking doctors. Shoe stores, pawnshops, and clothing stores owned by Jewish merchants attracted interested buyers, while theaters entertained the masses with silent films and later Spanish-language movies.[155] At times, bars or social clubs erected temporary boxing rings on the street or in alleyways, where men would watch and bet on cigar workers as they flexed their muscles and threw punches. On Saturday evenings, "boys and girls would crowd Seventh Avenue" and promenade down the street while they "[tried] to attract attention" from each other. Girls, accompanied by a chaperone, would walk on one side of the street and the boys on the other. "These continuous concentric circles" were opportunities to "meet and flirt."[156] Peddlers and vendors offered everything from fresh fruit to fish to ice cream.[157] Children flocked to the *"piruli* man," who sold "hard candy made in a cone shape" that boasted a "taste [similar] to rock candy." As the *piruli* man walked down Seventh Avenue with his candies displayed on a banana stalk, he yelled "Con dinero, sin dinero!" (With money or without money). A person could buy a *piruli* for a penny or redeem one with three coupons, "which appeared on Octagon Soap, Clabber Girl baking powder, and Golden Key evaporated milk."[158] Spanish-language signs lined La Avenida Séptima and the sounds of Spanish filled the street. "In a way, [walking down Seventh Avenue] was like taking a dream trip to Cuba," reported the *Tampa Daily Times* in 1924.[159] This space—which was at once social and commercial—provided entertainment, escape, and excitement to the people of Ybor City while also providing employment and entrepreneurial opportunity to hundreds of Latinas/os who labored within the community's service economy.

Cuban cigar work was the foundation of this community. As the scholar Kenya C. Dworkin y Méndez explains, Cuban cigar production "did not involve new technologies but a tradition [of labor] that required individual and collective expertise and workmanship."[160] Ybor City's Cuban cigar workers took pride in their craft, and it reflected in their appearance. "Collectively, the cigar makers dress very well," reported the *Tampa Daily Journal* in 1890.[161] When these women and men went to work they looked as though they were in their finest attire. Men wore crisply pressed long-sleeve shirts paired with clean slacks, while women donned shirtwaists with floor-length flowing skirts. Between 1886 and 1890, the day of a cigar worker began in the factory at six o'clock in the morning. At nine they took a short break for breakfast and then started working again at ten. They "work[ed] incessantly" until three in the afternoon, "when the day of eight hours finished."[162] By the turn of the century, however, this humane schedule shifted to one that mimicked U.S. standards of efficiency and maximum production.

"[Cigar workers] start[ed] at six o'clock in the morning," remembered José Vega Díaz, "[and we worked until] six o'clock in the evening—twelve hours in the factory." Vega, a Cuban immigrant of mixed Spanish and Cuban parentage, began his apprenticeship to become a cigar maker in 1897 at the age of twelve, rose to the cigar makers' benches in 1899 at the age of fourteen, and left cigar work in 1926 at the age of forty-one. To Vega, his time in the cigar factories was little more than a "bad dream." "When I dream about the cigar factory, I dream it's late [and] I cannot finish," then "everything breaks—the wrapper [ruptures] or [the picker says] I had too many scratches [on the outer leaf, which caused the cigar to be discarded]" and resulted in a deduction in wages. Vega explained that "at first, [he] liked the cigar factories" because the earning potential was good. "You know [manufacturers] used to pay . . . fourteen dollars for one thousand small cigars," he said, "[but then they would move] you from the main hall, to another hall downstairs [where you would work] the same job [making] the same size cigars [but] they [paid] you less."[163] The shifts in production practices and the harsh treatment of workers by employers pushed Vega to leave cigar work and become a delivery man for a furniture company, a job he did for more than twenty years.

While Vega experienced oppressive workplace practices as a cigar maker during the years he labored in the Cuban cigar industry, he was a part of a multiracial, multiethnic, and mixed-gender workforce. There was not an exclusive restriction on the training of Black Cubans for cigar work, yet fewer Black women and men became tabaqueras/os compared to their light-skinned peers, who occupied the majority of spaces at the cigar makers' benches. Spaniards typically held the positions of *rezagador* and *escogedor* as well as jobs in upper management such as foreman, accountant, manager, or factory owner. Such divisions had the potential to create tension within cigar factories that paralleled colonial class and ethnic divisions in Cuba and had the ability to foment discontent and lead to strikes as a result of perceived, or real, abuses of power. While Italians did not arrive in Ybor with knowledge of cigar work, those who learned Spanish—a linguistic necessity in a Cuban cigar factory—labored alongside their Latina/o neighbors. Although Cuban cigar work was traditionally done by men, Ybor City women worked in factories alongside their husbands and their brothers, and even their children, although in lower-paid and lesser-skilled positions. Inside a factory it was not uncommon to find a "father, mother, sons, and daughters" working side by side, and in some instances "members of three generations [labored] together."[164]

Despite the fact that women contributed to the household economy in Ybor City, either through work in factories or through labor in the home, memory within the community does not consistently reflect this reality. "Husbands say their wives don't work," one Ybor community resident remembered, "but women always work." For example, Severina Patiño Cardo labored as a *despaldilladora* in the Ybor cigar industry until she left her position to provide care for her immediate and extended family. Patiño managed the needs of her eight children, her husband, her parents, her grandparents, and her elderly cousins. The family lived together in a rented duplex. Inside the home "there were so many people," recalled one of Patiño's children. Patiño enlisted her daughters—Dolores, Josephine, Ramona, Dora, and Delia—to assist with work in the home until they came of age and entered the Ybor cigar industry. Together the women of this family did laundry by hand in a tin basin in the kitchen and shopped, prepared, and cooked enough food to feed more than ten people three meals each day. To keep the house clean, they divided the labor. As a conscious consumer who sought to save money where she could, Patiño "kept a vegetable garden to help [cut food costs for the family]" and in the evenings rolled cigars in a chinchal to bring additional income into the home. The labor of women such as Patiño was essential to the function of community and the survival of families. An informal economy of wage work that included laundry, house cleaning, childcare, and midwifery emerged in Ybor City.[165] Women were essential to the success of the Cuban cigar industry whether through factory labor, wage work, or the economy of care.[166]

While cigar factories, independent businesses, and home-based labor afforded the wages and sustenance necessary to everyday life, women and men in Ybor City established mutual aid societies that provided cradle-to-the-grave support to all dues-paying members. These institutions—locally termed centros, *sociedades*, or clubs—represented the power of collective self-help. The mutual aid system that immigrants developed in Ybor City mirrored the mutual aid network in Cuba, as it provided health insurance, unemployment insurance, medical services, burial services, education, entertainment, and comradery through five primary organizations: the Círculo Cubano (white Cubans), La Sociedad de la Unión Martí-Maceo (Black Cubans), the Centro Español (Spaniards), the Centro Asturiano (Spaniards), and L'Unione Italiana (Italians). Both the Centro Español and the Centro Asturiano were local affiliates of Havana-based clubs, and the Círculo Cubano as well as La Sociedad de la Unión Martí-Maceo maintained a relationship with the Cuban government.[167] In the evenings and on the weekends these clubs welcomed members into their cantinas, their dance halls, and their theaters. In times of need, illness, injury, or job loss, the sociedades covered the expense of medical services and prescriptions and assisted with food costs and rent payments. Manuel Tamargo, an Ybor resident, explained, "When we got to this country we had to take care of ourselves, [no] one would do it for us."[168] From the perspective of Tamargo, as well as thousands of other Ybor community members, it was the mutual aid system that provided the infrastructure necessary to survive and to live in this new place.

Leftist radicalism and labor activism thrived in Ybor City, much as it had in Key West. Cuban cigar workers established revolutionary clubs to support the movement for Cuban independence and donated a day's wages to the fight for a free Cuba each week. José Martí, the famed poet and Cuban revolutionary, visited Ybor City on multiple occasions to give speeches, coordinate with revolutionary clubs, and fundraise for the coming revolution. Cubans, who lived in Ybor City and West Tampa, were not simply interested parties but people who had left their homelands because of the political and economic instability that rocked the island. To the Ybor community, the fight for Cuban independence was personal. As a result, both the cigar factory floors and the neighborhood streets of Ybor City were revolutionary spaces during the 1880s and 1890s. The energy of this period was so strong that it outlasted the struggle to excise Spain from Cuba and reverberated through the community for generations. "Ybor City was a radical, trade union town" where the cigar workers "kept alive the Cuban revolutionary tradition" while the "Spanish and Italian [kept alive the] anarchist ones."[169] Many women and men in Ybor joined the Socialist Party and the Communist Party, while others embraced the ideals of anarchism and anarcho-syndicalism. Famed leftists such as Luisa Capetillo and Carlo Tresca spent time in Ybor City, while Eugene V. Debs and Elizabeth Gurley Flynn visited the community to recruit supporters and encourage political mobilization. The people of Ybor City were, indeed, receptive to these messages. In line with their dedication to leftist ideologies and support of anti-imperialist politics, women and men in Ybor City largely defined themselves as spiritual or agnostic but vehemently anticlerical.[170] Rather than investing in religious institutions, the people of Ybor put their faith in one another.

Cigar workers established grassroots unions in Ybor City, while affiliates of national labor organizations such as the Knights of Labor, the American Federation of Labor, the International Workers of the World, and the Congress of Industrial Organizations courted and competed for the membership of these women and men. Major strikes brought the Ybor cigar industry to a halt in 1899, 1901, 1910, 1920, and 1931.[171] Over the years people struck for "higher wages, a closed shop, and sometimes simply for a better grade outer leaf for the cigars they made," as well as for improved factory conditions that demanded "factories be scrubbed once a month" and "supplies of water be kept constantly on hand" for the use of the workers. Cuban cigar workers exhibited remarkable solidarity in the midst of strike actions and over time developed a community infrastructure that could support temporary unemployment through the creation of a grassroots committee that provided strikers assistance with food and rent costs. While "the manufacturers had imported from Havana the skilled workers necessary to make luxury cigars" in what they believed to be a "new uninfected land," when powerful strikes and leftist radical politics emerged in this space, "they [wondered] what sea wind had carried [these] seeds from Cuba."[172]

When the members of the Tampa Board of Trade met with Vicente Martínez Ybor and Ignacio Haya in 1885, they never anticipated that this company town would become a place of radical, leftist, immigrant workers with a tradition of unionism powerful enough to control an entire industry. In fact, initial reports celebrated the coming of the Martínez Ybor and Haya enterprises with hope that they would bring jobs to native-born Anglo-Tampans. They did not. Cuban cigar work required skills that Anglos did not have and that Cubans were unwilling to share. Cigar workers refused to work alongside Anglos or accept them in their unions. This reality, however, did not affect the success of the cigar industry. Instead, Tampa became a one-industry town dependent on people southern Anglos deemed to be inferior. In some ways, both Martínez Ybor and Haya contributed to this problem.

On March 8, 1887, the founders of Ybor City called a meeting with the Tampa Board of Trade and requested assistance with their workforce. Although their community had existed for barely one year, it was clear to Martínez Ybor and Haya that they did not and could not control these women and men. The Board of Trade, which was eager to see profits continue to rise and the local economy expand, reached an agreement with the two manufacturers that stated: "Resolved: that the Board of Trade assures Mess. Ybor and Sánchez Haya, as well as the citizens of Tampa, generally, that they will guarantee their full support and protection for their lives and property by every legitimate means."[173]

Perhaps what Martínez Ybor and Haya did not realize was how broadly "every legitimate means" would be interpreted or that many members of the Board of Trade were also members of the KKK and the local citizens' committee. Martínez Ybor and Haya had a largely positive relationship with

Tampa's Anglo leaders. Members of the Board of Trade, which included the founding families of Tampa as well as the mayor, courted the favor of Martínez Ybor and Haya as each group worked to gain proximity to wealth and influence. Anglo elites invited these Cuban cigar manufacturers into their social circles and even accepted them into their families. For example, the daughter of Gavino Gutiérrez, the man who planned Ybor City, married Donald Brenham McKay, who owned the *Tampa Daily Times* and served multiple terms as mayor of Tampa, while Martínez Ybor secured a match for his daughter within Tampa's financial elite through her union with businessman Hugo Schwab who later became treasurer and secretary of the Florida Brewing Company.[174] The combination of wealth and Spanish birth had the ability to transcend whatever prejudice Anglo southerners held toward these immigrant men and their immigrant daughters who spoke accented English.

It is possible, however, that Martínez Ybor and Haya requested that the Board of Trade do what these manufacturers were unwilling to do themselves. The historical memory of Martínez Ybor is one of a benevolent *patron* (patron). People herald the time he invited workers to his home for a Noche Buena (Christmas Eve) feast, the days he delivered kerosene lamps to new residents of Ybor City, and the holiday he gave his cigar workers bonuses. Such actions, no matter how generous they may seem, were intended to assuage and regulate cigar workers. Assuming that these stories are true and not the result of hagiographic tales, Martínez Ybor may have grown frustrated, if not angry, with his inability to attain what he wanted most—control.

In April 1887, one month after Martínez Ybor and Haya gave Tampa leaders the authority to harness the radical, leftist workers of Ybor City, the Board of Trade drafted and supported a resolution to extend the boundaries of Tampa to include Ybor City. Although Martínez Ybor protested this action and resented the proposal that he lose authority over his own company town, Tampa political leaders took the matter to the Florida legislature and received state approval to annex Ybor City into the expanded municipality. The new city of Tampa immediately assigned police to impose law and order in this immigrant space and made clear that the "sturdy and determined citizenry of Tampa" would "protect its interests and its welfare" against "transient agitator[s]."[175] Such language and such action made clear that the Anglos who governed Tampa, as well as the Anglo population that supported them, understood Ybor City residents as people who had no place in this southern town and stood in opposition to the ideals that governed this place. While city leaders were eager to have access to the expanded tax base and profits of Cuban cigar workers, they were unwilling to recognize the humanity or the authority Ybor residents had over their community and their bodies.

In the years that followed, Ybor City cigar workers faced considerable resistance to labor activism and political action. Local newspapers encouraged, and at times demanded, that the citizens' committee or the KKK take action against insubordinate workers. Kidnappings, beatings, and lynchings became common in this southern space as white supremacy converged with anti-radicalism and nativist hatred to create the perfect storm of violent reactionism. To those who watched these events unfold it was, indeed, confounding. In 1893, a Tampa newspaper remarked: "To Cubans is owed the credit for the founding of the Fourth Ward of Tampa, that is Ybor City, where its residents produce wealth that is enjoyed by the very people who look upon Cubans with contempt. . . . This state of Florida previously impoverished is today one of the most prosperous states in the country, thanks to the development of Cuban cigars brought by the very people upon whom scorn is heaped."[176]

What is impressive about the Ybor City community, however, is that they did not stop striking, they did not stop organizing, and they did not stop living. While Anglos in Tampa sought to control and rebuke the authority that immigrants and U.S.-born cigar workers held over their workplaces and their neighborhood, the people of Ybor fought back. Unionism remained strong as did leftist political activism. Over time, the community looked for solutions and tactics to bypass violence and often found the solution in women. Unlike men, women did not experience direct violence at the hands of the citizens' committee or the KKK and therefore had space to exert their authority and the will of their community in times of heightened tension without retribution.

If we think back to the 1899 Labor Day parade, it was women who the community used to make a statement about interracial labor unionism and the right to equal work. Not only did the community choose to elevate a woman whose race confounded the Anglo journalist on assignment and to surround her with light-skinned Cuban women, but they chose to openly declare the principle that "labor knows no color, race, or creed." While this message was, in part, to the Cuban cigar workers who attended the parade that day, it was also a statement to broader Tampa that the ideals Anglos professed and the customs they sought to enforce had no authority within this Latina/o community.[177]

As long as the demand for cigars and the need for Cuban cigar work remained strong, so too did Ybor City. The women and men who lived in this community built a place that was theirs and a sense of self that was uniquely Ybor. Yet, as it did for working people around the globe, the Great Depression changed everything. In the years that followed, women became paramount to the survival of this place as well as its people.

CHAPTER TWO

Resisting

We have arrived at a moment where being neutral is being fascist.
—*La Gaceta*, Ybor City, 1937

When Rosa Rodríguez de León left her husband, the Communist Party (CP), and New York City in late 1935, she started a journey that redefined her life and the future of organized labor.[1] With her seven-year-old daughter, Mytyl, by her side, de León boarded a bus and headed south to Tampa, Florida, where she worked as an American Federation of Labor (AFL) organizer for nearly two years. It was due, in part, to de León's experience in this southern space that she sought to cast off the shadow of privilege that her light complexion, slender five-foot frame, formal education, perfect English, and elite birth afforded her to become the organizer internationally known as Luisa Moreno.[2] This personal and professional metamorphosis took place in Ybor City against the backdrop of a politic that made labor organizing, as Moreno initially envisioned it, difficult if not nearly impossible.[3]

The Depression-era Ybor City that Moreno walked into was a place with a formidable Latina/o community and a shattered economy. Due to the onslaught of the Great Depression in 1929, the local Cuban cigar industry—on which Ybor Latinas/os depended for work and Tampa leaders trusted to fuel the city—had declined at an alarming rate. Over the course of seven years, dozens of cigar factories closed their doors. The enterprises that remained operational reduced their overhead costs by downsizing their workforce and bringing in cheaper labor. In most cases this meant manufacturers fired tabaqueros and hired tabaqueras to turn Cuban tobacco into Cuban cigars. A few other factory owners began to wade in the waters of mechanized production and hired women to work the machines. Such shifts in Cuban cigar production resulted in mass Latino unemployment, a drastic decrease in the average Latina/o family wage, and the rise of Latinas as primary income earners and powerful leaders within factories, unions, families, and the Ybor community. Yet as the Cuban cigar industry struggled to survive and the unemployment rate of Latinos rose, the local Ku Klux Klan (KKK), the citizens' committee, and white supremacist vigilantes became increasingly violent. Many Anglos who belonged to and traveled between these groups were city leaders and people with access to political influence who sought to control Cuban cigar workers in an effort to keep the cigar industry alive, placate cigar manufacturers, and maintain political control over this space. In response, Latinas/os in Ybor City were among the millions of people who joined the Popular Front movement to fight fascism across the globe as well as in their own backyards. Moreno, who the AFL sent to Tampa to recruit Latinas into the Cigar Makers' International Union (CMIU), faced the challenge of negotiating between the demands of her employer and the needs, interests, and politics of the Latina workers she represented.

Moreno joined the Latinas of Ybor as they created a coalition of resistance against economic inequality in Ybor City and Tampa during the 1930s. Throughout the decade of the Depression, these women objected to the de-skilling and mechanization of the Cuban cigar industry; the effect of unemployment and underemployment on their sons, brothers, and husbands; the prejudicial conditions and restrictions of federal relief programs; and the United States' position on the rise of global fascism, most importantly, the Spanish Civil War. Although Moreno arrived in Ybor City prepared to recruit and negotiate labor contracts on behalf of the Latina cigar workers who belonged to the CMIU, during her time in the community she saw that the scope of the problems these women faced could not be solved with a labor agreement, no matter how advantageous it might be. Labor unionism, as the AFL understood it, was too narrow to address the big issues of Ybor City. As a result, Moreno abandoned the demands of her employer, the AFL, and collaborated with Latinas in Ybor to support a popular front movement that sought to overcome local economic inequalities and social injustices. As these women raised their voices in defense of the Spanish Republic, they denounced antidemocratic politics in Cuba as well as anti-immigrant, racialized oppression within Tampa—all actions they understood as fascist.

When it comes to discussions of fascism and antifascism, one of the perpetual challenges is understanding what these terms mean. As the historian Ariel Mae Lambe explains, to say "that antifascism is against fascism seems a straightforward assertion, but it leads directly to a notoriously difficult task: defining fascism." Fascism is an elusive political concept that historians and scholars contest today. Most reference Italy under Benito Mussolini as well as Germany under Adolf Hitler and Nazism to illustrate historical instances of such regimes. Fascism, however, does exist outside such classic cases. What fascist movements and political parties often have in common is that a group of "chosen people"—those who believe they have historic authority and supremacy over others—contend they are "under attack and must be vindicated." Such forces frequently develop when "a nation is in decline," when a subset of people experience the might of their social privilege contested, or when there is a rise in economic instability. Fascism can emerge as an answer to such problems through a vigorous and unifying form of nationalism, which unites people into a "militant party with an activist political style and a charismatic authoritarian male leader."[4] During the 1930s, amid the Great Depression, fascism spread throughout the world as strongmen energized the masses by pointing to political opponents as well as underrepresented racial, ethnic, and religious groups as responsible for the scarcity of jobs, economic resources, national stability, and personal pride. Antifascism stood in contrast to such ideologies and brought together those whom fascists blamed for social, political, and economic ills. Antifascists advocated that a broader multiethnic, multiracial, gender-diverse coalition that opened the political field and economic markets to more, rather than fewer, people was central to the creation of a just and stable world. The Popular Front—or Frente Popular, as it was known in Ybor City—was the movement that sought to create a people's front that fought against the rise of fascism throughout the world, within nations, and inside communities.[5]

The Popular Front in Ybor City blended a Latin American and European approach to resistance with U.S. iterations of the movement. As right-wing authoritarianism took hold of the Americas, the Caribbean, and Europe, Latinas in Ybor aligned themselves with international antifascist politics.[6] Regimes that sought to constrain human rights, civil liberties, and labor equality felt personal to immigrants in Ybor City, most of whom hailed from Cuba and Spain. While many immigrant women aligned with antifascist politics because their families and memories extended to places where oppressive authoritarianism sought to dominate popular authority, U.S.-born Latinas allied with antifascism out of community solidarity and a shared ethnic identity. Importantly, however, Latinas in Ybor recognized that the battle against fascism was not a problem contained "over there." Fascism, after all, can come in many shapes and sizes—at times in the form of a national dictator and at others in the form of a local politician. Fascism can emerge through a coup d'état or through democratic elections. Tampa's Anglo power holders, many of whom held positions of elected authority in the city, mimicked fascism in their violent efforts to quell the power of organized labor, to crush leftist radicalism, and to define Latinas/os as un-American foreign citizens undeserving of relief.[7] One result of these actions was the problem of mass Latino unemployment and the inability of these men to find work beyond Ybor or voice their concerns without the threat of visceral retaliation and lynching. Latinas in Ybor City created a movement that was the working-class and grassroots embodiment of *feminismo americano*—the commitment to "women's political and civil equality" and "social and economic justice" as well as the "political and civil rights of all people, men and women"—as they became the voices and bodies that rebuked the power of fascism in their own community.[8]

Moreno encountered the women of Ybor in the midst of this moment of global crisis and local reckoning. During her time in the community, Moreno focused her energies on mobilizing Latinas so they could project their own voices and stand together as the mouthpieces and representatives of Latina/o interests throughout Ybor City and Tampa. While Moreno was by no means a flawless heroine, she was an effective organizer. She took the time to understand the cultures of labor that collided in this borderland and to understand how to navigate oppressive and violent forms of vigilantism that vilified any iteration of politics or community organization that stood in the face of potential profit. In the process of movement making in Ybor City Moreno learned much about herself, because the women she organized influenced her even more than she influenced them. Latinas in Ybor City were born into a tradition of radical, leftist, working-class politics, whereas Moreno had chosen to adopt these principles and ideologies. The reciprocal nature of this relationship led to the emergence of a professional organizer who went on to lead the nation's most ambitious union and to the rise of Latina activists in Ybor City who sought to overcome the limitations of southern hierarchies in Florida on their own terms.

Colliding Cultures of Labor

Considering the circumstances of her birth, Moreno was an unlikely champion of labor and human rights. Born the daughter of a Colombian socialite and a Guatemalan coffee tycoon, Moreno grew up with five siblings on her family's grand estate. As a child she learned to speak and read Spanish and French from private tutors, and at age thirteen Moreno was well versed in English after spending four years at a Catholic boarding school in Oakland, California. By fifteen, Moreno aspired to a university education, but Guatemalan law prohibited women from the halls of academe. Moreno rejected this legal limitation and encouraged other elite daughters to advocate for women's rights through educational reform. In the early 1920s, as budding feminist and suffragist movements erupted and succeeded in the United States, the actions of Moreno and her fellow women's activists proved triumphant and Guatemalan universities accepted their first class of women.

While some Guatemalan women began to fill university classrooms, Moreno left her homeland for Mexico City and immersed herself in the world of "the bohemian cultural elite."[9] Moreno flourished in this new environment as she brushed shoulders with the artists Frida Kahlo and Diego Rivera and became a journalist and poet. In 1927, Moreno married Miguel Angel de León, a fellow upper-class Guatemalan. A year later, with Moreno pregnant, the couple traded the comfort of Mexico City's intelligentsia circles for the crowded vibrancy of New York City's Spanish Harlem tenements.[10]

Upon their arrival to the United States, Moreno and her husband struggled to find work in New York City. As the U.S. economy deteriorated and jobs became scarce, the couple's artistic talents did not help them earn enough money to pay rent and put food on the table. By early 1929, a desperate Moreno accepted a job as a seamstress at a garment factory, and her husband became the primary caregiver to their daughter, allowing him to continue to pursue his passion for painting while simultaneously nurturing his drinking habit. Moreno worked long hours on the shop floor to provide for her family and became intimately aware of the struggle her fellow women workers endured. Aside from low pay, dangerous working conditions, and grueling workdays, women workers found it nearly impossible to secure childcare and contribute to the family wage.

The historian Vicki L. Ruiz identified the moment Moreno decided to organize on behalf of Latina wage workers. After one particularly trying day at the factory, a friend and fellow seamstress asked if Moreno would like to meet her baby. Moreno obliged and followed her companion to the apartment the woman and her child shared. Like most of Moreno's colleagues, her friend struggled to find and pay for a caregiver. In the absence of a family member able to assume this role, her friend relied on an older woman in the building to watch the child. As Moreno and her friend entered the building and began to ascend the stairs, both women heard the scream of a crying baby, and "her friend started to panic [for] she recognized her child's voice."[11] The women rushed into the apartment and found "no babysitter was in sight." Her friend scooped her baby into her arms and stood in shock—"a rat had eaten off half the baby's face."[12] When Moreno shared this memory with Ruiz, she explained that "it was in that moment" that "she knew she had to do something to change the material conditions of her fellow workers."[13] To find a path to advocate for herself and the women who surrounded her, Moreno joined the Communist Party USA (CPUSA) in 1930 and founded La Liga de Costureras (League of Seamstresses), known as La Liga, a labor union to represent Latina seamstresses. Perhaps most importantly, Latina garment workers across Spanish Harlem followed her.[14]

For the next five years, and under the cloud of the Great Depression, Moreno organized New York Latina workers largely on her own. Upon the founding of La Liga, Moreno affiliated her union with the Needle Trades Workers Industrial Union (NTWIU), a labor organization established by communists and fellow travelers expelled from the International Ladies' Garment Workers' Union (ILGWU) in late 1928.[15] Moreno hoped the connection with the NTWIU would bring organizer training, staff assistance, and financial support. When it did not, Moreno disaffiliated La Liga from the NTWIU and aligned with the "more mainstream" ILGWU.[16]

The decision to shift union affiliation speaks to both the tenuous nature of Moreno's allegiance to the CPUSA and Moreno's desire to see La Liga succeed. As with many CPUSA members and fellow travelers of the 1930s, it was not dogmatic dedication to the Comintern or the goal of creating a Soviet United States that brought Moreno into the party but the possibility that the principles of Marxism could pave a path toward relief, equity, care, and equality in a society where capitalism created barriers to security through discrimination on the basis of ethnicity, race, gender, sex, and class difference. To Moreno, these intersecting inequalities were real, not theoretical. She and her fellow seamstresses struggled to purchase food, secure childcare, and pay rent in an economy and nation that depended on low-cost, disposable labor. As a wage-earning woman, Moreno was cheap because the value of her labor was less than that of a man. As a working-class immigrant, Moreno was replaceable because she was one of millions. During an era of heightened precarity, the CPUSA provided Moreno, and countless others, with the dream of an intangible utopia where the value of one's work, the sense of one's dignity, and the might of one's voice had nothing to do with one's sex, gender, skin color, or citizenship status. This dream was powerful and, no doubt, one worth having.[17]

Once Moreno affiliated La Liga with the ILGWU, she exchanged the romance of the party for recognition by labor's political elite. The ILGWU rose to prominence after the Triangle Shirtwaist Factory fire of 1911, when national media outlets captured images of women workers jumping out of windows and falling to their deaths just one block from Washington Square Park. Triangle was neither the first factory fire nor the first workplace tragedy to claim the lives of its workforce. It was, however, the first industrial disaster to result in the mass death of women workers within earshot and eyesight of middle-class and upper-class New Yorkers. Printed images of Manhattan sidewalks strewn with the mangled, burned bodies of seamstresses personified the human cost of unregulated capital to those who had long refused to acknowledge the problem, igniting a new phase of labor activism, labor law, and infrastructure legislation across the United States. In the wake of Triangle, the ILGWU emerged as a national force. The union teamed with the Women's Trade Union League—the cross-class women's organization that united the fortitude of working-class women's activists with middle- and upper-class women allies who had money, time, progressive politics, and political access—to enact labor reform, gain union support, and fight for women's suffrage. Working-class women's activists such as Fannia Cohn, Rose Schneiderman, Pauline Newman, and Clara Lemlich created a powerful network that illustrated the might and reach of immigrant, women organizers. By the time Moreno brought La Liga into the orbit of the ILGWU, some of these women had fought their way through the ranks of the union from member to organizer to vice president to secretary to director of education in the national organization, while others had been invited into the home and political circles of the then New York governor and later U.S. president, Franklin D. Roosevelt. Although affiliation with the ILGWU did not bring the money or staff support Moreno craved, it integrated La Liga into the matrix of working-class women's activists who knew how to improve worker conditions at the grassroots level and how to influence the future of national labor and welfare policy.[18]

While La Liga's newfound proximity to power lent a sense of legitimacy to the budding union, it did little to support day-to-day operations. Moreno, therefore, got creative. Rather than relying on funding and staff from the national organization, members of La Liga turned to volunteerism from friends and relatives, most of whom were men. Husbands, brothers, and neighbors supported their wives and sisters through La Liga's "fraternal auxiliary," which sold tickets to fundraisers, managed publicity, planned events, and supported strikes to keep the union afloat. Moreno was proud of this invention. During an interview with Ruiz, Moreno explained that she developed this strategy "at a time when only a few men's unions had 'ladies auxiliaries.'"[19] As a veteran organizer in the late 1970s, reflecting on her life in conversation with a young and eager historian, Moreno was pleased to stand among the vanguard of working-class women's activists, for she knew that her strategies were, and remained, revolutionary.[20] As a young organizer in the 1930s, Moreno found it exhilarating to build a woman-led union that represented Latina workers and rebuked a culture of working-class activism that placed men, rather than women, at the helm of administration and leadership. Over the course of the six years that Moreno worked as the leader and primary organizer of La Liga, her union remained small and centered on community affairs. No matter the size of La Liga, her organizing talent was visible. Moreno's skill caught the eye of the AFL in 1935, and the union offered her a job as an organizer of the CMIU in Florida.[21] Frustrated by her isolating, deteriorating marriage, as well as her genuine desire to change the culture of labor unionism and highlight the needs of working Latinas, Moreno accepted the position and began a new life in the U.S. South.[22]

When Moreno stepped off the bus and began organizing in Florida, the AFL hoped she would be the answer to its problems. The union tasked Moreno with the mission of organizing cigar workers in central Florida—the region between Lakeland and Jacksonville—but it was the recruitment of cigar workers in Ybor City and West Tampa that the AFL coveted most. In 1892, six years after Cuban cigar factories opened their doors in Ybor City, the CMIU established its first Tampa local.[23] Yet by the time Moreno arrived in the area, roughly forty-three years after the first local's founding, the CMIU had seven locals but continued to struggle to build a loyal membership base among Latina/o cigar workers.[24] CMIU organizers reported that Ybor cigar workers were disorganized and had little interest in the union.[25] At times Ybor cigar workers seemed apathetic toward the CMIU and at others openly hostile. Despite the decades-long recruitment dilemma, the union never dissolved its locals and continued to pursue its goal of bringing all Cuban cigar workers into the CMIU. Ybor City, and by extension Tampa, was the crown jewel of the U.S.-based Cuban cigar industry. Cuban cigar workers who lived and worked in this place had the reputation of producing the highest-quality, handmade Cuban cigars in the world, thereby earning Tampa the title of "Cigar City."[26] Even as the economy wavered during the Depression, the Cuban cigar industry remained the largest, single-industry employer in the city of Tampa. If the CMIU, and the AFL, was to become a political force in the Sunshine State—one that could influence and shape labor legislation—it had to recruit, represent, and gain the respect of Ybor cigar workers.[27]

Moreno likely knew this general history when she accepted the job in Florida, but she may have wondered if there were more to the story. Upon hire, the AFL made clear that it was not just Moreno's talent but also her identity that made her an attractive organizer.[28] The fact that Moreno was an immigrant, Latina, and Spanish speaking mattered to the union. Her experience with La Liga and its alignment with the ILGWU illustrated that, at least on some level, she was open to a U.S.-centric brand of labor unionism and knew how to translate such principles to Latinas in Spanish Harlem, or so the AFL hoped.[29] It is possible that the AFL yearned for Moreno to replicate in Ybor City what she did in New York City, even though it never said so explicitly.[30]

Organizers sent to Ybor City in years past—most of whom were non-Spanish-speaking, Anglo men—reported to the AFL that Latina/o cigar workers "[were] opposed to all American institutions" and "could not understand reason."[31] It is likely that under their leadership few Cuban cigar workers joined the union roster because of the failure to communicate, both literally and figuratively, what the union could provide to these women and men. Neither the CMIU nor the national AFL leadership were blind to this problem. During the 1910s, the union filled the position of CMIU organizer from within the Ybor community. Men such as José de la Campa, a Spanish anarchist turned socialist, and Giovanni Vaccaro, a Sicilian socialist, led CMIU locals and called Ybor home.[32] These union leaders had worked in the Ybor cigar industry and carried an understanding of the community's sense of political consciousness. Much like their fellow cigar workers, they were first and foremost radical leftists, not allegiant, obedient AFL employees. While these organizers believed, ardently, in the mission of trade unionism, to them union work was part of an immediate effort to improve the lives of those in the Ybor community and grew from a larger, internationalist political vision.[33] The CMIU, by contrast, understood labor organizing from the perspective of a nationalist, U.S.-centric philosophy—a concept that was not historically welcoming to non-Anglo, noncitizen, and non-male workers. The conflict between these two viewpoints was endemic.[34] One group wished to advocate for workers while consolidating its national power within the United States, whereas the other wished to remake the world. It is unlikely that either the CMIU or the upper leadership of the AFL explained this reality to Moreno. Instead, she had to discover it on her own.

Moreno worked long hours in Ybor City. She visited factories, introduced herself to management, met with Spanish-language newspaper editors, and led union meetings at the Centro Obrero (Labor Temple).[35] Her days were ceaseless and her schedule was unpredictable. Moreno made the decision to "board her daughter [Mytyl] with a pro-labor Latin[a/o] family" in Ybor City, while Moreno lived separately in a rented room at a local boardinghouse.[36] At the time, Moreno assumed this arrangement provided Mytyl with the consistency, the stability, and perhaps even the love she needed. The reality, however, was more complicated. The head of the first foster family who hosted Mytyl in Ybor City molested her when she was seven years old. Moreno, who had run La Liga like a family, may have seen the communities she organized as an extension of the household she wished she had but could not provide. Blind trust, coupled with infrequent visits to see Mytyl, left her daughter vulnerable and the target of sexual exploitation. This trauma never subsided. Ruiz explained that Mytyl "related these incidents with a rawness that had not abated with time" and characterized Mytyl's childhood as one filled with "a sense of profound loneliness."[37] Neither documentary evidence nor oral history testimony suggests that Moreno knew of the suffering her daughter endured.

The relationship between Mytyl and Moreno exposes a side of activism historians prefer to ignore—the reality that while "women are capable of everything and anything," nobody can be everything to everyone at the same time in a capitalist system without access to wealth or a system of assistance.[38] Moreno made the decision to be an activist first and a mother second. In some ways, this decision grew from the circumstances of her life. Moreno was estranged from her husband, disowned by her family, and had no money.[39] On a practical level, Moreno may have made the choices she did because she had neither a network of support nor the means to rent a home large enough for her and Mytyl while shouldering the cost of full-time child-care and doing her job. Moreno needed an income to provide for her daughter—a central component of mothering—and did so as she followed her passion to make the lives of all working-class women better. We could understand Moreno as a resourceful, determined young mother who did the best she could by herself and with limited resources. We could assume that this was a part of her life she regretted and, given the chance to do it differently, she would search for other solutions. Perhaps many of these assumptions are true, but to accept them unequivocally would require that we overlook who Moreno was during this season of her life.

Moreno's decision to prioritize activism over motherhood was a choice she made before she arrived in Florida. In New York, it was Miguel, her husband, who stayed home and cared for Mytyl while Moreno worked a double day as a seamstress and a union organizer. Miguel, we should not forget, was no star parent. He was often drunk and struggled with the task of raising himself and his child.[40] The division of labor within the de León household initially emerged out of necessity, yet later it provided Moreno with an escape—an escape from her husband, an escape from her marriage, and an escape from her reality.[41] It pained Moreno to watch her once talented, handsome husband devolve into a drunken depression. Although Moreno did not disclose physical abuse within her marriage, she did share that Miguel could be violent.[42] The union, and her time away from home, reinvigorated

Moreno and reminded her who she was. Moreno may not have been able to change the dynamic inside her Spanish Harlem tenement, but she could change the lives of others with her voice and her organizing. This power was, no doubt, addictive and energizing. When Moreno left New York, she took parts of herself with her. No matter her change of address or her change of name, during this point in time, the core of Moreno was the same in Ybor City as in New York—a labor organizer above all else.

In Ybor City, Moreno immersed herself in the community.[43] She knew that if she were to succeed at recruiting new members into the CMIU and organize on behalf of these cigar-working women and men, she had to understand them. Moreno likely spent time in the cantinas and cafés of Ybor City and West Tampa as she researched the community. These spaces were typically masculine but not officially gender segregated.[44] Upon her first visit, the men in the room may have seen her as a curious oddity, but over time she became a welcome eccentric. As Moreno absorbed the atmosphere of her new city, she may have ordered crispy, salty Cuban bread that she dipped into a cup of sweet, creamy *café con leche*—the perfect duo for a morning of anthropologic eavesdropping. When Moreno stopped by for an evening of research, she likely followed the lead of the local clientele. For a cheap drink she may have ordered a ten-cent beer, but if she had some extra money that week, perhaps she selected a whiskey on the rocks or a rum and cola, both of which flowed openly since the repeal of Prohibition.[45] Organizers from competing unions, such as the Industrial Workers of the World, as well as activists and members of leftist radical political groups from Mexico, the Caribbean, Spain, and Italy may have introduced themselves to Moreno while she sipped her drink du jour and gained a sense of the ideologies that guided the community.[46]

Understanding the perspective of Latinas in Ybor was not as straightforward. When Moreno walked into the neighborhood's cafés and cantinas, she would not have seen groups of Latinas huddled around domino tables arguing about politics and discussing the latest news. To learn about the needs, struggles, and ideas of women in Ybor, Moreno had to earn their trust and receive invitations to their homes. Each evening after men ate dinner and drank their nightly *cafecito* (small coffee, typically a demitasse), they left their homes and poured into neighborhood cantinas such as La Tropicana.[47] In the absence of men, women walked onto their porches and welcomed each other with cool lemonade in the summer and warm coffee or homemade wine in the winter. No matter the season, this space transformed from utilitarian to sacred at sundown.[48]

The front porch served as a refuge where women gossiped, shared ideas, and confided in each other. Moreno may have been asked to join these women after meeting in the factory or the Labor Temple.[49] The cigar-working women of Ybor may have wanted to know more about this Latina from New York whom the CMIU had sent south to represent them. If Moreno joined in the nightly front porch ritual, she would have learned, much as she had in New York, of these women's worries about income and rent. Ybor Latinas would have shared their fears about mechanization and the anxiety they had over changes in the industry. They would have explained that these shifts affected not only their wages but also the tradition and pride of cigar work itself.[50] Some of these Latinas may have felt hopeless in the 1930s. When the historian Nancy A. Hewitt interviewed Ybor Latinas in the 1980s, many women refused to discuss the Depression in detail. The memory was too painful.[51] As these women sat with Moreno in the moment, however, they would have wanted her to know more than their fears; they would have wanted to share their strength, and they would have wanted her to understand their culture—the things that made them proud to say they were from Ybor City. It was through interactions in places like this that Moreno would have learned more about the local history of labor, a tale that likely conflicted with the official story she received from the CMIU.

From all the time Moreno likely spent listening and having conversations with Latinas/os in Ybor, she learned that one thing the CMIU got right was that cigar workers in Ybor City were wary of U.S.-based institutions, labor unions included. This distrust was not without reason. In the past, the union operated under a banner of "pure and simple" unionism that cigar workers understood as exclusionary, in part because it was.[52] During the early years, the AFL separated workers on the basis of race and sex and operated according to openly xenophobic and nationalist visions of immigrant workers. Within this structure, there was little room for an immigrant, multiracial, multi-ethnic workforce that wished to maintain the integrity of their craft within their community to defend their skill and their culture of labor. What the CMIU did not see during the early years of the Ybor cigar industry was that cigar workers did not wish to become U.S. workers whose labor was defended by U.S. principles.[53] Instead, they wanted a union that would defend their principles, their traditions, their craft, and their wages.

What made the Cuban cigar industry in Tampa powerful and distinct was the fact that it had an immigrant workforce. One could not claim to make true Cuban cigars without a workforce of Cubans—all of whom produced clear Havana cigars and had been trained in the Spanish hand process.[54] Most factories that claimed to make Cuban cigars, beyond Florida and the island, used Cuban leaf for the exterior of the cigar but relied on cheaper, domestic tobacco for the filler, the innermost portion of the cigar.[55] This mattered not only to consumers but also to Ybor cigar workers. In order for the industry to sell, and for tabaqueras/os to produce, the highest-quality cigars, it required the highest-quality Cuban tobacco. Moreover, the Spanish hand process required apprenticeship and expertise. This method of cigar making flourished on the island and required that all cigar workers involved in the process of cigar making do their job by hand. Therefore, every person who worked within Ybor factories was a skilled worker, whose replacement was not simple.[56]

What made the immigrant status of Ybor cigar workers most powerful was the fact that they could leave if they chose. In times of strike, unrest, or dispute with manufacturers, a portion of cigar workers of Cuban and Spanish descent often left Ybor City and went to Key West or Havana, where they found temporary work in other cigar-making communities or simply stayed with family and friends until the tension subsided. Sometimes the number of cigar workers who left the city was marginal, but other times it was in the hundreds.[57] This reality terrified manufacturers and Tampa civic leaders. Factory owners could not produce their product without workers trained in the Spanish hand process, and the city of Tampa, which was a one-industry town, could not thrive without a workforce that knew how to produce a clear Havana cigar. Ybor cigar workers had the ability to bring the local industry and the city to its knees if they so wished. And, at times, they did. As one *despaldilladora*, Luise Herrera, said in the midst of a strike at the turn of the century, "[We] should all leave Tampa and allow it to rot like a grinning skeleton."[58] Even though many of the first-generation immigrant cigar workers had retired by the time Moreno arrived, these women and men trained the next generation in the old style.[59] Not only did this generation expect the same level of respect, but manufacturers knew their workforce maintained their international relationships across this southern borderland.

Cigar workers believed their skill came with specific privileges that their employers had to respect and their union organizers had to defend. Ybor cigar workers guarded their right to set their own pace of work, have open access to cigars to smoke during the workday, and bring home raw tobacco if they chose.[60] Workers expected their employers to permit a *cafetero* (a person who sold and served *café con leche* and espresso) to have access to the shop floor so they could access essential stimulants without interrupting their labor. Among the most important of all traditions, however, was the

Lector reading to cigar makers at the Corral Wodiska factory, Ybor City, 1929.
Burgert Brothers Collection, University of South Florida Libraries — Tampa Special
Collections, Tampa, Florida.

right of workers to select, hire, and fire a *lector* (reader) of their choosing. It
was the cigar workers, not the factory owners, who paid the salary of the lector. This person read what the workers selected, because it was the cigar
workers who employed them. On the surface, the purpose of the lector was
to entertain people throughout the workday, but within the community those
who occupied this position held considerable political and cultural authority. It was not unusual to meet an illiterate Ybor cigar worker who could quote
Victor Hugo, debate Karl Marx, and explain the latest in international affairs
with equal fervor and conviction.[61]

Moreno may have never entered a Cuban cigar factory before she was an
organizer, but she would have been familiar with the *lectura* (the reader tradition and position) and understood the power of its influence. As a young
feminist, Moreno was well versed in ideas of women's autonomy, equality,
and independence from Latin America and the Caribbean. It is further likely

that she intersected in spaces where U.S.-centric feminism thrived, especially in socialist and communist spaces in New York City. To Moreno, feminism was more than suffrage, legal rights, and the vote—it was a concept that encapsulated the self, the family, the workplace, and the community that neither nation nor citizenship confined as it moved across borders and bent to the needs of women according to place and time. Moreno was likely inspired by one particular feminist, Luisa Capetillo, the famed Puerto Rican labor organizer, writer, and anarcho-syndicalist. Roughly twenty-two years before Moreno arrived in Ybor City, Capetillo walked the streets of the community and ascended to the position of *lectora*, the only woman documented to have held the position in this community. As lectora, Capetillo dressed like her male peers, in a white shirt, black pants, dark jacket, and panama hat—an atypical wardrobe for a woman in 1913—and her voice boomed throughout the factory as she read the published material that her mixed-sex employers requested, as well as some of her own writings. Capetillo herself was a feminist author. She had published her book *Mi opinión sobre las libertades, derechos y deberes de la mujer* (My opinion on the liberties, rights, and duties of woman) before arriving in Ybor City, but it was her time in the community that pushed her to revise the monograph and to compose essays for a second book, *Influencia de las ideas modernas* (The influence of modern ideas). Moreno likely read the works of Capetillo and pondered, much as the author had, the conflicting experiences of women's political authority, free love, labor organizing, and working motherhood. Perhaps, as Ruiz postulates, the intersecting experiences of these two women inspired Moreno to shed her birth name Rosa and professionally embrace the name Luisa—an ode to the lectora, labor organizer, and feminist whom she wished to follow in spirit.

Given this context, Moreno would have understood how such a tradition could mean so much to so many and why cigar workers felt the lectura was worth fighting for. Amparo Valdés, a Black Cuban woman who worked in Ybor cigar factories during the 1920s and 1930s, looked forward to the daily readings of novels in the afternoon. What resonated with her and her friends was not the feminist treatise of Capetillo, but the reading of *Les Misérables*. Themes of revolution, struggle, inequality, and working motherhood felt personal to Valdés, a widowed single mother of three who labored to feed and care for her family independently. Valdés's son later remembered that his mother and her friends spent weeks asking each other, "Faced with the starvation of your children, what would you do?" While he assumed his mother and her friends were "stumped" by this "skillfully posed dilemma," it is most likely that the question felt personal and may have even filled Valdés and her friend with a sense of fear.[62] Many women, such as Valdés, were the primary breadwinners of their households, and it was their responsibility to provide both emotional and physical care for their families. To these women, the themes read from the lector were not fictional theories but personal problems that defined their lives and their anxieties.

As Moreno spent more time in Ybor City, she likely learned that cigar workers seemed to be on a consistent search for a union that understood them. On the days she sat in cafés and listened to other people's stories, she may have heard men of the older generation remember fantastic strikes.[63] Despite the prevalence of unions in Ybor City, cigar workers had not categorically won a mass strike, without compromise, since La Huelga de Pesa, the Weight Strike, in 1899, a strike waged without any union representation. That year, management of the Ybor-Manrara factory introduced scales in an effort to improve efficiency by weighing the amount of tobacco given to each cigar maker and specifying the number of cigars that should be produced from a specific portion of tobacco—a practice that was commonplace in northern U.S. cigar factories.[64] Cuban tabaqueras/os in Ybor City, however, saw the invention as an insult to their craft. It was an offense that transgressed Cuban cigar workers' rights to control the means of production within their workplace, a fundamental tradition to their trade. In response, cigar workers walked out of nearly all factories in Ybor City and brought the industry to a halt for weeks. Manufacturers eventually bent to the demands of the Ybor workforce, agreed to remove the scales from the factories, and welcomed all strikers back to work. Thirty-six years later, as Moreno toured the cigar factories of Ybor and West Tampa, she would have been surrounded by the power of this strike, even if she did realize it, for the scales had not returned.[65]

Women and men of the immigrant generation may have told Moreno of the brief period when they created a union in their image. After the victory of La Huelga de Pesa, the informal leadership committee that guided this strike created a formal union called La Sociedad de Torcedores de Tampa (Cigar Makers Society of Tampa), best known as La Resistencia (the Resistance). This grassroots, Latina/o-led union accepted all cigar workers no matter their race or their sex—something U.S. unions, up to this point, had refused to do. For these workers, not only was an organization without division on the basis of "color or creed" inherently stronger, but it was a form of unionism that felt natural, as it fit within their internationalist, cross-border, anti-imperial paradigm. La Resistencia drew organizational and strategic inspiration from La Liga de Trabajadores de Cuba (League of Cuban Workers), a labor organization that represented cigar workers on the island and fought for increased wages, the maintenance of traditions, and worker autonomy within factories. Over 4,000 people joined La Resistencia at a time when the CMIU struggled to attract roughly 300 members, nearly none of whom had a Latina/o surname.[66] The ability of La Resistencia to gain such a robust membership illustrated that these women and men could be organized, but it required that unions embrace, rather than reject, immigrant understandings of workplace and politics. Cuban cigar workers did not strive to become U.S. citizens and good U.S. workers, but they did seek to achieve and maintain an equitable and dignified workplace.[67] In the end, La Resistencia burned bright and brief. While the union successfully negotiated contracts that led to higher wages, its decision to pursue a strike with the goal of a closed shop policy drained the union of its resources. In 1902, after a mere three years of passion-filled organizing, La Resistencia dissolved.[68]

The power of La Resistencia reverberated beyond the union's formal existence. While Moreno may have heard women and men of the immigrant generation wax poetically about *their* union, the children and grandchildren of these workers—those Moreno organized and with whom she spent the most time—likely shared secondhand memories of La Resistencia when asked.[69] The more Moreno learned, the more she would have recognized the legacy of La Resistencia in the decisions made by the CMIU in Tampa. Although national leaders never explicitly stated that they shifted their policies due to the culture of Ybor cigar workers or the example of La Resistencia, the changes the CMIU underwent illustrate that they listened and endeavored to understand the workers whose membership it courted. By the 1910s, the CMIU abandoned segregated unionism, on the basis of both gender and race, in Ybor City and West Tampa. Instead, the union established a multi-local system that organized and extended membership to this multiracial, multiethnic, gender-diverse workforce. The new locals "divided along craft lines for cigar [workers]," a structure that mirrored the *gremio* (guild) system of La Resistencia, which divided workers according to the skilled position they performed in the cigar factory.[70] Eventually, the CMIU founded seven locals in the area that represented workers in Ybor City and West Tampa. In addition to these changes, the CMIU agreed to the creation of the Joint Advisory Board. Much like the committee system that guided the actions and decisions of La Resistencia, the board consisted of "a minimum of three [elected] delegates," who served as representatives between members and the appointed organizer. The board took up residence, along with the union, in the Centro Obrero, where they met for joint meetings, between each other and the broader community. With these changes in place, the CMIU held membership drives that lowered the cost of entry to one dollar. As a result, Ybor cigar workers joined the union by the thousands, and its membership surged to 6,000 members during this decade.[71]

Despite these changes and the increase in membership, Cuban cigar workers often played by their own rules. Wildcat strikes and general strikes that lasted up to ten months were not uncommon in the neighborhood. The CMIU, however, preferred to negotiate and reach an agreement with manufacturers due to the capital that a strike required from the national organization and the goodwill it expended with factory owners.[72] Cigar workers in Ybor disagreed. These women and men had the tolerance, will, and community infrastructure necessary to endure lengthy work stoppages in demand for better pay and worker dignity. Most importantly, they were willing to strike with or without union endorsement. For the next decade, a series of strikes continued. At times these clashes resulted in the outcome Ybor cigar workers desired, but at others they ended in violence. Ybor City's Cuban cigar workers understood both the value of their craft and the demand for their product. As a result, they were neither willing to accept low wages nor willing to abandon their traditions in exchange for U.S. efficiency.

Cigar workers in Ybor had the intellectual fortitude and the strength needed to defend their craft and their wages because of community institutions and community solidarity. Centros provided unemployment insurance, while local anarchist and socialist auxiliaries created *cocinas economicas*, soup kitchens, to feed those who could not pay for food.[73] Likewise, Ybor residents who owned pharmacies, markets, and restaurants often extended a line of credit to desperate patrons. Peter Parrado, a community member born and raised in Ybor City, remembered that if customers did not have enough money to pay their bill, they could simply say "apuntamelo" (take note).[74] In response, the owner of the market would record the spending and expect reimbursement after a strike concluded or once a community member found employment again after being laid off or resigning in protest. To keep spirits high during times of unrest, strikes, or unemployment, local Spanish-language presses printed manifestos of support that a community member read during evening meetings at the Labor Temple or in the theater of a mutual aid society if a larger venue was essential. A culture of working-class entertainment likewise emerged in Ybor City. Community-inspired dramatic plays, poetry, and *zarzuelas* (lyrical comedies) written by women and men in Ybor celebrated the working-class, cross-border lives of Cuban cigar workers.[75] While hundreds of people packed the grand theaters of mutual aid societies to watch these performances, they likewise welcomed the stage dancers, opera singers, dramatists, and political activists from Cuba, Puerto Rico, and Spain. These events kept Ybor Latinas/os connected to their homelands, their heritage, and a borderland where neither labor, culture, nor tradition was confined by nationhood or citizenship.

Moreno likely admired the solidarity she found in Ybor City, for it reflected her own approach to organizing and her own sense of political consciousness. Although the AFL understood the connection of La Liga de Costureras to the ILGWU as an indicator of Moreno's acceptance of U.S. unionism, in practice she embraced the ethos of latinidad that thrived in Spanish Harlem and stretched across borders. As Moreno learned more about the culture and the politics of Ybor City, she may have seen the collective community approach to organization in this place as a more intricate version of the family-centric mobilization model she developed in New York. Moreno may have even studied the Ybor community's infrastructure and political culture as something she wished to replicate if her career took her beyond the Sunshine State or the AFL. Yet while Moreno may have admired aspects of Ybor, she almost certainly understood that neither the community nor its people were perfect.

When Moreno joined Ybor Latinas on their front porches at night, she may have asked how the union could better serve them as women. Much like the women Moreno sought to represent, she understood that the choice to divert a portion of a person's weekly wage during the Depression was a big decision—the service had to be worth the investment. The most obvious response Moreno would have received was for the union to make the needs of women and the defense of women's wages a priority. Despite the shifts the CMIU made during the early 1900s and 1910s, the support of Latina labor was seldom a high priority to the union or the community itself.

Latinas typically occupied the position of *despaldilladora*—the person who stripped the stem from the tobacco leaf—which in the hierarchy of Cuban cigar work was essential but less skilled, despite requiring an apprenticeship to do the job and join the CMIU.[76] Unlike the union-supported uproars that ensued when manufacturers attacked men's wages or men's skills, there was rarely a response when women experienced the same injustice. This exhausted Latinas and made them question whether union representation was essential or even beneficial to their lives. These women did not, however, accept the dismissive reaction lightly. For example, in 1916 when the CMIU refused to support a strike demanding an increase in wages for women in the stemming department, Latina workers walked off the job and called a wildcat strike. The historian Hewitt revealed that these women walked from factory to factory encouraging others to join the strike. Although women joined by the thousands, many men refused to leave their benches and stand beside Latinas in solidarity. In response, women "offered their skirts," hooted catcalls, and declared these men "afeminadas" (effeminate women). This homophobic slur—intended to mock the masculinity of the men who remained seated—queer-baited and attacked the sexuality of those unwilling to join the strike, declaring them neither friends of labor nor real men.[77]

Just as gender-based inequality and a gendered pay gap were not unusual in this place, neither was homophobic language and ideologies. Despite the leftist philosophies that underlined the politics and paradigms of those in Ybor, understandings of gender and sex walked a traditionalist, cisgender, heterosexual line. Even Capetillo, remembered and praised for her intellectual progressivism, denigrated queerness from the platform of the lectora and from the essays of her feminist treatises.[78]

In contrast, Emilio Gonzalez-Llanes, a writer and poet, revealed the experience of being gay in Ybor through his *Cigar City Stories*, a testimonio. Within the pages of this semiautobiographical novel, Gonzalez-Llanes details how he navigated love, politics, and sexuality in a place that publicly condemned who he was and who he wished to be. Among the tales of a boy coming of age and accepting his sexuality is a conversation between Abel, the character who embodies Gonzalez-Llanes, and a man named Tito—the partner and lover of Abel's uncle (Julian), a missing leftist organizer and CPUSA member. In this story, Tito telephones Abel to share that the Ybor community has uncovered the details of Julian's disappearance. A shrimp boat captain, notorious for black market activities, has confessed that he accepted payment from two plainclothes police officers to maroon Julian on a sandbar near Key West. As the boat captain explained, Julian was bound and gagged. He drowned as the tide rose, murdered by the state for his work as a labor activist and advocate of communist principles. Before the phone call ends, Tito shares with Abel that he has left his wife, his double life, and moved into the rented room he and Julian once shared—a statement of love, loss, and acceptance. While Tito could not "be with Julian anymore," he takes solace in the company of his lover's "books, his tools, his clothes." Little more than mere items, these things keep alive the memory of "the only man [Tito] ever loved." In the book, the character Abel empathizes with Tito during the conversation as he shares, "I'm so glad I left Ybor City. I could never be myself there." Abel—who had moved to Miami, the physical and imaginary "fairyland" of Florida—finds himself in his new city, where he lives with "a wonderful man" with whom he is "very much in love."[79] Abel's fictional experience mirrors the lived reality of Gonzalez-Llanes. He too had to leave Ybor City in order to live the life of Tito's dreams. In reality, Gonzalez-Llanes found acceptance in California.[80]

When Moreno heard stories of moments like the women's wildcat strike, she may have read the actions and language of those involved as empowering, perhaps even entertaining or feminist. She may have been impressed that more than 1,500 people joined the strike and another 8,500 threatened to join. As it seems, existing sentiments of working-class solidarity coupled with public shame could be quite effective. Words such as *afeminada*, in the context of a strike, defamed the men who did not join collective action and marked them as outsiders, perhaps even traitors, to the culture of labor unity—an unsubtle parallel to the juxtaposition between traditional family structures and the lives led by queer women and men in Ybor City during this period. Although this was a place where one could be an anarchist, a socialist, or a communist in public, the same radical acceptance did not extend to sexuality. In the context of this strike and the use of this slur, it did little to improve the lives of *despaldilladoras*. In the end, it was those who worked on the main factory floor, predominantly cigar makers who were men, who saw an increase in wages. This, it seems, was a trend. One year later, in 1917, when Latinas called another wildcat strike to protest the introduction of stemming machines and the de-skilling of their trade, it was the men who joined the collective action who reaped the benefits.[81]

Stories such as these would have shown Moreno the limits of sex-based equality within Ybor City's union structure. When it came to political action, Latinas and Latinos worked together as they donated money in support of the Russian Revolution and raised defense funds for political prisoners such as Nicola Sacco and Bartolomeo Vanzetti, Italian immigrants and anarchists accused of murder (for which there was no conclusive evidence) and later executed by the state in Massachusetts. Together Ybor Latinas/os founded and funded roughly "two dozen food and clothing cooperatives." Women who worked in the home stood up for those they loved as they led a "campaign against an ordinance that threatened to increase the price of bread" and later a boycott of "potato, meat, and onion" to keep food affordable for the community.[82] Latinas risked their jobs and forwent their paychecks to stand beside Latinos on the picket line in defense of men's wages and men's dignity within the Cuban cigar industry. Yet when it was women's work, women's value, and women's skills that were in question, men did not reciprocate. The few instances when women did not stand alone, men co-opted their cause with their own grievances, leaving women's call for a living wage sidelined. In 1884, the AFL rhetorically recognized the value of women's labor when it approved its "Statement on Women," which affirmed that "women should receive the same pay as men for equal work performed" as long as it did not "impair [women's] potential motherhood" or "prevent the continuation of a nation of strong, healthy, sturdy, and intelligent women and men."[83] It was the qualifying portion of this statement that contrib-uted to the union's lack of enthusiasm when it came to negotiating on behalf of women's labor and women's wages. Instead, what emerged both in Ybor City and throughout the nation was advocacy for a "family wage"—a term that allowed employers to increase men's pay and power within the home and workplace and limit women's independence and self-sufficiency through a rationalization of fitness. Moreno, herself a single working mother, would have understood why these women needed higher wages regardless of whether or not they had a spouse, partner, or child. As she thought about how best to organize this place, she may have examined other contradic-tions of the community with equal scrutiny.

Although the CMIU, city leadership, and non-Latina/o factory owners may have seen the creation of interracial union locals as outstanding, to women and men in Ybor City this was not a novel invention. Unions that rep-resented cigar workers in Havana accepted all people who labored in the industry, regardless of race, and Ybor City's Cuban cigar workers expected the same organizational structure in Florida. From the perspective of Ybor Latinas/os, unions were strongest if all cigar workers across the industry united in the same labor organization. CMIU leadership took note that in-terracial unionism mattered to Latinas/os in Ybor and West Tampa. With the dissolution of La Resistencia, and an opening in the labor field, the AFL per-mitted CMIU locals in Tampa to end their policy of segregated unionism in the city. As a result, these locals became and remained the only interracial union locals between Florida and Louisiana. When Moreno traveled to Jack-sonville and Lakeland, she operated in a segregated environment that made her keenly and, uncomfortably, aware of the power of racial inequality both in and outside of progressive spaces in Florida and the broader U.S. South. Yet as Moreno stood in the Centro Obrero of Ybor City and addressed Tampa membership, she would have seen a room filled with Latinas/os of all races and of different ethnicities.[84]

It is essential to bear in mind, however, that Ybor cigar workers and com-munity members were not anti-racist activists and Ybor City was not a hidden anti-racist paradise.[85] Racial difference played an important role in the community, even if those lines blurred, in some ways, on the shop floor and within unions. Commitment to interracial unionism emerged from customs held on the island and the energy of movements for Cuban independence. Those who migrated to Ybor City from Cuba during the 1880s and 1890s were, predominantly, separatists who supported the end to Spanish rule on the island. Many declared themselves exiles upon arrival and stressed that they fled their homelands as a result of political persecution and resulting economic inequality. This perspective differed from that of leaders, ideologues, and activists who, as the historian Gerald E. Poyo asserts, believed the best path toward independence was through unity rooted in patriotic nationalism, the investment in the *cubanidad* (the condition of being Cuban), and an independent Cuban state above all else. José Martí, the famed Cuban revolutionary, managed to walk a rhetorical line that "fus[ed] nationalist and social concerns" and endeared him to cigar workers in Ybor.[86] Between 1891 and 1895, Martí made multiple visits to Ybor, where he worked with Cuban women and men to establish revolutionary clubs, met with community leaders, and gave speeches.

As the years passed, the memory of Martí, his words, and his visits to Ybor City took on a life of their own. In the testimonio *The Truth about Them*, Jose Yglesias wrote about the day his aunt reenacted her ceremonial meeting with Martí. According to Yglesias's aunt, during one of Martí's visits in the 1890s the Cuban revolutionary committee of Ybor selected her as its ambassador because she had a "strong voice that carried far," a voice Yglesias remembered as being of "great use in later years when she was the mother of twelve children."[87] Seventy years after the original event, Yglesias's aunt took to her feet and from the front porch of her casita in West Tampa proclaimed to family and friends:

> Here on this sister island
> A place has been made for me
> By a little band of men
> Who say—Our flag will fly free![88]

As his aunt spoke the last line, she waved an invisible Cuban flag and then stretched out her sepia-stained hands, the result of decades of work in the cigar factories, to offer the figurative flag to a ghost.[89]

From oral histories with women and men of the Ybor community, it seems that many people have stories of Martí similar to those of Yglesias. Long-lived tales of the moment a person stood next to Martí, of the evening a friend organized with Martí, of the day a cousin spoke to Martí, or of the time a family member shook hands with Martí. Moreno likely heard such anecdotes as she sat in cantinas and visited cafés.[90] Perhaps Moreno was even privy to a performance, such as that by Yglesias's aunt, when she sat with women on their front porches, for the legacy of Cuban independence was something that made those in Ybor feel proud. Proximity to Martí allowed these women and men to believe, years later, that they had the authority to claim this place as one where the promises of revolution and the ethos of the Cuban independence movement endured, untarnished by corruption that continued on the island. If this were so, then not only could their resistance to manufacturers act as a symbol of anti-imperialism, but their embrace of interracial unionism could obscure the racism Black Cubans experienced in the neighborhood. While women and men in Ybor City rejected organized religion because of its vicinity to political oppression, they worshipped Martí and embraced the "ideology of raceless nationality" evangelized from his pulpit of liberty.[91]

When Moreno wandered the streets of Ybor City she would have noticed that this place was not raceless, for the neighborhood would have seemed segregated despite the absence of any regulation that mandated such division. Most Afro-Cubans lived along the western outskirts of Ybor, the area that abutted the Scrub, one of Tampa's historically African American neighborhoods and a present-day site of public housing within Tampa. This form of de facto segregation extended into social spaces and daily life. Evelio Grillo, a member of the Black Cuban community of Ybor who came of age during the 1920s and 1930s, remembered the union meetings he attended with his mother as the only instances he interacted with any white Latinas/os. His mom—who was the head of the household, the primary breadwinner, and a *bunchera*—struggled to make ends meet. As a result, the family moved frequently within Ybor City. Grillo recalled that the tighter their family budget became, the farther they lived from the center of the neighborhood and the closer they got to the Scrub. At the turn of the century and into the 1930s, Afro-Cuban women and men occupied positions within the cigar industry that made less money—a factor that determined the type of housing one could afford and the type of social spaces one had discretionary funds to frequent.[92] Examples of systemic racism such as this were something that the culture of interracial unionism in Ybor should not obscure. Although Ybor Latinas/os, both Black and white, advocated for the maintenance of a shared union, other forms of discrimination against Afro-Cubans did not gain mass traction. This was most likely because interracial unionism made the union stronger for everyone, white Latinas/os included. In order to resist other forms of racial discrimination, white Latinas/os had to be willing to march, protest, advocate, boycott, and walk off the job in defense of others. They were not.

During the time Moreno watched, listened, and learned about the women and men in Ybor City, she found multiple cultures of labor that competed and necessitated navigation. U.S.-centric unionism, the form of labor organizing her employer advocated, had to bend to internationalist ideas if it were to be successful. Those who lived and worked in Ybor City did so in the nexus of a borderland where one's sense of self was fluid and in constant negotiation with anti-radical and anti-immigrant powers within the U.S. South and politically leftist ideologies that linked Latinas and Latinos to working-class networks beyond Florida. The more Moreno listened, the more she saw that what was at stake was not just union membership cards and due payments; it was the viability of the community and its survival.

Negotiating Radicalisms

By mid-1936, Moreno likely felt as though she had a better understanding of her new home. She had met community members and community leaders and taken the time to comprehend the cultures of labor that defined this space. As she visited cigar factories to meet with owners and began the process of negotiating a new contract for cigar workers, she could feel the effect the Depression had on the Ybor industry and its workforce. Not only had some of the major clear Havana manufacturers transitioned from the Spanish hand method to machine production, but the lector platform had disappeared from all factories. The clicking sounds of the *chavetas* were hardly audible above the hum of mechanic efficiency and radio static.[93] Moreno, who never got to see a Cuban cigar factory in its glory, had been told of the ways the Depression weakened cigar workers' ability to resist manufacturers. This fact came to life as she looked around the factory floor.

During her conversations with Latinas/os in Ybor, Moreno learned that the year 1931 was a major turning point that marked a shift in the balance of power between cigar workers and manufacturers. It was in April of that year when the Tobacco Workers Industrial Union (TWIU) arrived in Ybor City to recruit members and compete with the CMIU. Cigar workers had grown weary with the "slow pace of the International Union" and were eager to explore options with a new labor organization.[94] The TWIU, a union affiliated with the CPUSA, represented a fresh and enticing option. As a result, Ybor

Latinas/os joined by the thousands. By November 1931, the TWIU managed to add roughly half of the cigar industry workforce, 5,000 cigar workers, to its union roster and to the CPUSA membership rolls. For the next seven months, communists made their presence known in Tampa as they took the city by storm. Unlike the CMIU, which contained its negotiations to workplace concerns, the TWIU operated as an advocate for labor and a crusader against inequality as it "campaigned for improved unemployment relief, led protests against evictions, held rallies, and staged plays like 'Downfall of the Classes'" in Spanish and English at the Centro Obrero.[95]

Moreno likely understood why the TWIU attracted Ybor cigar workers. She, herself, knew that neither the CMIU nor the AFL was perfect, and in her conversations with women and men from Ybor she learned that the union had a fraught relationship with the community. But most of all, Moreno intimately understood the power of the CPUSA. When Moreno was in the process of building her own union in New York City, it was the NTWIU that she turned to first, not the ILGWU. She believed in the message and the politics of Marxism and would have understood how a labor union with such a different tone and vision appealed to the people of Ybor City.

Trouble began on November 7, 1931, however, when the TWIU held an event to honor the anniversary of the Russian Revolution. The rally, which took place at the Labor Temple in Ybor City, was so popular that attendance exceeded the capacity of the venue, and the crowd spilled out into the neighborhood's streets. The *Tampa Morning Tribune* reported that "the crowd had been worked into a frenzy by red speeches," evidenced by the sounds of Latinas/os "singing and yelling."[96] City police officers arrived on the scene, and moments later the sounds of gunshots filled Ybor City. As police busted into the building, women and men dashed to the closest possible exits. Bodies poured out of windows and into the nearby alleys. Although the police alleged that workers attacked them, the workers who attended the event claimed that Tampa's finest opened fire on the event's attendees first. Officers arrested twenty-two people that night.[97]

In the midst of the melee, city of Tampa police raided the home of Frank Crawford, a painter and member of the CP, who had been beaten and flogged for his radicalism a week earlier.[98] On this night, police arrested Crawford as well as the six other men found in his home.[99] Police confiscated supposed subversive materials and claimed the Crawford residence to be the headquarters of the local CPUSA. The historian Robert P. Ingalls explained that the Anglo press, the Tampa police, and the mayor of Tampa unilaterally emphasized that communist activity in the city was the result of "paid organizers and outside agitators," a form of rhetoric those in power had used for decades when it came to leftist activism.[100]

When the city of Tampa filed charges against those arrested and set bail at $10,000, Ybor cigar workers jumped into action to mobilize a donation effort to assist with bond and legal expenses. A few manufacturers attempted to outlaw such activity within their factories, but cigar workers waged strikes in protest. On November 26, 1931, Thanksgiving Day, cigar factory owners met with one another and collectively agreed they would prohibit the continuation of the lectura, as they believed that "all of the trouble" the city and the manufacturers experienced emerged from "the readers' stand where fiery Communistic translation[s] from anarchistic publication[s] ha[d] been constantly poured into the [cigar] workers."[101] As cigar workers arrived at the factories the next day, "they found the readers' platforms dismantled." In response, cigar workers staged a walkout, which reached the level of a general strike. Bakers, grocers, and other business owners closed their doors in solidarity with cigar workers, which brought the entire city to a stop.[102] Three days later, when Latinas/os tried to return to their workbenches, they were unable to enter the factories—manufacturers had locked the doors. Cigar workers continued their strike effort by picketing outside of factories and holding nightly strategy meetings at the Labor Temple.

Three weeks passed before the cigar factories reopened. When they did, however, much had changed both in terms of the landscape of labor and the landscape of the city. Unlike previous strikes, this time manufacturers refused to negotiate with cigar workers and required acceptance of their terms before consideration of rehire. According to manufacturers, anyone who worked in their factories had to abide by an ethic of "true Americanism," which meant agreeing to an open shop union policy as well as to a ban on monetary collections and fundraising within factories; acceptance of manufacturers' refusal to recognize the TWIU or "any other group with communist affiliation"; and, perhaps the most painful condition of all, the end to the lectura within all Tampa factories.[103]

Moreno would have empathized with the emotional result that such a loss in tradition had on Cuban cigar workers. To these women and men, the lector was not simply a form of entertainment but a form of education. Moreno herself had been touched by the influence of the lectura even if she never experienced its might within a Cuban cigar factory. Nearly fifty years later, the historian Gary R. Mormino asked José Vega Díaz, a former Ybor cigar maker, why he thought manufacturers understood the lector to be so dangerous. Vega explained that while "the reader l[it] the candle . . . [the cigar factory owners and the church] want[ed] to blow away the light."[104] Perhaps he shared such insight with Moreno, and organizers like her, as they listened to the needs of the community.

Vega believed in 1980, as he did in 1931, that factory owners, city officials, and religious leaders wished to limit the access of cigar workers to information so they could control their knowledge, their politics, and their collective power. To Vega, this event did not stand in isolation. He had seen it before. As a young man, Vega watched as priests worked to govern what people were taught in school, to prevent them from gaining enough knowledge to question the injustices that surrounded them. Likewise, during the Cuban War for Independence, the Catholic Church supported the Spanish government and rejected separatist calls for autonomy by operating as an extension of the empire rather than an advocate of the people whose souls it claimed to protect.[105] Manufacturers could not control the lector because the lector was not their employee. The lector worked for cigar workers and read the materials they selected. By ending this tradition, factory owners hoped they could create a less militant work environment and perhaps workforce.

Moreno understood that while women and men such as Vega had the ability to walk away from the doctrine of organized religion, it was more difficult to turn their backs on the factories because people had to earn a wage in order to eat. Neither the robust mutual aid system nor generous credit extensions could support all community members in perpetuity. As a result, cigar workers begrudgingly agreed to the terms manufacturers set and watched as the lectores went to the factories to "pick up the pieces of [their] platform[s] that had been destroyed by thugs hired by the cigar-factory owners."[106] One community member remembered that as the lectores gathered what remained of their pulpits, they "worked slowly and silently, caressing each board as if it were an old friend, a chapter from one of [their] novels."[107] While the lectura never returned to the Cuban cigar factories of Ybor City, the tradition lived in other ways. Some lectores worked for or founded Spanish-language presses in Ybor, while others spread their message through the community's theater culture and later continued their subversion with taxpayer dollars through the Federal Theatre Project.[108] Moreno even hired some of these unemployed lectores to speak and perform at union meetings as a way to draw people into the CMIU and to keep them connected to a tradition and culture their employers attempted to strip away.[109]

In addition to the cultural impact of the 1931 strike, Moreno saw other elements of this event's legacy in Ybor cigar factories as she toured the shops and introduced herself to owners. Thirty percent of the Cuban cigar workers who walked out of the factories in November 1931 never regained their positions. While in the four years after the strike the number of jobs available to the women and men who relied on the industry continued to shrink as a result of market shifts and the Depression, in 1931 the reduction of the workforce was due to decisions made by a "secret committee of 25 concerned citizens" assembled by the mayor. This committee, endorsed by cigar manufacturers, had the authority to determine who had the ability to be a *true* American worker and who did not.[110] Latina/o cigar workers deemed unhirable carried the stigma of being foreign, un-American disturbers whose bodies and ideas threatened the safety of the city and the minds of supposed good U.S. citizens. The city flexed its muscles further through a sweeping decision by a Tampa federal court that outlawed "seditious literature or speeches," which directly prevented the TWIU from operating within the city regardless of any future agreement or negotiation reached between cigar workers and manufacturers.[111]

When Moreno sat in cafés and on women's porches, she learned that what made this strike so powerful was not simply its traumatic outcome but the sense of precarity and anxiety this moment created within families. The writer Yglesias explained that the 1931 strike left him with a "psychological scar." Yglesias recalled that when his mother joined this strike and lockout he feared for her safety because he knew the KKK regularly broke into meetings at the Centro Obrero to terrorize, intimidate, and accost attendees.[112] He, and Latina/o children like him, understood that it was at such meetings and during such moments of explosive tension that people went to jail and others disappeared. Yglesias may have even been aware that days before his mom took to the picket line in defense of her job and her politics, men claiming to be police officers had struck, blindfolded, and flogged Frank Crawford.[113] To children such as Yglesias, their fear was not unfounded but grounded in the stories they inherited and the violence they saw. In this place, it was no secret that manufacturers and city leaders were willing to do anything to protect their investments and political power.

Moreno likely thought about such stories when she sat across from cigar factory supervisors, managers, and owners. While they understood that she represented cigar workers, they hoped she would be flexible and open to discussion of their needs too. From the perspective of cigar manufacturers, the CMIU owed them thanks for collaborating with Tampa city leaders and expelling the TWIU from Tampa, which created space for the CMIU to thrive in organizational isolation. In August 1933, cigar factory owners who had managed to weather the Depression, thus far, agreed to union recognition of the CMIU in accordance with the New Deal. As of December 1933, the CMIU boasted more than 5,000 members—a number it had not reached since the 1910s.[114]

While the leaders of the CMIU and AFL likely relished in this moment due to the resulting growth of the union, Moreno may have scrutinized a different detail of the 1931 strike and the resulting 1933 agreement—the reality that manufacturers in Tampa, much like the community's cigar workers, understood how to organize themselves. Factory owners operated through a local organization called the Manufacturers Trust, a group that included the owners of all major factories as well as city officials and business leaders. From a tactical standpoint, this made contract and strike negotiation incredibly difficult because it required Moreno, or any union representative for that matter, to work with the owners of all companies as well as city leaders to reach an agreement even if the grievance was with a singular factory. The alliance between manufacturers and city officials illustrated the centrality of the industry to the Tampa economy. Not only were politicians and business leaders eager to support cigar factory owners, but they were willing to endorse and enact violence in order to control cigar workers and protect the Cuban cigar industry.

As Moreno shook hands with manufacturers and shop representatives, she may have found it difficult to separate her need to establish a working relationship with them from the terror she knew they wrought on the city and the community for decades. Since 1892, the year the CMIU established a presence in Ybor City, union representatives watched as Latina/o workers, predominantly men, faced threats and violence from the KKK, the Tampa Police Department, and the local citizens' committee. Membership within these groups was not exclusive. Police officers were often Klan members, who stood beside each other in the citizens' committee, where they brushed shoulders with local business and political leaders, many of whom routinely wore the same white hoods.[115] Anti-labor, anti-immigrant, racist conservativism wielded such might in this city that the American Civil Liberties Union (ACLU) declared Tampa one of the nation's premier "centers of repression," as it was "under the control of public officials dominated by the KKK."[116] Mean things happened here because vigilantism was sponsored by the city and unchecked, if not endorsed, by the local legal system.[117]

Ybor community members never stopped talking about the time thirteen Cuban strike leaders were bound and gagged, placed on a ship, left on a beach in Honduras, and told if they ever returned to Tampa, they would be killed by the citizens' committee.[118] Likewise, people remembered the day a lynch mob handcuffed two Italians, accused of a murder they did not commit, and hung the men from a tree. Some women and men told stories of the time the Tampa police tarred and feathered, yet left alive, a Spanish immigrant who, a person claimed, exposed himself in public. Authorities placed the man on display inside a jail cell and did not allow him to leave until more than 2,000 people had come to view the spectacle. Each of these instances received support from the local Anglo press and endorsement from the broader Anglo community. In fact, some of these actions happened because local business leaders encouraged, even demanded, mob violence to teach a lesson to the foreign elements they believed plagued the city. Vigilante violence sought not to right the wrongs committed from an alleged crime but to act as a message and serve as a symbol of what happened when those assumed to be less powerful challenged the authority of those who believed themselves to be in power. Such moments illustrated the danger of resistance. Women and men in Ybor City, as well as the AFL, shared this information with Moreno because they wanted her to understand the violence she could encounter. Vigilantism was not something of the past but a form of control very much alive and active in Tampa.[119]

Joseph Shoemaker, a leader of the Modern Democrats, had been lynched weeks before Moreno arrived in Tampa with her daughter in tow. What caused this state-sponsored murder was the crime of daring to mobilize the voting power of working-class women and men. Local interest in leftist politics, and specifically socialist ideas, had expanded beyond the borders of Ybor City and into the neighborhoods of Anglo Tampa during the Depression. Unemployment and insufficient relief support left those in need, no matter their race, ready to organize in support of new local leadership that could better meet the demands of the Tampa community. Shoemaker collaborated with the Workers' Alliance in city campaigns that sought to unseat the White Municipal Party at the ballot box. Although candidates who ran for office as Modern Democrats did not win any elections in the 1930s, they were an active, visible force that symbolized the stirrings of a challenge to Tampa's political elite. If Modern Democrats had organized working-class women and men in Tampa as well as in Ybor City, this new progressive force would have been able to control local politics. The result of this threat was fatal.[120]

On November 30, 1935, police barged into a house where Shoemaker was holding a meeting of Modern Democrats along with four leaders of the Socialist Party and the Workers' Alliance. All five men were taken downtown and questioned about their alleged communist activities and asked "if [they] believed in racial equality"—a damning and un-American offense according to Southern Democrats.[121] After questioning, the police released these men one by one. As Shoemaker and two other men exited the police station, a group of officers forced these men into a squad car and then drove them to an empty, wooded lot on the outskirts of Hillsborough County. The vigilantes stripped the men of their pants and flogged them with "chains, straps, and hoses." Shoemaker recognized one of the men as a police officer and identified him by name in the midst of the attack. In response, the men whipped Shoemaker for nearly five minutes, then tarred and feathered all three victims before speeding away. The doctor who cared for Shoemaker explained that not only had he been severely mutilated as a result of the flogging but he was also paralyzed on half his body due to "blows to the head." While the other two men survived, Shoemaker died nine days after the attack.

Unlike other lynchings in Tampa, this crime garnered national attention. Women and men across the country wrote letters to the governor of Florida imploring him to take action against the vigilantes who orchestrated the kidnapping and subsequent murder. Likewise, the ACLU established a reward to encourage those with information to come forward, while the AFL threatened to withdraw its 1936 conference from Tampa if those who committed the murder remained unpunished.[122] National pressure coupled with calls for justice from those who lived in Tampa led to the arrest and trial of eleven men connected to the lynching of Shoemaker.[123] Moreno, who had been in Florida since January 1936, watched local and national reactions to the killing of Shoemaker.

While the AFL feared that the resurgence of anticommunism in Tampa was so strong that it seemed impossible for any union, no matter how patriotic or centrist it was, to operate without accusations of communist, anti-American action surrounding organizing efforts, what Moreno saw on the ground was something different. As the historian Ingalls asserts, the Shoemaker murder seemed to weaken anti-radical, anti-leftist, extralegal power in Tampa to a certain extent. Although national headlines centered on the fact that all of the men guilty of the crime evaded conviction, it was a small miracle that they faced charges and sat trial in the first place. Such a reality sent a message to the city's political elite, who had long relied on popular violence to control labor and politics in the city. They now saw that people were watching and that their actions could have consequences. With the spotlight of the nation shining on the corrupt nature of Tampa's city government, Moreno found flexibility in her capacity to organize, coordinate meetings, and even embrace her leftist politics without reservation.

Demanding Workers' Rights and Human Rights through Women's Actions

By mid-1936, Moreno's work in Tampa was well underway. Manuel González, a member of the Joint Advisory Board, wrote a letter to the president of the CMIU noting that Moreno was "on the job day and night."[124] He explained that not only had she embraced her role as an organizer, in line with the charge of the AFL, but she also introduced new strategies that brought excitement to union meetings and added names to the union roster. Moreno, who spent her first few months in Ybor City seeking to understand the cultures of labor and radicalisms that defined this space, made personal visits with membership a permanent function of the union by establishing committees to meet with cigar workers when she could not do so herself.[125] She also "had the very good idea" of bringing entertainment to meetings at the Centro Obrero to make "those events more interesting."[126] Moreno invited local musicians and theater groups as well as former lectores and political speakers. Dialogue between the Joint Advisory Board and the national union illustrate that Moreno worked to show cigar workers in Ybor that the CMIU did not have to be an organization that took their money and gave nothing back. Instead, it could be a space where the dynamic cultures of their workplaces and the politics that had long guided their lives could live in the union hall even if they could not thrive in the same way they once had on the factory floor.[127] CMIU leadership was, indeed, pleased with the work of Moreno. Not only had she made meaningful changes to the union, but she had managed to survive in a place where unionism was akin to communism and the threat of violence was palpable. Moreno herself later admitted that she encountered few problems on this front. The fact that she was a woman, had light skin, spoke perfect English, and could pass as white in this southern space helped cloak her in an air of respectability that neither the Klan nor the citizens' committee sought to disrobe.[128] It seemed that the decision of the AFL and CMIU to hire a woman was effective.

Moreno spent the summer and fall of 1936 on trains and buses commuting between Tampa, Jacksonville, and Lakeland to renegotiate an industry-wide contract that would improve the lives of cigar workers across central Florida. These hours alone gave her time to think and rest. As miles of pine trees and green prairies whipped by the window, Moreno likely sat back and thought about the changes the Ybor cigar industry had undergone and the challenges she faced in negotiation. Unlike organizers who came before her, all of whom struggled in some way even when the industry was at its height, Moreno faced a different challenge—finding a way to maintain employment status and increase pay while the Cuban cigar industry was losing money and retreating from Florida.

Between 1929 and 1940, cigar work changed drastically. In Ybor City, the cigar-making workforce declined by 56 percent, and, by 1939, women composed 55 percent of the total industry workforce.[129] Cigar work became women's work, a trend that continued through the 1960s as mechanization overtook the industry. Moreno understood the reasons for this change. The Great Depression decimated the industry as people's pocketbooks precluded them from purchasing the luxurious cigars Ybor City was known for. Cigarettes, which surged in popularity after World War I, offered a cheaper, addictive, and more fashionable option to tobacco enthusiasts the world over.[130] Just as cigar workers looked at the balance of their checking accounts with longing and despair, so too did cigar factory owners. An economic survey of the Cuban cigar industry of Tampa, published in 1940, found that the annual profit margins of local factories had consistently declined throughout the 1930s. Such a reality did not bode well for Ybor cigar workers or the future viability of the Cuban cigar industry.[131]

Moreno knew things were glum. Ybor City, which once boasted more than a hundred factories that produced clear Havana cigars in the Spanish hand method now had fewer than fifteen factories that did things the old way. An estimated twenty-five factories remained in Ybor; however, these introduced stripping machines, bunching machines, wrapping machines, and cellophaning machines. The factory with the largest number of employees, Hav-a-Tampa, abandoned any form of hand rolling and employed only machine operators.[132] Seventy-five percent of the people who worked in this factory were Anglo women.[133] Cheap cigars, which sold for as little as two to five cents each, were the most popular item produced in the factories during the Depression years. At one time, cigar factories considered "cheap cigars as merely a by-product," a cigar created to prevent wasting scraps of tobacco, but now "the by-product [had] become . . . their major product."[134]

While Moreno understood the reality of the market, she also understood that the women and men of Ybor City were struggling. As she walked into meetings with factory owners and sat before the board of the Manufacturers Trust, she kept in mind the experiences of women like Dolores Patiño Río, a cigar maker and mother from Ybor City who weathered industry changes to feed her family.[135] Río worked at the Corral Wodiska factory, one of the six clear Havana shops that survived the Depression, and was among the thousands of women who rose to the position of tabaquera during these lean years. As a woman, Río's labor was cheaper. Factory owners hoped that she, and Latinas like her, would be more amenable to industry changes than Latinos, who felt as though the tradition and dignity of their work had been stripped from them. Río explained to the historian Nancy A. Hewitt that during the 1930s cigar manufacturers not only shifted the focus of production but also adjusted hours and placed cigar workers on a limit.[136] Unlike the pre-Depression period, during which tabaqueras/os' income reflected the number of cigars produced in a day and the quality of the cigars produced, the limit system meant women and men could produce only a set number of cigars each day. Furthermore, most cigar makers had a part-time schedule. This decision was made so the industry could employ more people despite changes to their budgets.

As Río looked backed on this experience, she recalled that even though none of these shifts were ideal, she was willing to do anything she needed to survive. "Everyone made less," Río said, but it was "better to earn less than to be on the streets."[137] The U.S. Women's Bureau confirmed in a report that "it [was] obvious that many [women in Tampa were] subsisting on less than what [was] recognized . . . as a reasonable American standard of health and decency."[138] In 1931, cigar worker earnings averaged $16 a week—the recognized minimum wage for an "adequate budget" in 1918.[139] By 1938, the average wage of Ybor tabaqueras had fallen to $13.86 per week, despite the fact that the cost of living had risen.[140]

As Moreno walked through the streets of Ybor City, she saw the effect these changes had on the lives of women and men in this community. The vast majority of those without jobs in Ybor City were tabaqueros who had been displaced by either tabaqueras who worked cheaper or by machines that worked faster. Gerardo Cortina Pinera, a former lector and waiter, explained that although he tried to find "a stable position in any place, and in anything," all of his efforts seemed to fail.[141] Cortina was among the estimated 5,688 "surplus cigar workers" who lived in Ybor City and stood in line at the office of the Works Progress Administration in hopes of getting a relief position.[142] Like thousands of other Latinos from Ybor, Cortina was unable to secure relief work. Although the New Deal sent funds to support those who needed assistance in Tampa, the local administration of these programs was imperfect and discriminatory. While initially there was no policy that barred Latinas/os from access to relief, changes to federal policy later excluded

Cigar makers (mostly women) at a factory in Ybor City, 1958. Burgert Brothers Photographic Collection, Tampa–Hillsborough County Public Library System.

noncitizens from the program, which compounded the struggle of Ybor Latinos. Those without U.S. citizenship received denials on the basis of their documentation status, while those with U.S. citizenship—but who perhaps did not speak English, spoke with an accent, or simply seemed too different—received relief denials as a result of ethnic and racial prejudice.[143]

The rise in Latino unemployment pushed cigar-working families to consider what other options they might have for survival. Like the cigar factories that left Ybor City for New York, New Jersey, and Philadelphia, many families moved northward because of the stories they heard about open access to relief and the availability of jobs outside the U.S. South. John Cacciatore, a resident of Ybor City, noted to an employee from the Federal Works Project that in Ybor City men received "50 cents a week for the maintenance of a whole family" and "the single person [was] not given relief what[so]ever," whereas in New York City people were "given a home, groceries, coal to warm themselves in the winter, and electric lights."[144] Those such as Domenica Ginesta, a former tabaquero who also spoke to the Federal Works Project, echoed Cacciatore's idealistic notions about the northern United States and expounded that "New York [was where] . . . those without work [could] find opportunities."[145] Ginesta explained that "th[e] exodus [of people leaving Ybor City was] primarily of the younger generation who [paid] caravan drivers $10 to $12 to drive them to the Big Apple." Sometimes families left Ybor City together, other times Latinas with jobs stayed in Florida with their children. Older, former cigar workers did not have the same energy and hope for a move up the East Coast, but as Ginesta detailed: "[We were] in contact with the Cuban government in an effort to have them take us back to Cuba and allow us a pension for the few remaining years of our life."[146] Even in the midst of such a report, the Ybor resident shared, they had "little hope" that anything would result from this effort.[147]

The men who remained in Ybor City and continued to search for work often found it through self-employment. Dolores Patiño Río remembered that although her father had lost his job in the factory, he opened a chinchal in their family home. The cigars he made he sold on the street, to avoid over-head costs and circumvent taxes. Other men found temporary jobs in cigar-box-making factories or by working as cigar label makers. These unskilled positions had an impact not only on Latinos' sense of self-worth but also on the family wage. As this trend continued for nearly a decade, Latinas and Latinos became increasingly frustrated and angered by the inaction of lo-cal community members, and they began to speak out. *La Gaceta*, the local Spanish-language newspaper, published the article "The Problem with Women in Tampa," as both an open letter and a plea to the cigar industry: "Thank you to our municipal authorities that allowed mechanization to ruin industry; thank you to the egotistical industrialists who have discredited our hands and our skill, and thank you to the Chamber of Commerce who failed to see that the machine and industry would consume our market and lead to our complete demise, thus causing our men to leave Tampa looking for work so we can eat."[148] While stress of male unemployment disrupted the inter-nal dynamics of Latina/o families, it also made it nearly impossible for people to earn enough money to support their dependents without a dual income. As women futilely pleaded with city officials to find solutions for their un-employed husbands and brothers, they turned to the CMIU to represent not only their interests as cigar workers but also their political needs as Latinas who vied for authority in Tampa and the broader United States.

Moreno's quest to renegotiate cigar workers' contracts coincided with the eruption of the Spanish Civil War in July 1936. While this conflict was ultimately a battle between the elected Spanish Republic—a government that supported labor unionism, Catalonian independence, and a broad progressive democratic agenda—and the Falange, the extreme right-wing, nationalist party upheld by the Spanish military and endorsed by the Catholic Church, the civil war became a global symbol of the fight against fascist oppression.[149] Within weeks after this conflict began, all Ybor centros stood together as they declared that this moment was not a "war of national independence" but one against the power of "international fascism."[150]

Those who lived in Ybor City, of course, had historic ties to Spain. Some Spaniards left the continent and came directly to Ybor City, but many lived, worked, and had families in Cuba before they crossed the Florida Strait. No matter their route, the people who made their way to Tampa left Spain because of their experience with poverty and political oppression at home. They expressed their rejection of the Spanish Crown and the Catholic Church through their embrace of anarchism and anarcho-syndicalism as well as support for the Cuban War for Independence. Many Spanish immigrants felt that what the empire had done to Cubans was akin to what the monarchy had done to them.[151] Cuban immigrants had been subjects to the Spanish Crown and shared, oftentimes more passionately, the rejection of monarchist policies that had sought to squash their right to self-determination. Yet as strongmen leaders emerged in Cuba during the 1920s and 1930s, as well as in places such as Brazil, Peru, Chile, and the Dominican Republic, the rise of the Spanish Republic signaled hope.[152] What women and men in Ybor saw in the election of the Spanish Republic and the implementation of its reformist policies was that the strength of fascism and dictatorial authoritarianism was not absolute. It could be popularly beaten with ballots if people united through a popular front. Yet when General Francisco Franco allied with Nazi Germany and Fascist Italy to overtake the democratically elected Spanish government, people in Ybor, as well as around the globe, stood in shock as they feared for the reemergence of an oppressive Spanish state and the expansion of fascism into their own backyards.[153]

The internationalism of the Spanish Civil War drew women and men from Ybor City into the Popular Front—the people's movement and people's coalition that stood in opposition to the growth of fascism around the world. While initially a movement connected to the CP, the Frente Popular took on a life of its own depending on where one lived. In Ybor City, the Popular

Front was at once a collective effort to mobilize in support of the Spanish Republic and a movement to challenge the aspects of fascism Latinas/os believed surrounded them in Tampa and in the broader United States. The Ybor community understood the assassinations of Spanish union leaders, progressive politicians, and working-class women and men as an extension of the battle they fought in Florida against the Klan, the citizens' committees, and the manufacturers who sought to quell the free expression of their politics and undermine the value of their labor through intimidation and violence. In Ybor City, the Popular Front was a mode through which women and men sought justice and fairness abroad and at home.

Moreno likely joined the Latinas/os of Ybor City at the Labor Temple in early August for the first community-wide meeting in support of the Spanish Republic. To her, such an event would have been unforgettable. Despite the grandeur of the mutual aid societies' buildings and the stories she heard about the power of mutualism in Ybor, she had not seen it in action. Moreno may have even wondered, before this point, whether the Depression had weakened the spirit of collectivism just as it had the Cuban cigar industry. Inside this meeting, however, the community strength she had heard of came to life. In attendance were women and men from organized labor, the Socialist Party, the CP, fellow travelers, Protestant religious leaders, and representatives of the Cuban, Spanish, and Italian mutual aid societies. As all people in attendance discussed how best to support the Spanish Republic, they concluded that a separate committee was necessary. Two days later, the community announced the founding of the Comité de Defensa del Frente Popular Español (Spanish Popular Front Defense Committee), which remained active and robust until 1939.[154]

Within Ybor City, the loudest and most visible voice in support of the Spanish Civil War was Victoriano Manteiga. Like so many other members of the Ybor community, Manteiga was born in Cuba and, in 1913, came to Ybor City to work in the cigar industry. Rather than taking a seat at the cigar maker's bench, Manteiga climbed the lector platform and worked as a reader in various factories for nine years. As manufacturers began to clamor against the presence of lectores, he decided to climb down from his perch and establish in his vision a Spanish-language newspaper. He called it *La Gaceta*.[155] Manteiga used his newspaper as he had the lector stand as he shared the latest global affairs in Spanish and expressed his opinions on everything from local political campaigns to union activity to vigilante violence. Manteiga was brash and unapologetic, as was *La Gaceta*.

Over the course of the Spanish Civil War, Manteiga used the pages of his publication to keep the Ybor community updated on the latest occurrences abroad and to mobilize women and men at home. He published all announcements from the *comité* (committee) in a section of the newspaper titled "La Retraguardia de Tampa" (Rearguard of Tampa) and featured his opinions on the war as well as popular reactions to it on the front page under the heading "Chungas y no chungas," the local opinions section. Yet perhaps the most informative, and entertaining, was the weekly publication of the names of all people and all businesses that contributed to the fundraising effort of the comité, which appeared in the newspaper alongside a list of the names and addresses of all businesses and religious institutions that neither condemned the Spanish Civil War nor donated to the local antifascist effort. Manteiga encouraged women and men to boycott the latter, and they did.[156] The stories Manteiga featured in his newspaper about the atrocities of the war in Spain sat alongside reports on the Shoemaker murder trial, the struggle Latinas/os from Ybor faced as they looked for work, and the opposition of the city of Tampa to organized labor. While indeed this information was what the community wished to read and learn about most, the juxtaposition of the news of oppression at home adjacent to the news of oppression abroad created a visual and intellectual connection between the two different forms of fascism.

Moreno had a professional, working relationship with Manteiga. When Moreno initially made the rounds through the neighborhood, she learned that Manteiga needed to support her organizing efforts and to advertise events she planned at the Labor Temple. Manteiga obliged. Over the course of Moreno's time in Tampa, Manteiga highlighted the meetings she orchestrated and the efforts she made. While his initial reports described Moreno as "la joven organizadora" (the young woman organizer), by the end of her time in the community she was "nuestra Luisa Moreno" (our Luisa Moreno).[157] In some ways, it was the Spanish Civil War and the collective mobilization that shifted this relationship. While Moreno was no longer a card-carrying member of the CPUSA, she endeared herself to the thousands of people in Ybor as she sat beside them in comité meetings and supported their politics, something other CMIU organizers from beyond Ybor City had not done. After months of frequent trips between Jacksonville and Tampa, and protracted meetings with workers, the Joint Advisory Board, and the Manufacturers Trust, Moreno finally negotiated a wage increase, only to have the CMIU capitulate to the complaints of the factory owners. In this moment, Moreno recognized the split between the union's priorities and the needs of the women and men she represented and made the decision to organize on her own terms. For the remainder of Moreno's time in Florida, she embraced a form of unionism that blended political advocacy with labor-based goals.

In November 1936, the annual AFL convention took place in Tampa. At this event, the issue of politics and unionism collided in public. While the city of Tampa condemned the politics of labor, city leaders were more than happy to gain revenue from the thousands of attendees who flocked to their corner of the Sunshine State. A weekend of booked meeting spaces, reserved hotel rooms, and packed restaurants was enough incentive to share this place with the radical, "militant vermin" that Anglo leaders believed occupied the Labor Temple and union halls.[158] The atmosphere on the convention floor was particularly contentious, for the AFL executive council had suspended the Congress of Industrial Organizations (CIO) unions in September, roughly two months before the convention. Because the AFL was publicly anticommunist and anti-interventionist, the political alliance between CIO unions and the Popular Front challenged the authority of AFL leadership. At the convention, the AFL voted to officially bar the CIO from its ranks and split the union.[159] With this action, the AFL lost a third of its membership, cutting away at the power of the national federation. The *Tampa Morning Tribune* painted CIO leader John L. Lewis as a "rebel" guilty of treason for defying the AFL.[160]

In the midst of the fray, Moreno delivered an impassioned speech at the convention urging women and men to reject any AFL-negotiated contract and connecting the oppression of manufacturers and the lack of strength from the union to the fight against all forms of fascism.[161] Just as the Latinas who had raised their voices through *La Gaceta* and advocated for the need of labor equality as "mothers with children" who "did not want to see [their] families broken," Moreno painted the union's refusal to support the fight to maintain the Spanish Republic as akin to a greedy manufacturer who privileged profit over the well-being of women, men, and children.[162] Throughout the conference, Moreno supported Ybor cigar workers as they petitioned the AFL to permit Isabel de Palencia, the Spanish journalist and diplomat, to speak on the convention floor. Just as William Green, the president of the AFL, rejected Lewis's efforts to expand the political focus of the union, he refused to allow de Palencia to address AFL membership. In response, the Comité de Defensa del Frente Popular hosted a dinner for de Palencia at the Columbia Restaurant in Ybor City and arranged for her to speak at the Círculo Cubano, the Centro Obrero, and L'Unione Italiana. As de Palencia entered the ballrooms of these mutual aid societies and the open room of the union hall, hundreds of women and men "erupted into applause" and welcomed her with a toast in recognition of her work for "justice in Spain."[163] During her address to Ybor cigar workers and community members, de Palencia took a moment to address a broader non-Latina/o audience as she explained, in perfect English, that "communism [was] being used to describe everything democratic, everything opposed to fascism," but to remember that even "President Roosevelt himself . . . was called a communist by his political enemies."[164] In this statement, de Palencia communicated that to be an antifascist was neither a crime nor, in her mind, something that was radically leftist; instead, it was something to embrace without fear or qualification.

No doubt taken aback by Moreno's stern position and brash support of nonunion-sanctioned actions and policies, AFL leadership concluded she might prove detrimental to the CMIU in Florida and began to arrange to transfer her to Pennsylvania after the summer of 1937.[165] Moreno's protest and rejection of AFL authority at the national convention was not the only tension that plagued the event. As the press from across the nation reported on the explosive meeting, the friction between Lewis and Green became palpable. Like Moreno, Lewis maintained his support of the Popular Front and criticized the AFL's accommodationist actions. Meanwhile, Green denounced the CIO as "industrial rebels," and the *Tampa Morning Tribune* noted that, as Green spoke, his "pink face turn[ed] a little pinker" while he "shout[ed] his indignant assaults on the A. F. of L.'s solidarity."[166]

While the CMIU made plans to end Moreno's organizing activities in Tampa and transfer her northward, she abandoned the AFL's official line and began to work alongside cigar workers and community members in Ybor City on political matters. Between 1936 and 1937, Moreno joined the people of Ybor City in their public support of antifascist, prodemocratic politics at home and abroad. She supported the nearly 1,000 women who created and joined the Anti-Fascist Women's Committee, and watched as members, such as Margarita Pita, became strategic leaders who helped organize protests, food collections, donation drives, and boycotts.[167] Pita, who was born in Tampa in 1898, was the eldest of six siblings and the daughter of a cigar maker. Like many Latinas in Ybor City, she was of blended heritage. Her father was born in Cuba, and her mother was born in Key West to Cuban cigar-working parents. Pita never married. She became the primary caretaker of her siblings' children and contributed to the family wage by earning money as an independent tutor and educator through mutual aid societies. This flexibility allowed Pita to help her recently widowed sister,

Maria Luisa, who worked in the cigar industry to provide for her young daughter as a single mother in the midst of the Depression.[168] Pita's alliance with the Comité de Defensa del Frente Popular and her dedication to the Women's Committee echoed the actions of women in Cuba who aligned with antifascist organizing on the island.[169]

Moreno must have been amazed by the strength of fundraising and collective action in Ybor. Over the course of three years, the community sent 30 tons of beans, 20,000 pounds of clothing, 1,000 cans of milk, 20,000 cigars, 4 ambulances, an X-ray machine, and upwards of $7,000 in medication.[170] Women such as Pita planned picnics to raise funds, while those who worked in Cuban cigar factories donated a portion of their weekly paycheck to support the republican cause, just as they had in support of Frank Crawford's bail fund in 1931 and the Cuban War for Independence throughout the 1890s.[171] Latinas likewise networked with community organizations to establish profit-share events, where either a portion or the entirety of the money earned from movie screenings, sporting events, and theater performances contributed to the collective coffers to support the republic.[172] Monthly collection efforts typically ranged between $5,000 and $9,000, an impressive sum considering the national and local economic strains these women and men weathered. In addition to monetary support, roughly twenty-four young men from Ybor joined the International Brigades and traveled to Spain to contribute their bodies and their strength.[173]

After Hitler's bombing of Guernica in late April 1937, Moreno worked with the women at the García y Vega factory to organize a march that "protest[ed] the ruthless killing of women and children by Franco's forces" and to publicly illustrate that the international fight against fascism was just as personal as their local fight against labor inequality.[174] Latinas declared, "Our hearts bleed for all civilized women; fascism shreds our sentiments and we will protest with the vigor of our bodies as we call for justice."[175] Latinas wrote pledges to the local newspaper calling all community members to bind together. While local vigilante violence and control of the labor movement had sought to make women and men in Ybor City quiet and compliant, these people pledged alongside women and men in New York, Harlem, Chicago, Los Angeles, and San Antonio to agitate local and national sentiments.

We disagree with all fascists.
We disagree with all "neutrals" regardless of ethnic group or mutual aid society.
We have arrived at a moment where being neutral is being fascist.[176]

At 3:00 P.M. on May 6, 1937, Ybor City fell silent as weeks of protest preparations fell into place.[177] As tabaqueras stood from their workbenches, a lull swept across the city. Rarely were the streets of Ybor this quiet, but on this warm Thursday afternoon stillness signaled action.[178] The tall, mahogany double doors of the García y Vega factory swung open, and 300 women emptied out onto the brick-paved streets. Quickly and calmly, these women walked one block to the Labor Temple located on Eighth Avenue. This building's Moorish architecture echoed Ybor City's Spanish roots, while inside its rich legacy of Cuban unionism came to life. Latinos from the fraternal delegation of the Popular Front met these Latinas, as well as Latina cigar workers from other factories and public works projects, and together they made their way to Seventh Avenue.[179]

By 5:00 P.M., Moreno was one of the 5,000 Latinas from Ybor City, dressed mainly in black, who lined up in rows of four, linked arms, and began to march. The demonstrator in the front row of the procession, identified as Rosa Prado, carried an American flag, while Anglo police officers on motorcycles flanked each side of the marching women.[180] The rhythmic, almost synchronized, rapping of nearly 10,000 high-heeled shoes made it impossible to ignore the women marchers or their messages. With their heads held aloft, the proud demonstrators rounded the corner onto Seventh Avenue. An estimated 2,000 sympathizers lined the streets of Ybor City and some Latina/o-operated businesses closed their doors in solidarity with the marchers.[181] In all, more than 7,000 people—women, men, and children—participated in this protest either as women marchers or as community supporters. As the women reached the end of the main thoroughfare, the loud cheers of their allies faded and the women slowly left Ybor City and entered potentially dangerous terrain.

At 5:30 P.M., the Latina marchers were in the heart of Tampa. Anglos' stares replaced supportive Latinas/os' cheers.[182] Anglo police officers stood along Franklin Street's sidewalks, allegedly prepared to guard the Latina marchers from any possible threat. In light of Tampa's long, ugly history of racial and ethnic violence, however, it is most likely that Tampa's finest were present to remind the women of Anglo authority. As the Latinas reached downtown Tampa, the city's political and financial center, their ranks tightened as their pace slowed. Like a well-organized and disciplined brigade, the women came to a halt at the steps of Tampa's city hall. Ybor City's Latinas patiently waited for their spokeswoman to step forward and address the mayor in English.[183]

When Tampa mayor Robert E. Lee Chancey emerged from the building, he was greeted by a sea of women who packed the streets. One person broke ranks and stepped forward to submit a petition to the mayor and read a statement on Ybor City's support for the Spanish Republic and antifascist politics.[184]

> In the name of the thousands of U.S.-born *americanas*, Spaniards, Italians, Cubans, workers, professional and business persons, who are horrified by the hideous and horrendous slaughter of non-combatants, and defenseless women and children by Hitler and Mussolini's invasive forces, we ask you as mayor of Tampa to publicly condemn this monstrous crime against humanity.
>
> As citizens and residents of a peaceful and democratic nation, we feel morally obliged to give all possible aid to Spanish cities that defend their democratic government against fascist aggression, thus maintaining the standard of peace and democracy in the world.[185]

Once the representative concluded the reading, the crowd of Latinas/os erupted with applause as Mayor Chancey came down the steps of city hall, thanked the women marchers, and promised them he would send a letter to Florida's congressional delegation in Washington, D.C. During his response, Chancey invoked President Roosevelt as he expressed his desire for the United States to act as a "good neighbor" to Spain rather than as a "passive enemy."[186] However, like the AFL at the national convention, Chancey never opposed U.S. neutrality or acknowledged the importance of the women's actions, and there is no evidence that he ever sent a letter to Washington about the day's events. As it was for the majority of native-born Anglo Tampans, antifascism in Spain was for Chancey directly aligned with foreign radicalism, which was an element he consistently worked to combat by any means possible. Despite the mayor's casual indifference toward the women's politics, presence, and claim to power in the city of Tampa and the broader nation, Latina marchers publicly, and rhetorically, confronted Tampa's traditional southern notions of femininity as they ended their march on the front steps of the Tampa city hall. From place to language, these women made an open claim of Latinas/os' support of the Popular Front and their position as residents of Tampa and citizens of the United States, no matter their documentation status.

As the summer of 1937 continued, protests against labor inequality and political suppression erupted throughout central Florida. While Moreno indeed helped Ybor community members plan the antifascist march in May, it is difficult to unravel her direct role in the events that followed. Although the AFL reassigned Moreno to Philadelphia following her speech at the national convention, it seems that she never arrived at her new post. Between January and June 1937, CMIU leaders questioned Moreno's whereabouts and speculated that she was attending to family issues with her daughter, until the union concluded that Moreno had "joined the side of evil" and moved to the CIO.[187] While it would be comfortable and endearing to imagine that Moreno maintained a relationship with those she organized in Ybor City, there is no evidence that she returned to Ybor or stayed in close communication with any of the women from whom she learned so much. But what Moreno did take with her was a knowledge of what kind of union she wanted to work for and what kind of union she wished to create. Moreno went on to be a founding member of the United Cannery, Agricultural, Packing, and Allied Workers of America (UCAPAWA)—perhaps the most ambitious union to exist in the United States. Women held the majority of leadership positions within UCAPAWA and constituted the majority of UCAPAWA membership. In some ways, Moreno used UCAPAWA to apply what she learned in Florida. Women workers needed women organizers to communicate their needs, and when that happened their work as political agents soared. In Ybor City, allegiance to any union was never a top priority; instead, solidarity was built through political ideas and a sense of shared experiences.

When Moreno left Tampa, activism did not stop. After all, it was the cultures of labor within the community that drove Latinas to resist fascist forces in their workplaces, their communities, and throughout the world, not the presence of a singular person. For the next two years, Latinas worked with the comité to support the Spanish Republic through letter-writing campaigns to politicians in Washington, D.C.; fundraisers; and impassioned speeches. They assisted in the coordination and execution of parades and marches that drew public attention to the cause of the Spanish Republic and the problems cigar workers faced as the industry they relied on contracted and their ability to earn a living wage to support a family became increasingly difficult. Perhaps most powerful of all, the Frente Popular provided an avenue through which the leftist ideologies of Latinas/os could interact with the mumbling of progressive politics in Tampa. By September 1938, a parade that marched from Ybor City to DeSoto Park included local musicians, cigar workers, the comité, the maritime workers' union, the bakers' union, and the Workers Alliance. Together these women and men marched alongside and behind Latinas of the Anti-Fascist Women's Committee as they held signs that demanded the right to a fair wage, the right to union recognition, and the need to recognize and support the Spanish Republic.[188] Latinas persisted as leaders in the cigar industry and leaders in movements for antifascism until

1939, when the Spanish Republic fell and Franco's government assumed control of Spain. This result sent the community into a state of collective mourning. While the U.S. government chose to recognize the Franco regime, those in Ybor City refused to follow suit. The Centro Asturiano de Tampa communicated with its parent organization in Havana that the Ybor club had chosen to remove all references of allegiance and support for Spain from its membership materials. The mutual aid society took down the flag of the Spanish Republic and in its place raised the U.S. flag. A different signal, and in some way a necessary one, it sought to highlight which ideologies those in Ybor City valued against a rising tide of anti-radicalism and anti-immigrant reactionism that surged as World War II neared.

CHAPTER THREE

Surviving

Have these 100% Americans noticed the names of some of Tampa's heroes—Villa, Nicoletto, Murgado, Valdez just to name a few? If they did, they would see that telegrams beginning with "The War Department regrets—" are delivered to the Gonzalezes and Alvarezes as well as the Smiths and Jones.

Disgusted.

—*Tampa Morning Tribune*, 1944

On December 31, 1938, Estrella and Pedro walked out their front door a few minutes before midnight. Together they stood on their decaying wooden porch with their niece Edith Ogden Kennedy and her new husband Stetson Kennedy.[1] Kennedy—who worked as a folklorist for the Federal Writers' Project (FWP), the relief program that employed out-of-work writers, journalists, and academics—was not on assignment that night yet could not help but analyze the world around him. Sounds of children shouting in English, Spanish, and Italian filled the streets as the pop of firecrackers pierced the air. While both couples absorbed the sounds and sights of adolescent excitement, they silently stared into the distance. The Regensberg Cigar Factory, known as El Reloj because of the giant clock atop its watchtower, hovered above the community and made time seem inescapable to the women and men who lived in this place.[2]

As the couples waited for midnight, Estrella and Pedro confided in their visitors that time had not been kind to them in recent years. Like their neighbors, however, they made the most of it. Throughout the Depression the couple weathered the ups and downs of the cigar industry as they moved from the cigar makers' benches to the cigar box assembly lines to trying to secure a position on the Works Progress Administration (WPA) relief rolls. Each shift meant less money. But the couple explained they were grateful for President Franklin D. Roosevelt and they welcomed the availability of bulk grapefruit juice, canned meat, and flour from the "relief station."[3] No matter their struggles, Estrella and Pedro dreamed of more. Once the couple saved enough money, Pedro hoped to open his own cigar enterprise and Estrella assumed she would work beside him. Neither one of them hoped for something as grand as a factory, just a chinchal—one of the small, family-owned businesses that allowed tabaqueras/os to make cigars the old way, with care and passion, and sell them to tourists in Tampa and St. Petersburg.[4] As the couple stared into the distance they may have thought of how they hoped to give their children more than what they had and provide their young ones with a better and more secure life.[5]

When El Reloj struck midnight, a police officer who stood on the balcony of L'Unione Italiana, the Italian mutual aid society, raised his arm toward the sky and fired his revolver five times. The sound of gunfire snapped the couple out of their trance and jolted them back to reality. Children raced through the streets, shouting as they huddled together and lit ten-cent Roman candles. The mini-explosions echoed through the streets and accentuated the percussion of rumba as the music spilled from the ballroom of the Círculo Cubano, the white Cuban club. Both couples gazed into the sky as they smiled, yelled, and laughed with a holiday-induced performance of joy. As Kennedy later remembered this moment, he remarked that it was "only the children" in the streets who "[did] not sound forced [or] artificial" that night. Once the firework flares dimmed and the scent of gunpowder faded, an oppressive silence lingered in the air. Pedro, who could no longer handle the tension, looked at everyone and said: "Well, I guess that's all. It's 1939 and it don't feel no different to me."[6] Estrella likely looked at her husband and chuckled with dismissive amusement.

It would have been impossible for Estrella and Pedro to anticipate the changes their community would undergo over the next six years. The eruption of World War II, and the entry of the United States into this global conflict, led to a surge of patriotism and nationalism that called into question the moral character of people perceived to be foreign. To Latinas and Latinos in Ybor City, this meant proving themselves as neighbors worthy of inclusion in the place they now called home. This task, at times, must have felt herculean.

Between 1939 and 1946, Latinas/os from Ybor City fought to survive in a shifting world where public perception mattered. Latinas, who had moved into visible positions of power in the 1930s, encountered accusations of anti-Americanism that itself manifested through stereotypes that marked these women as unmotherly and unwomanly because their actions and their politics stood in opposition to what the nascent welfare state, and by extension the federal government, defined as acceptable behavior.[7] Such stigmas grounded in Latina bodies, extended to men and children in the community as well. From the perception of state officials, as well as Anglo outsiders in

Tampa, Latinas were inherently unable to provide the ethic of care essential to nurture their families, while Latino husbands were dismissed as lazy. Latina/o children, consequently, were little more than delinquents—products of their amoral parents and un-American upbringing. While in previous years, such reports from welfare officials, sociologists, and the local Anglo news would not have mattered profoundly, in the Depression and during wartime it did. The decline of the mutual aid networks on which these women and men long relied—along with the growing effort to identify and deport noncitizens assumed to have un-American politics and to discipline those who did not align with state-defined concepts of normative gender roles—created new conditions for determining who had the right to residency, who had the right to citizenship, and who had the right to belong in the United States.

Historians have debated the concept and meaning of citizenship in a quest to understand belonging. Most nations define citizenship according to law, which in the United States includes a complex immigration code that welcomes fewer immigrants than it rejects. These laws allow the state to define citizenship and assess an immigrant's ability to adhere to such expectations. Such a rigid interpretation of citizenship, however, does not address self-perception or belonging from the position of the individuals themselves.[8] By the late 1930s, the Latinas and Latinos of Ybor City, both immigrant and U.S.-born, felt that they belonged in Florida and, by extension, the United States, regardless of their paperwork and their documentation status. It was in this place where they worked, where they loved, where they hoped, where they had families, where they joined unions, where they protested, where they attended political meetings, and where they created community. Yet while so much of their experiences were anchored in this place, their memories, extended families, and cultural networks reached across borders. World War II presented the opportunity for women and men in Ybor City to illustrate how an international sense of being was not at war with U.S. patriotic principles but lived alongside them through ethnic Americanism.[9] Throughout the wartime era, Latinos navigated a new relationship to the U.S. state as they joined the armed forces and became active in the defense effort, while Latinas defended their identities—as well as those of their sons, brothers, and husbands—through volunteerism and community advocacy. While such actions fought against stereotypes of who the broader Anglo community and U.S. nation assumed Ybor Latinas/os to be, these actions also began to change how Ybor Latinas/os understood themselves.

The Limits of Mutual Aid and the Stigma of Latinidad

Prior to the Great Depression, the residents of Ybor City developed a system of self-help through the founding of mutual aid societies. These institutions—locally referred to as sociedades, centros, or clubs—celebrated the cultures of the people who lived there and provided an infrastructure essential to their survival. In some ways, finding a strong mutual aid culture in Ybor City is hardly surprising. Ethnic associations stood at the center of cultural life in immigrant communities throughout the United States. New York City, Hoboken, Chicago, Philadelphia, Boston, and Los Angeles, as well as other immigrant centers, boasted impressive webs of mutual aid in the late nineteenth and early twentieth centuries.[10] In Ybor City, the five core mutual aid societies—the Círculo Cubano (white Cubans), La Sociedad de la Unión Martí-Maceo (Black Cubans), the Centro Español (Spaniards), Centro Asturiano (Spaniards from Asturias and northern Spain), and L'Unione Italiana (Italians/Sicilians)—provided essential social services as they worked to maintain cross-national connections between members and their homelands. Yet perhaps, most importantly, these institutions established a way for the women and men of Ybor City to maintain authority over themselves and their community in a Jim Crow city that relied on law, vigilantism, and racial and ethnic exclusion to control and restrict Latinas/os from most channels of social support and public assistance.[11]

Ybor City's centros defined the physical landscape of the immigrant neighborhood. These buildings were massive structures that stood proudly on Seventh Avenue and Eighth Avenue. Following the architectural traditions of Cuba and Spain, the exteriors of the buildings featured Moorish arches, alabaster columns, and ornately tangled wrought iron. The interiors of the sociedades rivaled the grandeur of their facades. Elaborate dance floors, marble staircases, and hand-carved moldings illustrated the pride and importance of these institutions to Ybor City's working-class residents, who donated their money to construct them and paid monthly dues to operate them. After the completion of the Centro Asturiano, for example, the *Tampa Morning Tribune* heralded the structure as the "most beautiful building in the South," a high compliment for an Anglo newspaper to pay to something on this side of town.[12] The home of the Centro Asturiano featured a 1,200-seat theater, a cantina and ballroom, a library stocked with works from authors such as Miguel Cervantes and Luisa Capetillo, and a state-of-the-art hospital.[13] The other centros were no less impressive. The palazzo exterior of the Centro Español welcomed members to a mosaic foyer and mahogany salon.

A grand double staircase led to the second floor of the building, which boasted a ballroom and meeting space where the sociedad provided cultural and language classes as well as weekly dances and socials. Much like the Centro Asturiano, the Centro Español owned and operated a hospital for members. The provision of medical care by the sociedades was essential to people in Ybor City because Tampa hospitals refused to treat Latina/o patients. Women and men of Ybor City celebrated the strength of their independent hospital system and took pride in their ability to receive care and medical services from people of their community who spoke their language and treated them with respect and dignity.[14]

The Círculo Cubano functioned as a "cathedral for workers," decorated with intricate tile work and vibrant stained-glass windows. Members of the Círculo Cubano paid monthly dues for access to benefits such as the cantina and pharmacy, as well as the library and the lavishly painted 70,000-square-foot dance hall. While the Círculo Cubano did not own its own hospital, membership included access to clinics and doctors within Ybor City—a health care structure that mimicked present-day health insurance by permitting members to go to a doctor within its network for zero fee or a nominal copay. L'Unione Italiana drew inspiration from traditions of the Mediterranean with its neoclassical style and white Romanesque columns. This three-story building housed a theater, cantina, library, dance hall, bowling alley, gymnasium, doctor's clinic, and laboratory.[15] For immigrants who were working class, the desire to dedicate a portion of their earnings to support these beautiful and expensive buildings highlights the importance of these institutions and the services they provided. Mutual aid structures gave immigrants a sense of place in a seemingly foreign environment. Walking through the streets of Ybor, surrounded by redbrick Cuban cigar factories and massive centros, one could forget one was in the United States.

The only centro that deviated from this origin story was La Sociedad de la Unión Martí-Maceo, the Afro-Cuban club. Initially, there was one club for Cubans no matter their race, El Club Nacional Cubano. This association emerged from the principles of the movement for Cuban independence, which championed interracial cooperation through rhetoric and symbolic actions.[16] By 1899, however, this club dissolved. What emerged were two distinct ethnic organizations—one for white Cubans and one for Black Cubans—the Círculo Cubano (founded in 1900) and La Sociedad de la Unión Martí-Maceo (founded in 1904).[17] As the historian Nancy Raquel Mirabal notes, there are few published or archival accounts by Afro-Cubans on the history or experience of their expulsion from El Club Nacional Cubano.

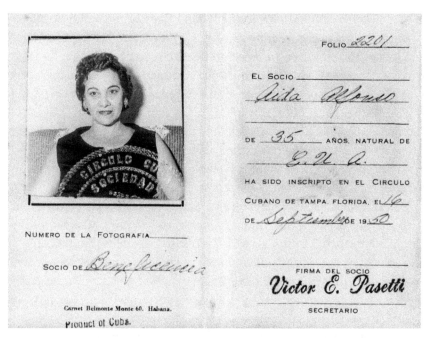

Aida Alfonso's Círculo Cubano membership card, 1950. Author's collection.

Instead, what survives is the perspective of white Cubans. According to these accounts, it was the city of Tampa and the expanse of Jim Crow that necessitated and required that the association disband.[18] This explanation could, indeed, hold currency. José Rivero Muñiz, a white Cuban from Ybor City, emphasized that "there had always been the most cordial relationship among Cubans [in the immigrant neighborhood]," but "in this part of the United States, it was necessary to face the facts." From his perspective the creation of two clubs allowed each group to proceed "in the manner that best suited their collective interests."[19]

The dissolution of El Club Nacional Cubano says as much about who white Cubans wanted to be in Ybor City as it does about who white Cubans thought they could be in the United States. In this southern space, these women and men wished for equality and respect, two things some hoped could be achieved through the embrace of their whiteness. While white Cuban cigar workers fought for interracial unionism, which served to benefit them directly, they were all too willing to bend to the exclusion of social spaces.[20] As Sylvia Griñan reflected on the experience and history of being Black and Cuban in Ybor City, she explained: "When the white Cubans started getting Americanized, they became more like white Americans in their attitudes toward [B]lacks, including [B]lack Cubans. And that extended to discrimination from all sides—from white Cubans and white Americans and also from [B]lack Americans who didn't really understand us. You can't comprehend how painful that can be."[21]

With the creation of La Sociedad de la Unión Martí-Maceo—a club name that honored the lives of the Cuban revolutionaries José Martí, the famed orator and leader, and Antonio Maceo, the Afro-Cuban general—Black Cubans fundraised and purchased a parcel of land, where they built their own clubhouse.[22] This structure was two stories high and included a dance hall, meeting rooms, and a theater large enough to hold 900 people.[23] The leaders of the Unión Martí-Maceo made sure the club, and its membership, was visible within the community, as they "sponsored virtually every social and cultural event celebrated" by the residents of Ybor City.[24] In a building adjacent to the clubhouse, the organization founded a school to preserve the heritage of Black Cubans. At night women, men, and children took Spanish-language and Cuban history classes from older members of the sociedad. Juan Maella remembered that while the elders of the Unión Martí-Maceo encouraged that he and his comrades learn English, they "would not allow English to be spoken in the clubhouse" in an effort to preserve language and culture for the next generation. "You see," Maella explained, La Sociedad de la Unión Martí-Maceo "was the only offering [B]lack Cubans had."[25]

All centros provided valuable services to members. Initially, the organizations restricted membership to those who shared their nationalities and required that members take an oath of allegiance to the country the sociedad represented.[26] In later years, however, these mandates fell by the wayside and the clubs allowed women, men, and families (considered to be white within Ybor City) to choose which centro to join based on the benefits available and the price of membership. All sociedades acted as social clubs where men could play dominoes, sip *café con leche*, debate politics, and organize labor. Women also found space within these institutions as they created *comités de damas* (women's committees) that coordinated May Day celebrations, arranged cultural activities, and planned community picnics.[27] These events took place at locations such as Rocky Point, Ballast Point, Palmetto Beach, and De Soto Park—all beachside locations where the gulf breeze swung through the air as cigar workers and community members dipped their toes in the salty water and feasted from "cauldrons full of food."[28]

Although community events were moments of celebration, at times they attracted hostile attention from Tampa Anglos. M. Santos, who lived and worked in Ybor City, explained that "many times there was trouble" at picnics

Dance at La Sociedad de la Unión Martí-Maceo in Ybor City, ca. 1940s. Robertson and Fresh Collection, University of South Florida Libraries—Tampa Special Collections, Tampa, Florida.

organized by the mutual aid societies, "because the American felt some kind of hatred towards us." These unwanted visitors would get drunk and "tease women in order to start a quarrel." Santos recalled one specific moment when three Anglo men "grabbed a girl and seized her breasts." To these men, this Latina's body was something they believed they had the right to access and assault in an attempt to exert their authority over both her person and this space. When the young woman's boyfriend told Santos what happened, he walked over to the unwanted visitors and demanded an explanation. One of the men answered "in a contemptuous way and at the same time closed his hands to threaten [Santos]." In response, Santos "threw the first blow with all [his] might," and the man "fell behind a door which was half open." The other two Anglo men rushed for Santos, and he "answer[ed] the attack with all the anger and indignation [and] power of [his] 19 years." Moments like this may not have happened at every event beyond Ybor City, but when they did such incursions were remarkable enough for a person to remember and recall years later.[29]

The employees of the FWP who examined the Ybor City mutual aid societies could not help but offer praise: "The institutions which have been the greatest agencies in giving help . . . in the community are the social clubs."[30] Centros offered loans, death benefits, health insurance, medical services, and optional unemployment insurance to dues-paying members, making the clubs one of the most reliable forms of aid to working-class women and men in Ybor City.[31] "The only detrimental effect of these clubs on its members," wrote one FWP employee, "is the tendency to keep [Latinas/os] together so that the probabilities of learning the English language and acquiring habits proper for the complex environment outside the club [are] lowered."[32]

Anglos from Tampa criticized the clubs for their culture of, what they understood as, "'socialistic, 'un-American,' and 'radical'" contract medicine.[33] The Hillsborough County Medical Association barred fifteen doctors who worked for hospitals and clinics within the Ybor health care network from admitting privileges in Tampa hospitals as well as the medical association itself. At times, this tension became violent. A group of men attacked J. R. Avellanal, the first doctor to work for the Centro Español, in response to his refusal to leave his position.[34] Mutual aid societies in Ybor City received recognition for the important role the institutions played in the lives of Latinas/os in Ybor City as well as denigration from those who critiqued these women and men's refusal to assail their cultural authority and assimilate into Anglo Tampa.

As women rose as the primary or exclusive breadwinners of their families, unemployment insurance through the centros was essential to survival, at least as long as the funds lasted. The dues to these institutions for a basic membership were, on average, $1.50 per month for the primary member plus an additional $0.60 per week for each dependent. Unemployment insurance, an optional benefit, cost an additional $0.50–$0.60 per week for each person who wished to add this service to their membership. In exchange, a woman or man with dependents had access to unemployment insurance for up to $55.00 per month, while single persons without dependents could receive $24.00 per month.[35] This benefit came with free medical care and prescriptions and, until the Depression, was available to persons who were unemployed, regardless of gender or marital status.

The problem with unemployment insurance and mutual aid societies, however, was that these institutions could not afford to support members if a high quotient of members could not afford to pay dues. Latinas/os could miss three months of dues payments before a mutual aid society suspended their membership.[36] As a result of declining membership and the rise in elderly people in need of health care, sociedades required that new members be under fifty years of age upon application. If elderly people lost their membership, they would be unable to rejoin the association by the 1930s. Such a policy sought to prevent people from withdrawing their membership to save money and rejoining only in times of medical need.[37] Mr. Garcia, an elderly resident of Ybor, explained to the FWP that his greatest fear was losing membership at the Centro Asturiano. As a man over fifty, he and his wife would have been unable to rejoin the sociedad if their membership discontinued.[38] Mrs. Garcia, who was likely the primary member of her household with steady employment in the late 1930s, would have felt particularly responsible to provide for her family and may have feared losing unemployment and medical support for her partner.[39]

As the Depression deepened, mutual aid membership rolls thinned as jobs within cigar factories became more difficult to find and the need for aid increased. Such support, however, was no longer available from the institutions on which the women and men had long relied. Mutual aid societies made the difficult, yet essential, decision to narrow their social services to medical support, care for the gravely ill, death benefits, and, of course, social activities and entertainment events necessary for morale. These organizations simply did not have the money to support the number of people who were out of work or underemployed.

Neither married nor single Latinas, many of whom were the primary wage earners in their homes, could afford personal illness, pregnancy, or the loss of employment without this benefit. Dolores Patiño Río remembered being a young, pregnant, working-class woman with a household full of dependent family members during the Depression: "I worked until six, seven months before I had Sylvia [my first child]. And then I left because [the cigar factory] fired me. . . . With Gloria [my second child], I worked until the last day."[40] Like most Latinas in Ybor City, Río could not afford to be without work because the unemployment insurance, which could function as maternity support in an earlier era, had vanished, as did ample opportunity for work in Ybor cigar factories. Because Río's labor cared for her husband, mother, grandmother, two cousins, and two children, all of whom lived under one roof in a small rented home, she could not afford to refuse work. "As soon as they gave me the chance . . . I was back [at the factory] again," Río recounted. "They call me, I say I cannot lose the [opportunity]. I got to work. I need the money," she added.[41] Río's mother and elderly cousins cared for her children while her husband hopped between chinchales and WPA work when he was lucky enough to get it. When Río thought back on her life and remembered this period, she said: "People say, 'Give me the good old days.' I don't want those good old days. Forget it." For Río, as well as the broader Ybor community, the Great Depression was brutal.[42] The fragile state of mutual aid combined with the difficulty of finding and securing enough steady employment to pay bills pushed women and men in Ybor City to seek assistance beyond their community institutions. For the first time, the residents of Ybor looked to the federal government.

The Social Security Act of 1935 redefined the role of the federal state in the lives of residents and the citizens of the United States. This legislation, developed and passed in the midst of the Great Depression, provided essential assistance to those in need. Collective memory surrounding this law varies. Some remember the food subsidies it made available to the hungry, the checks it sent to the elderly, the money it provided to families, the jobs it gave to those able to labor yet unable to find employment, and the system it developed to support retirement for future generations. Others, however, remember its limitations. This law denied assistance and future benefits to those who labored in agriculture and domestic work, it rejected requests for placement in federal work programs to those assumed to be capable of finding employment elsewhere, and it refused support to women who did not appear to be womanly or motherly according to welfare officials. The shortcomings of the Social Security Act famously led to the mass exclusion of Black Americans, but it also had wide-reaching implications for immigrants and those perceived to be outsiders even if they were U.S. citizens. After all, the implementation of this law was local.[43]

Women and men in Ybor City at once praised the Roosevelt administration for the New Deal and lamented how difficult it was for them to benefit from these new programs. On the surface, the advent of relief and federal work programs could fill the gap that the loss of mutual aid unemployment benefits left. But, central to one's ability to access relief, presently understood as welfare, was whether or not administrators of community-based relief offices viewed relief applicants as worthy citizens and members of the deserving poor. In Tampa, federal funds for public assistance programs most readily went to Anglos in need of work or supplementary income. From the perspective of those who managed relief offices within the city of Tampa, most of whom were Anglo, it was people such as themselves who most deserved assistance in these hard times. To them, Anglos were the true Americans while Latinas/os were foreigners, regardless of whether or not they were foreign-born.[44]

Few documents or accounts make clearer the meaning of difference or the power of stereotypes that thrived in this space and motivated exclusion from public assistance and social spaces more than the sociological report "The Cuban Family in Ybor City." This investigation, funded by the WPA and conducted by researchers employed by the FWP, illustrates the stigma latinidad carried within Tampa. Latinas/os' history of leftist ideologies, labor unionism, cross-border activism, rejection of religion, and support of collective community institutions marked them as un-American from the perspective of Anglos. Such actions, which had long ensured the survival of these women and men, became powerful barriers as Latinas/os waded into waters beyond the confines of Ybor City. The sociological report, while damaging to the entire community, was particularly damning when it came to women. Much like the New Deal — grounded in Anglo-protestant values that supported a welfare structure that celebrated stay-at-home mothers and male breadwinners — sociologists judged the working women of Ybor City harshly and concluded they were little more than neglectful mothers, amoral wives, and foreign tramps, a stigma that carried power beyond this era.

According to "The Cuban Family in Ybor City," a woman who spent her day at the factory "was too tired to give her child the necessary attention needed." Therefore, "from the start, [Cuban] children were handicapped in their education and their upbringing."[45] While these Latinas had no choice but to work in order to ensure the survival of their families, public officials linked women's dedication to labor with inherent unmotherly characteristics and unruly children. One account noted: "Home education of children was very meager after school. What [young Cuban children] kn[e]w, they merely learn[ed] from school and the gang."[46] FWP employees detailed in public reports that the absence of parents from the home "most of the day and the night" resulted in "evil effects" and "vulgar habits" in both young Cuban men and young Cuban women. Likewise, this observer explained that these young Latinos "would go out to the corner grocery store, café, etc., where the neighborhood gang met . . . [to] indulge in play, conversation, and other things with boys of [their] age and older men." Without the vigilant eye of a mother, "the young boys learned from the other ones, all about the sexes, and their mysteries."[47] Tampa FWP officials assumed that the absence of working mothers from their households resulted in "delinquent" boys and "fallen" girls.[48] The report detailed that in Ybor City "instead of [parents] explaining to the child the difference in sexes and their habits," Cuban mothers and Cuban fathers "merely kept [young boys] guessing at such an important subject."[49] Likewise, officials stated that despite the advancements in public health, "young girls [were] not told anything about sex and [its] consequences" by their mothers, and therefore "many of the girls' delinquencies started from grammar school." The report's writers added that "what girls learned [was] through hearsay in which the evils . . . [of sex were] not known to them," and young Latinas and Latinos "without the vigilance of their parents, formed plans and finally carried them out in some secluded place."[50] As a result of unplanned pregnancies, young Latinas were trapped by "unsatisfactory matchings," and young Latinos were "treated daily for venereal disease."[51]

Anglo government officials viewed these Cuban laborers as unfit parents who did not have the cultural capacity to raise productive, law-abiding, virtuous children. Furthermore, some of the FWP employees who wrote and published these reports may have understood immigrant Cubans as leftist radical laborers and assumed their children to be extensions of their parents' supposed corrupt values. To welfare officials, such characterizations confirmed the exclusion of Cubans from relief rolls. By using supposedly unbiased social scientific methods to explore the community, officials painted Cubans as hopeless—a state of being that could not be overcome by relief from government funds. Justifications such as these led relief officials to preference needy Anglos in Tampa over struggling Latinas/os in Ybor City.

The public perception of the failure of Latina mothers dually legitimized Anglos' stereotypes of Latinas as distrustful wives and sexual objects. FWP officials argued that these working mothers not only failed their children morally but also disrupted their homes with insincere marital commitments and inherent desires for extramarital sex. In the compiled FWP study on Tampa, the commission explained that the "Depression ha[d] caused many married men to lose their jobs," and as a result "these unemployed men not having anything to give their wives, their marriages usually ended in separation, each going back to their families respectively to live as best as possible." A Cuban woman "being free, considered [herself her] own keeper and went so far as to go out with any man that please[d] her without her father's consent." The report continued that as a result of this seemingly independent and unconscionable behavior, Cuban fathers allegedly refused to endorse such "disgrace" and ordered the young women "to obey or move out of the house." As a result, "the young girls usually became mistresses or went to a house of prostitution. Those [who] became mistresses end[ed up] in the same place sooner or later."[52]

While there were some women in Ybor City who labored in sex work, the author of this study does not examine such a reality with interest or understanding. Instead, the author employs a moral perspective and establishes a declension narrative that reinforces stereotypes of Latinas as unfit daughters, sisters, wives, and mothers. All Cuban women in Ybor City were not sex workers. However, for those who did labor in sex, this work provided an avenue for women to support themselves or provide additional income to their households, a layer of deftness and understanding the report does not provide.[53]

Cuban husbands, fathers, and single men fared little better within the study of the Ybor community. Characterized as members of the "poor miserable class" and men who were not "given the means of developing their energies, abilities, and intellect," Latinos were seen by Tampa officials as "instruments to political machinations" who solely sought "an easy way to predominance."[54] According to the FWP, while these Cuban men "were received, [upon arrival to Tampa], with affection and sympathy, they never thought of the future," because "Cuba was near at hand." The report stated, "The actual condition to which the Cubans in Tampa have reached cannot be blamed on anyone. . . . All errors must be made answerable to the one who commits them." Furthermore, the author of this report described Latinos as irresponsible heads of households who, despite their unending dedication to Cuban idealism, brought with them the "defects" of "indifference." The FWP writer likewise believed that the "virtue of thrift was something completely strange" to Cuban men, for "whatever they earned they would spend. . . . They lacked the willpower of retaining and knowing the full value of a dollar earned."[55]

As a result, officials opined that because Latinos were without work, savings, or the ability to contribute to the family, they invested their energy in the dream of a better life through reorganization of the political system. As the FWP wrote of Ybor Latinos with little education, "[They] believe that they have a right to live from the national budget, and entirely disregard their own means of livelihood. [And,] [w]ithout the necessary preparation, they believe they have the right to govern and command others, without knowing how to govern themselves."[56] These supposed unemployed, dependent men were further cast as unfaithful husbands who "ha[d] temptations; possibly due to climate." Regardless of the reason, continued the official, "It is a fact that [the Cuban] is never satisfied with his wife, and is always desirous of having a mistress: that is, another one that is not united to him by the indissoluble bonds of matrimony."[57]

From the perspective of FWP officials, Latinas defied, in body and action, what Anglo onlookers considered womanly, just as Latinos challenged what Anglos believed was responsible and manly. As neglectful parents, the moral corruption of Latina daughters and Latino sons was believed to be inevitable—if the mother and the father lacked any sense of morality, how could the children be any different? Latina sexuality became a key component of FWP reporting in Tampa, for it sparked interest and fear. In attacks on Latinas' roles as workers and mothers, these foreign women became hypersexualized by the people who observed them. The women's ethnic and racial differences, compounded by their dedication to paid labor, tested Anglo American southern sensibilities. Latinos, conversely, were the antithesis of what Anglo officials considered American and masculine, and FWP officials assumed them to be little more than foreign radicals, disloyal husbands, and irresponsible fathers.

While this report could be dismissed as an outlier, something written by an unknown racist and sexist FWP employee, there are reasons it is more significant than initially meets the eye. This account lies within the final, compiled sociological study of Ybor City—a version of the report that received approval from the author's colleagues and supervisors at the WPA. Within the broader report there is evidence that accuracy was of the utmost importance to those who oversaw the study. For example, the FWP employee who examined the role of the church in Ybor City waxed poetically about the importance and centrality of religious life, especially that of the Catholic Church, to the community. This account, however, conflicted with life histories of community members collected by other FWP workers who found high levels of anticlericalism and distrust of the Catholic Church within the neighborhood. In response, the WPA conducted a survey of religious life in Ybor City. Sixty percent of respondents identified as "definitely agnostic," 20 percent stated they had "no special bias or belief," and the final 20 percent indicated they were "devout." Although the practices of this survey may not meet the standards of present-day sociologists and other social scientists, the information collected complements the life history accounts the FWP compiled during the 1930s and early 1940s as well as oral history interviews conducted by historians throughout the twentieth and twenty-first centuries. The results of this survey, as well as the analysis surrounding it, sits as the introduction to the broader article on religious life within Ybor City. Such effort illustrates that the WPA encouraged its FWP employees to reflect accuracy to the best of their ability and likely had an editorial approval process. In the case of Ybor City, the WPA worked to illustrate that this community study reflected what officials knew, learned, and understood about the neighborhood and its people.[58]

The stigmas embedded within "The Cuban Family in Ybor City" become even more important, however, when we consider what being Cuban meant to outsiders in Tampa. The term *Cuban*, when used by Anglos in Tampa, was often a universal classification. In other words, from the perspective of Anglo outsiders, anyone who lived in Ybor City was Cuban, regardless of their actual ethnicity or self-identification. This generalization grew from the predominance of Cubans and Latinas/os of Cuban heritage in the community as well as the presence and power of the Cuban cigar industry in Tampa. Furthermore, this reality speaks to why the FWP profiled only the Cuban family in the sociological report. No other ethnic group received individual study to this extent or analysis of their personal lives.

In addition to the generalizing nature of the term *Cuban* in Tampa was the reality that this word could act as a pejorative that indicated someone was from Ybor City—a place many Anglos believed to be "dirty and a disgrace to the city," which therefore made that person from the neighborhood "a dirty, lazy, and ignorant" individual who did not belong in Tampa or, by extension, the United States.[59] Most egregious, however, was the creation and use of a local epithet. "If crackers [a pejorative term for Anglos] really wanted to make us mad," Frank Urso (an Italian) recalled, "they'd call us Cuban Niggers."[60] This racial slur simultaneously invoked foreignness and anti-Blackness, two intersecting categories that united into a singular phrase of hate and derision. As Anglos would "tighten their loose sweet drawl to spit out" these words, their vitriol illustrated the status of Ybor Latinas/os as non-white in this southern space as well as the contempt and ostracization that accompanied it.[61] Such language combined the aspects of Ybor City that outsiders believed made these women and men un-American—their dedication to radical leftist politics, their refusal to readily accept Anglo authority, their use of Spanish and Italian as well as accented English, their apathy toward or rejection of Christianity, their commitment to unionism, and their skin colors. *Cuban* was the catchall word for these supposed undesirable traits, which made the local stigma of latinidad a wide-reaching and mighty barrier that was difficult to overcome both when it came to attempts to access relief and when it came to interactions with Anglo Tampa.[62]

By the time the full sociological study of Ybor City was complete in 1942, many administrators in the Tampa offices of the WPA may have felt that their report was just and representative. From the perspective of Anglos, Latinas/os seemed to have proved FWP employees right when it came to the question of whether or not they deserved a spot on the relief rolls during the Depression. Latinas/os who managed to find entry onto the relief rosters organized strikes and sought to unify the unemployed through the Workers Alliance throughout the 1930s. While WPA administrators understood such acts as evidence that these women and men were ungrateful and undeserving of assistance, perhaps even dangerous to the mission of the New Deal, Latinas/os in Ybor City saw such modes of resistance as essential to improving the life and welfare of themselves and their fellow workers. At a time when Latinas and Latinos desperately needed to leave the confines of their community for help, Anglos resisted inclusion of these women and men on relief rolls as well as residents, community members, citizens of Tampa, and members of the United States.

Of Good Moral Character

On March 8, 1940, the front page of the *Tampa Morning Tribune* declared, "Dies Will Quiz Tampans in His Probe of Reds."[63] The headline's oversize script made the letters jump off the page as if to caution readers of the coming storm. In the article the author reported that Martin Dies, a "lanky, drawling Texan," congressman, and chairman of the House Un-American Activities Committee (HUAC) refused to indicate "the nature of the information he expected to receive," but emphasized that the presence of this committee "was connected with an inquiry into Communists in Florida and the entry of foreign agents from Latin American countries."[64] Tampa—a city with an active Popular Front, a vibrant culture of labor, an immigrant community, and a population that was majority non-Anglo—caught the attention of conservative politicians in Washington, D.C. The women and men who adhered to these supposed anti-American ideals had publicly supported the fight against fascism, marched through the streets in protest of U.S. isolation, and declared themselves members and allies of the antifascist movement as they advocated for international democracy. Likewise, Latinas/os from Ybor corresponded openly with the ambassadors of Cuba and Spain and frequently traveled between Florida and the island to coordinate with cross-national organizations.[65] While, in theory, such actions align with the tenets of the democratic ideals that underline what the United States purports itself to be, in 1940 they conflicted with national policies of isolationism. As paranoid politicians like Dies watched Germany and the Soviet Union sign the nonaggression pact, conservative U.S. politicians believed it was their duty to secure the porous borders of the United States to prevent the entry of potential spies. Ybor City's Latinas and Latinos, whose cross-border politics challenged the southern racial order and whose internationalist sensibilities criticized U.S. foreign policy, were among those Dies intended to scrutinize and question during his visit to the Sunshine State.

The mayor of Tampa and other local government officials, both of whom routinely rallied against Latina/o leftist radicals, had a surprising reaction to the HUAC investigation in their own backyard. In public interviews, Mayor Chancey insisted, "If Representative Martin Dies . . . is looking for alien smuggling, he probably will find more on the Canadian border than Florida."[66] Citing reports by local immigration officials, the mayor continued: "It is true that Havana and other Caribbean cities are thronged with [Jewish] war refugees eager to get to the United States." The mayor, however, assured the public that Tampa officials had contacted Jewish organizations in Cuba and "warned them not to try to smuggle their way in."[67] Chancey's response was an attempt to direct fear and suspicion toward potential new immigrants and deflect from the strength of homegrown leftist movements within Tampa. When pushed by a reporter to comment on un-American radicalism in the city of Tampa, the mayor replied: "Communism is something else . . . [and] it is generally accepted there are Communists in Florida [yet] not but a few in Tampa."[68] In truth, there were more than "a few" communists who lived among the palms in 1940, and Chancey knew it. As he gave his statement to the reporter, he likely thought about his own fight against, what he saw as, anti-American values and un-American activities over the course of the previous decade.

During Chancey's tenure as mayor of Tampa, he waged a political campaign against the rise of the Communist Party (CP) and approved of vigilante violence to quell the influence of the Communist Party USA (CPUSA) in this place, but such action was often in vain. Although Chancey and his political allies sought to repress the might of communism in this city, Tampa became an active center of communist activity. In response, Chancey supported and enacted an anticommunist city ordinance in 1935 and supported the efforts of the Tampa sheriff to detain and arrest anyone who participated in supposed anti-American, radical activity—be that assembly in support of the CPUSA or strikes and protests by workers who sought higher wages in the Cuban cigar factories. To Chancey, the efforts of organized labor were the same as communist influence, for both challenged the supremacy of the city's Anglo powerholding elite and the principles that guided the city. Like the anti-radical and anti-labor raids that targeted Latinas/os in Texas and California, vigilante violence by deputized community members left a legacy of anti-radical terror.[69] Chancey—who had long approved of the work done by the local police force, the citizens' committee, and the Ku Klux Klan (KKK) to repress the power and presence of communists in the city—applauded the day his men broke in to the home of the organizer Arnesto Soto and confiscated "all the important documents of the Party, including dues, stamps and [the] Party book."[70] During the raid, police officers arrested as many CP members as they could identify and jailed them for a month.

Despite such action, Chancey struggled to control communist influence and labor unionism throughout the city during the Depression. When cigar manufacturers announced they would abandon the Spanish hand-work system and move to either partial or full mechanization in their factories, Cuban cigar workers struck and protested in mass. Tensions between workers and their employers grew to such heights that officials from the Department of Labor came to Tampa to mediate the issue. This conference lasted two weeks, and, in the end, the two parties could not reach an agreement. Chancey watched as Cuban cigar workers responded to the situation by waging a campaign to disassociate from the Cigar Makers' International Union—an affiliate of the American Federation of Labor that decried communist and socialist politics and had long represented the Cuban cigar industry in Ybor City—in favor of representation by the CPUSA-adjacent Congress of Industrial Organizations (CIO). As a result, the city of Tampa "charged [those who led and supported this action to change unions with] the customary reactionary gag of 'Communism'" and arrested these workers as the KKK paraded through Ybor City to show that they did not want "talk of communism going on." Chancey, who allied with cigar manufacturers in the midst of this clash, succeeded while Cuban cigar workers, who had rallied to avoid additional loss of pay and damage to their craft, experienced standardization of their labor and additional cuts in wages.[71]

While Chancey may have felt as though he were an expert in the suppressive tactics needed to control the influence and expanse of communism in political organizations and the might of labor unions, he struggled to navigate the rise of antifascism within the city. Chancey watched as the eruption of the Spanish Civil War and the movement for the maintenance of the Spanish Republic captured the attention of women and men in Ybor City between 1937 and 1939. As Ybor community members decried the rise of global fascism, they proclaimed themselves to be the vanguard of democracy at home and abroad. Latinas marched through the streets of Ybor City and Tampa as they garnered allies from CIO-represented industries and coordinated with the American Red Cross. These local "premature anti-fascists," a classification created by the U.S. government, pushed Chancey into uncharted waters. On the one hand, these people supported the exact principles Chancey and the Dies committee proclaimed to protect; yet, on the other, their actions conflicted with the official position of the U.S. government toward the Soviet-supported Spanish Republic and the Spanish Civil

War. After all, what mattered most to politicians in the United States before 1941 was the maintenance of a foreign policy that stood in opposition to the Union of Soviet Socialist Republics and the alleged threat of communist influence. When Franco's regime raised the flag of the Spanish Falange over Madrid in April 1939, the primary newspaper of Ybor City, *La Gaceta*, pledged to continue to support allies of the Spanish Republic. In Tampa, however, this event seemed unremarkable. Chancey did not make a public a statement, and there was only one headline in the *Tampa Morning Tribune*, which read "U.S. Recognizes Franco, Regime Lifts Embargo." Such a position stood in staunch opposition to the politics of women and men in Ybor City.[72]

Chancey was well aware that Dies was in his city as a result of this history. The women and men of Tampa, specifically those in Ybor City, seemed like foreign subversives with dangerous politics in a climate of heightened anticommunism. Yet what neither Chancey nor Dies seemed to understand was that these supposed "un-American" actions committed by Latinas/os in Ybor felt very "American" to them. Latinas/os who lived in Ybor City saw President Roosevelt as a friend of organized labor and believed that because "he put good men on the Labor Board and the Supreme Court . . . he prove[d] he like[d] the CIO."[73] In the midst of strikes over wages and struggle over union representation, Latina cigar workers wrote to Eleanor Roosevelt and pleaded: "As citizens of this great nation, as admirers of the mottoes of the Government of Franklin D. Roosevelt; as mothers that wish with our honest work to bring up our children under decent conditions and to have work to support parents and minor brothers and sisters; we beg of you not to allow that dishonest conditions be established in Tampa; nor to reduce our wages . . . the change would destroy our homes . . . and increase [the number of] the unemployed; our conditions would become at once [full] of misery."[74] The actions of Ybor Latinas/os, some of whom were foreign-born but many of whom were birthright citizens, illustrated their investment and belief that the U.S. state had an obligation to listen, protect, and represent their interests as workers, residents, and citizens of the nation.

As the children of Cuban cigar workers watched the city of Tampa retaliate against their parents and representatives of the federal government "meet with patriotic organizations" to determine if their family members were enemies of the state, they may have felt confusion and even fear.[75] These young Latinas/os understood, however, that their Latina/o parents wanted them to have the opportunity to navigate the United States differently. "[My mother] was determined that [my siblings and I] were going to be American above all. No question about that," Sylvia Vega recalled.[76] Her mother, like many other Latina/o parents, praised the importance of education amid this era of industrial collapse and sought to prepare her children with the skills necessary to earn a living without the Cuban cigar industry. Vega's generation, those who came of age in the 1930s and 1940s and were predominantly U.S.-born, attended public schools and learned English from Anglo teachers as they prepared for a life beyond Ybor City. They grew to love baseball and cheered for local heroes such as Al López—the first person from Ybor City to play Major League Baseball—as he swung his bat for the Brooklyn Dodgers, the Boston Bees, and the Cleveland Indians. Young Latinas/os signed up for neighborhood Boy Scouts and Girls Scouts troops, joined clubs at school, tried out for the high school cheerleading teams, and ate sandwiches made with American white, rather than Cuban, bread.[77]

César Marcos Medina, the son of Cuban and Spanish immigrants, saw opportunity in this new generation and their work to navigate broader Tampa. Medina, who had originally followed in the footsteps of his lector father, worked in the Ybor cigar industry but found a better-paying job as a bookkeeper for the Bank of Ybor City in 1924. After saving enough money, Medina purchased the Two Brothers Bakery and quit his job at the bank. "At that time, if they had had a psychiatric hospital they would have locked me up," Medina recalled, "'cause everybody thought I had a very good job with the bank, and was making, in those days, what was considered to be a lot of money, and this was a very small bakery, but I could see the potential." Initially, the bakery got by. It sold "about a thousand dollars' worth of cakes and pies and cookies [in a year]," but most of the profit came from the sale of Cuban bread. In the early 1930s, however, there were "twenty-six or twenty-seven little bakeries making Cuban bread" and competition was tight. Bakery owners "[fought] among themselves and [undercut] prices"; they would even "put a couple bombs in the ovens" of competing bakeries. After that, Medina said "no more Cuban bread for me . . . I'm going to make American bread." People close to him reacted and said, "But you're a Cuban and a Spaniard . . . you can't do that!" To which Medina responded, "Yeah . . . well, this Cuban is going to make American bread."[78]

To encourage sales, Medina undercut his competitors by pricing his product at five cents and baking a penny in the center of the American loaf. This marketing tactic paid off. Not only did Latina/o parents purchase the product, but their children requested it. "We were responsible for teaching the Latin[a/o] to eat American bread," Medina explained, and over time the product became important to children in the neighborhood. "Kids didn't want to take Cuban bread to school anymore by the [late 1930s and 1940s] because other [Anglo] kids would laugh at them, see?" Not only did Medina's bakery survive his transition from Cuban bread to American bread production, but his business became the largest bakery in the city of Tampa. In the 1930s, he renamed the company BAMBY, Best American Bread Made Yet, and, by 1940 he rebranded it Wholesome Bakery, in response to accusations by a competitor across Hillsborough Bay in St. Petersburg, that his product was "unsanitary because it was made in Ybor City." Under the new name, sales skyrocketed, and he opened "eight or ten" bakeries along Florida's west coast. This company provided not only bread to children in Ybor City and across Tampa but also employment to Latinas/os in Ybor City who struggled to find work as the cigar industry declined. Pedro Blanco, a friend of Medina's and the son of Cuban and Spanish immigrants who struggled to find steady work throughout the Depression, got a position as a sales representative for Wholesome Bakery. Blanco, whose first language was Spanish, joined Toastmasters to improve his language skills, confidence, and sales numbers. Over time Blanco became a top seller and used the money to buy a home in Tampa. Years later his granddaughter, Andrea Alfonso McNamara, remembered the smell of freshly baked yeast bread that permeated her grandfather's car and the way this job changed his life. By 1961, Wholesome Bakery merged with the Continental Baking Company, the owner of Wonder Bread.[79]

Despite the ability of Latina/o children to speak English, participate in American pastimes, and carry sandwiches made with American bread in their lunch boxes, they encountered significant discrimination as they waded beyond the territory of Ybor City. "Having a Latin[a/o] name was a tough undertaking" during the 1930s and 1940s, remembered a former Ybor City resident. There were "signs in this city that said 'no Cubans or dogs allowed,'" which restricted anyone from Ybor City from entering that space. For many people, the idea of leaving Ybor City meant they had to be prepared for a fight, and some young men became expert boxers to protect themselves. Living in this space and navigating life in Tampa meant that one "had to be able to protect [oneself]."[80]

While many Latina/o parents from Ybor City emphasized the importance of education to their children, the experiences of these Latina/o children in the Hillsborough County public education system were rocky. Afro-Cuban children entered segregated education within the broader county. Evelio Grillo, a former resident of Ybor, explained: "For all our sharing of language, culture, and religion with white Cubans, we Black Cubans were Black." When Grillo entered the public education system, he "joined the streams of children headed toward the 'colored' schools." This experience, he later said, "resolved all of my confusion about my color, my Spanish tongue, and my culture." To the outside world in Tampa, and to white Cubans in Ybor, he was "a Black boy . . . [and] that was what was important." As Afro-Cuban children such as Grillo prepared their lunches of bologna sandwiches and crossed the border from Ybor City into African American neighborhoods in Tampa, predominantly the Scrub or the Central Avenue neighborhood, where Black public schools were located, they "walked in groups . . . to socialize with friends and [seek] protection from threats, imagined and real." Black Cuban students, whose first language was Spanish, constituted a minority of the population in Tampa's segregated schools and experienced "derision" as a result of being a "[linguistic] minority." African American students referred to Black Cuban students as "tally wops," a locally created racial slur, in "loud and jeering voices" across the schoolyard. Grillo reported that although he did not recall physical violence from his schoolmates, he did remember "substantial hurt to our feelings."[81] Black Cuban children navigated a sense of exclusion from multiple spaces as they pursued education. Not only did the public school system inculcate and deepen a sense of difference between Afro-Cubans and their white Cuban peers, but it highlighted distinctions between Black Cubans and African Americans. With time, the latter division softened but the former hardened.

Latina/o children with light skin entered Tampa's schools created for white children. While this experience taught many students the power of their whiteness, it likewise illustrated the power of difference that language, culture, work, and class created. At times Anglo teachers publicly mocked the Ybor neighborhood, Latina/o parents, and the accented English of Latina/o pupils, which "openly embarrass[ed] the Latin[a/o] children" but "amuse[d] . . . the Anglo Saxon" students in the classroom.[82] By the 1940s, the extent of discrimination in local public schools became so egregious that Latina/o parents sent opinion columns to the *Tampa Morning Tribune*, one of the Anglo newspapers. "I'm a Latin-born American citizen," one mother wrote, "and [I] do not like the mistreating of Latin[a/o] children [in our schools]. This proves that there is so much ignorance in the world. Teachers are supposed to teach equality, love, and the golden rule."[83] The center of many parents' issues with the local education system was teachers' use of corporal punishment toward students who spoke Spanish in school or on the playground. After one particularly brutal beating of a student at Cuesta Elementary, located near West Tampa, the Hillsborough County School Board assembled and decided that "Tampa teachers must not inflict corporal punishment upon Latin American youngsters who converse with their playmates on the school grounds in languages other than English." Despite this decision, however, trustees of the board encouraged principals and teachers to maintain a policy that "discourage[d] as much as possible the speaking of any language other than English on school property."[84]

In an effort to build a more functional relationship between Ybor City and the city of Tampa, Latina/o leaders within the immigrant neighborhood collaborated with cigar manufacturers and the office of the mayor to create festivals that facilitated cross-cultural interaction, the most notable of these events being La Verbena. Between 1935 and 1942, this celebration took place at Plant Park, a local fairground located in Tampa, and welcomed thousands of visitors from both sides of town. In the inaugural year of La Verbena, which corresponded with the fiftieth anniversary of the Cuban cigar industry in Tampa, the Anglo press was candid about the purpose of the festival: "Perhaps Tampans, living here, are too close to the cigar industry picture to appreciate to the full extent its size and importance. In a way, we know about the industry, its inception, its growth, and its meaning to the city; but we take these things for granted. Then comes an event such as this Golden Jubilee, celebrating the 50th anniversary of the industry's beginning here, and we gain a better understanding."[85]

The city of Tampa, which remained dependent on the weakened cigar industry, promoted this event to raise local and national awareness of its signature commodity, while Cuban cigar workers welcomed the opportunity to gain recognition for their work from a local government that treated them as second-class citizens. Central to bridging the cultural divide at such events were Latinas. Rather than celebrating the centrality of women cigar workers to the local economy, La Verbena promoted a vision of exotic beauty intended to tempt Anglo onlookers and recast Latinas as beautiful, desirable, and accessible women and the broader Ybor community as something people beyond the immigrant community should embrace. Women from Ybor City attended this event in skin-tight dresses that showcased their figures and were adorned by lace tablecloths, intended to serve as mantillas, positioned on their heads or draped across their shoulders. Mutual aid societies organized performances by flamenco and salsa dancers, while young Latinas paraded across the stage to compete for the title of La Reina de la Verbena (Queen of the Verbena Festival). As the years passed, the grandeur of this event became transnational. The committee of La Verbena flew in Miss Cuba from Havana to crown the winner of the beauty contest as a symbol of the connection between Ybor City and the island. In 1941, just before the start of World War II, Miss Cuba met with airmen stationed at Tampa's new

MacDill Air Force Base, where men hovered by her side as she ate baked beans.[86]

The queens of La Verbena were always white Latinas from the neighborhood, whose skin color and beauty sought to defy the stigma of latinidad by promoting an image of whiteness acceptable in this Jim Crow city. Throughout the 1930s and 1940s, both the city of Tampa and Cuban cigar manufacturers used young, white Latinas to promote their products as they fitted them in costumes, posed them in photos, and put them on display in booths at events such as the Florida State Fair and even the World's Fair. Although Mayor Chancey, as well as Anglo powerholding elites, sought to control the efforts of Latina/o workers to gain a fair wage, access to relief rolls, and equal entry into social spaces, city leaders and cigar factory owners were willing to use Latina bodies to rebrand Tampa as a Havana on U.S. soil—a place full of fun, beauty, and respectable exoticism yet devoid of the leftist politics or the racial diversity that lay at the heart of the community's history and its people's identity.

While Congressman Dies and the HUAC left Ybor City unscathed in 1940, the same could not be said of the Department of Justice and the Immigration and Naturalization Services. Congress passed the Alien Registration Act in 1940, which required "all aliens 14 years of age or older" to register their presence in the United States with the federal government. The language of this law defined "aliens" as "foreign-born persons who have not become citizens of the United States," which included "persons with first citizenship papers and work permits." To register, a man or woman had to complete an extensive form that detailed their personal, professional, and political lives and submit to being fingerprinted and photographed. Furthermore, the Alien Registration Act mandated that all noncitizens repeat this process annually in order to maintain current records of all immigrants and noncitizens living and working in the United States. Failure to comply with the law could result in "a fine of $1,000 and imprisonment for 6 months."[87] In four short months, the Department of Justice sought to register and locate all 3.6 million "aliens" living in the United States.

Immigration officials made sure Latinas and Latinos in Ybor City were aware of this law and its requirements. Federal officials and local liaisons reserved space at the Centro Asturiano to capture the attention of the Ybor community and inform these women and men of their duty to register as aliens living in the United States. On November 6, 1940, nearly 1,000 Latinas and Latinos filed into the mutual aid society's theater and sat on the red velvet seats to listen to the local immigration official explain how the U.S. government would legally exploit their privacy. As the evening's events

Tobacco Queens at La Verbena Festival in Ybor City, ca. 1937. Burgert Brothers Collection, University of South Florida Libraries—Tampa Special Collections, Tampa, Florida.

began, the Centro Asturiano—a space that embodied and symbolized the power of self-help, community, and ethno-cultural autonomy—became a site of state-sponsored policing and surveillance. A transcription from a speech composed by Senator Dennis Chávez was read to the attendees, which sought to assuage the anxieties of the residents of Ybor City.[88] While the words of the senator acknowledged that the "Spanish speaking peoples have contributed their share to the growth of the United States" and that Latinas/os had "nothing to fear from registration," the address made clear that the process was not optional and consequences would apply to those who refused to comply with this law intended for the "protection of all."[89]

As U.S.-born *tampeñas/os* (native-born Latinas/os from Ybor City) helped their foreign-born parents and grandparents fill out the forms necessary for "alien registration," this younger generation may have thought about the seeming injustice of the process. This law, which sought to judge whether someone was a "good and moral citizen," did not consider the labor these women and men did to sustain the city, why these women and men organized against the city, or the ways these women and men sacrificed for the survival of their children. Those of the U.S.-born generation from Ybor City, who had sought to bridge the cultural divide as they entered public schools, learned English, and posed at municipal events, may have wondered what would be enough to illustrate their commitment to both the city and the state. On December 7, 1941, following the bombing of Pearl Harbor, an opportunity arrived.

World War II and a Sense of Belonging

Luisa Alonso lived between two worlds in 1941, hers and that of her son's. Luisa, who was born in Florida in 1899, worked in the Cuban cigar industry of Ybor City her entire life. While neither she nor husband Braulio Alonso Sr. lost their jobs during the Depression, the pay they earned was not enough. Mechanization and the decrease in wages meant the couple made less money even though life was more expensive. Whenever possible, Luisa picked up additional hours at the factory, while her husband worked odd jobs. The couple must have felt accomplished, for they managed to weather the Depression without requiring that their eldest child, Braulio Alonso Jr., leave school and join them at the cigar maker's benches or the cigar worker's machines. Luisa and Braulio Alonso Sr. watched as their son learned English, excelled in coursework, and graduated valedictorian of his high school class in 1935. While Alonso Jr. dreamed of attending the University of Florida in

Gainesville and becoming a doctor, he enrolled in the University of Tampa, where he pursued a liberal arts education — staying home was the wise course for this working-class family. Alonso Jr. continued to live with his parents in their rented casita throughout his undergraduate years and worked at the Information News Stand in Ybor City, where he earned fifteen dollars a week, a "good sum [for] the time" and enough to help him "get through college." Luisa Alonso must have been consumed with pride and hope in 1939 when her son completed his college degree, again as valedictorian, and got a good job as a public school teacher in Tampa. Alonso Jr., however, assumed this career would be temporary. For the next two years he studied, prepared, and made plans to attend medical school, but in December 1941, after the bombing of Pearl Harbor, his draft notice arrived and everything changed. In the midst of wartime chaos, Luisa Alonso watched as her son hurriedly married his girlfriend, Adelfa Díaz, and reported to basic training at Fort Bragg in North Carolina.[90]

As young Latinos like Braulio Alonso Jr. entered the military, some by draft and others by choice, their families contended with the transformation of Tampa as well as their collision with a shifting economy and U.S. state. Only a handful of the original Cuban cigar factories, in a place that once had over 150, remained in operation at the start of World War II. Although Cuban cigar production was still the foundation of the local economy, manufacturers had replaced the practiced dexterity of tabaqueras/os for the standardized efficiency of mechanic cigar production, for fewer than nineteen of the remaining factories used the Spanish hand method by the start of the war. Tampa's municipal leaders, eager to expand the city and economy, welcomed the officials from the War Department as they scouted this place as a site for new airfields. While pilots praised the simplicity of maneuvering aircrafts across these flat and sandy lands, their superiors approved the construction of three airfields in this Gulf coast town that strategically linked the United States to the Caribbean — MacDill Air Force Base, Drew Field, and Henderson Field. These bases housed more than 43,000 service persons during the war and redefined Tampa as a place where Cuban cigars and the nascent military industrial complex collided. In 1941, the year MacDill field became operational, city leaders celebrated this new economic partnership as they displayed a scantily clad Latina cigar queen next to a bomber built from cigars in the booth dedicated to the city of Tampa at the Florida State Fair. Shipbuilders with government contracts flocked to this place, as did women and men eager to fill the companies' payrolls. Latinos from Ybor City, who struggled with unemployment throughout the 1930s, eagerly accepted

Latinas representing the cigar industry at the state fair, ca. 1941. Burgert Brothers Collection, University of South Florida Libraries—Tampa Special Collections, Tampa, Florida.

jobs at the shipyards, where they earned hourly wages (as opposed to cigar piecework pay), had ample hours (at times as many as forty-eight per week), and hearty union benefits. New faces crossed the border to Ybor City, as the people who fueled this wartime economy ate arroz con pollo and drank Havana Club on the rocks before they rushed the dance floors and celebrated into the early hours of the morning. The insularity that had long united the residents of Ybor City seemed to buckle against the changing tide.[91]

While the city of Tampa expanded and shifted during this era, so too did the Latinas/os who broke through the confines of Ybor City to serve in the U.S. military and contribute to the war effort. The young men who came of age in an immigrant neighborhood and developed a "combustible" commitment to "machismo," "invincibility," and desire to prove their equality as U.S. citizens, "marched off to war with a collective chip on their shoulders" and were "eager to show the public that they were as American as the twelfth-generation descendant from the Plymouth Plantation."[92] No two Latinos, however, experienced this period the same way. Some men such as Jose Yglesias understood World War II as an extension of the fight against fascism and the struggle for international democracy that had baptized him in the secular waters of communism and socialism throughout the 1930s. Yglesias entered the navy by choice. "The draft board classified me 3A [extreme hardship]," he explained, "because I was my mother's support, but I volunteered anyway because I believed in the war, in the PF [Popular Front] against fascism, in the New Deal, in socialism, in brotherhood of man." While this perspective "made [him] unique in [his] aviation unit, if not the entire cruiser," such ideas were not unique within Ybor City.[93] *La Gaceta*, one of the community's Spanish-language newspapers, rallied Latina/o residents as it declared that the "enemies of humanity are the Nazis, the fascists, the militarists, the Japanese, the Spanish Falangists," and it was the obligation of "democratic citizens and their allies" to unite and "ensure the destruction of totalitarianism" and the "enemies of democracy."[94] The Centro Español, which had refused to replace the flag of the Spanish Republic with that of the Spanish Falange at the conclusion of the Spanish Civil War, followed in the footsteps of the Centro Asturiano as it raised the U.S. flag over its buildings in Ybor City and West Tampa as a symbol of the war's extension of their antifascist democratic values and allegiance to the United States in this fight.

Luisa Alonso's son, Braulio Alonso Jr., recalled his experience in the U.S. Army through the lens of duty and realism. As a result of his university education as well as his "progress in [basic training] and [high] test scores," commanders at Fort Bragg recognized his leadership potential and sent him to officers' training at Fort Still, in Oklahoma.[95] While Alonso Jr. served as captain of the 328th Field Artillery Battalion, under the 85th Infantry Division, and was part of liberation efforts in Italy during the war, he did not romanticize his experience and described it as "unpleasant, vicious, bloody, and sacrificial." One memory he cherished, however, was his experience watching German troops surrender to his division in the French Alps. According to Alonso Jr., this moment must have been a "humiliating experience for the master race," for rather than "surrendering to high [ranking] officers" they "had to surrender to our Black troops, who ordered them where to place their arms and escorted them to internment."[96] To Alonso Jr., there was something satisfying in watching ethnocentric white nationalism and racism kneel, even if just for a moment, on the other side of the Atlantic.

While men such as Alonso Jr. found measured contentment in their military experience, Black Latinos from Ybor City did not remember any semblance of racial justice or personal satisfaction in the U.S. Armed Forces. Evelio Grillo was resolute as he detailed what he remembered of the war in his memoir: "When I write that I do not remember VJ Day and VE Day, I do so with complete candor. My amnesia is total. I did not feel Germany and Japan as palpably as I felt the United States Army. The Army's oppression was direct, immediate, and constant."[97]

Grillo had a university education and hope for a big future the day his draft notice arrived. Yet as he began his service in the 823rd Engineer Aviation "Colored" Battalion, he felt he was at "war not only against a foreign enemy . . . but also against the segregationist 'enemy' within the U.S. military." Grillo and other Black men ate in segregated spaces, lived in squalor during missions, and received "mistreatment by superior officers," all of which acted as a "constant reminder of the second-class citizenship [status of him] and his fellow Black soldiers."[98] Francisco Rodríguez Jr. also detailed his personal war with racism during World War II as he thought back on his life. Rodríguez—named after his father, Francisco Rodríguez Sr.—grew up in a home where labor activism and dedication to Afro-Cuban culture thrived. Within Ybor City, his father was a leader of La Sociedad de la Unión Martí-Maceo and active in the burgeoning civil rights movement in Florida. After the bombing of Pearl Harbor, Rodríguez Jr. joined the U.S. Marines. Yet during his time in the service, he witnessed discrimination and racism radiate throughout the so-called integrated armed forces to such a degree that he decided to "write something about segregation in the military," which "almost got [him] court marshaled." Inspired to right the wrongs he endured throughout this era, Rodríguez Jr. enrolled in law school at Howard University and became the first Black Latino leader of the National Association for the Advancement of Colored People in Tampa.[99]

As the sons of Ybor City served in military units across the world, the women of the neighborhood contributed to the war effort through volunteerism and community advocacy. Latinas transformed the Círculo Cubano into their own site of wartime production as they collaborated with the American Red Cross to knit and sew. Providence Velasco, a Latina born in Ybor City, remembered managing a team of "ten or fifteen women" who met weekly to "sew blankets and garments," at the request of military relief officials, for use in the barracks as well as in sites of medical care and convalescence. Meanwhile, younger women such as Eneida Fernández and Antonia González, both daughters of Ybor City, joined the Women's Army

Corps (after illustrating their physical fitness and passing an entry exam), where they operated switchboards and worked as mechanics, acted as stenographers and completed clerical tasks, repaired arms and heavy munitions, and became drivers and even bakers. Sylvia Vega became the head of the women's division of the Volunteer Port Security Force, a position that required she manage a unit of clerical workers. Women who were single and had medical credentials and training reported for duty as nurses essential to help doctors in the field.[100] Although letter writing and sending of care packages were not officially sanctioned forms of labor through the U.S. Armed Forces or adjacent war relief organizations, Latinas also maintained essential connections with their husbands, sons, and brothers through these activities. According to the historian Gary R. Mormino, Latina mothers "stuffed cans of *boliche* (roasted eye of round stuffed with chorizo) and *caldo gallego* (soup of white beans, ham hock, kale, potatoes, and chorizo)" into boxes and mailed them around the globe. Young men stationed in northern Africa and southern Italy received "beautiful packages of hand-rolled cigars" from their mothers, wives, and girlfriends to "replace [the cheap] cigarettes" the military provided, while others who stood guard in Adak, Alaska, shared "*pignolata*, an Italian dessert [fried dough lathered in caramelized, orange blossom honey]" with their unit. In return, many of these young men sent the Latinas in their lives a portion of their paychecks to contribute to their family's income to help make ends meet in their absence.[101]

Despite the seemingly total mobilization of the Ybor City community, tensions between Anglos and Latinas/os persisted in Tampa. Yglesias had an interaction he could "never forget" when he returned to Florida to visit family while on leave. As Yglesias sat in a car with two other servicemen, both of whom assumed him to be a native New Yorker, he listened as the men "praised the virtues of Tampa." When it came to the topic of Ybor City, however, the men issued a warning. "Don't go, it's a dangerous place," they said, "full of spics."[102] Interactions like this did not stand in isolation. Throughout World War II there were reports of "deplorable, violent incidents between young American men of Anglo-Saxon origin and Latinos." *La Gaceta*, forever the antifascist stalwart, declared that such problems must be the result of "the 'Fifth Column,' the enemies of democracy" that seek to encourage "bad blood between citizens who defend the same flag and fight for the same principles."[103] Such drama likewise played out in the *Tampa Morning Tribune* when a local Anglo mother wrote an opinion piece demanding that Latinas/os learn "to be American" and stop "jabbering away in Spanish, Latin or whatever it is," as she reinforced long-standing stigmas of latinidad by blaming Latina/o parents for the perceived delinquency and lack of patriotism of their children.[104]

In response to the slander, Latinas initiated a letter campaign and penned articles to the *Tribune*, in English, to stand against the accusations. These women reminded the "honest-to-goodness American" author that if those whom she considered to be "100 percent Americans" were to drive through Ybor City or West Tampa "they would see white and gold stars . . . at the windows of countless Latin[a/o] homes." After all, the "Villa[s], Nicoletto[s], Murgado[s], [and] Valdez[es]" were "heroes" too, and the telegrams that began with "'The War Department regrets—' [were] delivered to the Gonzalezes and Alvarezes as well as to the Smiths and Jones." Finally, the women asked if their sons, brothers, and fathers were "fighting for the rights of all peoples" or were "they making the supreme sacrifice that their kind may be socially ostracized?"[105] Latinas, as in years past, did not remain silent against accusations of un-Americanism, poor mothering, or anti-Latina/o hate during World War II; instead, they acted as powerful mouthpieces for their community as they published defenses of themselves, and their fellow community members, in Anglo-controlled spaces by laying claim to their right and the right of their children to belong.

For nearly five years, the city of Tampa thrived on the energy of the war, while families across the city collectively held their breath. Just as the mothers who wrote into the newspaper cited, it was the news of a loved one's death that they all dreaded. Juanita Salcines and her husband Emiliano owned the Salcines General Store in West Tampa, which was located across the street from the Western Union office. When Western Union received a telegram of a young man's death, one of the agents notified Juanita Salcines to "[alert] neighbors [and prepare them] to comfort the soon-to-be gold star mother." Although the couple's son, E.J., was a young boy at the time he never forgot the "hollering, screaming, crying, [and] weeping" as mothers crumbled with the news of their child's death.[106] While community members rallied as they purchased bonds, ran aluminum collection drives, and planted victory gardens, nothing could overcome the palpable sense of death that permeated the community and the broader city.[107] When World War II came to an end in 1945, Latinas and Latinos in Ybor City finally exhaled.

To the men who returned home, and the women who embraced them, neither Ybor nor Tampa looked the same as it did four years prior. While the broader city expanded and boasted new opportunities for jobs and municipal development, the Ybor City neighborhood felt like a relic of a distant past. The old casitas that Vicente Martínez Ybor and Ignacio Haya built looked like sun-bleached shacks, while the majority of the factories that once bustled with the sounds of thousands of hurried hands were empty and quiet. Rather than renting or buying homes in Ybor City, these young veterans moved into West Tampa, which served as a "halfway house to suburbia" and offered "growing families inexpensive housing, room for new [construction], and a Latin[a/o] infrastructure of Spanish-Cuban-Italian stores, cafes, mutual aid societies, and butcher shops."[108] With the funds from the G.I. Bill these young Latinas/os built their American dreams ten minutes away from where their immigrant grandparents and parents started theirs decades earlier. Community member Jorge García remembered this moment as a "mass migration from the inner city to the suburbs . . . for the members of my generation . . . it was the thing to do."[109]

As young Latinas/os decided their future did not lie in Ybor City, they looked to higher education and trade schools to provide them with the skills necessary to survive without the Cuban cigar industry. Many of the returned Latino veterans used the G.I. Bill to enroll in college and earn university degrees. By the late 1940s, roughly 50 percent of the 800 students who attended the University of Tampa were veterans and 20 percent of the student body were Latinas/os.[110] These women and men invested in university culture just as they had in their community as they served as class president, homecoming queen, and later the head of the alumni association. Many Latinas, much like their Latino counterparts, enrolled in universities and pursued degrees in teaching and social work. For example, Delia Sánchez received her degree in social work and during that era established a pilot program, which eventually became, what is known today, as the national Head Start program. While Latinas/os who attended college became lawyers, judges, teachers, and writers as well as principals, accountants, and business owners, those who attended trade schools began careers as mechanics, beauticians, plumbers, and contractors as well as firefighters and even police officers. Many Latinas labored as homemakers and used their language skills and activist traditions to represent their children at school and through Parent-Teacher Associations and provided care and advocacy to their extended families and aging relatives, who often did not speak English and could not navigate this new world with ease. Over the course of the war, and in its immediate wake, these women and men became the new faces of Tampa as they worked to show through service, volunteerism, and community work who Latinas/os could be, what kind of authority Latinas/os could hold, and the fallacy of the stigmas that had long applied to people like them. While this era was one of struggle and survival, it paved the way for a new phase—a period of remaking.

CHAPTER FOUR

Remaking

What made Ybor City in the past was not the architecture,
it was the people.

—TONY PIZZO

On the morning of November 18, 1963, five-year-old Marlene Maseda brimmed with excitement. Her father, Marcelo Maseda, received an invitation to meet President John F. Kennedy during his visit to Tampa, and it was she who got to join him. Before the young Maseda left the house with her father that day, she slipped into a traditional Spanish costume complete with a long skirt, a white blouse, and a lace mantilla draped over her shoulders. After all, she was the symbolic ambassador of Ybor City and the representation of the future of latinidad in this place.

The big event took place at the International Inn Hotel, a venue located on Westshore Avenue near downtown Tampa, in the Crystal Ballroom. That day, the hall sparkled with "all the colorful dressings needed to welcome an extremely popular president." As Marlene Maseda entered the room with her father and his colleagues, she joined hundreds of business leaders and lawyers as well as politicians and union members eager to brush shoulders with the mystique and power of Camelot. Then, at 3:35 P.M., the crowd stood as they chanted "JFK! JFK!" and the president entered the room. Once Kennedy took his place behind the podium with the presidential seal, Maseda followed her father to the stage, where he passed the president a box of Ybor-made Cuban cigars and she gave Kennedy a Spanish doll in a flamenco dress. "Mr. President," she said, "this doll is for your daughter, Caroline." The president thanked her and smiled widely for the cameras.[1]

To the Kennedy administration and the city of Tampa, the role of Marlene Maseda at this event illustrates how important Latinas/os were to politicians by the 1960s as well as how the city of Tampa wished to sell itself. Kennedy, who failed to capture the electoral votes of the Sunshine State two years earlier, wished to mobilize the support of Latinas/os in anticipation of the next election—a strategy with which local political organizers agreed. In this new era, no longer were the women and men of Ybor City a radical leftist inconvenience for both the state and the nation; they were Democrats and hopeful citizens who had crossed the border from the immigrant neighborhood into Tampa, where they settled and remade their lives as well as their sense of self. This process of remaking, however, was not so simple, for it required much forgetting. In order for Latinas/os from Ybor City to enter mainstream politics as a commanding force, they had to obscure their radical leftist past and celebrate a moderate, yet progressive, present. Maseda and her father offer a glimpse into this phenomenon.

Marcelo Maseda was the *alcalde* (mayor) of Ybor City in 1963, a ceremonial position established by the Ybor City Rotary Club that carried no government authority but much political influence. Throughout his campaign, and indeed throughout his life, public coverage of Maseda in mainstream Anglo newspapers praised his Spanish roots and his connection to the historic Spanish manufacturing elite of Ybor City and West Tampa. But the reality of his family history was more complex than this streamlined narrative. Maseda was the son of a Spanish father, José Maseda, and a Cuban mother, Julia Maseda, both of whom immigrated to Ybor City in the 1880s and 1890s.[2] The status of José Maseda as a *peninsular* indeed helped him curry favor with Spanish manufacturers and secure high-paying, salaried employment as a *rezagador* and later a foreman within the cigar industry. Like many families in Ybor City and West Tampa, the money earned by José Maseda had to provide for a large household—at times his home had as few as six people and at others as many as twelve. The Great Depression changed the fortune of Maseda, yet he persevered by opening a chinchal, for he refused to yield to the de-skilling of the industry and the devaluing of his expertise. Throughout these lean years, the Maseda family worked beside one another in the modest cigar enterprise located behind their home. Just before Maseda passed away in 1939, his oldest son, Modesto, took over the family business.[3]

With his father gone, the world of Marcelo Maseda looked different by 1941, but he balanced his obligation to contribute to the family wage with his pursuit of life beyond the confines of the Cuban cigar industry. This young man, a U.S.-born tampeño of mixed Spanish and Cuban parentage, came of age like many of his generation. He watched Latinas march through the streets in opposition to fascism and in support of international democracy, while he observed Latinos strike as cigar manufacturers stripped away the culture of Cuban cigar work. He learned to speak Spanish at home and English in school, as he earned an education in Tampa alongside Anglos who questioned if he belonged. He loved sports but excelled at baseball and even played for minor league teams such as the Tampa Smokers and the St. Pete Saints. He attended college at the University of Tampa and supported himself through work at an eatery, the Union Shipyard Cafe, which catered to the thousands of wartime workers who built ships in Tampa during the 1940s. Maseda then married his beloved Marina López, whose parentage was identical to his. Together they lived in West Tampa and reveled in their Latina/o version of a suburban "blue heaven." After some time, the couple welcomed their only child, Marlene—a tampeña of the next generation with an ethnicity as complicated as that of those who came before her.[4]

Marcelo Maseda spent his life within Tampa and Florida politics but never ran for political office himself (except, of course, as alcalde). He spent eighteen years working for the Public Service Commission of Hillsborough County, a position that taught him how the city of Tampa worked and gave him the political contacts necessary to influence it. Maseda poured his energy into making sure the interests of Ybor City and West Tampa Latinas/os were met by supporting the election of tampeñas/os from the old neighborhood as well as politicians who seemed to take their concerns seriously. Maseda became the executive administrative assistant for two senators and participated in the campaigns of dozens of other political hopefuls. Those who knew Maseda described him as a "West Tampa guy, an Ybor City guy," who understood how to get support from "both sides of the aisle" despite the fact that he was, like most from the neighborhood, "a staunch Democrat." Toward the end of his lifetime, as Maseda reflected on his career as a "political mover and shaker," he asserted, "No one put more [campaign] signs all over the state of Florida than I did."[5]

While Maseda was cognizant of how to play his part in order to gain political influence and recognition within greater Tampa, so too were the tens of thousands of Latinas/os who came from the neighborhood. Outwardly, and while in contact with Anglo Tampa, these women and men celebrated a Spanish heritage and a "Latin" or "Latin American" sense of self that safely ensconced them and their neighborhood in the romance of Europe and renounced the leftist, radical, revolutionary spirit of the Caribbean. Even those who came from Cuba could, if they wished, claim the legacy of their Spanish roots as core to their sense of being. This tactic was intentional and, in some ways, effective. For those able to stand adjacent to whiteness, it broke through the stigma of latinidad that had long universalized and vilified cubanidad in this space, as they managed to convince greater Tampa to forget the militant, working-class, internationalist culture that lay at the heart of Ybor City. The decision to dress Marlene Maseda in a Spanish costume before she met President Kennedy exemplifies this strategy, for in that moment she was the physical embodiment of a kind of latinidad Ybor Latinas/os hoped that Tampa and the broader United States could accept.

Between 1948 and 1970, the people of Ybor City remade the image of themselves as well as that of the neighborhood they came from. This chapter illustrates their remaking through three distinct moments: the 1948 Henry Wallace campaign, the 1955 visit of Fidel Castro to Ybor City and the Cuban Revolution, and the effort to save the immigrant neighborhood from the wrecking ball of urban renewal in the 1960s. Each moment exemplifies a different component of the remaking process and demonstrates that such an undertaking was not simply about redefining but also about accepting and rejecting. Latinas played their part in this remaking as they used their voice and bodies selectively. For women who came from a legacy of activism and political participation, it was the combination of their presence and absence from this process that determined their place in a remade world.

The Henry Wallace Campaign and the 1948 Election

World War II parted the clouds the Great Depression cast over Ybor City. Women and men, once again, walked down Seventh Avenue as they absorbed the aroma of coffee roasting at La Naviera and the scent of fresh Cuban bread baking at La Segunda. Some people bought deviled crabs (a local *croqueta*, made from reduced crab *enchilado* rolled in Cuban bread crumbs then fried) from a man named Miranda, who sold the local delicacy from the sidecar of his motorcycle. Others, however, preferred the sweetness of a guava pastry or the comfort of a piece of *scacciata* (an Ybor-invented version of pizza with a dough base of plush, sweet Cuban bread topped with tomato sauce and Parmesan). There were also new faces on the street, such as the taffy man, an Anglo who displayed candy on a white tray suspended by a strap worn around his neck. People dashed into the classic Silver Dollar Cafe at lunchtime, where they bought a Cuban sandwich to fuel them through the workday, as others rested at Las Novedades or the Columbia Restaurant for a leisurely afternoon and elegant fare. The Spanish-language movie theater was full of patrons, as were the dance floors of the centros and the stools at streetside bars. The end of wartime brought the return of the annual cigar festival, where the young, light-skinned, Latina daughters of Ybor City—worshipped for their dark, exotic features juxtaposed with their white skin—served as the symbol of everything a Latina should be in this new era.[6]

Yet between the eating and the dancing and the drinking and the celebrating was the reality that the landscape of labor and the landscape of the community had changed. Young veterans who had used the G.I. Bill to build homes on empty lots in West Tampa, Seminole Heights, and Tampa Heights became a part of a local Latina/o diaspora as they crossed the border from Ybor City into greater Tampa. These tampeñas/os attended college or found jobs in blue-collar positions that offered benefits and a decent salary. Women and men with Latina/o surnames, who searched for life beyond Ybor City and the Cuban cigar industry, were often public school teachers and social workers as well as managers and administrators in government offices. Some worked as salespeople or accountants, while others used their wartime expertise to become mechanics at the new air force base or even open their own businesses. The immigrant generation and working-class U.S.-born Latinas/os, however, stayed in Ybor City as they continued to work in the cigar factories that remained in the old neighborhood.[7]

Cigar factories, after the war, were almost entirely mechanized, and the people who worked within them were almost entirely women. Only 7,000 people labored in the Ybor cigar factories by 1949, yet these factories produced "the same number of cigars as had 13,000 workers twenty years previously." Of the 159 cigar factories that once thrived in this place, only 18 remained. While many of the workers in the old (though now mechanized) factories were primarily Latinas, new enterprises such as Hav-a-Tampa preferred to hire Anglo women. These women, manufacturers knew, did not come with the history of international labor organization and production disruption like their Latina/o contemporaries. As Anglo women crossed the divide from Tampa into Ybor City, they redefined the culture of work that Latinas/os had long fought to protect within this place. Gus Alfonso, an Ybor City native who grew up near Hav-a-Tampa, remembered a sea of blonde and red-headed women filter out of the factory at the day's end. As he put it, those women were "more machine operators than cigar workers." Yet even if machine work was not the same as the famed Spanish hand method, it was steady labor and offered working-class women—both Latina and Anglo—access to a reliable paycheck in an economy that seemed to have left them behind.

Latinos had a different experience. Men who were, in years past, the famed tabaqueros, skilled selectors, and discerning packers and pickers were now out of a job unless they were among the lucky few who managed to secure a position in a factory where the owner did not believe that machine work was just for women or at one of the few factories that still did things the old way. Some of the people who were not ready to abandon the handmade cigar industry, took matters into their own hands and opened chinchales. These upstart enterprises turned papaya-tree-laden backyards into production sites, and, at times, the risk paid off. Arturo Fuente, who opened his home business in 1946, worked alongside friends, family, and employees from six in the morning until midnight and sold his cigars "only in the Tampa area and only on a cash basis." This modest business model laid the foundation for one of the most renowned cigar brands that exists today.[8]

The old cigar workers on whom fortune did not shine looked for work wherever they could find it. Some became dishwashers, clerks, and waiters, while others found employment as janitors in public schools or trash collectors for the county. One past resident remembered how their family loved when an uncle secured a job as a sanitation worker at the hospital of a mutual aid society. "He liked to diagnose people," they remembered as they laughed, "but it was great, if you ever needed anything [medicine] he could get it." The jobs these men took typically did not require English-speaking skills. After having lived in a community surrounded by people who spoke Spanish and having worked in the Cuban cigar industry where Spanish was the linguistic currency of their craft, many Latinas/os of the older generations did not have the English-language skills necessary to move beyond the confines of the community into higher-wage positions as their children and grandchildren did.[9]

In this postwar world that touted the strength of consumerism and the power of the economy, many women and men from Ybor City felt as though they had been left behind. The old ways of commanding representation and demanding fair wages through unionism and strikes carried great risk in this local economy. It was clear that there were ample, eager laborers willing to take the place of anyone who refused to work according to the terms set by manufacturers. The children of immigrant and working-class Latina/o parents likewise recognized the inequality that the war wrought as they looked at the jobs available to their loved ones and the state of the cigar industry. These young tampeñas/os, many of whom had chosen careers that centered on education and community assistance as a result of their experiences in childhood, wished to improve society for themselves and for others but needed the support of a government willing to stand for such principles and fund it. The women and men of Ybor City, both those who lived there and those who came from there, were among a growing population of people who searched for new avenues to workplace and community advocacy in the wake of World War II. In the late 1940s, both the immigrant and U.S.-born generations of Ybor and West Tampa found their answer through participation in national party politics.[10]

Latinas/os from Ybor City were no strangers to electoral politics in the 1940s. Throughout the early twentieth century women and men, who were born in the United States or became naturalized citizens, registered to vote and exercised their franchise at the polls despite opposition and intimidation from Tampa Anglos. Tampa's power-holding elite established the White Municipal Party in 1910 to restrict from the ballot anyone who was not a southern, segregationist Democrat, in an effort to elect white supremacist politicians and enact white supremacist laws that would make the influence of Black and Latina/o voters powerless within this space. This tactic worked. Because "winning a primary was tantamount to winning an election," the White Municipal Party effectively ran the city until 1944, when the Supreme Court of the United States ruled the practice of white primaries unconstitutional in *Smith v. Albright*. Some Latinas/os in Ybor City, however, resisted the Tampa political machine before this landmark decision. Those who were members of the Communist Party or the Socialist Party ran local campaigns, supported by unions, that publicized candidates and encouraged voters to write in their names rather than cast their ballot for a politician who sought to minimize Latina/o and working-class political interests. While none of these efforts led to an election of their chosen representatives, they did encourage backlash from those who wished to maintain their authority over this place at any cost. The local citizens' committee, the Ku Klux Klan (KKK), and the police department marched through Ybor City to show what strength and politics looked like in this town, while others stuffed or stole ballot boxes to minimize the influence of votes that may have challenged their corrupt reign. In national elections, when local politicians could not control which candidate appeared on the ballot, Anglos who worked for the city would "reverse the candidate order so as to confuse voters [in Ybor City, the Fourth Ward,] who might have been told to vote for the second [socialist] candidate." Tampa's Anglo elite likewise had an intimate relationship with illicit gambling rings and mafia bosses, who rose to prominence in the 1920s and lived in the shadows through the mid-twentieth century. Through the work of relationships such as these, votes were for sale. Families that needed assistance during the Depression accepted bribes and agreed to cast their ballots in support of politicians who shielded local mobsters from legal consequences.[11]

While the corrupt nature of local politics in Tampa gave Latinas/os little reason to believe the city had any interest in representing them, they did have faith in the potential of national politics and the federal government by the 1930s. The election of Franklin D. Roosevelt brought Latinas/os in Ybor City and West Tampa into the national political fold, for both the policies of the New Deal and the appointment of veterans of the labor movement to cabinet positions signaled to women and men in Ybor City, as well as those of the working-class throughout the United States, that this president understood them. As long as Roosevelt sat in the White House, the majority of Latinas/os in Ybor City invested hope in him, even if they struggled to access the benefits of his programs due to local barriers such as the racism of Works Progress Administration officials. They, like many others, believed that FDR cared and that FDR listened. Beyond New Deal programs, Ybor Latinas/os wrote letters to the president and lobbied politicians in Washington, D.C., to support the fight against fascism through the Spanish Civil War. Although such pleas went unanswered, Latinas/os in the neighborhood linked World War II and the strength of Roosevelt throughout this era as evidence that he too supported the ideals of international democracy and the global fight against fascism. The death of Roosevelt and the struggle these women and men experienced in the wake of wartime left them searching for a politician who they felt could represent their modern needs in this new era. Although President Harry Truman had brought their sons home, Latinas/os looked for a president who did more than make statements about anticommunism and assistance for Europe; they looked for one who regarded the state of the working class and who understood their needs— they found that candidate in Henry Wallace and in the Progressive Party.

Wallace announced his decision to break from the Democratic Party and run for president of the United States on the Progressive Party ticket in December 1947. Wallace, a dedicated liberal and champion of the New Deal, had become disillusioned by Truman's failure to embrace the legacy of Roosevelt. Frustrated by anticommunist rhetoric (which Wallace believed sought to divide the globe) as well as the Marshall Plan (which Wallace believed benefited Wall Street at the expense of working-class U.S. citizens), the Iowa-born former farmer, vice president, and secretary of agriculture focused his attention on the need to dismantle systemic racism and anti-labor forces at home, as well as champion a foreign policy that promoted diplomacy through the United Nations. Many Latinas/os, African Americans, and white working-class women and men across the nation embraced Wallace's call as they rallied for a candidate who they believed followed in the footsteps of FDR, the last president they trusted.[12]

Latinas/os in and from Ybor City were not so different from people who found inspiration in Wallace's platform across the nation. Never before had they seen a national presidential candidate who "spoke out against racism, called for integrated housing, and [equal access to] education," while also "support[ing] the Good Neighbor policy" and organized labor. For women and men who were veterans of the labor movement, longtime champions of international democracy, working-class laborers with low wages, and people who saw the infrastructure of their community in decline, the Wallace platform seemed compelling and personal. For the Ybor Latinas/os who had watched their community and workplaces change over the course of a decade, the Wallace campaign presented the opportunity for them to engage in national politics as voters at a time when it seemed essential.[13]

Wallace hit the campaign trail in 1948 as he trekked from California to New York and Pennsylvania to Florida. He sought to win votes and inspire people who searched for a better standard of U.S. politics by showing them that the promise of the New Deal was still possible and that peace did not require that the United States become the hegemonic police of democracy. In New York, Wallace established campaign headquarters and took to the airwaves as he called for a popular people's resistance against the wealthy few who invested their capital in global control. Wallace met with Black women and men as he discussed the centrality of anti-segregation and anti–Jim Crow policies to his platform. In Philadelphia, he joined people from across the country to mark the founding of the Progressive Party and addressed 3,200 party delegates and alternates, as well as 8,000 visitors, at the Philadelphia Convention Hall in order to invigorate new party members. On the West Coast, Wallace spoke to a crowd of 100,000 supporters at Lincoln Center in East Los Angeles and met with the grassroots organizers who made the campaign possible. He likewise walked the agricultural fields with Mexican American farmworkers as he listened to their stories and acknowledged the injustice of their treatment and the ingratitude they received for their work. From the perspective of Wallace, the Progressive Party and his 1948 campaign had the potential to create the multiethnic, multiracial coalition he wished the Democratic Party had the bravery to support.[14]

To mobilize Latinas/os as supporters of Wallace throughout these spaces, organizers within the Progressive Party established the Amigos de Wallace (Friends of Wallace) campaign. By producing campaign materials in Spanish and hiring Latina/o organizers within Latina/o communities to represent the Progressive Party, this effort sought to capture the attention of Spanish-speaking women and men eager for a politic that represented them through the U.S. electoral system. The lives of Latinas/os throughout the nation, much as in Ybor City, had been shaped by a postwar economy that left them earning poverty wages in an increasingly expensive world and contending with political policies that vilified resistance to workplace discrimination as akin to un-Americanism and communism. While the Progressive Party offered solutions to such issues, on-the-ground, pavement-pounding outreach was essential if organizers were to communicate the Wallace platform to these women and men.

At the Amigos de Wallace headquarters in New York City, campaign strategists published a manifesto by Wallace, which they distributed through Latina/o communities in the United States. This statement called for "Mexican-Americans, Puerto Ricans, Spaniards, and Latin Americans" to join him in the "fight for civil rights" as it embraced an internationalist platform that urged, "We cannot allow this nation to become an imperialist power that exploits us and wrecks us for the benefits of the banks." The manifesto warned that if U.S. citizens allowed the nation to continue down its current path, it would extend its "oppressive tentacles" and "provoke another world war." Looking to excite Latinas/os and encourage their participation, the proclamation continued:

> *Spanish-speaking citizens and Hispanic Descendants:*
>
> In the electoral fight of 1948 there is nothing more than two parties: that of Truman with his republican allies, Hoover and the like; and the *NEW PEOPLES PARTY LED BY APOSTLE HENRY A. WALLACE.* We, the people of Hispanic origin, cannot be on the side of Truman and his devilish political scheme whose triumph would be the ruin and enslavement of the American people and the entire world. As progressives, we must support Henry Wallace and his New Party with all our soul, heart, and life, whose program contains positive plans to solve the serious and pressing problems that confront the American people, and in particular our ethnic group.[15]

As the campaign sought to share its principles, it likewise spoke to Latinas/os as stakeholders in a shared future: "Forward then fellow citizens and *Amigos de Wallace*, join the New Party. . . . We will fight valiantly in the army of Peace that Henry A. Wallace so gallantly leads." Rhetoric and invitations such as this echoed the impassioned tone of anarchists, socialists, communists, and labor organizers that once reverberated through the cigar factories and the streets of Ybor City. Latinas/os in Ybor and West Tampa politically identified with such ideas and found excitement in the Wallace platform. As a result, campaign officials hired Mariano Rodríguez to serve as the vice-chairman of the Progressive Party in Tampa and Ida Pérez to serve as the secretary of the Progressive Party in Tampa. The campaign hoped that Rodríguez and Pérez, both the children of cigar workers, would build a bridge between this community of Latinas/os and the national party.[16]

Although Wallace found national support within leftist circles — such as in organized labor, civil rights organizations, and communities such as Ybor City and West Tampa — he struggled to build a national coalition. Many "journalists and politicians dismissed Wallace as a bitter and confused man," while "cartoonists portrayed him as a marionette, mindlessly delivering the latest Moscow line while Stalin pulled the strings."[17] Northern liberals viewed him as the "unwitting ally of 'reaction'" and a threat to postwar growth, while white southerners invested in white supremacy believed Wallace to be the second coming of Reconstruction-esque Yankee oppression.[18] When the Wallace campaign toured the U.S. South — something neither Truman nor Thomas Dewey dared to do during the 1948 election — people launched "eggs, tomatoes, and a torrent of ugly invectives" at the candidate as he delivered speeches about the importance of racial equality and the need to desegregate the region. Paul Robeson, the Black American singer and self-proclaimed antifascist, stood by Wallace on the trail and sang songs such as "Let My People Go" and "Old Man River" to integrated audiences. This did little to ingratiate Wallace to southern Dixiecrats eager to vote for Strom Thurmond, but it did much to inspire Black audiences who embraced a candidate who treated them with humanity.[19]

Segregationists in Florida welcomed Wallace with the same vitriolic treatment he received in other southern states. While self-proclaimed "men of good will" and "defenders of the [S]outh" declared Wallace a "[S]outh hater" because he "proclaimed that segregation was a sin," others marked him as a dangerous Red because he advocated a peaceful relationship between the United States and the Soviet Union.[20] In some areas of the state, the presence of Wallace and support for his campaign encouraged the disturbing resurgence of KKK activity. Hooded men, cloaked in anonymity and fragile masculinity, burned crosses in the front yards of supporters as they sought to quell a movement that threatened to dismantle Jim Crow and white supremacist politics in the Sunshine State. Yet despite the threats of people who wished to control politics through racial oppression and anticommunist paranoia, Wallace traveled throughout the state and shook the hands of those willing to meet him.[21]

Wallace arrived in Tampa during the early hours of the morning on February 17, 1948. He began his whirlwind tour of the city with a press conference at the Floridian Hotel located in downtown Tampa. Unlike most candidates who addressed the press from grand ballrooms or commanding podiums, Wallace ushered journalists into his hotel room. While sitting on his bed with the sleeves of his white buttoned-down oxford shirt rolled up,

Wallace took questions from reporters of the *Tampa Morning Tribune* and the *St. Petersburg Times*. Perhaps unsurprisingly, the interview began with an inquiry into accusations of the presidential candidate's communist ties and un-American politics. In response, Wallace made clear that he "specifically reject[ed] support from anyone who wished to overthrow the government . . . but welcomed anyone who believe[d] in [the] promot[ion] [of] understanding between nations as requisite for peace." "I am not the one with Communism on the brain," Wallace reminded the journalists. The presidential hopeful then explained that his approach to international relations would center on diplomacy rather than the dropping of an iron curtain and the escalation of a cold war. Wallace optimistically shared with the Tampa press that if he were in the White House, he would encourage "Stalin to come half way with us just as he did with FDR." Most importantly, however, the hopeful progressive asserted that it was "high time we think in terms of American problems" rather than invent threats to international security. To Wallace, such issues were the same problems that occupied the minds of Latinas/os in Ybor City and broader Tampa—how to survive in a growing economy and an expanding capitalist state that allowed the elite to strike it rich at the expense of the many who earned far less than a living wage.[22]

Before the interview closed, however, reporters turned away from questions of "foreign affairs and domestic issues" to one of "local import." National Guard Major General Sumter L. Lowry, a community leader, had urged "all right thinking people" in Tampa to boycott Wallace's speech scheduled for later that evening. When the journalists asked Wallace what he thought of the matter, the candidate simply grinned and replied: "It is like when they ban books, it immediately increases circulation." Wallace, in many ways, was correct. According to local newspaper reports, many people in the Tampa area were interested in what the presidential candidate had to say. Some people shared with journalists that "curiosity was always worth the 50 cent admission fee" and they planned to spend their evening listening to the candidate's words even though they "did not anticipate to be convinced." Other potential voters planned to attend the rally with more enthusiasm. Frank González shared with the *Tampa Morning Tribune* that he planned to "string along with [Wallace] if convinced that he followed FDR's principles," while A. J. Jiménez asserted that Wallace was "just another candidate like Truman" and believed that the "communist charge against [him] was" little more than "propaganda intended to scare people who are easily led."[23]

As local Progressive Party organizers finalized preparations for the night's rally, Wallace traveled throughout the city and met with potential voters.

Mariano Rodríguez and Ida Pérez arranged a campaign stop at the El Paraiso cigar factory, where the presidential candidate met with Latinas who worked at the factory and were members of the Cigar Makers' International Union. While some of these women had already pledged to register as members of the Progressive Party, Rodríguez and Pérez understood that the Latina/o vote in Tampa was essential to Wallace's presidential bid.[24] Not only did this visit have the potential to encourage votes that could positively influence the election outcome, but it had the ability to show Latinas in Ybor City that their struggles and their politics were important to presidential candidates. Wallace was the first presidential hopeful to shake hands with Latinas/os in Ybor City or West Tampa and show these women and men that they mattered as U.S. voters.

According to reports from *La Gaceta*, cigar workers greeted Wallace enthusiastically and showed him the cigars they made. As Wallace learned about their trade and the pride these women took in their labor, he may have listened to them explain the need for fair wages and the problems their families and their community faced. These women may have even discussed antifascism and the Popular Front, both at home and abroad, for Ybor Latinas believed this presidential candidate shared their perspective. Wallace, a key member of the New Deal coalition, understood the importance of labor rights and government benefits to Ybor's working-class Latinas/os and likely offered encouraging words of support. Much as he did during other meet-and-greet events, the presidential candidate may have even pledged that he would not recognize Franco's government and would seek to dismantle fascist policies at home, such as Jim Crow. Before Wallace left the factory, cigar workers took to their feet and gave the presidential candidate a standing ovation. *La Gaceta* recounted that Wallace seemed moved by the spontaneous show of gratitude and support from the workers.[25]

At 8:00 P.M. that February night, an estimated 2,500 women and men converged on Plant Field in downtown Tampa to hear Wallace address the public. This event, in many ways, was unlike any other political rally the city had seen. Central to the Wallace platform was the principle of anti-racism. Wallace, who advocated the end of segregation and the dissolution of all Jim Crow legislation, refused to speak to segregated audiences no matter where he was or what local laws dictated throughout his campaign. Despite the grumblings of some Tampa Anglos, the city approved the permit for the event and allowed Wallace to hold an integrated rally in this Jim Crow space. The press reported that "a great majority of the listeners was of Latin extraction, many of them cigar workers," but "the strangest sight of all was the mingling of white and [Black] people in the grandstands." To maintain order, ten police officers patrolled the area in case "rowdyism" erupted. The event, however, was peaceful. When a member of the local press asked an attendee why they believed the night was calm, the person explained the event lacked violence or harassment because "everyone there, except the reporters and the police, were brothers and sisters under the skin . . . the solid class of citizenry both native born and emigrants" who had "labored since [R]econstruction days to make the South what it is today." Furthermore, the attendee emphasized to the reporter that members of the Progressive Party would "not be interested in crackpot politicians whose ambitions lead them to all kinds of foolish extremes in leading the foolish ignorant [masses] to belie[ve] in false and fanatic ideologies."[26]

Unable to report discord, journalists described the night's event as a joyous festivity reminiscent of the Florida State Fair. "A hot dog stand," which stood on one side of the entrance, "did brisk business in cold drinks and sandwiches" while "a popcorn stand," positioned at the opposite entrance, "didn't do as well." Pillow salesmen walked through the stands and "hawked their cushions in strident voices" to anyone who wished for a plush and comfortable seat. The tunes of "lively band music" blared through "loudspeakers" as "ushers for the Progressive Peoples Party darted through the stands taking up collections during one part of the rally." It was this portion of the event, the fundraising, that impressed journalists most. Before the rally began, a New York commentator and lecturer, William Gallinor, reportedly "showed Tampans a thing or two about raising quick funds for a candidate." As Gallinor took to the loudspeaker with fiery enthusiasm, he began with requests for "$100, [and] he got 11 [donations] in a row — right quick like," then moved on to a call for $50 and $25 gifts. "Then came a flock of 10s and still more scores of 5s eventually adding up to an even 2000 in cash and pledges." Finally, Gallinor "invited 'a parade of $1 bills' and the audience with its upraised hands turned into a sea of waving green." The press estimated that the combined value of all donations, including the $0.50 event entrance fee and accounting for expenses, likely neared $7,000. "Not bad for a one-day stand!" the *St. Petersburg Times* reported.[27]

With the pledges made and the cash donations collected, it was time for the event to begin. First, a "[Black] woman from Tampa" sang the National Anthem and the "non-segregated crowd applauded." Next, everyone "stood silently with bared head when a [Black] minister spoke the benediction" to bless the event and the candidate. After the singer and the minister sat down next to the campaign staff, it was time for Wallace to address the Tampa public. As the presidential candidate walked out onto the stage, the crowd chanted, "VI-VA WAL-LACE! VI-VA WAL-LACE!"[28] In response, Wallace "grin[ned] slightly" and "stepped up to the microphone" as wisps "of [his] greying hair ruffl[ed] in the cool night air." Once the candidate reached his mark, he looked at the audience and "waved his hands and shouted back, 'Amigos mios!' (my friends)." The women and men in the stands erupted into laughter, applauded again, then took their seats so they could listen to what the candidate had to say.[29]

During the speech, Wallace addressed issues of domestic and international concern. When it came to the home front and the state of the U.S. worker, the presidential candidate charged both political parties of conspiring with "monopolists" to gain "super profits," which resulted in an inflated economy and the depressed wages working-class women and men experienced. When Wallace mentioned the House un-American Activities Committee and the accusations that he had been "adopted by a party made up of enemies of [the] country," attendees and supporters "booed." The presidential hopeful then charged both political parties "with grand larceny" as he asserted that they "[stole] citizens' civil rights, workers' wages, and people's hopes" as well as the "people's hard-won victory in the war against foreign fascism." From the perspective of Wallace, as well as many people in the crowd, the Popular Front coalition they built in the 1930s through unionism and community action had the promise of improving the lives of women and men around the globe. This hope, however, was little more than a dream if politicians did not invest in economic and racial equality at home as well as the pursuit of international democracy and cross-national cooperation as central components to the foreign policy platform of the United States. By the end of the night, after speaking to the crowd for over an hour, Wallace made his case for president of the United States by positioning himself as the person who would bring the New Deal into the modern age. As one attendee said, it was clear that Wallace was "the greatest friend to humanity" and the candidate "with a philosophy closest to Roosevelt's."[30]

Latinas and Latinos from Ybor City remembered Wallace on Election Day. While the majority of Tampans cast their ballot for Truman, as did the majority of Floridians and U.S. voters, Wallace captured "seven of the eleven precincts" between Ybor City and West Tampa, which translated to over 50 percent of the vote in this area. The majority of the remaining votes in these Latina/o neighborhoods went to Truman. Out of the 10,293 ballots cast for the Progressive Party in the state of Florida, roughly 40 percent of the vote came from Hillsborough County alone. This was an impressive show of voter power, not just for Florida but nationwide. As the historian Jared G. Toney explains, "While [Wallace] gained more actual votes in New York" than in Florida, "the concentration of Progressive Party supporters relative to population was significantly higher (in fact double) in Tampa." *La Gaceta* reported this news proudly, for it equated the support of the Progressive Party among Latinas/os in Ybor City and West Tampa to a triumph of the people over "the weak company kept by the political bosses of the Democratic Party in this city."[31]

Wallace was, indeed, a radical presidential candidate, but he was still a person who sought to reform the United States within the existing structure of the state.[32] The central message of his campaign was that U.S. politics can work for everyone—white working-class, racially and ethnically marginalized peoples, immigrant and U.S.-born. Yet such function was only possible if those in power dared to make space for all who were a part of the nation's citizenry. This concept was so controversial in 1948, and in many ways remains to be so, that accusations of anti-Americanism and red-baiting followed because Wallace and his supporters dared to envision a different kind of country. Latinas/os from Ybor City and West Tampa, prior to this election, operated on the margins of the U.S. political system as they relied on unionism to represent their interests to local employers and leftist political parties to address their concerns. Neither the White Municipal Party nor members of the local and political Anglo elite were willing to make space for them and, in the past, had resorted to extreme and violent measures to illustrate this fact. Yet with the decline of the Cuban cigar industry, the aging of their houses and community infrastructure, and the experience of their children crossing the border into greater Tampa for education as well as traveling the globe as servicepersons during World War II, the relationship between Latinas/os in and from Ybor City had been remade. Henry Wallace represented the kind of politician these women and men needed—one who seemed to listen to them and consider their needs with sincerity.

In the years that followed, Latinas/os throughout Tampa took the lessons of the 1948 election seriously as they mobilized the community as a political entity and even ran for political office themselves. The action of running for office, in most cases, was done by men, typically tampeños of the U.S.-born second and third generations. The action of voting, however, was a community affair and women's labor and time was essential. Potential candidates from Ybor City and West Tampa went to cigar factories to shake hands with and listen to the Latinas who worked there. Tampeñas helped their parents submit naturalization papers and register to vote, and on Election Day these women drove family and friends to the polls while their children were at school. Together women and men from the neighborhood sat in Ybor City and West Tampa cafés (their own political headquarters) as they stuffed envelopes and mailed flyers to share with their networks information about the candidates they supported. Businesses throughout the Latina/o communities plastered signs and information about voting day. In order to turn these Ybor and West Tampa Latinas/os into U.S. voters, these women and men had to see a need for representation and believe that participation in the U.S. electoral system could improve their lives — by the 1950s, they did.

As women and men from Ybor City and West Tampa harnessed their power as a local voting bloc, they reshaped Tampa's municipal politics and the state of Florida. Latinas/os from Ybor City joined and used the Democratic Party as their primary vehicle to seek municipal and national recognition. Countless tampeños, and later tampeñas, became members of the Tampa City Council, the Hillsborough County Commission, the Board of Education, and nearly every other elected position within the city. Nick Nuccio, the son of Sicilian immigrants and a native-born Ybor resident, ascended to the position of mayor in 1956 and again in 1963. As the first person who lived in and was from Ybor City to reach this position, Nuccio received significant racial backlash from Tampa Anglos during his first term. He relished, however, in the praise he earned from those in his neighborhood. Another Ybor community member, Dick Greco, followed in Nuccio's footsteps and became mayor of Tampa in 1967, as did Bob Martínez in 1979, who went on to become governor of Florida in 1983. E. J. Salcines, the son of Juanita Salcines, who served as community support for West Tampa mothers in World War II, became the state attorney of Florida and later a federal judge. A statue that commemorates E. J. Salcines's service to the city of Tampa and the state of Florida now stands outside the Tampa courthouse.[33]

The Cuban Revolution in Ybor City

Fidel Castro arrived in Ybor City in November 1955. The twenty-nine-year-old revolutionary was in the midst of a tour of the United States to raise money and establish stateside support through the creation of the 26th of July Movement clubs (the organizations that supported and funded the Cuban Revolution). Before Castro reached Tampa, he delivered speeches in Pennsylvania, New Jersey, Connecticut, New York, and Miami — all locations with notable Cuban populations — where he worked to mobilize a cross-national network of people dedicated to the overthrow of

Fulgencio Batista, the dictator who ruled Cuba through suppression, corruption, and violence as well as the auspices of the U.S. government. Castro approached his visit to Ybor City as a symbolic walk through time. He and his comrades assumed temporary residency at the old Pedroso boardinghouse—the same location where José Martí once stayed—and replicated the strategy of the "apostle of Cuban liberty" as Castro made connections with local community leaders and established a satellite of his revolutionary organization within Ybor City. This place, he believed, would be as essential to his revolution as it had been to the movement for Cuban independence.[34]

Yet while Castro declared that "the Republic of Cuba is the daughter of the cigar makers of Tampa," he overlooked that much had changed since the 1890s. The people whom Martí once called "new pines" had lived in Florida for two to three generations. It was in Ybor City—not Cuba—where they married, created families, established community, and labored as they weathered nativist violence, anti-union suppression, the Great Depression, and a present-day shifting economy. While many local Latinas/os embraced their Cuban heritage as foundational to themselves as well as what it meant to be from Ybor City, they were no longer as invested in the politics of the island as they had been decades prior. After all, they had their own problems here. Although Castro may have expected the people of Ybor City to anoint him as the new leader of *Cuba libre*, he instead found a few ardent supporters and many apathetic observers.[35]

As the historian Ada Ferrer states, "People interested in Cuba often make the mistake of thinking too much about Fidel Castro." In the case of Ybor City, nothing could be more accurate. While in hindsight Castro looks "tall, solid, confident" and "larger than life, as if preordained for victory and power," in 1955 he was "but one revolutionary among many," or, as a member of the Ybor community plainly put it, he was "unknown."[36] During the month Castro spent in Ybor City, he did not wear the green fatigues or sport the full, unkempt beard he became famous for years later; instead, he wore "civilian clothes" and had a clean-shaven face. At times, Castro stood on the corner of the street, "where he would talk, and people would listen" to his tale of rebellion and his experience in prison.[37] No doubt Castro told and retold, in spectacular fashion, the story of July 26, 1953—the day he and ninety-four fellow defenders of Cuban liberty stormed the Moncada Barracks at Santiago de Cuba and battled the "soldiers of the tyrant Batista."[38] In reality, forty-five of Castro's fellow rebels are documented as having arrived at that barracks. Some members of his group, many of whom were out-of-towners, got lost in Santiago de Cuba or "found their intended routes blocked by a carnival." While Castro likely left out this part of the story, he may have detailed the violent reaction of the Batista government to the July 26 assault. After Cuban soldiers arrested those connected to the event, Batista's army killed and tortured "more than fifty of the rebels." Some of these men "were buried without their eyes or teeth," and "the two women who participated in the attack were burned with cigarettes." One woman, Haydée Santamaría, received "a tray holding her brother's eyes and her boyfriend's testicles." According to journalists and historians, the reaction of the Batista government to the Moncada attack was the "largest mass killing of prisoners [by the ruling Cuban government] since the War of Independence."[39]

Many people agreed with Castro, both in Ybor City and throughout the United States, on the subject of Batista. They recognized that Batista rose to power in 1952 through a coup d'état and secured an extension of his presidency in 1954 "in a sham election" where "he was the only candidate."[40] People understood Batista was ruthless and corrupt. But, as the anthropologist Susan D. Greenbaum asserts, from the perspective of Latinas/os in Ybor City, "[These] were not unusual characteristics in Cuban politics."[41] To many people who lived in Ybor and West Tampa, the story Castro shared, while horrific and gruesome, may have felt as though it were a tale as old as time in 1955. Castro, who spent nearly two years in prison before Batista granted amnesty to all political prisoners, experienced much confusion and frustration from the reception he received in Ybor City. The people who made this place the "cradle of Cuban liberty" seemed unmotivated by the stories he told and the plans he shared. As Castro wandered down Thirteenth Street and Seventh Avenue, he likely wondered when the "new pines" Martí claimed to have taken root in this corner of the Sunshine State had been felled.[42]

While Castro was able to envision his revolution and articulate hope for his homeland, he was unable to understand the needs or motivations of women and men in Ybor City. By 1955, roughly 30 percent of the people who lived in Ybor were Black Americans, who sought refuge in the decrepit casitas after historically African American neighborhoods—namely, the Scrub and Central Avenue—had been leveled as part of a citywide improvement plan for a new interstate and a public housing project. The buildings that lined Seventh Avenue, which once echoed the architecture of Havana and the romance of Sevilla, had begun to crumble. There was little hope for their replacement or their renovation. Countless Cuban cigar factories sat empty throughout the city, and the cigar workers who labored in the enterprises that lingered were aging, retiring, and moving in with their children, who had crossed the border into broader Tampa and lived their lives as ethnic U.S. citizens rather than committed leftist radicals. The pillars of the community, the mutual aid societies, were in dire need of assistance and funding. The clubhouse of both the Círculo Cubano and La Sociedad de la Unión Martí-Maceo needed repairs that the institutions could not afford. Much as with the Centro Español and L'Unione Italiana, membership in the Cuban socie-dades had dwindled since the Depression years. The women and men who remained on the rosters mainly used medical services and attended talks, performances, and events. Tampeñas/os, however, no longer gathered in the clubs as often as they had in years past. The cantinas and domino tables, once reliable sources of income for the centros, were less crowded in the evenings than they were in the neighborhood's heyday. Latina/o families that left the old community had shifted the focus of their collective action from an effort to remake global politics to an effort to redefine the position they held in broader Tampa. Ybor City was the foundation of tampeña/o culture, heri-tage, and history, but, to many members of this community, neither the old neighborhood nor its past political principles were the center of their lives by the time Castro arrived.[43]

Perhaps nothing illustrates the clash of culture between Castro and the people of Ybor City more than the drama that unfolded when the young rev-olutionary attempted to give a public talk in the community. In late Novem-ber 1955, Castro approached the leadership of the Círculo Cubano and La Sociedad de la Unión Martí-Maceo with the request that they allow him to use one of their ballrooms to deliver an address to the people of Ybor City. Both clubs refused. According to Armando Dorta, president of the Círculo Cubano, and Juan Casellas, president of Martí-Maceo, political talks and po-litical fundraisers violated the bylaws of their organizations. Furthermore, each mutual aid society leader explained, both of their institutions required recognition of the Cuban government regardless of whether or not they agreed with the president in power. One community member who belonged to La Sociedad de la Unión Martí-Maceo recalled that Castro became enraged and called them "stupid" and said "[they] didn't understand what he was doing for Cuba."[44] The citation of bylaws by both Dorta and Casellas was, indeed, an excuse to prevent the possible backlash these institutions could receive from their membership, the broader Tampa community, and the U.S. government if the mutual aid societies were assumed to be in support of Castro's politics and revolutionary efforts, for both organizations had per-mitted and sponsored political events and discussions in recent years. Furthermore, both centros were willing to accept membership from anyone who wished to join regardless of their ethnicity, nationality, or loyalty to the Cuban government.[45] In fact, Casellas himself was Puerto Rican. While Castro perceived the request to donate space to his event as a rightful obligation of anyone who opposed the Batista regime and believed in a free Cuba, to the leadership of the Círculo Cubano and La Sociedad de la Unión Martí-Maceo this was not a risk they were willing to take. Both Dorta and Casellas understood that regardless of the politics Castro proclaimed his revolution endorsed, any action seen to stand in opposition to official U.S. foreign policy carried the risk of accusations of anti-Americanism in a Cold War world. When it came to choosing between a new future for Cuba and the safety of their community, the leaders of both the Círculo Cubano and La Sociedad de la Unión Martí-Maceo chose to protect the legacies they built in Ybor City.[46]

Despite rejection from both Cuban mutual aid societies, Castro seemed to have secured himself space in the ballroom of L'Unione Italiana by November 25, 1955. That day, La Gaceta announced the event on the front page of the newspaper as it encouraged all who were a part of this "Cuban colony" who had not forgotten "the ideologies of Martí" as well as "all people no matter their nationality" who believed in "the ideas of democracy and liberty" to attend the address.[47] The St. Petersburg Times followed the next day with a headline that read "Anti-Batista Revolutionist to Speak Here" and detailed that the talk would take place at 3:00 P.M. on November 27 at the Italian Club. However, twenty-four hours before the event, the president of L'Unione Italiana, Joseph Maniscalco, informed Castro that the organization could not host his address because its political nature conflicted with the club's bylaws. In an interview with the Tampa Sunday Tribune, Maniscalco explained that he and the board of directors of the Italian Club were under the impression that the event was to be a "social meeting," but once they learned of its "true purpose" they decided it was essential to pull their support. "We don't feel we should be mixed up in political affairs," Maniscalco stated, "for [we] think we should stay away from anything that may embarrass the government of the United States."[48] Both Castro and Victoriano Manteiga—the editor and owner of La Gaceta, who also led the local 26th of July Movement club—erupted into a fury and accused all mutual aid societies of bending to the will of the Batista government and accepting dirty money from Batista himself; such accusations were not without merit.

Between 1948 and 1956, the Círculo Cubano and La Sociedad de la Unión Martí-Maceo received hearty donations to their benevolent organizations from the Cuban government and, at times, from Batista himself.

To each organization these donations were, as the anthropologist Greenbaum explains, "a godsend," for they provided funds essential to perform maintenance on the buildings of the Cuban sociedades and begin historic preservation efforts in Ybor City.[49] For example, the Pedroso boardinghouse—once owned by Paulina and Ruperto Pedroso, an Afro-Cuban couple—had been purchased for "its historic importance" by a Cuban businessman in 1951. In 1956, the man "deeded the property to the Cuban government, and Batista announced his intention to transform the house into a museum and sent "$18,235 . . . to pay for the costs of restoring the house." To those who worshipped the ideals and the lore of Cuban independence, this site held great significance. It was in this house where José Martí slept during his visits to Ybor City and where Paulina Pedroso provided him with medical care after he experienced an assassination attempt. But, perhaps most importantly, the Pedroso boardinghouse represented the idea of an anti-racist, color-blind Cuba and Cuban people—a foundational concept to Martí's rhetoric and a myth both the Cuban government and the people of Ybor City wished to purport and believed to be central to their identities. While the structure of the Pedroso boardinghouse burned down before the museum came to fruition, the funds Batista sent to Tampa sponsored the creation of El Parque de José Martí (José Martí Park). Much like Castro, Batista wished to position himself as the benefactor of *Cuba libre*.[50]

By the morning of November 27, 1955, Castro and Manteiga secured the Congress of Industrial Organizations union hall on Seventh Avenue as the new location of the afternoon's event. Unlike the grand ballrooms of the sociedades, which featured large stages, velvet-covered seating, and space for nearly 1,000 guests, the union hall was humbler—an open room with folding chairs and a maximum capacity of 400 people. While *La Gaceta* reported a full room, both the *St. Petersburg Times* and the *Tampa Morning Tribune* noted that 300 inquiring minds attended the event. During the meeting, Castro declared that he would "fight to the death to free his country" from the "dictatorship of President Fulgencio Batista." "My movement will end only when tyranny is dead or we are dead," Castro shouted with passion in Spanish from the floor of the union hall. "If Batista does not resign there will be revolution," he promised, but "if he does [resign], there will be no bloodshed." Throughout the three-hour address, Castro invoked imagery of the movement for Cuban independence. Castro reminded the audience that the day's date, November 27, was the same day Martí spoke to an audience in Ybor City. As Castro's eyes fell on the unoccupied seats in the room, he made a point to say, "The empty chairs hold the spirits of my comrades who fought with me and died [at the Moncada Barracks]" on July 26, 1953.[51]

Before the event ended, Castro and the leadership of the local 26th of July Movement club requested donations to support the coming revolution. As a straw hat, "characteristic . . . of the Cuban countryman," circulated around the room, several people donated hundred dollar bills while others tossed fives and tens into the hat. By the end of the event, the press estimated that the meeting "netted $110.02, after expenses." While one newspaper captured an image of Castro and local 26th of July Movement leadership looking longingly at a small pile of money crumpled on a table, the revolutionary leader took questions from the press with confidence. When asked what he would do with the donations, Castro "quoted José Martí, the apostle of Cuba as he said: 'The results are public but the methods are secret.'"[52]

Castro departed Ybor City on November 28, 1955, and left the responsibility of community mobilization in the hands of the local 26th of July Movement club. Manteiga used his newspaper to spread the word of the revolution and garner support (and particularly money) from the community for the next three years. The majority of the funds collected from this organization went to Mexico, where revolutionaries purchased food, weaponry, and medical supplies. According to the St. Petersburg Times, a number of members from this local organization were part of a convoy intercepted by the Port Authority off the coast of the Everglades as they attempted to smuggle "howitzers, submachine guns, rifles, carbines, walkie-talkie radios, mess kits and clothing" across the Florida Strait. Yet despite these notable moments, the effort of the 26th of July Movement in Tampa illustrated the disconnect between the Ybor community and the island. According to the historian William Watson Jr., the 26th of July Movement club had sixty members at its height, and the majority were not the ardent rebels Castro envisioned he would recruit. Protests and public events often yielded few participants, and the 26th of July Movement was never able to harness mass dedication or enthusiasm from the Cuban cigar workers. While in the 1890s, the cigar workers of Ybor City made a weekly donation of one day's wages to support the fight for Cuban independence from Spain—a ritual they replicated during the 1930s to defend the Spanish Republic and Ybor City from fascist forces—in the 1950s, these workers and their descendants were unwilling to do the same for the Cuban Revolution. This reality frustrated and angered Manteiga, who proclaimed, "In Tampa we regret the apathy of the young who eat much and think less and the old people who lick the hooves of Batista."[53]

The effort of the 26th of July Movement, in many ways, represented an older way of doing things. The local movement, much like the revolution on the island, was a space of men's work rather than women's efforts. Women's positions within this organization were not as movement makers but as supporters and bystanders—something that stood in direct opposition to what Ybor City and the community had become. Although nineteenth-century ideals of manhood and masculinity may have inspired Castro and his fellow rebels who waged war in the Sierra Maestra, in Ybor City the people who had managed to survive changes in the economy, the assault of national political policies, and the ostracization by Tampa Anglos from political access required taking women seriously as participants and agents of change. For the families who continued to rely on cigar work as their primary form of income, it was Latinas' wages that kept their rents paid and their stomachs full. Not only had Ybor City changed in terms of its needs and interests, but the culture of activism and collective organization had moved beyond models that relegated women to the sidelines.

Yet even more than the role of women in the structure of the 26th of July Movement and its U.S.-based organizations was the status of the Cuban cigar industry in Ybor City. From the 1880s through the 1930s, the Cuban cigar factories of Ybor City and West Tampa were the primary sites of collective organization within this community. The culture of leftist activism that once fueled the immigrant neighborhood lived on the shop room floors, came to life inside the Centro Obrero, coalesced in unions, and thrived at family dinner tables. Both the Cuban cigar industry and the radical, leftist culture of Cuban cigar work was central to the politics that made this place. By the 1950s, not only had integral community institutions, such as the lectura, faded from Ybor City but so too had the might of the Cuban cigar industry itself. During earlier decades, the reason Ybor Latinas/os were so powerful was that their skill and their industry were central to the local economy. If cigar workers called a strike, they could bring the city of Tampa to a halt—a fact known to cigar manufacturers and Anglo politicians alike. The might of labor emboldened the women and men of Ybor to withstand much resistance, and even violence, from broader Tampa because these workers knew the influence they had in this southern town. In 1955, things were different. Tampa was no longer a one-industry town, and the Cuban cigar industry was more a nostalgic novelty than an illustration of the city's future. As a result, it was difficult for the leftist politics and broad visions of global change that once united women and men on the factory floor to thrive in this space, for the primary concern of the dwindling Cuban cigar workforce was merely the maintenance of the cigar industry itself. With each passing year, it seemed more and more cigar workers either left the industry and found work elsewhere in Tampa or retired and moved into the homes their children purchased in the suburbs of Hillsborough County.

There was, however, one other important factor that explains why more people from Ybor did not publicly defend and join the 26th of July Movement—generational difference. Victoriano Manteiga immigrated to Ybor City in the 1910s, and Raúl Villamia, another leader and influential voice within the local movement, came to the United States to play baseball in the late 1940s and made Ybor his home in 1953. While Manteiga was drawn to the 26th of July Movement as a result of his immigrant experience, his decades of work as a lector, his labor as a newspaper editor, and his position as a leftist movement maker, Ybor community members like him were few and far between by the 1950s. People such as Villamia, in contrast, were part of a small migrant group that arrived in Florida decades after the majority of the Ybor community. The ties that men such as Manteiga and Villamia, as well as their families, maintained with Cuba were stronger in the 1950s than those of their peers in Ybor City and West Tampa—the majority of whom immigrated to this place before 1930, when the local Cuban cigar industry was at its height. Furthermore, the politics and economic circumstances that motivated the migration of those who arrived in Ybor City after 1930 were directly linked to the issues Castro spoke out against and that the 26th of July Movement sought to remedy. Creating a coalition of people willing to support Castro and dedicate money to a revolution that the United States opposed in the midst of the Cold War was a tall order, especially when the majority of people Manteiga and Villamia sought to mobilize had a more distant relationship with the island and a closer relationship with the United States. To tampeñas/os, those of the second and third generation, Cuba was a place they visited to see relatives or take short vacations, but Tampa was where they lived and built community. While evidence suggests that many people from Ybor City sympathized with the politics of the 26th of July Movement, few were willing to put their bodies, their money, and their safety on the line in this political moment.[54]

On January 1, 1959, when news of the triumph of Castro over Batista reached Tampa, more than 1,000 people throughout the city rushed to Ybor. In a show of support, cars jammed the streets and people honked their horns to illustrate their hope for a new Cuba. Some people waved flags and pendants with pride as others gave speeches and placed flowers at the bust of Martí just outside the Círculo Cubano. It seems that although Latinas/os from Ybor City may not have cared enough about the Cuban Revolution to invest their time, money, and effort in a struggle that did not directly affect their lives, many hoped that this new government would bring positive change to the island.[55] The lack of enthusiasm and ardent support of the majority of the Ybor community lent to the 26th of July Movement did not mean that they were anti-Castro or that they stood in opposition of the Cuban Revolution; it meant that their sense of self and the politics most tampeñas/os believed were worth actively fighting for had changed.

While members of the Ybor City community watched to see what kind of leader Castro would be, Cubans who lived on the island and opposed the new government's policies fled the country. Roughly 10,000 Cubans came to Tampa in the immediate wake of the revolution, a number that pales in comparison to those who went to Miami "by a ratio of about 40 to 1." These two communities—the "new Cubans," as they were called in Tampa, and the tampeñas/os—did not mix well and maintained a division over time. Initial outward displays of support for the revolutionary regime by Latinas/os from Ybor City resulted in "scuffles," some of which included gunfire. Although the 26th of July Movement club dissolved by 1960, a Fair Play for Cuba Committee emerged, which sought to combat anti-Cuban propaganda and political policies developed by the U.S. government. This organization, likewise, included stalwart supporters but did not have a large quantity of card-carrying members from Ybor City. Despite this reality, the new Cubans who opposed the Castro government and the circumstances that forced their recent migration filled light bulbs with red paint and launched them at the houses and workplaces of those they knew supported or sympathized with the revolution and even at the Círculo Cubano clubhouse. A "war of the roses" emerged in José Martí Park as anti-Castro supporters laid white roses at the feet of the statue of Martí, while those who supported Castro and the new government placed red roses in the same location. Each camp discarded the offering of the other upon arrival to this hallowed ground. Frank Valdez, the president of the Círculo Cubano, accused the newcomers of attempting to take over the mutual aid society. He explained that the provision of the bylaws, which "banned political and religious discussion," kept them out. Instead, the new Cuban arrivals built their own society, the Club Cívico, located near MacDill Air Force Base, which resembled a country club more than one of the working-class centros. As two tampeños explained, "[The new Cubans] don't think like we do . . . that club doesn't belong to the low class people . . . that club belongs to those who have money." With time, many of women and men from Ybor City became disillusioned with the Cuban Revolution; but it was the difference of class, heritage, and politics that maintained a barrier between these two communities. While the new Cubans defined their lives in opposition to Castro and the revolution, most of the tampeñas/os of Ybor City simply moved on. To the Latinas/os who had lived and labored in Ybor and Tampa for generations, the Cuban Revolution was ideological, but it was not as personal as past political movements.[56]

If the Henry Wallace campaign illustrated the type of politic that tampeñas/os would accept and support as part of their remaking, then the Cuban Revolution illustrated what the ideas and causes most members of the community would shy away from. Although many people supported the ideas of the 26th of July Movement and the hope that Castro's government might bring positive change to the island, the majority of tampeñas/os were unwilling to donate their money, their intellectual energy, or their physical selves to a political cause hundreds of miles away. What they were dedicated to, however, was protecting and maintaining a sense of self that was distinctly of Ybor City.

Urban Renewal

On a hot, humid, Florida afternoon in September 1966, Blanca and José Vega heard a knock on the front door of their casita. Like many women and men of the immigrant and first generations who still lived in Ybor City, the Vegas had called the same house on the same street home for over fifty years. When the couple opened their front door, likely expecting to greet a neighbor, there stood a man they did not know who identified himself as an official from the Urban Renewal Authority. In a matter-of-fact manner, the man informed the couple that their house, located on 1515 Thirteenth Avenue, was in the territory marked for redevelopment and revitalization. As a result, the couple would have to move because their home would be torn down to make way for what the Tampa Urban Renewal Authority claimed was something better. To lessen the blow, the man explained that the couple would receive compensation for their cooperation. Blanca and José Vega stood in shock as they watched the man strut to his car and drive away.[57]

Blanca Vega closed the door and walked over to the window. As she placed her hands on the sill, the wood absorbed her history and her sadness. Vega's palms, which were thick and tough, told the story of a woman who labored as a cigar worker for over thirty years. She, however, was one of the lucky women—relatively well paid and skilled—who rose to the cigar makers' benches by the 1910s and remained there until she retired by the 1940s. Yet during those years, Vega did more than work; she built a life. To her, nothing represented that life more than her home. She remembered the day her husband José planted two sapling palms in the front yard. Over the years, those trees took root and grew as her family did. The walls of the couple's casita held the memories of the screams Blanca Vega released as she gave birth to three children in a bedroom—Nicio, Silvio, and Ligia—all of whom finished high school and went on to create a life beyond Ybor City. As a young woman, Vega spent her evenings on her wide front porch, within reach and earshot of her children, as she visited with other women and neighbors. By the time Vega was middle-aged, she stood on that same front porch when she said good-bye to her son Silvio, who shipped off to basic training and joined the U.S. Army Air Corps in 1942. Unlike some of the other families in the neighborhood, Blanca and José Vega knew they were fortunate, for they got to celebrate their son's return home from World War II by 1946. While many cigar-working families saw the Cuban cigar industry as a job filled with passion and care, in the Vega household it was a means to an end. Over the years Blanca and José Vega discussed politics in their living room and at the dining table as they moved between anarchist, socialist, and communist circles, but in recent years, their passions tempered along with the rest of the neighborhood. In retirement, Blanca Vega used her home as a production site for volunteerism. She crafted costumes for the local Spanish-language theater and donated items she sewed to the American Red Cross at the request of her daughter, who was a member of the organization. Blanca Vega loved the days her grandchildren came to her house so she could share with them the traditions she held dear and be sure the next generation knew what it meant to be from Ybor City, even if they never lived there.[58]

After some time, Blanca Vega backed away from the window, turned to her husband, and began to sob. "I can't, I can't, I can't," Vega cried as she gasped for air. In an attempt to calm herself down, Vega went into the bathroom, filled the tub, and slipped into the warm water. Following her bath, José Vega helped his wife out of the tub and then led her down the hall to their bedroom, where he tucked her "into the bed they'd honeymooned in," so she could rest. When Vega entered the bedroom to check on his wife sometime later, he realized she was no longer there. That afternoon, as Blanca Vega napped, she had a heart attack and passed away as a result of crippling sorrow. Following the death of his wife, José Vega turned his home over to the Urban Renewal Authority. "I didn't care about not selling the house anymore," he said. "Fifty years we lived there. I didn't care." By the end of 1966, the structure that was once the Vega home had disappeared and all that remained was an empty lot with two tall palm trees. The land on which Blanca and José Vega built a shared life remained barren until the city of Tampa extended the interstate exit ramp in the early 2000s.[59]

The story of urban renewal and Ybor City is one of deindustrialization, unfulfilled promises, and failed plans that resulted in the demolition of a place and the physical remaking of Ybor City. Ybor was always more than just cigars and capital—it was a place where people sought refuge, created political movements, organized against exploitative labor, and fought to be heard. Just as the bulldozers that leveled the Vega home ruptured the soul of a family, the destruction that urban renewal wrought—a process that spanned more three decades—disconnected Ybor City from the history that made this community.

While the wrecking balls and bulldozers did not arrive in Ybor City until the later 1950s, the effort to remake this community reaches back to the 1930s and 1940s. During the Great Depression, the Home Ownership Loan Corporation assessed the condition of Tampa real estate with funds from the federal government. The result of this initiative was a map and study that detailed the state of all neighborhoods within Hillsborough County. According to the report, Ybor City was among the areas of the county at risk for "blight." Therefore, assessors redlined this space and marked it as a potential priority for, what they called, slum clearance to make way for infrastructural expansion.[60]

Women and men in Ybor City were not ignorant of such developments. When Stetson Kennedy visited the Ybor Latina/o community on behalf of the Federal Writers' Project in 1939, he interviewed a woman named Amanda Pollato, who lived on Twelfth Avenue, down a "narrow dirt alley lined with unpainted framed shacks." As Pollato invited Kennedy into her home, she explained, "[The city] is planning to tear down a lot of these old 'shotgun' shacks." Indeed, she was right. The city of Tampa, which sought to take advantage of the Federal Housing Act, established the Tampa Housing Authority to gain access to federal monies and modernize the city through the vision of local politicians and city planners. The first priority for this group was the Scrub, a historically Black community that abutted Ybor City. The second priority, however, was Ybor itself. John Pacheco, an alderman from

Ybor City during the 1930s, recognized the link between Blackness and community destruction.[61] In 1936, he drafted a petition that stated the following:

To the Honorable Board of City Representatives.

Gentlemen: The undersigned Citizens, residents and tax payers of that portion of the City of Tampa, which bounds between Ninth Avenue and Columbus Drive do most sincerely petition your Honorable Body that some Act or Resolution be adopted by your body eliminating negroes living within this boundary.

We respectfully solicit the aid of authorities to stop the intermingling of negroes with the white population avoiding thus that our children, wives, and immediate families be embarrassed with such condition.

To avoid such a condition, we are certain that proper steps can be taken, as all of the negro tenants in this immediate surrounding are not property holders but tenants at will.

Thank you in advance for the relief that we are at this time asking of your body. Respectfully submitted.[62]

While Alderman Pacheco received only twenty signatures on his petition, it was the political act of submitting a document to Anglo leaders in a Jim Crow city, which requested that segregation be applied to Ybor, that was significant. Pacheco sought to protect his community by wrapping it in a shroud of whiteness as he declared the difference between Black and Latina/o residents in this space. Such an anti-Black action did not go unnoticed by the local chapter of the National Association for the Advancement of Colored People (NAACP). NAACP leaders wrote to Pacheco and urged that he recognize the shared struggle that Latina/o and Black women and men faced in Hillsborough County. This organization further suggested that the two communities work together rather than against each other. There is no record that indicates Pacheco responded to the NAACP or that he met with leaders of the organization. Instead, this action was part of a series of events that set the tone for the future of Black and Latina/o relationships in the coming decades. Black women and men, including some Black Cubans from Ybor and West Tampa, went on to organize and wage a local civil rights movement, while white Latinas/os worked to remake the image of themselves and gain access to Anglo political circles.[63]

During the 1950s, Ybor City encountered a new problem—the Cuban cigar industry was no longer the economic backbone of Tampa because Tampa was no longer a one-industry town. The city produced "ships and steel, cement and electrical equipment, and tin cans by the billons." It established an industrial park that "compris[ed] a thousand acres" and accommodated "multi-million dollar brewing plants, two of which [were] the largest in the world." Tampa emerged as the leader of phosphate and citrus production, for it "shipped seventy percent of the world's supply" and hosted "ninety percent of Florida citrus processing plants." Of the original 159 Cuban cigar factories, only twelve major enterprises remained and most produced cigars with machines. The average cigar worker was over the age of forty-five, spoke no English, and had a sixth-grade education, and nearly all were women. In order to obtain a handmade cigar, the product that led to the establishment of Ybor City and built the city of Tampa, a person had to visit an independently owned chinchal.[64]

The diminished power of the Cuban cigar industry meant that Ybor City was no longer the place where tampeñas/os lived, worked, and built community as they labored in a shared industry. Roland Manteiga, the son of Victoriano Manteiga and the next generation of *La Gaceta* leadership, detailed the state of Ybor City in a series of publications in 1955 titled "The Vanishing Latin Quarter." According to his reporting, "Ybor City [was] doomed to vanish within 10 to 15 years unless drastic steps [were] taken to prevent this . . . unavoidable fate." Manteiga understood that shifts in the local economy as well as the state of the community meant that "those who ha[d] been financially able" had left Ybor City and "only the poor remain[ed.]" He cited both the "migration of . . . the sons and daughters of the original cigar makers to other areas of the city" after and since World War II and the lack of investment and new construction in the area as primary causes for this condition. Despite this accusation, the journalist explained that he understood why tampeñas/os chose to live beyond the boundaries of the community: "The average home is some 50 years old . . . and the area is termite ridden. . . . To invest [one's] small savings by building a home in this infected area would be to buy something that cannot keep its value because of the surrounding devalued and dilapidated houses." Likewise, Manteiga followed in the footsteps of Alderman Pacheco and blamed Black women and men, who, from his perspective, bent to the will of exploitative landlords who did not care for the neighborhood or their properties, as a major cause of Ybor City's decline. This issue led to meetings with Anglo elected officials during which the young writer proposed removing Black families from Ybor, for, from his perspective, these residents were part of the problem with the neighborhood and were unworthy residents. By August 1955, the NAACP and the Tampa Urban League requested a meeting with Manteiga, to which he agreed. During this session the two entities sought to develop a plan that could preserve Ybor City and honor the humanity of the neighborhood's Black residents. Francisco Rodríguez Jr., the Afro-Cuban World War II veteran who attended Howard Law School and became leader of the Tampa NAACP, attended this event and told Manteiga: "You can't tell people to stand their ground and not pay exorbitant rents." Rodríguez reminded Manteiga of the reality of being Black and Cuban in Ybor, as he said: "I'm Latin[o] myself and have lived in both cultures, but don't tell me that a man with a wife and six children is going to stand out in the streets and refuse high rent when he has no other place to go. Pretty speeches are made to people when their mouths are full and they have a roof over their heads." The provisional agreement of the meeting was that the Ybor City Chamber of Commerce would encourage Tampa to adopt a plan that would build quality public housing and restore the old architecture of Ybor City.[65]

The meeting between Manteiga and the NAACP, and specifically the exchange between the newspaper editor and Rodríguez, illustrates how race within Ybor City influenced the way tampeñas/os interacted with broader Tampa and understood themselves as they moved beyond the old neighborhood. Manteiga, who was a white Cuban, centered his focus on the preservation and revitalization of the community that built a culture that was distinctly of Ybor City. To him, certain people belonged in this space—those with a specific history of migration—while African American women and men in Ybor City, in his eyes, did not. Manteiga, because of the space he occupied as one of the potentially acceptable, non-Black members of Ybor City, had the privilege of being able to walk into municipal government organizations, be seen as a community leader, and stand among those Latinas/os from Ybor who yielded considerable authority in Tampa. Rodríguez, in contrast, did not have the same experience and knew all too well the power of racism within, and beyond, Ybor City. As Rodríguez left the immigrant neighborhood and encountered the full extent of U.S. Jim Crowism, he understood how this system barred him from equal access to voting and citizenship rights, from the ability to purchase a home where he chose, from securing a fair and equal wage in Tampa-based industries, and from attending well-funded schools. Rodríguez had to fight even harder than Manteiga to exist in Tampa. While Afro-Cuban cultural connections endured in Tampa, political organizations such as the Democratic Party did not accept these women and men as readily as they did light-skinned Latinas/os from Ybor. Instead, Black Latinas/os increasingly fought for inclusion alongside African Americans through groups such as the NAACP and contributed to the creation of a local civil rights movement.[66]

One year after Manteiga published his exposé on the state of Ybor City, Nick Nuccio became the first tampeño mayor of Tampa. During Nuccio's tenure as leader of the city, he took seriously plans to remake Ybor in order to ensure its survival. The Latin Plaza plan reigned supreme while Nuccio was in office. This effort sought to transform twelve acres of Ybor City into a Latina/o version of New Orleans and refashion the industrial community into a portal that could transport visitors to old Spain and colonial Havana. While Manteiga maintained that any plan to revitalize Ybor City should respect its industrial, working-class heritage, the majority of business and tampeña/o community leaders supported turning Ybor into a tourist destination, thereby overlooking the needs of the neighborhood's Black residents as well as the historical integrity of the Ybor Latina/o community.[67]

Central to the appropriation of funds for the Latin Plaza plan was approval from the Tampa City Council. The Alcalde Program of Ybor City, an effort that began as a joke between men at a Rotary Club meeting, became a political lobbying group and Ybor booster organization. The women and men who held the position of *alcaldesa* and alcalde between 1955 and 1958 began an outreach initiative to gain support and interest in Ybor City culture. Such an effort included the creation of an Ybor City "Pledge of Affection" as well as a declaration that this place was not only a city within a city but a country within a country. One could apply for an Ybor City passport and even go through a naturalization process to become a member of the community if one was not born within it. The message was simple—Ybor City was for everyone and anyone could be tampeña/o, at least symbolically and for a price.[68]

Ybor business leaders, city boosters, as well as alcaldesas and alcaldes marketed a vision of latinidad they hoped the public would buy. To achieve such a goal, which required that the community overcome the long-standing stigma latinidad carried in this place, these groups collaborated as they designed advertisements and produced promotional videos that featured beautiful Latinas and suave Latinos. Unlike the kitschy, tobacco-clad outfits women wore in the 1930s and 1940s to encourage interest in the cigar industry, this new tactic embraced during the 1950s and 1960s sought to entice interest in tampeña/o culture as well as tampeñas/os themselves. Latinas in these advertisements and promotional films had light skin and jet-black, perfectly coiffed hair and wore dresses of the latest fashion. Men featured in these marketing efforts swooned over these women's exotic, yet American, beauty and longed for their attention. This version of Ybor City sought to remake the image of who tampeñas/os were in the eyes of Tampa Anglos and in the minds of those who controlled government funds. This version of latinidad disconnected the leftist, radical, working-class, immigrant foundation of the neighborhood from its cigars, food, pastimes, and music to cleanse Ybor of its "original sin" and transform the community's essence into something Tampa could sell and claim as theirs.[69]

While one could criticize this marketing technique as a tool employed by hopeful politicians and desperate community leaders whose actions diluted and cheapened the culture of Ybor City, it is important to remember that for many tampeñas/os of the second and third generations such images represented who they wanted to be and the type of power they wished to have. For example, when Marcelo Maseda stood before President John F. Kennedy as alcalde of Ybor City—dressed in a tuxedo complete with a top hat, accompanied by his daughter, Marlene, who donned a Spanish costume—he wanted to show the world, the nation, the city, and his daughter that he and his community belonged and that they were important as citizens as well as human beings. Maseda likely wished for his daughter to have opportunities he did not have as a child and to grow up in a place that did not discriminate against her for who Anglos perceived her to be because she was a tampeña. As this father and daughter duo stood together prepared to meet JFK in 1963, they did more than meet the president of the United States; they introduced the world to what it meant to be from Ybor City.[70]

Maseda does not stand alone in this effort. There are humbler and more common examples of such sincerity. Ligia Artal, the daughter of José and Blanca Vega, attended Hillsborough High School during the 1930s and participated in the women's basketball team as one of three non-Anglo women. Artal excelled in school, and her parents sent her to college, where she earned a degree in education and then got a job as a public school teacher, had children, and became a civic leader. Artal volunteered her time to the American Red Cross and later chartered the local chapter of the Pan American University Women's Club. This organization, which promoted middle-class values, stood in stark contrast to her father's membership in political societies such as Atorcha (the Light), a local anarchist organization led by the Spanish anarchist Pedro Esteve. Artal was proud of her achievements, as were her parents. Throughout Artal's life, she illustrated what many members of a new generation of tampeñas wished and believed themselves to be—accepted and acceptable. From her perspective, the leftist politics and activism of her parents' generation seemed to come at great risk, yield few benefits, and induce much violence and hatred. The women of Artal's generation wanted to live a different life regardless of whether or not the political choices that facilitated such paths were paved by concepts and paradigms with which their parents and grandparents' generation would have agreed.[71]

Despite the popularity of the Latin Plaza plan, and the labor done to promote the project, the proposal never came to fruition. In 1958, the Tampa City Council received notice that the cost of the project would far exceed the original $1.5 million estimate. According to the historian Brad Massey, roughly 3,000 people "signed a petition protesting" the decision of city leaders to divert funds into other initiatives. The Tampa City Council, however, refused to reverse its decision. Instead, the city used these funds to update Tampa's water treatment facilities and begin construction on Interstate 4—a city improvement project that called for the destruction of a portion of Ybor City and nearly all historically Black communities in Tampa.[72]

The 1960s ushered in a new decade and a new plan for Ybor City. While Ybor City's Cuban cigar industry had long been in decline, the 1962 embargo against trade with Cuba killed what was left of the industry. Without access to Cuban tobacco, the factories that remained in business could no longer claim to produce Cuban cigars. In response, many closed their doors. Protests and pleas from the remaining Ybor cigar workers did not change federal policy, and the last generation of Ybor cigar workers faded from the industry that put Tampa on the map. Local politicians attempted to negotiate with the federal government to find assistance for those who lost their livelihoods as a result of this policy. The answer, however, did not come in the form of work assistance but in the form of public housing and plans for community revitalization. In 1965, after three years of extensive research, the Tampa Urban Renewal Authority "outlined its 'idea to rehabilitate, clear and redevelop slum areas,'" which it claimed would allow the city to "preserve and strengthen the distinctive qualities of Tampa's Latin[a/o] heritage and present-day Latin[a/o] community." According to the analysis of Tampa Urban Renewal Authority officials, 92.9 percent of the dwellings that remained in Ybor were substandard. While some community members, such as the Vegas, were original owners who cared for their homes, the majority of the old casitas were in a state of disrepair and owned by exploitative landlords who overcharged for rent and refused to renovate their properties. The plan, however, did not leave space to discern between homes that should be condemned and homes that should be preserved. Instead, it called for the demolition of all structures between Seventh Avenue and Nebraska

Avenue as well as Seventh Avenue and the new Interstate 4. The Tampa Urban Renewal Authority office stated that it would build new, state-of-the-art public housing for residents who had been displaced and reserve five and a half acres to build a "Walled City," a Spanish-style tourist attraction featuring bloodless bullfights and "authentic fiesta entertainment" that would supposedly produce $20 million in profit a year. However, before the Tampa Urban Renewal Authority secured the funds to support this plan, it sent bulldozers into the neighborhood. While the houses came down and the land was cleared, nothing took its place. By the end of the decade, Ybor City "look[ed] much as it did when Mr. Ybor came here" in 1885.[73]

Ybor City laid barren for nearly three decades. Hillsborough County Community College became the largest landholder in this space, for Hillsborough County had neither the will nor the capital to invest in the preservation of Ybor and the memory of the people who built Tampa and the state of Florida. Yet as Ybor City remained in a state of traumatic isolation, what remained of the neighborhood provided shelter to those who needed it. Ybor became a place for artists in the 1970s and a haven for queer men by the 1980s. When the old tampeñas/os realized that neither the state nor the city was going to save their neighborhood, they mobilized to preserve what was left of Ybor City. Together they managed to stop the Tampa Urban Renewal Authority from leveling most mutual aid societies. The bulldozers, however, claimed one victim—La Sociedad de la Unión Martí-Maceo—which fell along with the casitas that its members once called home. The effort of tampeñas/os to prove that their history and their neighborhood mattered pushed the state of Florida to declare Ybor City a historic site and state park in the 1980s. The state appropriated enough money to purchase and relocate a casita, one of the few that had not been destroyed, and renovate this structure to resemble the original cigar worker housing, for tourists to visit. Likewise, the state invested funds into the renovation and conversion of the old Ferlita Bakery into a museum intended to tell the story of who the cigar workers of Tampa were. Yet if one were to take a tour of this museum that seeks to tell the tale of Florida's first sustained Latina/o community, the stories one would hear would be of contented immigrants who loved to work and embraced the American way, rather than the history of the building, the resisting, the surviving, and the remaking that defined who these people were and who they became.[74]

Finding

Norma Alfonso dressed her five-year-old daughter as Miss America for Halloween in 1963. Norma—who was a stay-at-home mom and a self-professed homemaker—designed, sewed, and crafted the costume herself. Completing the outfit with a homemade sash and a handcrafted crown, Norma took pride in her creation, and, this year, she wished to document the occasion. Although Norma and her husband Gus were on a tight budget, the couple decided to invest in a professional portrait to preserve the image of their daughter in this costume and the promise it represented. To these young parents, their child was their Miss America—a U.S.-born, native English speaker who lived beyond the borders of Ybor City and had the ability to grow up with all the advantages they never had. The hopeful couple in this story are my grandparents and the American child is my mother.

The life of my grandmother and the stories she told me inspired the history within this book. Born in Ybor City as Norma Blanco in 1931, my grandmother was a member of the forgotten and unsung third, U.S.-born generation. While it was her grandmother, Amelia Alvarez, and her aunt, Margot Falcón, who protested fascism and marched through the streets of Ybor City, it was Norma who had to find a way to navigate life as a Latina and Spanish-speaking child in the Jim Crow South as she crossed the border into Anglo Tampa as the Cuban cigar industry declined and the power of her community began to wane. The leftist politics and activism that her parents and grandparents understood as an avenue to achieve equal work, higher pay, and a more just world were the same actions that stigmatized children like herself as dangerous, foreign, and un-American. My grandmother—much like the women and men of the U.S.-born generations within the pages of this book—embraced a vision of herself, of her culture, and of Ybor City that obscured the legacy of leftist radicalism as central to her community in an effort to survive. While history teaches us to celebrate those who fought against oppression rather than those who accommodated its pressure, both processes are worth understanding and both are central to this story.

The women and men of Ybor City had the power and the might to resist the anti-immigrant, nativist forces that sought to control them, as long

Andrea Alfonso McNamara as Miss America on Halloween, 1963. Author's collection.

as the Cuban cigar industry remained vital to the local economy. During the late nineteenth century, it was the arrival of Cuban tobacco and the arrival of Cuban cigar workers that transformed Tampa from a scarcely populated Gulf coast town into the industrial center of the state of Florida. While Anglo politicians, business leaders, and members of the social elite condemned the threat these newcomers posed to the ruling white supremacist, Jim Crow order, they also understood that Tampa could not exist without them. Cuban cigar workers built this southern city and a culture that was distinctly of Ybor City—a sense of self that championed the experience of being working class, Spanish speaking, anti-imperialist, and part of a cross-border community with a Cuban foundation and a multiethnic, multiracial legacy. Leftist activists and intellectuals from around the world circulated through this space to recruit members to their cause as well as learn from the women and men of Ybor.

Cuban cigar work, however, was a particular kind of labor, for it required skill, Spanish-language proficiency, quality Cuban tobacco, and a consumer who was able and eager to pay for the luxury of a clear Havana smoker. As the economic consequences of the Great Depression encouraged the public to turn away from high-priced, handmade Cuban cigars and turn toward cheap, mass-produced cigarettes, Cuban cigar manufacturers in Ybor City either closed their doors or replaced the high-paid Latino cigar makers with low-paid Latina tabaqueras, and some introduced machine production. This shift pushed nearly 50 percent of the men in Ybor City into unemployment and made women, in many cases, the head of household and primary wage earner of their families. Yet with the weakening of the Cuban cigar industry came a rise in nativist reactionism and vigilante violence. As Latinas/os turned to leftist unions, the Communist Party, and the Socialist Party for support to gain access to equal employment and higher wages, they increasingly became the targets of white supremacist, anti-radical brutality at the hands of the Ku Klux Klan, the citizens' committee, and the Tampa Police Department. It was within this environment that Latinas rose as leaders and activists of the community. In the midst of the Jim Crow South, womanhood had the ability to navigate this Jim Crow city without the vicious and brutal consequences men faced as they challenged Anglo authority. The rise of the Popular Front and the fight for the Spanish Republic energized women and men in Ybor City not just because of their ethnicities and internationalist politics but because the fight against global fascism mirrored the struggle against, what they perceived to be, domestic fascist forces. As women marched through the streets in protest of Franco and the Falange, they likewise challenged the control of Anglo authority as they demanded that Anglo politicians and Anglo city leaders recognize the rights of Ybor Latinas/os as residents and citizens in this space.

While the women of Ybor City emerged as public community advocates and strategic political leaders, Tampa officials reacted to Latinas' perceived unwomanly acts as evidence that neither they nor their children were or could be "good and moral citizens." A stigma of latinidad emerged that vilified immigrant and first-generation Latinas as amoral wives, deficient caregivers, and foreign citizens to justify the exclusion of Latina/o families from wide-reaching access to New Deal programs and economic assistance during the Depression. However, as U.S.-born Latina/o children waded beyond the boundaries of Ybor City and crossed into Tampa to receive an education during the 1930s and 1940s, Latina mothers began to dream that their daughters and sons could have a future ungoverned by the Cuban cigar industry and the stereotypes that sought to control their lives. During this era, it was my grandmother's generation that learned new lessons of the forms marginalization and racism could take. Rather than receiving threats from groups such as the KKK and the citizens' committee, these children experienced ostracization from Anglo peers and exclusion from public spaces as they endured racial epithets and abuse from Anglo teachers who accosted them for speaking Spanish. Latina mothers reacted to such acts by writing to Tampa newspapers to make the case that neither their children's bilingualism nor their latinidad made them any less "American" and by lobbying the Hillsborough County School Board to outlaw corporal punishment and language-based discrimination. World War II and the years that followed offered new opportunities for young Latinas/os who longed for a different life. As young men received their draft notices and enlisted in the army, young women joined the war effort at home through volunteerism and community support. Together this generation demonstrated through service and action that they too were American and had a stake in the nation as ethnic Americans and as birthright citizens.

When Latinos returned home as veterans and the community woke up from its patriotic-induced fervor, Ybor City did not look the same. While Seventh Avenue, the heart of the community, still bustled with life, more than half of the cigar factories had closed and the old casitas looked weathered and aged. These young women and men, tampeñas/os of the U.S.-born generation, used money from the G.I. Bill to buy and build homes in the suburbs of Tampa. As this new generation moved out of the old neighborhood, they sought to build a different kind of life. Many enrolled in college and earned professional degrees, which gave them access to careers and a standard of living that exceeded their parents' wildest dreams. These young women and men used their new position in the community to enter politics and remake the image of what it meant to be Latina/o and from Ybor City. Many distanced themselves from the leftist politics that allowed their parents and grandparents to resist workplace exploitation and survive attempts by Anglo Tampa to control Latina/o authority through white supremacy and instead embraced a moderate, yet progressive, sense of self that allowed them to enter mainstream society. In the midst of urban renewal and the effort to find a future for the community, this new version of latinidad became central to community strategy. Latinas with light skin became beautiful yet exotic American women, while men emerged as handsome and swoon-worthy Latinos in marketing materials and promotional efforts that sought to build a bridge between this new Ybor City and Anglos in Tampa. Despite such work and the presentation of plans that illustrated why Ybor City was worth preserving, the bulldozers arrived and leveled the majority of the neighborhood. By the 1960s, the culture that people created in Ybor City became a form of latinidad that existed outside its original place.

Historians who examine Ybor City often speak as though the culture the people of this neighborhood created died as its leftist radicalism faded in the 1930s. The story of Ybor City, however, is not just the experience of building and resisting, it is also the history of surviving and remaking. It is a sense of self that reaches across generations and lives in the traditions that passed through families and the stories told at dinner tables. It is a culture that has a foundation in the experience of leftist, radical politics as well as one that illustrates a sense of endurance against great obstacles. Being tampeña/o, or of Ybor City, is a form of latinidad indigenous to this place and one that indeed lives. The story of the people who lived here and the work of the women who fought for its survival tells us much about what it means to be Latina/o in the U.S. South. While women and men on the West Coast and in the Northeast created civil rights movements that challenged the political order, those who lived here battled different political machines that caused them to adapt to their surroundings in different ways. This fact in no way makes their latinidad less worthy or authentic, but it does make it a product of a borderland where people vied for authority against the tide of shifting economies and violent reactionism. Not only did Ybor City and the women and men from this place find ways to endure, but they managed to pass along their culture and their sense of self to future generations. The history of Ybor City, the community that laid the foundation of what became Latina/o Florida, illustrates that the experience of being Latina/o in the U.S. South is neither new nor singular. It is, however, part of a regional and national story that encourages us to consider how people, places, and politics become who and what they are.

Acknowledgments

This book was a labor of love and a test of determination. I am forever thankful to those who believed in me, to those who supported the project, and to those who taught me how to question the places and people we hold most dear.

I am grateful to the vibrant intellectual community at the University of North Carolina at Chapel Hill that taught me how to study and write history. Jacquelyn Dowd Hall pushed me to be the best writer I can be and introduced me to the world of feminist history, as both a discipline and a community, which continues to guide my work and my life to this day. Zaragosa Vargas accepted me into the Carolina community as the first and only Latina/o studies student in the history department and dedicated himself to my work and professional success in a way few mentors would. Sarah Deutsch, although at Duke University, never failed to bridge the vast divide of 15-501 to provide support and kindness over coffee and a cookie. It was a privilege to learn from mentors who showed me that kindness and scholarship are not mutually exclusive. Katherine Turk provided incisive comments on early versions of this book and attended the workshops I participated in and the talks I gave during the years I spent writing and thinking about Ybor City. She never failed to send useful comments and edits after each event. I am grateful to Katherine Mellen Charon and Juliana Barr—both of whom are mentors and women's historians who became good friends—for their care, feedback, and guidance. Louise McReynolds and Don Raleigh provided encouragement throughout this process even though my work could not be more different than theirs.

Throughout my time in Chapel Hill my friends became my second family. I am especially grateful to call Liz Ellis my best friend—she is the person who has read more versions of this book than anyone else. I cannot imagine a better person to power walk through life with. Jessie Wilkerson provided an example of how to navigate academia and in the process became, and remains, one of my closest confidants. Yuri Ramírez, who was the only Latina/o history and Latin/o studies student at Duke University, is a dear friend. I am thankful for the connection we forged in the Triangle and maintain to this day. I am likewise grateful to the friendships of Jeanine Navarrete and Shannon Eaves, both of whom read portions of this book and provided comments, but most of all I appreciate their support and friendship. I thank Jaycie Vos for all she taught me about oral history digitalization and archiving. As I worked with old tape cassettes, I often thought about our time shared at the Love House and the connection we formed through oral history. I am grateful for the collegiality of Adam Domby who taught me how to use digital databases and took the time to provide comments on the first chapter of this book.

I benefited from the kindness of Latina/o history and Latina/o studies scholars across the nation, whose support made all the difference. I thank, first and foremost,

Vicki L. Ruiz, who provided instructional feedback on early versions of this work and who opened her personal archives to me. I am grateful for her intellectual generosity as well as her creation of a network of scholars committed to the ongoing missionary labor of writing and shaping Latina history. Perla Guerrero served as a source of encouragement throughout the writing process. I appreciate her feedback on writing, her foundational work on Latinas/os in the U.S. South, and, above all, her mentorship and friendship. Julio Capó pushed me to rethink organization and presentation. I thank him for his support of this project and for his enthusiasm for a reconsideration of Florida, our shared home state, and the place of Latinas/os within it. Max Krochmal provided essential feedback on my work through review, conversation, and context on the Southwest. He served as a sounding board as I worked through ideas that guided political evolution, and he provided essential feedback on my work through review, conversation, and context on the Southwest. Cecilia Márquez commented on portions of this manuscript and never failed to be a supportive reader. It has been a pleasure to blaze the trail of the next generation of Latina/o South scholarship with her. I thank the keen eyes of Katie Benton Cohen, Cindy Hahamovitch, Sarah Stanford-McIntyre, and the Carolina Working Group in Labor and Working-Class History, who commented on various versions of my introduction. I am grateful to, most notably, Nancy Hewitt, Gary Mormino, and Robert Ingalls, all of whom wrote books that guided my understanding of Ybor City's early years and shared their personal archives with me. I thank them for their generosity and their scholarship. I gained much from the studies of Nancy Raquel Mirabal, whose work on Afro-Cubans in Florida provided the groundwork for my understanding of race in the community and whose insistence to look "beyond the Miami monolith" provided inspiration and direction.

The completion of this research and writing would not have been possible without the work of the librarians and archivists who assisted me and the institutions that funded my work throughout the research and writing process. Jennifer Dietz of the Hillsborough County Division of Archives and Records and Andrew Huse of Special Collections at the University of South Florida were instrumental in my research process. Both directed me toward collections as new documents were processed and helped in any way possible during the years I trudged from archive to archive. I am likewise grateful to the research assistance of Sofia Paschero, graduate student at the University of South Florida, and to Tomaro Taylor, the university librarian at the University of South Florida, who moved mountains to digitize collections and documents needed to finish this book in the midst of the COVID-19 pandemic. Emanuel Leto, whom I met at the Tampa Bay History Center and later became a good friend, was instrumental in assisting me forge crucial community connections and in creating opportunities to share early iterations of this work and discuss its evolution as it reached its final formation. I thank the National Endowment for the Humanities, the American Association of University Women, the American Historical Association, the Institute for Citizens and Scholars at Princeton University, the Samuel Proctor Oral History Program at the University of Florida, the Center for the Study of the American South at the University of North Carolina at Chapel Hill, and the Tulane Center for the Gulf South. Each of these institutions provided funding necessary to conduct research at the Library of Congress and the National Archives in Washington, D.C.; the State of Florida Archives in Tallahassee; and the Hillsborough County Archives and the University of South Florida Special Collections in Tampa. They also provided me with the support needed to think and write.

I am grateful to the Department of History at Texas A&M University. Carlos Blanton believed in me and this project throughout its development—I thank him for his incessant encouragement. David Vaught, who led our department at the time of my hire, provided essential guidance. Although I appreciate all my colleagues, I am especially grateful to Cynthia Bouton for her support, April Hatfield for her kindness, Kate Unterman and Brian Rouleau for their friendship, and Sonia Hernández and Felipe Hinojosa for their mentorship. I am thankful for my students, whose engaged questions, excitement for history, and interest in the book-writing process pushed me to lead through example and write a book that they will want to read (or so I hope). I thank the College of Liberal Arts for its generous start-up package as well as the Glasscock Center for Humanities Research for its publication support grant. These funds were essential during the research and production process.

It was an honor to work with the University of North Carolina (UNC) Press. I thank my editor, Brandon Proia, for his undying advocacy of this book. It is difficult to imagine a more supportive editorial experience. I am grateful to Jessica Newman, who acquired this book for UNC Press and helped me work through its conceptualization and bring the project to completion. The design team at UNC Press created a book cover that I will treasure forever. I thank them for their vision and creativity.

To my oldest and dearest friends from Tampa—Karen Baker, Brooke Organ, and Shawna Matthys—I thank you all for supporting me through the writing process and being some of my loudest cheerleaders. I look forward to our next getaway and the years of friendship to come.

I owe the existence of this project to my family. Stephen Badalyan Riegg, my husband and best friend, loved me through this process and championed the project at every stage. I thank him for the pages he read, the paragraphs he listened to me recite, the meals he cooked, the house he cleaned, the laundry he washed, and the home office he assembled so I could write in peace. This book is, in part, for you and for us. I decided to write this book because of the memories my grandparents, Norma Alfonso and Gus Alfonso, shared with me. However, I persevered through the research and writing process because of my family's encouragement. My sister, Katie McNamara, was the best research assistant and writing partner I could hope to have. She supported me on at every stage of the project's development and never failed to come through as a last-minute document scanner or an urgent chapter reader. I thank her and her husband, Oswaldo Medina Ramírez, for all they did as this book evolved. My mom, Andi McNamara, stood by my side as I trudged through documents and claimed home-office space during research trips. She also culled through family photographs and artifacts, helped me to avoid parking tickets at the University of South Florida Library, and never failed to answer questions about her side of the family, which inspired new avenues of research. This book would not have been possible without her and the memories she shared with me.

Nobody was prouder of this book (or the fact that I became a professor) than my dad, Jim McNamara. If my dad was in line at the bank, at the bagel store, at Home

Depot, or at the local Cuban sandwich shop, he never failed to share who I am and what I do with an unsuspecting patron (and as far as he was concerned, a new friend). My dad was my biggest fan. As I entered the final stage of writing this book, he sent me a song a day to help me reach the finish line. I like to think this book has its own playlist as a result of his efforts. The sounds he selected from Stevie Wonder, the Beatles, Jessie Winchester, Steve Miller Band, Louis Armstrong, Gram Parsons, the Bellamy Brothers, Tom Petty, and so many others inspired me when I was most exhausted. While my dad passed away on September 9, 2022—a few months shy of this book's release—*Ybor City* came to fruition, in part, because of him. My dad was an artist and one of the most creative people I have ever met. It brings me joy that he lived to see the book's cover. As he said, "it's perfect." Thanks for all you did, Daddy-o.

Notes

Archival Abbreviations

CMIUC	Cigar Makers' International Union (CMIU) Collection, Special Collections, Hornbake Library, University of Maryland, College Park, Md.
CMOJ	*Cigar Makers' Official Journal*
CPUSAR	Records of the Communist Party USA, Library of Congress, Washington, D.C.
CSR	Center for Southwest Research, University Libraries, University of New Mexico, Albuquerque, N.Mex.
DOL	General Records of the Department of Labor, National Archives Annex, College Park, Md.
GMM	George Meany Memorial AFL-CIO Archive, Special Collections, Hornbake Library, University of Maryland, College Park, Md.
HMAMD	Historical Manuscripts, Archives and Manuscripts Department, University of Maryland Libraries, Hornbake Library, College Park, Md.
NARA	National Archives and Records Administration, College Park, Md.
SAF	State Archives of Florida, Tallahassee, Fla.
SCUSF	Special Collections, University of South Florida, Tampa, Fla.
SPOHP	Samuel Proctor Oral History Program, University of Florida, Gainesville, Fla.
TBHC	Tampa Bay History Center, Tampa, Fla.
TPC	Tony Pizzo Collection, Special Collections, University of South Florida, Tampa, Fla.

Introduction

1. Amelia was born in San Antonio de los Baños, Cuba, a rural town roughly fifteen miles from Havana. Louis A. Pérez Jr., *Cuba and the United States: Ties of Singular Intimacy*, 3rd ed. (Athens: University of Georgia Press, 2003); Louis A. Pérez Jr., "Incurring a Debt of Gratitude: 1898 and the Moral Sources of United States Hegemony in Cuba," *American Historical Review* 104, no. 2 (April 1999): 356–98. Note to readers: I use Spanish-language sources throughout this monograph. All translations, unless otherwise noted, are mine.

2. *Passenger Lists of Vessels Arriving at Key West, Florida, 1898-1945*, Records of the Immigration and Naturalization Service, 1787–2004, Record Group 85, NARA, accessed via Ancestry.com, *Florida, Passenger Lists, 1898-1963*. The SS *Olivette* was part of the Plant System of steamships and railroads; see "Map of the Plant System of Railway, Steamer and Steamship Lines and Connections," 1899, Touchton Map

Library Digital Archive, TBHC, Accession Number L2009.093.021, M Number M1529, accessed November 2020, http://luna.tampabayhistorycenter.org/luna/servlet/detail /TBHC~3~3~4606~4823: Map-of-the-Plant-System-of-Railway,?qvq=q:Plant;lc:TBH C~3~3&mi=30&trs=52.

3. For detailed information on the construction of the SS *Olivette* and information on cargo hold and capacity, see Irwin Schuster, "SS *Mascotte* of the Plant Line 1885–1931," *Nautical Research Journal* 61, no. 4 (December 2016): 246–48; Arsenio M. Sanchez, "The *Olivette* and *Mascotte* of the Plant Steamship Line," *Sunland Tribune* 20 (1994): 49–50.

4. Nancy A. Hewitt, *Southern Discomfort: Women's Activism in Tampa, Florida, 1880s–1920s* (Urbana: University of Illinois Press, 2001), 1. The term *cigar worker* refers to anyone who worked within the Cuban cigar industry, whereas *cigar maker* refers to someone who was a skilled cigar roller. The term in Spanish for cigar maker is *torcedor* but in Ybor City the most common colloquial term was, and is, *tabaquera/o*. In this book, I use tabaquera/o most frequently but torcedor is most precise. See Nicholas Foulkes, *Cigars: A Guide* (London: Penguin Random House, 2017), 146; Robert P. Ingalls and Louis A. Pérez Jr., *Tampa Cigar Workers: A Pictorial History* (Gainesville: University Press of Florida, 2003), 67.

5. Gary R. Mormino and George E. Pozzetta, *The Immigrant World of Ybor City: Italians and Their Latin Neighbors in Tampa, 1885–1985*, 2nd ed. (Gainesville: University Press of Florida, 1998), 43.

6. Between the late nineteenth and early twentieth centuries, the streetcar system was called the "street railway system," as it ran not on electricity but on coal or steam and embedded railway tracks. In 1907, a more formal and citywide system of streetcars emerged. However, because the distance between the Port of Tampa and Ybor City is six miles, it is likely that the Alvarez family took the railway car to Ybor City. For more, see Meeghan Kane, "Tampa's Trolleys: Innovation, Demise, and Rediscovery," *Sunland Tribune* 30 (2005): 31–43; *Passenger Lists of Vessels Arriving at Key West, Florida, 1898–1945*.

7. Louis A. Pérez Jr., "Cubans in Tampa: From Exiles to Immigrants, 1892–1901," *Florida Historical Quarterly* 57, no. 2 (1978): 129–40. Note: *Anglo* is the term used by Latinos in Tampa to describe people who are non-Latino, non-Black, native-born, and white.

8. While Cuba generally lacked legislation that codified the segregation of space based on race, outside of the slave codes, this does not mean that segregation on the basis of race was less real or that it did not take place. On how de facto practices of racial discrimination effectively and systematically segregated the urban landscape, see Bonnie A. Lucero, *A Cuban City, Segregated: Race and Urbanization in the Nineteenth Century* (Tuscaloosa: University of Alabama Press, 2019), especially 5–6.

9. Perla M. Guerrero, *Nuevo South: Latinas/os, Asians, and the Remaking of Place* (Austin: University of Texas Press, 2017).

10. Braulio Alonso Jr., *La Gaceta*, June 27, 1997; Federal Writers' Project, "Dominica Guinta, Interview" (unpublished manuscript, 1941), SCUSF; Sammy Argintar, interview with Yael V. Greenberg-Pritzker, March 29, 2000, quoted in Ingalls and Pérez, *Tampa Cigar Workers*, 152; see also Mormino and Pozzetta, *Immigrant World*;

Hewitt, *Southern Discomfort*; Susan D. Greenbaum, *More than Black: Afro-Cubans in Tampa* (Gainesville: University Press of Florida, 2002).

11. The history of the Cuban sandwich is hotly contested and debated. Cubans from Miami have a version of the sandwich (no salami), which some claim to be the original. Meanwhile Latinas/os from Ybor claim that the sandwich originated in Ybor City (with salami). New research from Andrew T. Huse, Bárbara C. Cruz, and Jeff Houck has documented the history of this sandwich and suggests that there was no singular or typified "Cuban sandwich" on the island, but instead there were many versions. However, the version of the sandwich I described in the text is what is recognized today as the Cuban sandwich in Ybor. For more, see Andrew T. Huse, Bárbara C. Cruz, and Jeff Houck, *The Cuban Sandwich: A History in Layers* (Gainesville: University Press of Florida, 2022). For a local perspective of this origin story, see "Our Family and Your Family: Where It All Begins," Restaurant Brochure, La Segunda Central Bakery, Ybor City, Florida, n.d.; "The Mayor's Hour—Tampa Traditions, La Segunda Bakery," May 4, 2017, City of Tampa, accessed September 2022, https://www.youtube.com/watch?v=M9_B9yWsR9c; Andrew T. Huse, "Welcome to Cuban Sandwich City," *Cigar City Magazine*, January–February 2006, https://issuu.com/cigarcity magazine/docs/jan_feb_2006/16. For assorted stories of Tampa food culture, see Andrew T. Huse, *From Saloons to Steak Houses: A History of Tampa* (Gainesville: University Press of Florida, 2020). Mojo is a marinade often used in Cuban cooking. In Tampa, it is made of sour orange juice, olive oil, garlic, salt, pepper, and oregano. This marinade breaks down meat and penetrates it with bright flavors.

12. Yael V. Greenberg-Pritzker, "The Princes of Seventh Avenue: Ybor City's Jewish Merchants," *Sunland Tribune* 28 (2002): 55–68; Huse, *From Saloons to Steak Houses*; Mormino and Pozzetta, *Immigrant World*. Note that over time Jewish and German immigrants were most likely to purchase cigar factories and move out of Ybor City as part of the merchant class and the middle class.

13. On Cuban dance and music traditions, see Ned Sublette, *Cuba and Its Music: From the First Drums to the Mambo* (Chicago: Chicago Review Press, 2004); Christina D. Abreu, *Rhythms of Race: Cuban Musicians and the Making of Latino New York City and Miami, 1940–1960* (Chapel Hill: University of North Carolina Press, 2015); see also Mormino and Pozzetta, *Immigrant World*; Hewitt, *Southern Discomfort*.

14. Greenbaum, *More than Black*; Nancy Raquel Mirabal, "De Aquí, de Allá: Race, Empire, and Nation in the Making of Cuban Migrant Communities in New York and Tampa, 1823–1924" (Ph.D. diss., University of Michigan, 2001); Frank Andre Guridy, *Forging Diaspora: Afro-Cubans and African Americans in a World of Empire and Jim Crow* (Chapel Hill: University of North Carolina Press, 2010). See also chapter 3, "Surviving," in this book.

15. Pedro Blanco and Amelia Alvarez, marriage license, Hillsborough County, Fla., 1907, Hillsborough County Marriage Records, Digital Collections, SCUSF, accessed June 2020, https://digital.lib.usf.edu/SFS0044124/00001?search=Blanco.

16. For a description of the neighborhood and the creation of women's communities, see Jose Yglesias, *The Truth about Them* (1971; repr., Houston, Tex.: Arte Público Press, 1999). Other *testimonios* by Yglesias that chronicle the neighborhood and provide historic texture of the community include Jose Yglesias, *A Wake in Ybor City*

(1963; repr., Houston, Tex.: Arte Público Press, 1998); Jose Yglesias, *Home Again* (1987; repr., Houston, Tex.: Arte Público Press, 2002). A testimonio is a first-person narrative that examines experiences of social and political inequality. At times, the author changes the names of main characters and fictionalizes certain aspects of personal experience to represent those of a broader community. This form of memory work is common in Latina/o and Latin American writing. Note: Jose Yglesias did not use accent marks in his name—the exclusion is intentional.

17. For more on the tradition of women and front porch discussions, see Yglesias, *The Truth about Them*; see also chapter 2, "Resisting," in this book. During the first ten years of Amelia's life in Ybor City, her neighbors were all Cuban women. See United States Census Office, *Thirteenth Census of the United States, 1910*.

18. Delia Blanco, Amelia's first daughter, did not survive. In the 1910 federal census, Amelia Alvarez noted that she had one child and zero living. Immigration documents reveal that she took Delia to Cuba when she was nine months old. See *Thirteenth Census of the United States, 1910*; Delia Blanco, February 7, 1910, Woodlawn Cemetery, Tampa, Fla., Ancestry.com, U.S., Find A Grave Index, 1600s–Current, accessed November 2020, www.findagrave.com/memorial/35241301/delia-blanco.

19. Amelia Blanco, December 17, 1952, Centro Español Memorial Cemetery, Tampa, Fla., Ancestry.com, U.S., Find A Grave Index, 1600s–Current, accessed November 2020, www.findagrave.com/memorial/57783120/amelia-blanco.

20. Amelia's grandson, Nelson Pino, remembers that when she passed away they found little bags of coins hidden throughout the house. These were pouches of her gambling money. Nelson Pino, discussion with the author, June 2020, field notes in the author's possession.

21. Gustavo Jesus (Gus) Alfonso, discussion with the author, June 20, 2020, field notes in the author's possession.

22. Sarah McNamara, "Borderland Unionism: Latina Activism in Ybor City and Tampa, Florida, 1935–1937," *Journal of American Ethnic History* 38, no. 4 (Summer 2019): 10–32; Hewitt, *Southern Discomfort*.

23. For more, see Ariel Mae Lambe, *No Barrier Can Contain It: Cuban Antifascism and the Spanish Civil War* (Chapel Hill: University of North Carolina Press, 2019); Ana Varela-Lago, "¡No Pasarán! The Spanish Civil War's Impact on Tampa's Latin Community, 1936–1939," *Tampa Bay History* 19, no. 2 (1997): 5–35; Ana Varela-Lago, "'We Had to Help': Remembering Tampa's Response to the Spanish Civil War," *Tampa Bay History* 19, no. 2 (1997): 36–56; Ana Varela-Lago, "Conquerors, Immigrants, Exiles: The Spanish Diaspora in the United States" (Ph.D. diss., University of California, Santa Barbara, 2008).

24. Sarah Milov, *The Cigarette: A Political History* (Cambridge, Mass.: Harvard University Press, 2019). For a description of El Príncipe de Gales cigars, the main brand of the Martínez Ybor factory, see Manuel González, "Jubilee Years of El Príncipe de Gales: Romantic History of the World-Famous 'El Príncipe de Gales' Brand of Havana Cigars," *Theater Magazine* 6, no. 65 (July 1906): 280a.; see also chapter 1, "Building," in this book.

25. United States Census Office, *Fourteenth Census of the United States, 1920*; United States Census Office, *Fifteenth Census of the United States, 1930*; United States Census

Office, *Sixteenth Census of the United States, 1940; Tampa City Directory*, 1931–39, TBHC *Clear Havana* is the term used to describe a cigar made purely of Cuban tobacco. See chapter 1, "Building," in this book.

26. For more on Latinas/os and the public school system in the U.S. South and the effect this had on race, see Carlos Kevin Blanton, *George I. Sánchez: The Long Fight for Mexican American Integration* (New Haven, Conn.: Yale University Press, 2015); Carlos Kevin Blanton, "George I. Sánchez, Ideology, and Whiteness in the Making of the Mexican American Civil Rights Movement, 1930–1960," *Journal of Southern History* 72, no. 3 (August 2006): 569–604; Carlos Kevin Blanton, *The Strange Career of Bilingual Education in Texas, 1836–1981* (College Station: Texas A&M University Press, 2004).

27. For examples, see Max Krochmal and Todd Moye, eds., *Civil Rights in Black and Brown: Histories of Resistance and Struggle in Texas* (Austin: University of Texas Press, 2021); Allyson P. Brantley, *Brewing a Boycott: How a Grassroots Coalition Fought Coors and Remade American Consumer Activism* (Chapel Hill: University of North Carolina Press, 2021); Johanna Fernández, *The Young Lords: A Radical History* (Chapel Hill: University of North Carolina Press, 2020); Dionne Espinoza, María Eugenia Cotera, and Maylei Blackwell, eds., *Chicana Movidas: New Narratives of Activism and Feminism in the Movement Era* (Austin: University of Texas Press, 2018); Juan Gómez-Quiñones and Irene Vásquez, *Making Aztlán: Ideology and Culture of the Chicana and Chicano Movement, 1966–1977* (Albuquerque: University of New Mexico Press, 2014); Lauren Araiza, *To March for Others: The Black Freedom Struggle and the United Farm Workers* (Philadelphia: University of Pennsylvania Press, 2013); Judy Tzu-Chun Wu, *Radicals on the Road: Internationalism, Orientalism, and Feminism during the Vietnam Era* (Ithaca, N.Y.: Cornell University Press, 2013); Gordon K. Mantler, *Power to the Poor: Black-Brown Coalition and the Fight for Economic Justice, 1960–1974* (Chapel Hill: University of North Carolina Press, 2013); Brian D. Behnken, *Fighting Their Own Battles: Mexican Americans, African Americans, and the Struggle for Civil Rights in Texas* (Chapel Hill: University of North Carolina Press, 2011); Maylei Blackwell, *Chicana Power! Contested Histories of Feminism in the Chicano Movement* (Austin: University of Texas Press, 2011); Jason M. Ferreira, "'With the Soul of a Human Rainbow': Los Siete, Black Panthers, and Third Worldism in San Francisco," in *Ten Years That Shook the City: San Francisco 1968–1978*, ed. Chris Carlsson with Lisa Ruth Elliot (San Francisco: City Lights Foundation Books, 2011), 30–47; Gaye Theresa Johnson, "Constellations of Struggle: Luisa Moreno, Charlotta Bass, and the Legacy for Ethnic Studies," *Aztlán* 33, no. 1 (2008): 155–72; Laura Pulido, *Black, Brown, Yellow, and Left Radical Activism in Southern California* (Berkeley: University of California Press, 2006).

28. For examples, see Paul Ortiz, *An African American and Latinx History of the United States* (Boston: Beacon Press, 2018); Max Krochmal, *Blue Texas: The Making of a Multiracial Democratic Coalition in the Civil Rights Era* (Chapel Hill: University of North Carolina Press, 2016); Alan Eladio Gómez, *The Revolutionary Imaginations of Greater Mexico: Chicana/o Radicalism, Solidarity Politics, and Latin American Social Movements* (Austin: University of Texas Press, 2016); Jeffrey O. G. Ogbar, *Black Power: Radical Politics and African American Identity* (Baltimore: Johns Hopkins University Press, 2005); Victor M. Rodriguez, "Boricuas, African Americans, and Chicanos in

the 'Far West': Notes on Puerto Rican Pro-Independence Movements in California, 1960s–1980s," in *Latino Social Movements: Historical and Theoretical Perspectives*, ed. Rodolfo D. Torres and George Katsiaficas (New York: Routledge, 1999), 79–109; Marisela R. Chavez, "'We Lived and Breathed and Worked the Movement': The Contradictions and Rewards of Chicana/Mexicana Activism in el Centro de Acción Social Autónomo-Hermandad General de Trabajadores (CASA-HGT), Los Angeles, 1975–1978," in *Las Obreras: Chicana Politics of Work and Family*, ed. Vicki L. Ruiz (Los Angeles: UCLA Chicano Studies Research Center Publications, 2000), 83–105. I thank the historian Eddie Bonilla for his discussion on this topic.

29. Natalia Molina, "The Power of Racial Scripts: What the History of Mexican Immigration to the United States Teaches Us about Relational Notions of Race," in "Race and Blackness in the Latino/a Community," special issue, *Latino Studies* 8, no. 2 (2010): 157; see also Natalia Molina, *How Race Is Made in America: Immigration, Citizenship, and the Historical Power of Racial Scripts* (Berkeley: University of California Press, 2014); Guerrero, *Nuevo South*, 13; Benedict Anderson, *Imagined Communities: Reflections on the Origin and Spread of Nationalism* (London: Verso, 1983).

30. Mormino and Pozzetta, *Immigrant World*; Robert Kerstein, *Politics and Growth in Twentieth-Century Tampa* (Gainesville: University Press of Florida, 2001); Huse, *From Saloons to Steak Houses*.

31. It was in 1937 that Amelia was noted as Spanish by an immigration official.

32. There is an ample historiography on the topic of white Latina/o exclusion from de jure forms of segregation. For a prime example of such work that engages this topic, see Neil Foley, *The White Scourge: Mexicans, Blacks, and Poor Whites in Texas Cotton Culture* (Berkeley: University of California Press, 1999).

33. Cesar Marcos Medina, interview with Gary R. Mormino, 1977, SPOHP; Phillip Spoto, interview with Gary R. Mormino, 1977, Oral History Program, SCUSF; Mormino and Pozzetta, *Immigrant World*, 239.

34. Robert P. Ingalls, *Urban Vigilantes in the New South: Tampa, 1882–1936* (Knoxville: University of Tennessee Press, 1988); Yglesias, *The Truth about Them*. See also Monica Muñoz Martínez, *The Injustice Never Leaves You: Anti-Mexican Violence in Texas* (Cambridge, Mass.: Harvard University Press, 2018).

35. The Fernandez family and the owners of Naviera Coffee Mill, interview and discussion with the author, May 2010, interview and field notes in the author's possession. For examples of expert discussions on the different experiences of Cuban diasporas and their cultures in the United States, see Ricardo L. Ortíz, *Cultural Erotics in Cuban America* (Minneapolis: University of Minnesota Press, 2007), 1–42; Nancy Raquel Mirabal, "'Ser de Aquí': Beyond the Cuban Exile Model," *Latino Studies* 1, no. 3 (November 2003): 366–82.

36. Mirabal, "'Ser de Aquí'"; María Cristina García, *Havana USA: Cuban Exiles and Cuban Americans in South Florida, 1959–1994* (Berkeley: University of California Press, 1996); Frank S. DeBenedictis, "The Cold War Comes to Ybor City: Tampa Bay's Chapter of the Fair Play for Cuba Committee" (master's thesis, Florida Atlantic University, 2002); United States Census Office, *Twenty-Fourth Census of the United States*, 2020, accessed May 2022, www.census.gov/quickfacts/fact/table/hillsboroughcountyflorida/PST120221. This book, *Ybor City*, is not a history of Miami, and therefore Miami is

not the central focus of this study. There are, however, other scholars who have studied the city and have forthcoming work about Miami. The politics of Latinas/os of Cuban descent in Miami is not as simple as the national conservative stereotype, and research has shown that this has not been the case since at least the mid-1990s. Additionally, it is essential to note that there have been four migrant waves of Cubans to Florida since the 1870s—each of these has a distinct history. For a sample of such work, see Julio Capó Jr., "Queering Mariel: Mediating Cold War Foreign Policy and U.S. Citizenship among Cuba's Homosexual Exile Community, 1978–1994," *Journal of American Ethnic History* 29, no. 4 (Summer 2010): 78–106; Alejandro Portes and Alex Stepick, *City on the Edge: Transformation of Miami* (Berkeley: University of California Press, 1993); Silvia Pedraza, "Cubans in Exile, 1959–1989: The State of the Research," in *Cuban Studies since the Revolution*, ed. Damián Fernández (Gainesville: University Press of Florida, 1992), 235–57; Silvia Pedraza, *Political and Economic Migrants in America: Cubans and Mexicans* (Austin: University of Texas Press, 1985). There is exciting new work on Miami from Jeanine Navarrete, "'Cubans Vote Cuban': Local Politics and Latino Identity in Miami" (Ph.D. diss., University of North Carolina at Chapel Hill, 2016, book in progress); Mauricio Castro, "Casablanca of the Caribbean: Cuban Refugees, Local Power, and Cold War Policy in Miami, 1959–1995" (Ph.D. diss., Purdue University, 2015, book in progress); Alexander Stephen, "Excludable: Cubans, Migration, and Carceral States" (Ph.D. diss., University of Michigan, anticipated completion 2025).

37. *La Traducción* and *La Gaceta* are the community newspapers that have survived and serve as the best examples, and such terminology is prevalent in each. There were many other Spanish-language community newspapers; however, most were damaged, and few have complete collections available today. For examples of Anglo terminology toward people from Ybor, see the *Tampa Morning Tribune* and the *Tampa Times* between 1885 and 1980. Some members of the Ybor City community, including writers, used *Latino* at times in later years as the term fell into use more popularly. See Jose Yglesias, "The Radical Latino Island in the Deep South," *Nuestro* 1 (August 1977): 71–74.

38. Peter Parrado, interview with the author, October 2012. Considering Florida as a place with Latina/o history relevant to regional and national trends presents much opportunity to expand and enrich the history of the United States. Much like Florida, Texas often receives similar exclusionary treatment when it comes to consideration of its historical importance to the South and the nation. This study encourages scholars to see such locations not as different cases but as places where concepts of race that later governed other southern states first emerged. For examples of those who note Florida and Texas as exceptional, see Julie M. Weise, *Corazón de Dixie: Mexicanos in the U.S. South since 1910* (Chapel Hill: University of North Carolina Press, 2015); Mary E. Odem and Elaine Lacy, eds., *Latino Immigration and the Transformation of the U.S. South* (Athens: University of Georgia Press, 2009). For examples of broader, inclusive geographies, see Sarah McNamara, "A Not-So Nuevo Past: Latina Histories in the U.S. South," *Labor: Studies in Working-Class History* 16, no. 3 (September 2019): 73–78; Julio Capó Jr., *Welcome to Fairyland: Queer Miami before 1940* (Chapel Hill: University of North Carolina Press, 2017); Sofia Enríquez, "Canciones de

los Apalaches: Latinx Music, Migration, and Belonging in Appalachia" (Ph.D. diss., Ohio State University, 2021). An example of new Latina/o history on Florida that pushes scholars to rethink migration patterns and interlinked Latina/o experiences in cases of non-Cuban migration in Florida is Terrell Orr, "'Now We Work Just as One': The United Farm Workers in Florida Citrus, 1972–1977," *Southern Cultures* 25 (Spring 2019): 140–57.

39. The work of Jean M. O'Brien inspired the organizational structure of this book, as well as its intention to be accessible to a broad audience. I thank her for her keen example of how to present complex scholarship in a form that encourages engagement from all. Jean M. O'Brien, *Firsting and Lasting: Writing Indians out of Existence in New England* (Minneapolis: University of Minnesota Press, 2010).

Chapter One

Epigraph from Federal Writers' Project (hereafter cited as FWP), "Life History of Enrique Pendas" (unpublished manuscript, 1936), SCUSF. For more on recent Indigenous histories of Florida, see "Indigenous Florida," special issue, *Florida Historical Quarterly* 100, no. 1 (Summer 2021). I thank Denise I. Bossy and Andrew K. Frank, the guest editors of this issue of the journal, for their work to encourage scholars of Florida to rethink the long history of the peninsula. Their effort, as well as the works of scholars in this issue, including Aubrey Lauersdorf, Jason Herbet, James Hill, and Kristalyn Marie Shefveland, pushed me to rethink the broader narrative of the state as I sought to place the history of Latinas/os within it.

1. Nancy A. Hewitt, *Southern Discomfort: Women's Activism in Tampa, Florida, 1880s–1920s* (Urbana: University of Illinois Press, 2001); Gary R. Mormino and George E. Pozzetta, *The Immigrant World of Ybor City: Italians and Their Latin Neighbors in Tampa, 1885–1985*, 2nd ed. (Gainesville: University Press of Florida, 1998); Susan D. Greenbaum, *More than Black: Afro-Cubans in Tampa* (Gainesville: University Press of Florida, 2002); Michael Gannon, ed., *The History of Florida* (Gainesville: University Press of Florida, 1996).

2. *Tampa Morning Tribune*, September 4, 1899. There is no written record or report of this event in any surviving Spanish-language newspapers from Ybor City or Tampa. Of the newspapers that survive, most are incomplete clippings within the Tony Pizzo Collection housed in SCUSF. For a different perspective on this event, see Hewitt, *Southern Discomfort*, 98–101.

3. Quotation in Kirk Monroe, "Gulf Coast City," *Christian Union*, January 19, 1982; also in Mormino and Pozzetta, *Immigrant World*, 45. See also Hewitt, *Southern Discomfort*; Mormino and Pozzetta, *Immigrant World*; Greenbaum, *More than Black*; Louis A. Pérez Jr., "Cubans in Tampa: From Exiles to Immigrants, 1892–1901," *Florida Historical Quarterly* 57, no. 2 (1978): 129–40; Gerald E. Poyo, "Tampa Cigarworkers and the Struggle for Cuban Independence," *Tampa Bay History* 7, no. 2 (1985): 94–105; Louis A. Pérez Jr., "Vagrants, Beggars, and Bandits: Social Origins of Cuban Separatism, 1878–1895," *American Historical Review* 90, no. 5 (1985): 1092–121.

4. Robert P. Ingalls, *Urban Vigilantes in the New South: Tampa, 1882–1936* (Knoxville: University of Tennessee Press, 1988), 24; Donald Brenham McKay, *Pioneer Florida* (Tampa, Fla.: Southern Publishing Company, 1952), vol. 2, located in SCUSF.

5. *Tampa Morning Tribune*, September 4, 1899. Note on terminology: There is a difference between cigar maker and cigar worker. A cigar worker is anyone who labors in the Cuban cigar industry, while a cigar maker is the specific job of making a cigar. The latter are often referred to as tabaqueras/os or a *torecedor*. Everyone in the industry was a cigar worker, but only those who rolled the cigars were cigar makers. This confusion of terminology was often made by the Anglo press, and the adjustment to the quotation reflects the above distinction.

6. For more on whiteness among Latinas/os in the U.S. South, see Neil Foley, *The White Scourge: Mexicans, Blacks, and Poor Whites in Texas Cotton Culture* (Berkeley: University of California Press, 1999); Perla M. Guerrero, *Nuevo South: Latinas/os, Asians, and the Remaking of Place* (Austin: University of Texas Press, 2017); Perla M. Guerrero, "Chicana/o History as Southern History: Race, Place and the US South," in *A Promising Problem: The New Chicana/o History*, ed. Carlos Kevin Blanton (Austin: University of Texas Press, 2016), 83–110; Cecilia Márquez, *Making the Latino South: A History of Racial Formation* (Chapel Hill: University of North Carolina Press, 2023); Julie M. Weise, *Corazón de Dixie: Mexicanos in the U.S. South since 1910* (Chapel Hill: University of North Carolina Press, 2015). See also Carlos Kevin Blanton, "George I. Sánchez, Ideology, and Whiteness in the Making of the Mexican American Civil Rights Movement, 1930–1960," *Journal of Southern History* 72, no. 3 (August 2006): 569–604; David R. Roediger, *The Wages of Whiteness: Race and the Making of the American Working Class* (New York: Verso, 1991).

7. Brian DeLay, ed., *North American Borderlands* (New York: Routledge, 2013), 9.

8. See Pekka Hämäläinen and Samuel Truett, "On Borderlands," *Journal of American History* 98, no. 2 (September 2011): 338–61; DeLay, *North American Borderlands*; Jeremy Adelman and Stephen Aron, "From Borderlands to Borders: Empires, Nation-States, and the Peoples in between in North American History," *American Historical Review* 104, no. 3 (June 1999): 814–41; Benjamin H. Johnson and Andrew Graybill, "Introduction: Borders and Their Historians in North America," in *Bridging National Borders in North America: Transnational and Comparative Histories*, ed. Benjamin H. Johnson and Andrew Graybill (Durham, N.C.: Duke University Press, 2010), 1–30; Bathsheba Demuth, "Labors of Love: People, Dogs, and Affect in North American Arctic Borderlands, 1700–1900," *Journal of American History* 108, no. 2 (September 2021): 270–95.

9. Alejandra Dubcovsky and George Aaron Broadwell, "Writing Timucua: Recovering and Interrogating Indigenous Authorship," *Early American Studies* 15, no. 3 (Summer 2017): 409–41; Alejandra Dubcovsky, *Informed Power: Communication in the Early American South* (Cambridge, Mass.: Harvard University Press, 2016); Denise I. Bossy and Andrew K. Frank, "Charting a Path toward an Indigenous History of Florida," *Florida Historical Quarterly* 100, no. 1 (Summer 2021): 1–22.

In the matter of Florida history, there is much work to be done. Assembling a general narrative that reaches from the sixteenth century to the present is a historiographic challenge. To date, there is no synthetic monograph on the state written by a scholar and drawn from peer-reviewed secondary works and primary sources. The most comprehensive study that meets such qualifications is Gannon's *The History of Florida*. I thank Michael Gannon for his work assembling and publishing this volume—his memory lives on through his independent work and this volume. I also thank the volume's authors, who together achieved what no scholar has done independently. Their essays in this volume, as well as their historiographic direction, were pivotal to my synthetic understanding of this history, specifically the pieces by Jerald T. Milanich, Paul E. Hoffman, Eugene Lyon, Amy Turner Bushnell, John H. Hann, Daniel L. Schafer, William S. Corker, Robin F. A. Fabel, Susan Richbourg Parker, Jane Landers, Brent R. Weisman, Robert A. Taylor, Jerrell H. Shofner, and Thomas Graham.

10. Dubcovsky and Bradwell, "Writing Timucua," 415; see also John E. Worth, *The Timucuan Chiefdoms of Spanish Florida*, vol. 2, *Resistance and Destruction* (Gainesville: University Press of Florida, 1998).

11. For territorial understanding of French Florida, see Woodbury Lowery, *The Spanish Settlements within the Present Limits of the United States: Florida* (New York: G. P. Putnam's Son, 1911), 34; for digital access, see "Exploring Florida," Florida Center for Instructional Technology, University of South Florida, accessed May 2022, http://fcit.usf.edu/florida/maps/pages/2000/f2077/f2077.htm.

12. Dubcovsky and Bradwell, "Writing Timucua," 416. See also Gonzalo Solís de Merás, *Pedro Menéndez de Avilés and the Conquest of New Florida: A New Manuscript*, ed. and trans. David Abresú (Gainesville: University Press of Florida, 2017); René Goulaine de Laudonnière, *Three Voyages*, ed. and trans. Charles E. Bennett (Gainesville: University Press of Florida, 1975); Jonathan DeCoster, "Entangled Borderlands: Europeans and Timucuans in Sixteenth-Century Florida," *Florida Historical Quarterly* 91, no. 3 (2013): 375–400.

13. For more on Native Florida, see Bossy and Frank, "Charting a Path."

14. Quotation in Dubcovsky and Bradwell, "Writing Timucua," 416; Bossy and Frank, "Charting a Path."

15. Amy Turner Bushnell, "Republic of Spaniards, Republic of Indians," in Gannon, *The History of Florida*, 78.

16. For more on Indigenous power in Florida, see Alejandra Dubcovsky, "Defying Indian Slavery: Apalachee Voices and Spanish Sources in the Eighteenth-Century Southeast," *William and Mary Quarterly* 75, no. 2 (April 2018): 295–322; Dubcovsky, *Informed Power*; Bossy and Frank, "Charting a Path"; Jane Landers, "The Geopolitics of Seventeenth-Century Florida," *Florida Historical Quarterly* 92, no. 3 (Winter 2014): 480–90; Sherry Johnson, "The Historiography of Eighteenth-Century Florida," *Florida Historical Quarterly* 93, no. 3 (Winter 2015): 296–326. For a comprehensive list of all missions in Spanish Florida, see John H. Hann, "The Missions of Spanish Florida," in Gannon, *The History of Florida*, 103–4. For more on Florida missions, see John H. Hann, *A History of the Timucua Indians and Missions* (Gainesville: University Press of Florida, 1996); Mark F. Boyd, Hale G. Smith, and John W. Griffin, *Here They Once Stood: The Tragic End of the Apalachee Missions* (Gainesville: University Press of Florida, 1983).

17. Eugene Lyon, "Settlement and Survival," in Gannon, *The History of Florida*, 55–75; Ida Altman, *Emigrants and Society: Extremadura and Spanish America in the*

Sixteenth Century (Berkeley: University of California Press, 1989); Paul E. Hoffman, "The Land They Found," in Gannon, *The History of Florida*, 41–54.

18. For more on early Native histories of Florida, see Jerald T. Milanich, "Original Inhabitant," in Gannon, *The History of Florida*, 3–17; Bushnell, "Republic of Spaniards, Republic of Indians"; Jerald T. Milanich, *Florida Indians and the Invasion from Europe* (Gainesville: University Press of Florida, 1995); Jerald T. Milanich, *Archaeology of Precolumbian Florida* (Gainesville: University Press of Florida, 1994); Randolph J. Widmer, *The Evolution of the Calusa: A Nonagricultural Chiefdom on the Southwest Florida Coast* (Tuscaloosa: University of Alabama Press, 1988).

19. Daniel L. Schafer, "Raids, Sieges, and International Wars," in Gannon, *The History of Florida*, 112–27.

20. For more on the history of slavery in Florida before statehood, see Edward E. Baptist, *Creating an Old South: Middle Florida's Plantation Frontier before the Civil War* (Chapel Hill: University of North Carolina Press, 2003).

21. Michael Gannon, "First European Contacts," in Gannon, *The History of Florida*, 38. See also Schafer, "Raids, Sieges, and International Wars"; Jane Landers, "Free and Enslaved," in Gannon, *The History of Florida*, 179–94.

22. "Treaty of Amity, Settlement, and Limits between the United States of America and His Catholic Majesty. 1819," in *The Federal and State Constitutions, Colonial Charters, and Other Organic Laws of the States, Territories, and Colonies Now or Heretofore Forming the United States of America, Compiled and Edited under the Act of Congress of June 30, 1906*, ed. Francis Newton Thorpe (Washington, D.C.: Government Printing Office, 1909), n.p.; also available through "Treaty of Amity, Settlement, and Limits between the United States of America and His Catholic Majesty. 1819," Avalon Project—Documents in Law, History and Diplomacy, Lillian Goldman Law Library, Yale Law School, accessed May 2022, https://avalon.law.yale.edu/19th_century/sp1819 .asp.

23. Susan Richbourg Parker and William S. Corker, "The Second Spanish Period," in Gannon, *The History of Florida*, 176.

24. Vicki L. Ruiz, "Nuestra América: Latino History as United States History," *Journal of American History* 93, no. 3 (December 2006): 656.

25. Ruiz, "Nuestra América."

26. Ruiz, "Nuestra América." For more, see Andrés Reséndez, *Changing National Identities at the Frontier: Texas and New Mexico, 1800–1850* (New York: Cambridge University Press, 2005); Raúl A. Ramos, *Beyond the Alamo: Forging Mexican Ethnicity in San Antonio, 1821–1861* (Chapel Hill: University of North Carolina Press, 2008); Arnaldo de León, *They Called Them Greasers: Anglo Attitudes toward Mexicans in Texas* (Austin: University of Texas Press, 2002); Lisbeth Haas, *Conquests and Historical Identities in California, 1769–1936* (Berkeley: University of California Press, 1995); Leonard Pitt, *The Decline of the Californios: A Social History of Spanish-Speaking Californians* (Berkeley: University of California Press, 1966); Antonia I. Castañeda, *Three Decades of Engendering History: The Selected Works of Antonia I. Castañeda*, ed. Linda Heidenreich with Antonia I. Castañeda (Denton: University of North Texas Press, 2014); Juliana Barr, *Peace Came in the Form of a Woman: Indians and Spaniards in the Texas Borderlands* (Chapel Hill: University of North Carolina Press, 2007); David Weber, *The Spanish Frontier*

in North America (New Haven, Conn.: Yale University Press, 2009); Ramón A. Gutiérrez, *When Jesus Came, the Corn Mothers Went Away: Marriage, Sexuality, and Power in New Mexico, 1500–1846* (Stanford, Calif.: Stanford University Press, 1991); Sarah Deutsch, *No Separate Refuge: Culture, Class, and Gender on an Anglo-Hispanic Frontier in the American Southwest, 1880–1940* (New York: Oxford University Press, 1987).

27. Quoted in Schafer, "Raids, Sieges, and International Wars," 112. See also Amy Turner Bushnell, *The King's Coffer: Proprietors of the Spanish Florida Treasury, 1565–1702* (Gainesville: University of Florida Press, 1981).

28. Parker and Corker, "The Second Spanish Period," 176.

29. Parker and Corker, "The Second Spanish Period," 176.

30. In the Adams-Onís Treaty, there were promises that the United States would recognize the rights of Spanish landholders to maintain lands they had been granted. As in the case of California and Texas, these land grants were difficult to track, as U.S. systems of land ownership differed from those of the Spanish. At times, people were dispossessed of the lands they owned, but more often they sold at a low price or the lands did not pass on generationally.

31. Parker and Corker, "The Second Spanish Period," 175.

32. The United States Congress passed legislation that protected the rights of white enslavers to maintain and regain the persons they enslaved in the event that they ran away. The use of the term *fugitive* implies criminality on the part of the enslaved person. Laws that gave white enslavers the right to recover the people they believed they owned are embedded in the U.S. Constitution, the Fugitive Slave Act of 1793, and the Fugitive Slave Act of 1850. See Article IV, Section 2, Clause 3, U.S. Constitution, 1783; Fugitive Slave Act of 1793, United States Congress, 1793; Fugitive Slave Act of 1850, United States Congress, 1850. For more scholarly work on this topic, see also Kathleen M. Brown, *Good Wives, Nasty Wenches, and Anxious Patriarchs: Gender, Race, and Power in Colonial Virginia* (Chapel Hill: University of North Carolina Press, 1996); Edmund Morgan, *American Slavery, American Freedom: The Ordeal of Colonial Virginia* (New York: W. W. Norton, 1975).

33. For more, see Stephanie McCurry, *Masters of Small Worlds: Yeoman Households, Gender Relations, and the Political Culture of the Antebellum South Carolina Low Country* (New York: Oxford University Press, 1995); Bertram Wyatt Brown, *Southern Honor: Ethics and Behavior in the Old South* (New York: Oxford University Press, 1985); Lorri Glover, *Southern Sons: Becoming Men in the New Nation* (Baltimore: Johns Hopkins University Press, 2007).

34. Landers, "Free and Enslaved," 189–90.

35. Landers, "Free and Enslaved," 189.

36. Landers, "Free and Enslaved," 184–86.

37. Jane Landers, "Gracia Real de Santa Teresa de Mose: A Free Black Town in Spanish Colonial Florida," *American Historical Review* 95, no. 1 (February 1990): 9–30; Landers, "Free and Enslaved," 184; Michael Mullin, *Africa in America: Slave Acculturation and Resistance in the American South and the British Caribbean, 1736–1831* (Urbana: University of Illinois Press, 1992); Daniel H. Usner Jr., *Indians, Settlers, and Slaves in a Frontier Exchange Economy: The Lower Mississippi Valley before 1783* (Chapel Hill: University of North Carolina Press, 1992). See also Jane Landers, "Acquisition and

Loss on a Spanish Frontier: The Free Black Homesteaders of Florida," in *Against the Odds: Free Blacks in the Slave Societies of the Americas*, ed. Jane Landers (London: Routledge Press, 1996), 85–101; Warren Eugene Milteer Jr., *Beyond Slavery's Shadow: Free People of Color in the South* (Chapel Hill: University of North Carolina Press, 2021).

38. Landers, "Free and Enslaved"; Brent R. Weisman, "Florida's Seminole and Miccosukee Peoples," in Gannon, *The History of Florida*, 195–219. For more on the history of the Seminoles, African Americans, and slavery, see Andrew K. Frank, "Red, Black, and Seminole: Community and Convergence on the Florida Borderlands, 1780–1840," in *Borderland Narratives: Negotiation and Accommodation in North America's Contested Spaces, 1500–1850*, ed. Andrew K. Frank and A. Glenn Crothers (Gainesville: University Press of Florida, 2017), 46–67. While there were Native peoples who enslaved Black women and men, this was not the typical practice among the Seminoles, yet outlying cases may exist. For more on the history of Native peoples who enslaved Black peoples, see Barbara Krauthamer, *Black Slaves, Indian Masters: Slavery, Emancipation, and Citizenship in the Native American South* (Chapel Hill: University of North Carolina Press, 2013); Tiya Miles, *Ties That Bind: The Story of an Afro-Cherokee Family in Slavery and Freedom* (Berkeley: University of California Press, 2015).

39. Landers, "Free and Enslaved"; Weisman, "Florida's Seminole and Miccosukee Peoples"; Daniel L. Schafer, "U.S. Territory and State," in Gannon, *The History of Florida*, 220–43.

40. Not only did the Florida peninsula pass between British and Spanish hands, but the colony was split in two—British West Florida and Spanish East Florida. For more, see Robin F. A. Fabel and Daniel L. Schafer, "British Rule in the Floridas," in Gannon, *The History of Florida*, 144–61; Parker and Corker, "The Second Spanish Period."

41. For more on free people of color in Florida, see Landers, "Acquisition and Loss"; Milteer, *Beyond Slavery's Shadow*.

42. *Ancient City* (St. Augustine, Fla.), July 12, 1851, quoted in Schafer, "U.S. Territory and State," 239.

43. Landers, "Free and Enslaved," 192; Schafer, "U.S. Territory and State," 238; Landers, "Gracia Real de Santa Teresa de Mose."

44. Schafer, "U.S. Territory and State," 238; Daniel L. Schafer, *Zephaniah Kingsley Jr. and the Atlantic World: Slave Trader, Plantation Owner, Emancipator* (Gainesville: University Press of Florida, 2013). As a note, while Schafer uses the term *wife* to describe Anna Kingsley, the mother of Zephaniah Kingsley Jr.'s children, additional research is needed to understand their relationship. Anna was purchased by Kingsley in Havana with the intention of making her his wife. The question of consent and Anna's understanding of their relationship provides ample room for additional study. For an exemplary example of such work, see Amrita Chakrabarti Myers, *Forging Freedom: Black Women and the Pursuit of Liberty in Antebellum Charleston* (Chapel Hill: University of North Carolina Press, 2011). For more on the history of African-owned plantations and slaves, see Jane Landers, *Black Society in Spanish Florida* (Urbana: University of Illinois Press, 1999).

45. While historians typically understand the Seminole Wars as three distinct conflicts, historians Denise I. Bossy and Andrew K. Frank assert that modern-day

Seminoles refer to this period as "the Long Seminole War" and reject the idea that these were separate conflicts because all focused on Indigenous removal policies. See Bossy and Frank, "Charting a Path," 17; Weisman, "Florida's Seminole and Miccosukee Peoples," 203.

46. Schafer, "U.S. Territory and State," 231. For more on the perspective of territorial militia and leaders of U.S. armed forces before the passage of the AOA, see "Thomas Sidney Jessup Diary," Florida Memory Digital Collection, SAF, accessed August 2022, www.floridamemory.com/discover/historical_records/jesup. To view land grants issued as a result of the AOA, see "Armed Occupation Act Permit Files," Record Group 00589, Series .S 1305, United States General Land Office, Microfilm, SAF.

47. Schafer, "U.S. Territory and State," 231. Many of those who took advantage of the AOA went to Hillsborough County, the present-day location of Tampa. For more, see James W. Covington, "Life at Fort Brooke," *Florida Historical Quarterly* 36, no. 4 (April 1958): 319–30; Mormino and Pozzetta, *Immigrant World*; Hewitt, *Southern Discomfort*; Greenbaum, *More than Black*; Robert Kerstein, *Politics and Growth in Twentieth-Century Tampa* (Gainesville: University Press of Florida, 2001).

48. Weisman, "Florida's Seminole and Miccosukee Peoples"; Schafer, "U.S. Territory and State."

49. Weisman, "Florida's Seminole and Miccosukee Peoples," 215–16. For more, see Brent R. Weisman, *Unconquered People: Florida's Seminole and Miccosukee Indians* (Gainesville: University Press of Florida, 1999); Jessica R. Cattelino, *High Stakes: Florida Seminole Gaming and Sovereignty* (Durham, N.C.: Duke University Press, 2008); James W. Covington, *The Seminoles of Florida* (Gainesville: University Press of Florida, 1993); Harry A. Kersey Jr., *An Assumption of Sovereignty: Social and Political Transformation among the Florida Seminoles, 1953–1979* (Lincoln: University of Nebraska Press, 1996); Patsy West, *The Enduring Seminoles: From Alligator Wrestling to Ecotourism* (Gainesville: University Press of Florida, 1998); Patsy West, "'Tiger Tiger': Miccosukee Rock 'n' Roll," *Southern Cultures* 14, no. 4 (Winter 2008): 127–40.

50. Schafer, "U.S. Territory and State," 238. Schafer explains that nearly every owner of six or more slaves in the state of Florida had been a Spanish colonial. Once Spanish colonials died, the lands did not pass on to their inheritors. Typically, these estates were liquidated as per conflicts between U.S. land rights and Spanish land grants. There were no Spanish planters in South Florida, as it remained under the control of Native peoples. Occupation of these lands was a U.S. imperial agenda. For more on the use of *settler* and on settler colonialism, see Patrick Wolfe, "Settler Colonialism and the Elimination of the Native," *Journal of Genocide Research* 4, no. 8 (December 2006): 387–409; Lorenzo Veracini, *Settler Colonialism: A Theoretical Overview* (New York: Palgrave Macmillan, 2010).

51. Schafer, "U.S. Territory and State," 232. For more on the history of Florida crackers, see James M. Denham, "The Florida Cracker before the Civil War as Seen through Travelers' Accounts," *Florida Historical Quarterly* 72, no. 4 (1994): 453–68; James M. Denham and Canter Brown Jr., eds., *Cracker Times and Pioneer Lives: The Florida Reminiscences of George Gillett Keen and Sarah Pamela Williams* (Columbia: University of South Carolina Press, 2000). For more on the history and politics of yeoman farmers in the U.S. South, see McCurry, *Masters of Small Worlds*.

52. Schafer, "U.S. Territory and State," 238; Peter H. Wood, *Black Majority: Negroes in Colonial South Carolina from 1670 through the Stono Rebellion* (New York: W. W. Norton, 1974).

53. Schafer, "U.S. Territory and State," 233.

54. This language, "slaveholding" and "non-slaveholding," in reference to states and regions is the verbiage used in the documents from the secessionist convention in Florida. See "Gov. Madison Starke Perry—Constitutional Convention 1861," Series 577, Carton 1, Folder 6, SAF, accessed May 2022, www.civilwarcauses.org/florida-dec.htm. See also "Ordinance of Secession," January 10, 1861, Florida Memory Digital Collection, SAF, accessed May 2022, www.floridamemory.com/fpc/memory/onlineclassroom/floridacivilwar/documents/secession/images/secession.jpg.

55. Schafer, "U.S. Territory and State," 236.

56. Schafer, "U.S. Territory and State," 236. Reconciling who supported the secession is difficult during this period. According to the 1860 census, 55 percent of Florida consisted of white women and men, and only white men (both with and without property) had the right to vote. In the 1860 election, the majority of votes supported the Southern Democratic Party candidate, John Cabell Breckinridge, but 10 percent of voters supported the Constitutional Union Party candidate, John Bell. Voter and census information does not illustrate whom white women supported at the time, since all women did not have the right to vote. However, historians have illustrated that after the passage of the Nineteenth Amendment the majority of women voters (the majority of whom were white women) voted as their husbands did.

57. Schafer, "U.S. Territory and State," 236.

58. Schafer, "U.S. Territory and State," 236.

59. *Journal of the Proceedings of the Convention of the People of Florida Begun and Held at the Capitol in the City of Tallahassee, on Thursday, January 3, A.D. 1861* (Tallahassee, Fla.: Office of the Floridian and Journal, printed by Dyke and Carlisle, 1861), 11. See also "The Civil War: When Florida Opened Up the Gates of Hell," *Forum: The Magazine of the Florida Humanities Council* 34, no. 1 (Spring 2010): 3.

60. Robert A. Taylor, "The Civil War," in Gannon, *The History of Florida*, 244. Florida, which at the time held only three electoral votes due to its low population, voted for Breckinridge, the Southern Democrat. For an example of an election return from Florida, see "Alachua County Returns for President 1860," Florida Memory Digital Collection, SAF, accessed May 2022, www.floridamemory.com/FMP/selected_documents/large/s21_b046_f12_01_01.jpg. On memory and the process of misremembering the Civil War, see also Charles B. Dew, *Apostles of Disunion: Southern Secession Commissioners and the Causes of the Civil War* (Charlottesville: University of Virginia Press, 2016); Adam H. Domby, *The False Cause: Fraud, Fabrication, and White Supremacy in Confederate Memory* (Charlottesville: University of Virginia Press, 2020).

61. "Gov. Madison Starke Perry—Constitutional Convention 1861." For more on Florida during 1861, its first year in the Confederacy, see *A Journal of the Proceedings of the House of Representatives of the General Assembly of the State of Florida, at Its Eleventh Session, Begun and Held at the Capitol, in the City of Tallahassee, on Monday, November 18, 1861* (Tallahassee, Fla.: Office of the Floridian Journal, printed by Dyke and Carlisle, 1861), Documenting the American South, Southern Historical Collection,

University of North Carolina at Chapel Hill, accessed May 2022, https://docsouth.unc.edu/imls/florida1/menu.html.

62. Taylor, "The Civil War."

63. "Constitution of the Confederate States of America," March 11, 1861, in *A Compilation of the Messages and Papers of the Confederacy, Including the Diplomatic Correspondence, 1861–1865,* ed. James D. Richardson (Nashville, Tenn.: United States Publishing Company, 1905), n.p., digitally available via Avalon Project—Documents in Law, History and Diplomacy, Lillian Goldman Law Library, Yale Law School, accessed May 2022, https://avalon.law.yale.edu/19th_century/csa_csa.asp. Note: Jefferson Davis was the provisional president of the Confederacy until 1862.

64. Taylor, "The Civil War," 246.

65. Taylor, "The Civil War," 246.

66. Taylor, "The Civil War," 246.

67. Taylor, "The Civil War," 250–51.

68. The vote to secede from the United States was 62–7. There were delegates who did not support this action, including Richard Call, a Whig Unionist, Florida resident, and former governor of Florida. Schafer notes that Call rose to condemn the vote in January 1861, stating: "You have opened the gates of Hell, from which shall flow the curses of the damned which shall sink you to perdition."' Herbert J. Doherty Jr., *Richard Keith Call, Southern Unionist* (Gainesville: University Press of Florida, 1961), quoted in Schafer, "U.S. Territory and State," 242. See also "Letter from Gen. R. K. Call," December 22 and 23, 1860, Florida Memory Digital Collection, SAF, accessed May 2022, www.floridamemory.com/fpc/memory/onlineclassroom/floridacivilwar/documents/call/large/call.jpg.

69. Darling and Sanderson, quoted in Schafer, "U.S. Territory and State," 242.

70. Jerrell H. Shofner, "Reconstruction and Renewal, 1865–1877," in Gannon, *The History of Florida,* 262. The Constitution of 1865 was neither approved nor ratified by the U.S. Congress, and instead Congressional Reconstruction commenced, which split the South into five military districts. Federal officials, the Freedmen's Bureau, and the U.S. military were sent to these regions to be sure they abided by the U.S. Constitution. The state of Florida was in Military District 3. For more on the rejected constitution, see Constitution of the State of Florida, 1865, Florida Memory Digital Collection, SAF, accessed May 2022, www.floridamemory.com/items/show/189093.

71. Quoted in Shofner, "Reconstruction and Renewal," 262. For details on the proceedings of the 1865 meeting of the Florida legislature, see *A Journal of the Proceedings of the House of Representatives of the General Assembly of the State of Florida, at Its Eleventh Session, Begun and Held at the Capitol, in the City of Tallahassee, on Monday, December 18, 1865* (Tallahassee, Fla.: Office of the Floridian, printed by Dyke and Sparhawk, 1865–66).

72. Shofner, "Reconstruction and Renewal," 262; Joe M. Richardson, "Florida Black Codes," *Florida Historical Quarterly* 47, no. 4 (1969): 365–79; Joe M. Richardson, "The Negro in the Reconstruction of Florida" (Ph.D. diss., Florida State University, 1963).

73. The Florida Constitution was not approved by Congress until November 1865. For the final form of this document, see Constitution of the State of Florida, 1865, Florida Memory Digital Collection. The path to the Civil Rights Act of 1866 was not simple. President Andrew Johnson vetoed the bill, but the House and Senate over-

rode the veto. For the final act as well as the statement on the override, see S. 61, "An Act to protect all persons in the United States in their civil rights, and furnish the means of their vindication (Civil Rights Act of 1866)," March 13, 1866, Thirty-Ninth Congress, First Session, Washington, D.C., accessed May 2022, www.visitthecapitol .gov/exhibitions/artifact/s-61-act-protect-all-persons-united-states-their-civil -rights-and-furnish. See also Fourteenth Amendment, U.S. Constitution; Fifteenth Amendment, U.S. Constitution.

74. For more on the history and experience of military reconstruction in Florida, see Merlin G. Cox, "Military Reconstruction in Florida," *Florida Historical Quarterly* 46, no. 3 (1968): 219–33.

75. Shofner, "Reconstruction and Renewal," 265; Jerrell H. Shofner, *Nor Is It Over Yet: Florida in the Era of Reconstruction, 1863–1877* (Gainesville: University Press of Florida, 1974). On the economy in Florida, see Paul Ortiz, *Emancipation Betrayed: The Hidden History of Black Organizing and White Violence in Florida from Reconstruction to the Bloody Election of 1920* (Berkeley: University of California Press, 1994).

76. Shofner, "Reconstruction and Renewal," 268.

77. Shofner, "Reconstruction and Renewal," 266–67; Ortiz, *Emancipation Betrayed*, 24.

78. Ortiz, *Emancipation Betrayed*.

79. Ortiz, *Emancipation Betrayed*. While the Freedmen's Bureau worked to supply African American women and men with jobs, reunite families, provide education, register people to vote, and more, it encountered considerable resistance in Florida. For more on the work of the bureau as well as other forms of Black resistance to white supremacy, see Heather Andrea Williams, *Self-Taught: African American Education in Slavery and Freedom* (Chapel Hill: University of North Carolina Press, 2005); Thavolia Glymph, *Out of the House of Bondage: The Transformation of the Plantation Household* (New York: Cambridge University Press, 2008); Tera Hunter, *To 'Joy My Freedom: Southern Black Women's Lives and Labors after the Civil War* (Cambridge, Mass.: Harvard University Press, 1997). While federal troops ceased the active work of occupation in 1877, they physically remained in Tampa, Pensacola, Key West, and St. Augustine. See Gregory P. Downs and Scott Nesbit, *Mapping Occupation: Force, Freedom, and the Army in Reconstruction*, published March 2015, accessed April 2022, http://mappingoccupation .org.

80. Ortiz, *Emancipation Betrayed*, 27.

81. On the elections of 1888 and 1892, see Shofner, "Reconstruction and Renewal," 284. For more on the importance of the election of 1888 and the resulting history of Florida post-Reconstruction, see Ortiz, *Emancipation Betrayed*.

82. Ortiz, *Emancipation Betrayed*.

83. Ortiz, *Emancipation Betrayed*, 232, 229–36.

84. Daniel R. Vollaro, "Lincoln, Stowe, and the 'Little Woman / Great War' Story: The Making, and Breaking, of a Great American Anecdote," *Journal of the Abraham Lincoln Association* 30, no. 1 (Winter 2009): 18, http://hdl.handle.net/2027/spo .2629860.0030.104.

85. Ortiz, *Emancipation Betrayed*.

86. Shofner, "Reconstruction and Renewal," 268–70. For more on Stowe and her conflicting comments on race in post-Reconstruction Florida, see Ortiz, *Emancipation*

Betrayed, 13–17, 28–29. For her writings while in Florida, see Harriet Beecher Stowe, *Palmetto-Leaves* (Boston: James R. Osgood, 1873); Harriet Beecher Stowe, "Our Florida Plantation," *Atlantic Monthly*, May 1879.

87. Julio Capó Jr., *Welcome to Fairyland: Queer Miami before 1940* (Chapel Hill: University of North Carolina Press, 2017), 29.

88. Kristalyn Marie Shefveland, "Remembering an Indigenous South: Regional Identity, Vero Beach, and Settler Tourism," *Florida Historical Quarterly* 100, no. 1 (Summer 2021): 106–27.

89. For more on Florida and tourism and the economic development of Florida after the Civil War, see Capó, *Welcome to Fairyland*; Thomas Graham, "The First Developers," in Gannon, *The History of Florida*, 276–95; Jack E. Davis and Raymond Arsenault, eds., *Paradise Lost? The Environmental History of Florida* (Gainesville: University Press of Florida, 2005); Patrick Sheridan, "Good Roads and the Dixie Highway: Connecting Florida with the Rest of the Nation," *Florida Historical Quarterly*, 98, no. 3/4 (April 2021): 253–80.

90. Graham, "The First Developers," 279–81.

91. For more on the history of Florida during the Gilded Age, see Susan R. Braden, *The Architecture of Leisure: The Florida Resort Hotels of Henry Flagler and Henry Plant* (Gainesville: University Press of Florida, 2002); Edward Williamson, *Florida Politics in the Gilded Age, 1877-1893* (Gainesville: University Press of Florida, 1978); Edward N. Akin, *Flagler: Rockefeller Partner and Florida Baron* (Kent, Ohio: Kent State University Press, 1988); Gary R. Mormino, "Florida's Gilded Year," *Gulf Coast Historical Review* 10, no. 1 (1994): 29–44; Hampton Dunn, "Florida: Jewel of the Gilded Age," *Sunland Tribune* 20, no. 6 (1994): 43–48; Sidney Walter Martin, *Florida's Flagler* (Athens: University of Georgia Press, 1949). For more on this process, and similar patterns, elsewhere in the U.S. South in the postbellum era, see Julie M. Weise, "Dispatches from the 'Viejo' New South: Historicizing Recent Latino Migrations," *Latino Studies* 10, nos. 1–2 (May 2012): 43–44.

92. Nancy Raquel Mirabal, "'Ser de Aquí': Beyond the Cuban Exile Model," *Latino Studies* 1, no. 3 (November 2003): 366–82.

93. Mormino, "Florida's Gilded Year." There has been debate over whether De Soto landed in Tampa Bay or near Fort Myers. Most recent studies determine that Tampa Bay is the most likely location. This determination concurs with the first study completed by the Smithsonian Institution in 1939; John R. Swanton, *Final Report of the United States De Soto Expedition Commission; Letter from the Chairman, United States De Soto Expedition Commission, Transmitting the Final Report of the United States De Soto Expedition Commission* (Washington, D.C.: Government Printing Office, 1939). For more on this debate, see Jerald T. Milanich and Charles Hudson, *Hernando de Soto and the Indians of Florida* (Gainesville: University Press of Florida, 1993); Gannon, "First European Contacts," 28.

94. Covington, "Life at Fort Brooke." For more on Fort Brooke, see "Records of the U.S. Army," Record Group 393, NARA.

95. Schafer explains that many of the crackers went to Hillsborough County and other regions in South Florida. During the nineteenth and early twentieth centuries, South Florida was considered to encompass the region south of Alachua County

(Gainesville). Today the term refers to the region south of Manatee County. See Schafer, "U.S. Territory and State."

96. Mormino and Pozzetta, *Immigrant World*, 43–62.

97. Mormino and Pozzetta, *Immigrant World*, 44.

98. Covington, "Life at Fort Brooke"; "Records of the U.S. Army."

99. Mormino and Pozzetta, *Immigrant World*, 45. For more on the Lost Cause and Civil War memory, see also Domby, *The False Cause*; David W. Blight, *Race and Reunion: The Civil War in American Memory* (Cambridge, Mass.: Harvard University Press, 2001); Barbara A. Gannon, *Americans Remember Their Civil War* (Santa Barbara, Calif.: ABC-CLIO, 2017); Kathleen A. Clark, *Defining Moments: African American Commemoration and Political Culture in the South, 1863–1913* (Chapel Hill: University of North Carolina Press, 2005).

100. For more on the history of vigilantism in Tampa, see Ingalls, *Urban Vigilantes*; see also chapter 2, "Resisting," in this book.

101. Mormino and Pozzetta, *Immigrant World*, 45.

102. Associated Railway Land Department of Florida, "The Plant System: Railway, Steamship, and Steamer Lines" (Buffalo, N.Y.: Matthews-Northrup, 1896), Touchton Map Library Digital Archive, TBHC, accessed May 2022, https://luna.tampabayhistory center.org/luna/servlet/detail/TBHC~3~3~4102~6879:Township-Map-of-Peninsular -Florida?qvq=q:Plant%20System;lc:TBHC~3~3&mi=31&trs=4; "Florida Resorts and Plant System," 1897, Touchton Map Library Digital Archive, TBHC, accessed May 2022, https://luna.tampabayhistorycenter.org/luna/servlet/detail/TBHC~3~3~5429~10383: Florida-Resorts-on-the-Plant-System?qvq=q:Plant%20System;lc:TBHC~3~3&mi =0&trs=47; *What to Say in Spanish and How to Say It*, Gulf Coast Booklet, no. 3 (Buffalo, N.Y.: Matthews, Northrup, 1899); Canter Brown Jr., "Tampa and the Coming of the Railroad, 1853–1884," *Sunland Tribune* 17, no. 4 (1991): 13–20; Tracy J. Revels, *Sunshine Paradise: A History of Florida Tourism* (Gainesville: University Press of Florida, 2011).

103. For clarity, I will refer to Vicente Martínez Ybor as Martínez Ybor throughout this chapter. The name of the community, Ybor City, is often referred to as Ybor. This terminology choice distinguishes the person from the place.

104. I thank L. Glenn Westfall for his work and research on the elusive founder of Ybor City. See L. Glenn Westfall, "Don Vicente Martínez Ybor, the Man and His Empire: Development of the Clear Havana Industry in Cuba and Florida in the Nineteenth Century" (Ph.D. diss., University of Florida, 1977); L. Glenn Westfall, "Latin Entrepreneurs and the Birth of Ybor City," *Tampa Bay History* 7, no. 2 (1985): 6–11; L. Glenn Westfall, "The Evolution and Development of Ybor City," *Sunland Tribune* 12, no. 5 (1986): 1017; Pérez, "Cubans in Tampa," 131. See also Mormino and Pozzetta, *Immigrant World*; Hewitt, *Southern Discomfort*; Greenbaum, *More than Black*; Ingalls, *Urban Vigilantes*.

105. Manuel Delofeu y Leonard, *¡Souvenir! Remembranzas de un Proscripto*, (Tampa, Fla.: Imp. M'Cluney y Co, 1900): 38; Westfall, "Don Vicente Martínez Ybor," 21–22. See also José Rivero Muñiz, *The Ybor City Story*, trans. Eustasio Fernández and Henry Beltrán (Dade City, Fla.: Lighthouse Books, 1976; Fernando Ortiz, *Cuban Counterpoint: Tobacco and Sugar* (New York: Alfred A. Knopf, 1947). Note that the distance

between Havana and Key West is 90 nautical miles, while the distance by air is 105 miles. Distance varies according to method of travel and point of departure. The exact point of departure of Martínez Ybor is unknown; for more detail, see Westfall, "Don Vicente Martínez Ybor"; Muñiz, *The Ybor City Story*.

106. Many cigar manufacturers used a blend of Cuban tobacco and U.S. tobacco to cut costs. Others blended Cuban tobacco with tobacco grown in Puerto Rico. Some did not use Cuban tobacco at all. The highest-priced, highest-quality cigars used pure Cuban leaf but as filler and as wrapper. These cigars earned the designation of "clear Havana." See A. Stuart Campbell, *The Cigar Industry of Tampa, Florida*, with W. Porter McLendon (Gainesville: Bureau of Economic and Business Research, University of Florida, 1939), Digital Collections, Special Collections of George A. Smathers Libraries, University of Florida, Gainesville, Fla., accessed November 2020, http://ufdc.ufl.edu/UF00055151/00001; Mormino and Pozzetta, *Immigrant World*, 100; Jean Stubbs, *Tobacco on the Periphery: A Case Study in Cuban Labour History, 1860-1958* (Cambridge: Cambridge University Press, 1985), 68–72; Robert P. Ingalls and Louis A. Pérez Jr., *Tampa Cigar Workers: A Pictorial History* (Gainesville: University Press of Florida, 2003), 1–2.

107. On the process of procuring Cuban tobacco, see FWP, "Ybor City: Sociological Study," State of Florida (unpublished manuscript, 1937), SCUSF; also quoted in Ingalls and Pérez, *Tampa Cigar Workers*, 60.

108. Pérez, "Cubans in Tampa," 129. For more on the history of the New York émigré group, see Nancy Raquel Mirabal, *Suspect Freedoms: The Racial and Sexual Politics of Cubanidad in New York, 1823-1957* (New York: New York University Press, 2017); Lisandro Pérez, *Sugar, Cigars, and Revolution: The Making of Cuban New York* (New York: New York University Press, 2018).

109. United States Census Office, *Ninth Census of the United States, 1870*; Gerald E. Poyo, "Key West and the Cuban Ten Years War," *Florida Historical Quarterly* 57, no. 3 (January 1979): 290. As a note, census numbers are likely an undercount. Cubans during this period were highly mobile, while others who lived in Ybor may have not participated in the census.

110. Westfall, "Don Vicente Martínez Ybor," 24–27.

111. Andrew Gómez, "Cubans and the Caribbean South: Race, Labor, and Cuban Identity in Southern Florida" (Ph.D. diss., University of California, Los Angeles, 2015); Gerald E. Poyo, *"With All, and for the Good of All": The Emergence of Popular Nationalism in the Cuban Communities of the United States, 1848-1898* (Durham, N.C.: Duke University Press, 1989); Poyo, "Tampa Cigarworkers," 94–105.

112. Pérez, "Cubans in Tampa," 130; Westfall, "Don Vicente Martínez Ybor," 24–25; Jefferson Browne, *Key West: The Old and the New* (St. Augustine, Fla.: Record Company Printers and Publishers, 1912).

113. Gómez, "Cubans and the Caribbean South"; Poyo, *"For the Good of All."* For more on early Key West and the response to this first wave of Cuban immigration, see Walter Maloney, *A Sketch of the History of Key West* (Newark, N.J.: Advertisers Printing House, 1876); Browne, *Key West*.

114. The names of the most prominent pro-independence newspapers were *El Yara* and *El Republicano*. According to Andrew Gómez, being in possession of these papers was grounds for imprisonment in Cuba under the Spanish colonial administration.

Gómez, "Cubans and the Caribbean South," 10. For more on revolutionary clubs and organizing in Key West, see Poyo, "Key West"; Poyo, *"For the Good of All."*

115. Poyo, *"For the Good of All"*; Gerald E. Poyo, "The Cuban Experience in the United States, 1865–1940: Migration, Community, and Identity," *Cuban Studies* 21 (1991): 19–36; Pérez, "Cubans in Tampa." For more, see Gómez, "Cubans and the Caribbean South"; Robert Kerstein, *Key West on the Edge: Inventing the Conch Republic* (Gainesville: University Press of Florida, 2012).

116. Westfall, "Don Vicente Martínez Ybor," 59; Mormino and Pozzetta, *Immigrant World*, 64.

117. Westfall, "Don Vicente Martínez Ybor," 56–57; Mormino and Pozzetta, *Immigrant World*, 64; *Tampa Sunday Tribune*, November 4, 1951; John P. Varnum, *Florida! Its Climate, Productions and Characteristics: A Handbook of Important and Reliable Information for the Use of the Tourist, Settler, and Investor* (New York: South Publishing Company, 1885).

118. Brown, "Coming of the Railroad."

119. Westfall, "Don Vicente Martínez Ybor," 61; Tony Pizzo, "Eduardo Manrara: The Cigar Manufacturing Prince of the Nation," *Sunland Tribune* 2 (1975): 31–37; L. Glenn Westfall, "Ignacio Haya: Pioneer, Cigar Entrepreneur," *Sunland Tribune* 6 (1980): 12–14.

120. Minutes, Tampa Board of Trade, October 5, 1887, TBHC. See also Westfall, "Don Vicente Martínez Ybor," 62; Mormino and Pozzetta, *Immigrant World*, 65.

121. *Tobacco Leaf*, July 10, 1886; Minutes, Tampa Board of Trade, October 21, 1885, TBHC; also quoted in Mormino and Pozzetta, *Immigrant World*, 65.

122. *Tampa Guardian*, April 14, 1886; *Tampa Guardian*, October 27, 1886; Mormino and Pozzetta, *Immigrant World*, 65; Westfall, "Don Vicente Martínez Ybor," 65–66.

123. Westfall, "Don Vicente Martínez Ybor," 64–65. For an example of the history on southern mill towns, see Jacquelyn Dowd Hall, James Leloudis, Robert Korstad, Mary Murphy, Lu Ann Jones, and Christopher B. Daly, *Like a Family: The Making of a Southern Cotton Mill World* (Chapel Hill: University of North Carolina Press, 1987).

124. Mormino and Pozzetta, *Immigrant World*, 66.

125. Westfall, "Don Vicente Martínez Ybor," 66; D. Paul Westmeyer, "Tampa, Florida, a Geographic Interpretation of Its Development" (master's thesis, University of Florida, 1953), 17, 58.

126. Fernando Lemos, "Early Days of Ybor City" (FWP, unpublished manuscript, 1941), SCUSF; FWP, "Life History of José Garcia" (unpublished manuscript, 1941), SCUSF; Mormino and Pozzetta, *Immigrant World*, 66.

127. *Tampa Guardian*, May 5, 1886; also in Westfall, "Don Vicente Martínez Ybor," 67.

128. Mormino and Pozzetta, *Immigrant World*, 65–66.

129. Mormino and Pozzetta, *Immigrant World*, 66.

130. Mormino and Pozzetta, *Immigrant World*, 67–68.

131. United States Census Office, *Tenth Census of the United States, 1880*; United States Census Office, *Twelfth Census of the United States, 1900*; Mormino and Pozzetta, *Immigrant World*, 55, 68.

132. Jennifer Simonson, "The Last Cigar Factory in Tampa," *Smithsonian Magazine*, August 5, 2021.

133. *Tampa Tribune*, February 14, 1890; also quoted in Ingalls and Pérez, *Tampa Cigar Workers*, 61.

134. *Tampa Daily Times*, December 14, 1924; also quoted in Ingalls and Pérez, *Tampa Cigar Workers*, 61.

135. Campbell, *Cigar Industry of Tampa*, 75; also quoted in Ingalls and Pérez, *Tampa Cigar Workers*, 62–63.

136. Campbell, *Cigar Industry of Tampa*, 17; also quoted in Ingalls and Pérez, *Tampa Cigar Workers*, 64; Foulkes, *Cigars*, 93.

137. Foulkes, *Cigars*, 93; *Tampa Daily Times*, December 24, 1924; also quoted in Ingalls and Pérez, *Tampa Cigar Workers*, 65.

138. *Tampa Daily Times*, December 24, 1924; also quoted in Ingalls and Pérez, *Tampa Cigar Workers*, 68.

139. Mormino and Pozzetta, *Immigrant World*, 69.

140. *Tampa Daily Times*, December 24, 1924; also quoted in Ingalls and Pérez, *Tampa Cigar Workers*, 67. There were several factors that determined the quality of a cigar; the quality of the tobacco and skill of the roller were the primary indicators. A roller with less skill could roll a cigar that was either too tight or too loose. Also, they may not follow the specific protocol necessary to roll a clear Havana and therefore have their work rendered less valuable. If a cigar was worthless, it was dismantled and the tobacco was used as filler for a future cigar.

141. Campbell, *Cigar Industry of Tampa*, 5; also quoted in Ingalls and Pérez, *Tampa Cigar Workers*, 104.

142. *Tampa Daily Times*, December 24, 1924; also quoted in Ingalls and Pérez, *Tampa Cigar Workers*, 67.

143. *Tampa Daily Times*, December 24, 1924; also quoted in Ingalls and Pérez, *Tampa Cigar Workers*, 69; "Flor de Tampa," Tampa Chamber of Commerce, 1958, TBHC.

144. Mormino and Pozzetta, *Immigrant World*, 67; Minutes, Tampa Board of Trade, September 29, 1905, Special Collections, TBHC.

145. Jose Yglesias, *The Truth about Them* (1971; repr., Houston, Tex.: Arte Público Press, 1999), 207–8; also quoted in Ingalls and Pérez, *Tampa Cigar Workers*, 77. Robert P. Ingalls, "Remembering Ybor City: The Life and Work of Jose Yglesias," *Tampa Bay History* 18, no. 1 (Spring/Summer 1996): 5–28.

146. Andrew T. Huse, *From Saloons to Steak Houses: A History of Tampa* (Gainesville: University Press of Florida, 2020), 18–19; "The Florida Brewing Company," Tony Pizzo Collection, SCUSF; L. Glenn Westfall, "Cigar Label Art: A Photographic Essay," *Tampa Bay History* 7, no. 2 (1985): 106–16.

147. *Tampa Morning Tribune*, January 30, 1896; Huse, *From Saloons to Steak Houses*.

148. *Tampa Tribune*, April 22, 1887; also quoted in Ingalls and Pérez, *Tampa Cigar Workers*, 22. Ybor City became the Fourth Ward of Tampa following incorporation.

149. Mormino and Pozzetta, *Immigrant World*, 67; Armando Mendez, *Ciudad de Cigars: West Tampa* (Tampa: Florida Historical Society, 1994). For more on Tampa infrastructure and internal development, see Kerstein, *Politics and Growth*.

150. United States Census Office, *Eleventh Census of the United States, 1890*; United States Census Office, *Twelfth Census of the United States, 1900*; United States Census

Office, *Fifteenth Census of the United States, 1930*. The Black Cuban population in Ybor City remained consistently between 18 and 15 percent during the years 1890–1930. It is likely, if not a certainty, that these numbers are an undercount. Census officials often had difficulty discerning the Blackness and whiteness of Cubans in Ybor City. For more, see Márquez, *Making the Latino South*; Greenbaum, *More than Black*.

151. Mormino and Pozzetta, *Immigrant World*, 70–91. See also Hewitt, *Southern Discomfort*; Greenbaum, *More than Black*; Nancy Raquel Mirabal, "De Aquí, de Allá: Race, Empire, and Nation in the Making of Cuban Migrant Communities in New York and Tampa, 1823–1924" (Ph.D. diss., University of Michigan, 2001); Jessica Jackson, *Dixie's Italians: Sicilians, Race, and Citizenship in the Jim Crow Gulf South* (Baton Rouge: University of Louisiana Press, 2020).

152. Jose Yglesias, "The Radical Latino Island in the Deep South," *Nuestro* 1 (August 1977): 71–74; Yglesias, *The Truth about Them*. For a full bibliography of Yglesias's work, see Robert P. Ingalls, "A Bibliography of Works by Jose Yglesias," *Tampa Bay History* 18 (1996): 107–11. On identity conjugation, see Vicki L. Ruiz, "Of Poetics and Politics: The Border Journeys of Luisa Moreno," in *Women's Labor in the Global Economy: Speaking in Multiple Voices*, ed. Sharon Harley (New Brunswick, N.J.: Rutgers University Press, 2007), 32; see also Guerrero, "Chicana/o History as Southern History"; Guerrero, *Nuevo South*; Natalia Molina, *How Race Is Made in America: Immigration, Citizenship, and the Historical Power of Racial Scripts* (Berkeley: University of California Press, 2014).

153. Lemos, "Early Days of Ybor City"; Westfall, "Don Vicente Martínez Ybor," 123.

154. Evelio Grillo, *Black Cuban, Black American: A Memoir* (Houston, Tex.: Arte Público Press, 2000), 8, 7–15; Greenbaum, *More than Black*; Mormino and Pozzetta, *Immigrant World*.

155. *La Gaceta*, June 27, 1997; Sammy Argintar, oral history interview by Yael V. Greenberg, March 29, 2000, quoted in Ingalls and Pérez, *Tampa Cigar Workers*, 152. For more on Jewish businesses in Ybor City, see Yael V. Greenberg-Pritzker, "The Princes of Seventh Avenue: Ybor City's Jewish Merchants," *Sunland Tribune* 28 (2002): 55–68.

156. *La Gaceta*, June 27, 1997; quoted in *La Gaceta*, March 23, 1990; also quoted in Ingalls and Pérez, *Tampa Cigar Workers*, 154.

157. "The Cigar and Manufacturing Industry in Tampa, Florida," United States Congress, Senate, Reports of the Immigration Commission, Immigrants in Industries, Washington, D.C., 1911.

158. *La Gaceta*, June 27, 1997; also quoted in Ingalls and Pérez, *Tampa Cigar Workers*, 165.

159. *Tampa Daily Times*, October 23, 1924; also quoted in Ingalls and Pérez, *Tampa Cigar Workers*, 151.

160. Kenya C. Dworkin y Méndez, "Latin Place Making in the Late Nineteenth and Early Twentieth Centuries: Cuban Émigrés and Their Transnational Impact in Tampa, Florida," *English Language Notes* 56, no. 2 (October 2018): 125.

161. *Tampa Daily Journal*, March 5, 1890; also quoted in Ingalls and Pérez, *Tampa Cigar Workers*, 53.

162. *United States Tobacco Journal*, July 25, 1896.

163. José Vega Díaz, oral history interview with Gary R. Mormino, August 24, 1980, Oral History Program, SCUSF; United States Census Office, *Fifteenth Census of the United States, 1930*; United States Census Office, *Sixteenth Census of the United States, 1940*; United States Census Office, *Seventeenth Census of the United States, 1950*.

164. FWP, "Seeing Tampa" (unpublished manuscript, 1937), SCUSF; also quoted in Ingalls and Pérez, *Tampa Cigar Workers*, 76. For more on Black Cubans in the Cuban cigar industry, see Grillo, *Black Cuban, Black American*; Greenbaum, *More than Black*; Hewitt, *Southern Discomfort*; Ingalls and Pérez, *Tampa Cigar Workers*, 24–25.

165. Dolores Patiño Río, interview with Nancy A. Hewitt, 1986, oral history in possession of the author; also quoted in Ingalls and Pérez, *Tampa Cigar Workers*, 74. This oral history, along with others conducted by Hewitt, will be donated to the Nancy Hewitt Collection at SCUSF in the future. See records of Severina Patiño and "Cerrina Cardo" in United States Census Office, *Twelfth Census of the United States, 1900*; United States Census Office, *Thirteenth Census of the United States, 1910*; United States Census Office, *Fourteenth Census of the United States, 1920*; United States Census Office, *Fifteenth Census of the United States, 1930*; United States Census Office, *Sixteenth Census of the United States, 1940*.

166. On care, see Jessica Wilkerson, *To Live Here You Have to Fight: How Women Led Appalachian Movements for Social Justice* (Urbana: University of Illinois Press, 2019).

167. Méndez, "Latin Place Making," 127. For more on mutual aid in Ybor City, see chapter 3, "Surviving," in this book.

168. Quoted in *Tampa Tribune*, September 15, 1977; also quoted in Ingalls and Pérez, *Tampa Cigar Workers*, 107.

169. Yglesias, "The Radical Latino Island"; also quoted in Ingalls and Pérez, *Tampa Cigar Workers*, 92; Hewitt, *Southern Discomfort*. For more on the history of anarchism and the Caribbean, see Kirwin Shafer, *Anarchists of the Caribbean: Countercultural Politics and Transnational Networks in the Age of US Expansion* (New York: Oxford University Press, 2020); Evan Matthew Daniel, "Cuban Cigar Makers in Havana, Key West, and Ybor City, 1850s–1890s: A Single Universe?," in *In Defiance of Boundaries: Anarchism and Latin American History*, ed. Geoffrey de Laforcade (Gainesville: University Press of Florida, 2015), 25–47.

170. FWP, "The Study of Religion in Ybor City" (unpublished manuscript, 1941), SCUSF; Hewitt, *Southern Discomfort*.

171. For more on the history of the culture of labor in Ybor City, see chapter 2, "Resisting," in this book. See also Mormino and Pozzetta, *Immigrant World*; Hewitt, *Southern Discomfort*; Ingalls, *Urban Vigilantes*.

172. Yglesias, *The Truth about Them*; also quoted in Ingalls and Perez, *Tampa Cigar Workers*, 89. For more on the culture of Labor in Ybor City, see chapter 2, "Resisting," in this book.

173. Minutes, Tampa Board of Trade, March 8, 1887, Special Collections, TBHC.

174. *Tampa Morning Tribune*, April 17, 1895; Clifford C. (Kip) Sharpe, "The Tampa Florida Brewing Inc., Florida's First Brewery," *Sunland Tribune* 18, no. 1 (1991): 59–66.

175. Kerstein, *Politics and Growth*, 26–27; *Tampa Morning Tribune*, September 22, 1910; also quoted in Ingalls and Pérez, *Tampa Cigar Workers*, 101.

176. *Cuba* (Tampa), September 9, 1893; also quoted in Ingalls and Pérez, *Tampa Cigar Workers*, 24.

177. *Tampa Morning Tribune*, September 4, 1899.

Chapter Two

1. I thank the research and kindness of the historian Vicki L. Ruiz. All biographical information herein about Luisa Moreno — born Blanca Rosa Rodríguez de León — is the result of Ruiz's work and her research. It is due to her writings and her generosity in source sharing that I am able to follow Moreno through Florida, understand who she was, and analyze her experience in Ybor. As Ruiz once wrote, the process of writing and doing Latina history is an effort of "ongoing missionary labor," an effort not only to do more than identify the presence of Latinas in the past but also to show how Latinas transformed the world around us. I have learned much from Ruiz's writings about Moreno, feminism, and labor activism. But I have learned even more through Ruiz's actions. I thank Ruiz for sharing her work publicly, sharing her sources privately, and leading by example. Vicki L. Ruiz, "Class Acts: Latina Feminist Traditions, 1900–1930," *American Historical Review* 121, no. 1 (February 2016): 1–16; Vicki L. Ruiz, "Of Poetics and Politics: The Border Journeys of Luisa Moreno," in *Women's Labor in the Global Economy: Speaking in Multiple Voices*, ed. Sharon Harley (New Brunswick, N.J.: Rutgers University Press, 2007), 28–45; Vicki L. Ruiz, "Luisa Moreno and Latina Labor Activism," in *Latina Legacies: Identity, Biography, and Community*, ed. Vicki L. Ruiz and Virginia Sánchez Korrol (New York: Oxford University Press, 2005), 175–92; Vicki L. Ruiz, "Una Mujer sin Fronteras: Luisa Moreno and Latina Activism," *Pacific Historical Review* 73, no. 1 (February 2004): 1–20; Vicki L. Ruiz, *Cannery Women, Cannery Lives: Mexican Women, Unionization, and the California Food Processing Industry, 1930–1950* (Albuquerque: University of New Mexico Press, 1987); Leisa D. Meyer, "'Ongoing Missionary Labor': Building, Maintaining, and Expanding Chicana Studies/History, an Interview with Vicki L. Ruiz," *Feminist Studies* 34, nos. 1/2 (Spring/Summer 2008): 23–45.

2. From this point forward in the chapter, I will use the name Luisa Moreno or Moreno for clarity. To learn more of why Moreno changed her name and to read a history centered on her personal evolution, see Ruiz, "Of Poetics and Politics." For more reference and general context, see Ruiz "Class Acts"; Ruiz, "Moreno and Latina Labor Activism"; Ruiz, "Una Mujer sin Fronteras."

3. Sarah McNamara, "Borderland Unionism: Latina Activism in Ybor City and Tampa, Florida, 1935–1937," *Journal of American Ethnic History* 38, no. 4 (Summer 2019): 10–32.

4. Ariel Mae Lambe, *No Barrier Can Contain It: Cuban Antifascism and the Spanish Civil War* (Chapel Hill: University of North Carolina Press, 2019), 2–3.

5. For an expert and succinct discussion of fascism and antifascism — including the debates and historiography surrounding this subject, see Lambe, *No Barrier Can Contain It*, 3–8. See also Lambe, *No Barrier Can Contain It*, 222–23nn10–25; Stanley G. Payne, *A History of Fascism, 1914–1945* (Madison: University of Wisconsin Press, 1995); Tim Mason, *Nazism, Fascism, and the Working Class: Essays by Tim Mason*, ed. Jane Caplan (New York: Cambridge University Press, 1995); Robert O. Paxton, *The*

Anatomy of Fascism (New York: Vintage Books, 2004); Federico Finchelstein, *From Fascism to Populism in History* (Berkeley: University of California Press, 2019).

6. For more on women-led, and specifically Latin American women-led, Popular Front organizing, see Katherine Marino, *Feminism for the Americas: The Making of an International Human Rights Movement* (Chapel Hill: University of North Carolina Press, 2019).

7. "Over There," song lyrics and music by George M. Cohan, 1917. On being foreign, or "alien," despite access to citizenship or naturalization, see Mae M. Ngai, *Impossible Subjects: Illegal Aliens and the Making of Modern America* (Princeton, N.J.: Princeton University Press, 2004); Linda Gordon, *Pitied but Not Entitled: Single Mothers and the History of Welfare, 1890–1935* (Cambridge, Mass.: Harvard University Press, 1998); Michael B. Katz, *The Undeserving Poor: America's Enduring Confrontation with Poverty* (New York: Oxford University Press, 1989); Hidetaka Hirota, *Expelling the Poor: Atlantic Seaboard States and the Nineteenth-Century Origins of American Immigration Policy* (New York: Oxford University Press, 2017).

8. Marino, *Feminism for the Americas*, 2; for a full discussion of *feminismo americano* and the concept of international human rights across the Americas, see 1–12. Moreno was intimately versed in what Marino terms *feminismo americano*. Ruiz, however, illustrates how Moreno's rejection of her elite life allowed her to pursue a version of this principle that not only theorized what *feminismo* was but also put it to work at the grassroots level through labor unionism and political actions. See Ruiz, "Class Acts," 5, 15–16.

9. Ruiz, "Moreno and Latina Labor Activism," 177.

10. Ruiz, "Moreno and Latina Labor Activism," 175–77; see also Ruiz, "Of Poetics and Politics," 29–32; Ruiz, "Class Acts."

11. Ruiz, "Moreno and Latina Labor Activism," 178–80; see also Ruiz, "Una Mujer sin Fronteras," 6; Ruiz, "Of Poetics and Politics," 32.

12. Ruiz, "Moreno and Latina Labor Activism," 178–80; see also Ruiz, "Una Mujer sin Fronteras," 6; Ruiz, "Of Poetics and Politics," 32.

13. Ruiz, "Moreno and Latina Labor Activism," 178–80; see also Ruiz, "Una Mujer sin Fronteras," 6; Ruiz, "Of Poetics and Politics," 32.

14. Ruiz, "Moreno and Latina Labor Activism," 178–80; see also Ruiz, "Una Mujer sin Fronteras," 6–7; Ruiz, "Of Poetics and Politics," 32.

15. Ruiz, "Moreno and Latina Labor Activism," 178–80; see also Ruiz, "Una Mujer sin Fronteras," 6–7; Ruiz, "Of Poetics and Politics," 32. For information on the NTWIU and its origin, see Daniel Katz, *All Together Different: Yiddish Socialists, Garment Workers, and the Labor Roots of Multiculturalism* (New York: New York University Press, 2011), 104; for a full examination of the NTWIU, its activism, and its relationship with the ILGWU, see 98–120.

16. Ruiz, "Moreno and Latina Labor Activism," 178; Ruiz, "Una Mujer sin Fronteras," 6.

17. On the CPUSA, its memory, resistance, and the South, see Jacquelyn Dowd Hall, "The Long Civil Rights Movement and the Political Uses of the Past," *Journal of American History* 91, no. 4 (March 2005): 1233–63; Ruiz, *Cannery Women, Cannery Lives*; Annelise Orleck, *Common Sense and a Little Fire: Women and Working-Class Poli-*

tics in the United States, 1900–1965 (Chapel Hill: University of North Carolina Press, 1995); Katz, *All Together Different*; Zaragosa Vargas, *Proletarians of the North: A History of Mexican Industrial Workers in Detroit and the Midwest, 1917–1933* (Berkeley: University of California Press, 1999); Zaragosa Vargas, *Labor Rights Are Civil Rights: Mexican American Workers in Twentieth-Century America* (Princeton, N.J.: Princeton University Press, 2007); Robin D. G. Kelley, *Hammer and Hoe: Alabama Communists during the Great Depression* (Chapel Hill: University of North Carolina Press, 1990); Michael Denning, *The Cultural Front: The Laboring of American Culture in the Twentieth Century* (New York: Verso, 1996); Robert P. Ingalls, *Urban Vigilantes in the New South: Tampa, 1882–1936* (Knoxville: University of Tennessee Press, 1988).

18. Orleck, *Common Sense and a Little Fire*, 35–50, 130–31, 117–65; Annelise Orleck, *Rethinking American Women's Activism* (New York: Routledge, 2015), 23–24, 35.

19. Ruiz, "Of Poetics and Politics," 32.

20. Vicki L. Ruiz, field notes from interview with Luisa Moreno, interview not recorded, July 1978, notes in Ruiz's possession, shared with the author; on interviewing Moreno, see Meyer, "'Ongoing Missionary Labor.'" Moreno did not allow herself to be recorded during oral history interviews—but she did permit notes. Ruiz took field notes following her discussions with Moreno and graciously shared them with me.

21. "To Whom It May Concern," confirmation of appointment of Luisa Moreno as CMIU organizer, January 27, 1927, CMIU Papers Microfilm, Folder 3-0054, "Frank Cassaro 1937," Frame 0055, GMM; there are no field reports between Moreno and the CMIU in the collection. It is possible they were purged following her deportation in 1950.

22. Ruiz, "Moreno and Latina Labor Activism," 178–79.

23. *Cigar Makers' Official Journal*, April 1892; Ingalls, *Urban Vigilantes*, 61; Gary R. Mormino and George E. Pozzetta, *The Immigrant World of Ybor City: Italians and Their Latin Neighbors in Tampa, 1885–1985*, 2nd ed. (Gainesville: University Press of Florida, 1998), 114; Durward Long, "Labor Relations in the Tampa Cigar Industry, 1885–1911," *Labor History* 12, no. 4 (1971): 551–59.

24. A. Stuart Campbell, *The Cigar Industry of Tampa, Florida*, with W. Porter McLendon (Gainesville: Bureau of Economic and Business Research, University of Florida, 1939), 51, Digital Collections, Special Collections of George A. Smathers Libraries, University of Florida, Gainesville, Fla., accessed November 2020, http://ufdc.ufl.edu/UF00055151/00001.

25. "Manifesto," CMIU Microfilm Collection, GMM, August 8, 1935. Ruiz shared this document with me.

26. Campbell, *Cigar Industry of Tampa*. See also Nancy A. Hewitt, *Southern Discomfort: Women's Activism in Tampa, Florida, 1880s–1920s* (Urbana: University of Illinois Press, 2001); Mormino and Pozzetta, *Immigrant World*; Ingalls, *Urban Vigilantes*; Susan D. Greenbaum, *More than Black: Afro-Cubans in Tampa* (Gainesville: University Press of Florida, 2002).

27. Campbell, *Cigar Industry of Tampa*, 51; Ingalls, *Urban Vigilantes*, 61–63; Hewitt, *Southern Discomfort*, 118, 204–5. A consistent theme within *El Internacional* (the CMIU newspaper), the *CMOJ*, and even annual AFL meeting reports is the need for recruitment among cigar workers.

28. Ruiz, "Of Poetics and Politics," 33.

29. Samuel Gompers, *Seventy Years of Life and Labor: An Autobiography* (New York: E. P. Dutton, 1925), 385, 386, 431–32. A survey of AFL conference reports, published annually, provides an excellent window into the vision of the AFL from the perspective of leadership. See also GMM.

30. There is limited documentary detail of Moreno's time as organizer from the CMIU-AFL. This is highly unusual for the collection. Most organizers who came before and after Moreno have files with contracts, field reports, budgets, and detailed correspondence. There are no existing field reports from Moreno; in fact, there is no correspondence between Moreno and the CMIU at all. Following the summer I spent looking for these documents at the George Meany Memorial AFL-CIO Archive in Maryland, I told and shared with Ruiz what I found and what I did not find. She and I discussed that, when it comes to Moreno, such an experience was not atypical. Moreno's radicalism and subsequent deportation in 1950 pushed the organizations she intersected to purge documents connected to her. So much of Moreno's life and early activism lives in the crumbs and the silences—the conversations Ruiz had with Moreno, the notes Ruiz shared with me, reports from those within unions about her actions, and newspaper articles with light reference. What remains are, predominately, a handful of documents about her rather than documents from her. Such is the case, too often, for those who aligned with leftist ideologies during the Red Scare and for women who had the will and confidence to challenge men in power—as Moreno did.

31. *Tampa Morning Tribune*, August 1899; see also Ingalls, *Urban Vigilantes*, 61; Hewitt, *Southern Discomfort*, 125–26, especially on the CMIU's anti-immigrant campaign. The issue of nativism ran deep within the CMIU. Between 1899 and 1902, there were frequent clashes between Latina/o cigar workers and the CMIU. This led to competitions for a closed shop and even attempts by cigar workers to preclude cigar factories from hiring CMIU members. See also *Tampa Morning Tribune*, *CMOJ*, and *Tobacco Leaf* during these years. Spanish-language newspapers detailing these clashes no longer exist.

32. For discussion of CMIU leaders from within the community, see Carmelo Rocca, oral history interview, October 1982, transcription only, SPOHP; Mormino and Pozzetta, *Immigrant World*, 122–23.

33. Mormino and Pozzetta, *Immigrant World*, 122–23. For more on the political philosophy of the AFL and the principle of "pure and simple unionism," see Gompers, *Seventy Years of Life and Labor*, as well as AFL annual meeting reports between 1900 and 1950. What is consistent is that the AFL understood radical leftist politics as an enemy of its nationalist, trade union project. Those in Ybor City, even organizers who worked for the CMIU-AFL, did not align with the political philosophy that governed the broader union. This did not deter the CMIU from working to recruit these workers. For more, see CMIUC.

34. A reading of the *Tampa Morning Tribune*, *Tobacco Leaf*, and *El Internacional* between 1910 and 1930 reveals this continuous tension. For times of especially heightened tension, see the years 1910, 1917, and 1920. See also Ingalls, *Urban Vigilantes*; Mormino and Pozzetta, *Immigrant World*; Hewitt, *Southern Discomfort*.

35. Manuel González, "Letter to R. E. Van Horn," October 28, 1936, HMAMD. Ruiz shared this document with me.

36. "Luisa Moreno," City of Tampa Directory, 1936, Special Collections and Archives, TBHC; see also Ruiz, "Of Poetics and Politics," 33; Ruiz, "Una Mujer sin Fronteras," 6; Ruiz, "Moreno and Latina Labor Activism," 178; Jacquelyn Dowd Hall, James Leloudis, Robert Korstad, Mary Murphy, Lu Ann Jones, and Christopher B. Daly, *Like a Family: The Making of a Southern Cotton Mill World* (Chapel Hill: University of North Carolina Press, 1987).

37. Ruiz, "Of Poetics and Politics," 34.

38. Luisa Capetillo, *A Nation of Women: An Early Feminist Speaks Out = Mi opinión sobre las libertades, derechos y deberes de la mujer* [My opinion on the liberties, rights, and duties of woman], ed. Félix V. Matos Rodríguez, trans. Alan West-Durán (Houston, Tex.: Arte Público Press, 2004), 103; original Spanish ed. published 1911. I was first alerted to this quotation by Ruiz when she gave me her article "Class Acts." For more on Capetillo in Florida, see also Hewitt, *Southern Discomfort*, 2–13, 204, 214, 215–16, 223; Nancy A. Hewitt, "Luisa Capetillo: Feminist of the Working Class," in Ruiz and Sánchez Korrol, *Latina Legacies*, 120–34.

39. For more on the relationship between Moreno and her family in Guatemala, see Ruiz, "Moreno and Latina Labor Activism"; Ruiz, "Una Mujer sin Fronteras"; Ruiz, "Class Acts"; Ruiz, "Of Poetics and Politics."

40. For more on Miguel de León and parenting, see Ruiz, "Una Mujer sin Fronteras," 6–7.

41. Ruiz, "Of Poetics and Politics," 32.

42. On the violence and abuse between Moreno and her ex-husband, see Ruiz, "Moreno and Latina Labor Activism," 179.

43. Manuel González, "Letter to R. E. Van Horn," October 8–28, 1936, HMAMD.

44. For a description of the cantina culture of Ybor, see Federal Writers' Project (hereafter cited as FWP), "Ybor City General Description" (unpublished manuscript, 1941), SCUSF; Restaurant Menu Collection, SCUSF; *New York Times*, January 18, 1903. See also Andrew T. Huse, *From Saloons to Steak Houses: A History of Tampa* (Gainesville: University Press of Florida, 2020), 11–17.

45. "Menu, Centro Asturiano," March 5, 1938, Centro Asturiano Library, Centro Asturiano de Tampa, Tampa, Fla.; FWP, "Ybor City General Description"; Restaurant Menu Collection, SCUSF; the Pizzo collections, TPC. Most menus in the Restaurant Menu Collection are from larger restaurants, but informal, historic menus from cantinas, bars, and special events are present in the libraries of mutual aid societies. See also SCUSF materials on mutual aid societies, including Centro Asturiano, Círculo Cubano, Centro Español, and Sociedad Martí-Maceo. On Prohibition in Florida, see Frank W. Alduino, "The 'Noble Experiment' in Tampa: A Study of Prohibition in Urban America" (Ph.D. diss., Florida State University, 1989). For more on the history of food and drink cultures in Ybor City and Tampa broadly, see Huse, *From Saloons to Steak Houses*.

46. Hewitt, *Southern Discomfort*, 205, 214; Mormino and Pozzetta, *Immigrant World*, 118–19; Ingalls, *Urban Vigilantes*, 116.

47. "1936 Sanborn Map," Division of Urban Planning, City of Tampa Municipal Archives, Tampa, Fla. There is no finding aid for the Division of Urban Planning. There are selected Sanborn maps available in SCUSF, TBHC, and the Hillsborough

County Municipal Archives, all of which are more accessible. On the culture of the porch, see Jose Yglesias, *The Truth about Them* (1971; repr., Houston, Tex.: Arte Público Press, 1999), 70, 138, 168; Maggie Fernández, interview by Nancy A. Hewitt, 1986, interview in the author's possession. This oral history will become a part of the Nancy Hewitt Collection at SCUSF in the future.

48. Yglesias, *The Truth about Them*, 70, 138, 168; FWP, "Amanda and Enrique" (unpublished manuscript, 1941), SCUSF.

49. Manuel González, "Letter to R. E. Van Horn," October 8–28, 1936, HMAMD. Ruiz shared this document with me.

50. Campbell, *Cigar Industry of Tampa*, 4.

51. On shifts in the cigar industry and the effects of the Depression, see Fernández, interview by Hewitt; Dolores Patiño Río, interview by Nancy A. Hewitt, 1986, interview in the author's possession; Angie Garcia, interview by Nancy A. Hewitt, 1986, interview in the author's possession; Providence Velasco, interview by Nancy A. Hewitt, 1986, interview in the author's possession; Carmela Carmelatta, interview by Nancy A. Hewitt, 1986, interview in the author's possession. These oral histories conducted by Hewitt will become part of the Nancy Hewitt Collection at SCUSF in the future.

52. Fernández, interview by Hewitt; Río, interview by Hewitt, 1986; Garcia, interview by Hewitt; Velasco, interview by Hewitt; Carmelatta, interview by Hewitt. For more on the political philosophy of the AFL and the principle of "pure and simple unionism," see Gompers, *Seventy Years of Life and Labor*; also AFL annual meeting reports between 1900 and 1950. What is consistent is that the AFL understood radical leftist politics as an enemy of its nationalist, trade union project. Those in Ybor City, even organizers who worked for the CMIU-AFL, did not align with the political philosophy that governed the broader union. This did not deter the CMIU from working to recruit these workers. For more, see CMIUC.

53. There were multiple clashes between the CMIU and cigar workers between 1892 and 1902 surrounding issues of distrust, including instances of anti-immigrant campaigns and efforts to make the industry "closed shop" for the CMIU only. One major issue was the CMIU's and AFL's desire to open cigar factories to Anglo workers; Cuban cigar workers, however, wished to defend their craft. They also wanted the union to fight for maintenance of culture and tradition, but this was beyond the purview of the CMIU. See Ingalls, *Urban Vigilantes*, 61–63; Hewitt, *Southern Discomfort*, 125–26, 204–5; *Tobacco Leaf*, August–September 1899; *Tampa Morning Tribune*, 1899, 1902, 1917, 1920.

54. For a map of tobacco-growing regions of Cuba, see Jean Stubbs, *Tobacco on the Periphery: A Case Study in Cuban Labour History, 1860–1958* (Cambridge: Cambridge University Press, 1985), xiv. For a description and explanation of the "Spanish hand method" of rolling cigars, see chapter 1, "Building," in this book.

55. Campbell, *Cigar Industry of Tampa*, 13–28.

56. Campbell, *Cigar Industry of Tampa*, 19; Ingalls, *Urban Vigilantes*, 31; Mormino and Pozzetta, *Immigrant World*, 100–102. For the experience of cigar making, see Alex and Josephine Scaglione, interview by Gary R. Mormino and George E. Pozzetta, April 2, 1980, SPOHP; Río, interview by Hewitt, 1986; Louis A. Pérez Jr.,

"Ybor City Remembered," *Southeastern Latin Americanist* 22, no. 1 (June 1978): 174–77. Recollections of cigar work are inherent to any oral history collection of Ybor City. See interviews with SPOHP and the Oral History Program, SCUSF.

57. During strikes, cigar manufacturers published articles in the *Tampa Morning Tribune* detailing the poor working conditions in Havana in an effort to deter migration. For an example, see *Tampa Morning Tribune*, August 1899; Mormino and Pozzetta, *Immigrant World*, 76–78.

58. *Tobacco Leaf*, August 23, 1901; also quoted in Hewitt, *Southern Discomfort*, 130.

59. Not only were apprenticeships mandatory among cigar makers, but they were required by the CMIU. This was an agreement made with manufacturers. See Campbell, *Cigar Industry of Tampa*, 43, 46; on the conflict with non-apprentice employees entering the clear Havana industry in 1917, a conflict that continued into the 1930s, see Hewitt, *Southern Discomfort*, 231.

60. Campbell, *Cigar Industry of Tampa*, 1–12.

61. Mormino and Pozzetta, *Immigrant World*, 101–2 (for reference to Hugo and Marx), 100–104 (for broader discussion of leftist intellectualism and lectores); Ingalls, *Urban Vigilantes*, 31–36; Louis A. Pérez Jr., "Reminiscences of a *Lector*: Cuban Cigar Workers in Tampa," *Florida Historical Quarterly* 53, no. 4 (April 1975): 443–49; Araceli Tinajero, *El Lector: A History of the Cigar Factory Reader*, trans. Judith E. Grasberg (Austin: University of Texas Press, 2010).

62. Evelio Grillo, *Black Cuban, Black American: A Memoir* (Houston, Tex.: Arte Público Press, 2000), 21.

63. Reminiscent discussions of Ybor City in the old days were not unusual and, in some ways, continue today. Gary R. Mormino and George E. Pozzetta, in the introduction to *Immigrant World*, write about the conversations they overheard. Today, these would be found not in the clubs but in the cafés of West Tampa—specifically, El Gallo de Oro, Cacciatore's Market, and the West Tampa Sandwich Shop. My favorite of all the conversations I have overheard happened in 2016 when a group of men from Ybor argued about who had the biggest impact on the city—Cubans or Italians. In the midst of the discussion, one of the men jumped on top of the table to make his point heard. This exchange took place at the West Tampa Sandwich Shop.

64. For context on cigar factories in the northern United States, see Patricia A. Cooper, *Once a Cigar Maker: Men, Women, and Work Culture in American Cigar Factories, 1900–1919* (Urbana: University of Illinois Press, 1987).

65. Durward Long, "'La Resistencia': Tampa's Immigrant Labor Union," *Labor History* 6, no. 3 (1965): 193–213; Ingalls, *Urban Vigilantes*, 62, 72–82; Hewitt, *Southern Discomfort*, 115–20, 125–26, 130; Mormino and Pozzetta, *Immigrant World*, 116–18, 125.

66. Long, "'La Resistencia'"; Ingalls, *Urban Vigilantes*, 62, 72–82.

67. Cuban cigar makers in Ybor City and West Tampa had a low rate of U.S. citizenship and naturalization when compared to other cities. United States Census Office, *Fifteenth Census of the United States*, 1930; *Tampa Morning Tribune*, February 8, 1912; also in Mormino and Pozzetta, *Immigrant World*, 301.

68. Long, "'La Resistencia'"; Ingalls, *Urban Vigilantes*, 62, 72–82; Hewitt, *Southern Discomfort*, 115–20, 125–26, 130; Mormino and Pozzetta, *Immigrant World*, 116–18, 125.

69. Long, "'La Resistencia'"; Ingalls, *Urban Vigilantes*, 62, 72–82; Hewitt, *Southern Discomfort*, 115–20, 125–26, 130; Mormino and Pozzetta, *Immigrant World*, 116–18, 125; see also Ybor and West Tampa Oral History Collection, SCUSF; Hillsborough County Oral History Collection, SPOHP.

70. Ingalls, *Urban Vigilantes*, 88; Long, "'La Resistencia,'" 196. The CMIU locals in Tampa in 1939 were as follows: 336, 462, 474, 493, 494, 495, and 500; see Campbell, *Cigar Industry of Tampa*, 51.

71. Campbell, *Cigar Industry of Tampa*; see also Ingalls, *Urban Vigilantes*, 88.

72. Hewitt, *Southern Discomfort*; Ingalls, *Urban Vigilantes*.

73. Mormino and Pozzetta, *Immigrant World*, 117; Huse, *From Saloons to Steak Houses*, 85–113.

74. Peter Parrado, interview by the author, June 2008, interview in the author's possession.

75. Hewitt, *Southern Discomfort*; Mormino and Pozzetta, *Immigrant World*. On the tradition of theater in Ybor City, see Kenya C. Dworkin y Méndez, "Before Exile: Unearthing the 'Golden Age' of Cuban Theater in Tampa," in *Writing/Righting History: Twenty-Five Years of Recovering the US Hispanic Literary Heritage*, ed. Antonia Castañeda and Clara Lomas (Houston, Tex.: Arte Público Press, 2019), 403–20; Kenya C. Dworkin y Méndez, "From Factory to Footlights: Original Spanish-Language Cigar Workers' Theatre in Ybor City and West Tampa, Florida," in *Recovering the U.S. Hispanic Literary Heritage*, vol. 3, ed. María Herrera-Sobek and Virginia Sánchez Korrol (Houston, Tex.: Arte Público Press, 2000), 332–50.

76. On apprenticeship requirements, see Campbell, *Cigar Industry of Tampa*, 43, 46; Hewitt, *Southern Discomfort*, 230–33.

77. Hewitt, *Southern Discomfort*, 222–23, 230–32; *Tampa Morning Tribune*, November 17, 1916; *Tampa Morning Tribune*, November 25, 1916; I thank Julio Capó Jr. and Miguel Cueller, who assisted in reading the context of "afeminadas" and its power as an anti-queer slur. For more on the history of queerness in Florida, see Julio Capó Jr., *Welcome to Fairyland: Queer Miami before 1940* (Chapel Hill: University of North Carolina Press, 2017). For more on anti-queer language in Mexico and Latin America, see Robert Irwin, *Mexican Masculinities* (Minneapolis: University of Minnesota Press, 2003).

78. Capetillo, *A Nation of Women*, 8, 124. Ruiz states, "Capetillo's sentiments about same-sex love mirrored such prejudice across Latin America"; Ruiz, "Class Acts," 10. See also Eileen J. Suárez Findlay, *Imposing Decency: The Politics of Sexuality and Race in Puerto Rico, 1870-1920* (Durham, N.C.: Duke University Press, 2000).

79. Emilio Gonzalez-Llanes, *Cigar City Stories: Tales of Old Ybor City* (Bloomington, Ind.: iUniverse, 2012), 59; Capó, *Welcome to Fairyland*. A testimonio is a genre of writing where one tells one's life story through narrative construction. Often, character names are different from what they are in reality. In *Cigar City Stories*, the author's character is named Abel. There are no existing oral histories that detail experiences of relationships that were not cisgender and heterosexual in Ybor City, but through poetry and testimonio these stories and experiences live.

80. "Obituary: Emilio Gonzalez," *Bay Area Reporter*, November 28, 2018, www.ebar .com/news/news//268818. The writings of Gonzalez-Llanes are valuable because they are so rare. Out of the hundreds of oral histories done with women and men from

Ybor, not one mentions queerness. In part, this could be a function of the questions interviewers asked. But it could also be a function of how interviewees are found. Oral history projects emerge from the networks oral historians cultivate. To tell a queer story of Ybor would require that a historian cultivate sincere relationships among older community members who likely feel ostracized, much as Gonzalez did. Ybor City has a rich queer history that intersects with gentrification. "Gaybor," a term that emerged in the 1980s, deserves more historical attention and a future study.

81. Hewitt, *Southern Discomfort*, 222–23, 230–32; *Tampa Morning Tribune*, November 17, 1916; *Tampa Morning Tribune*, November 25, 1916.

82. Hewitt, *Southern Discomfort*, 230–32. For more on Sacco and Vanzetti, see Jennifer Guglielmo, *Living the Revolution: Italian Women's Resistance and Radicalism in New York City, 1880–1945* (Chapel Hill: University of North Carolina Press, 2010), 136–38.

83. "Statement on Women," in *Report of Proceedings of the Thirty-Ninth Annual Convention of the American Federation of Labor* (Washington, D.C.: Law Reporter Printing Company, 1919), 111. All AFL convention reports detail the inclusion of women and reiterate the same policy until the late 1930s. While protocol changed, the shift within the union and the culture of labor did not. Policy and culture are two separate issues, and both must change in order for either to function.

84. CMIUC.

85. Greenbaum, *More than Black*; Nancy Raquel Mirabal, "De Aquí, de Allá: Race, Empire, and Nation in the Making of Cuban Migrant Communities in New York and Tampa, 1823–1924" (Ph.D. diss., University of Michigan, 2001).

86. Gerald E. Poyo, "Tampa Cigarworkers and the Struggle for Cuban Independence," *Tampa Bay History* 7, no. 2 (1985): 105. *Cubanidad* translates to "Cuban-ness" or "the condition of being Cuban," but the term implies more than these translations afford. Cubanidad refers to Cuba's unique culture or the cultural components that make the island and the people what it is. Cubanidad emerges from "both the process and the ever-changing results of the mixture of uprooted cultural elements," including African, European, and Native cultures. The appreciation and attachment to this cubanidad is "cubanía." In the case of Ybor City, there was a sense of cubanidad that emerged in exile and later evolved into a sense of latinidad. For an example of discussions on the concept of cubanidad, see Fernando Ortiz, "The Human Factors of Cubanidad," trans. by João Felipe Gonçalves and Gregory Duff Morton, *HAU: Journal of Ethnographic Theory* 4, no. 3 (2014): 445–80; quotation on 455. For a discussion of cubanidad and cultural evolution in the United States, see Ricardo L. Ortíz, *Cultural Erotics in Cuban America* (Minneapolis: University of Minnesota Press, 2007), vii–xix, 1–42.

87. Yglesias, *The Truth about Them*, 40.

88. Yglesias, *The Truth about Them*, 40.

89. Yglesias, *The Truth about Them*, 40. Yglesias discusses this aunt and her character in his discussion with Hewitt. For more, see Jose Yglesias and Dahlia Corro, interview with Nancy A. Hewitt, December 19, 1989, interview in possession of the author. This oral history will become a part of the Nancy Hewitt Collection at SCUSF in the future.

90. Ybor and West Tampa Oral History Collection, SCUSF; Hillsborough County Oral History Collection, SPOHP.

91. Lillian Guerra, *The Myth of José Martí: Conflicting Nationalisms in Early Twentieth-Century Cuba* (Chapel Hill: University of North Carolina Press, 2005), 26–27.

92. Grillo, *Black Cuban, Black American*, 7–15, 20. See also Greenbaum, *More than Black*; Mirabal, "De Aquí, de Allá"; Guerra, *The Myth of José Martí*, 70–72. Guerra notes the dedication of those in Ybor City and West Tampa to Cuban independence. There were over sixty-six Partido Revolucionario Cubano clubs in the area, which during that time included Black and white Cubans. Yet it was the memory of such collaborations that freed the community to face the power of racial inequality within. Consistent nods to inclusion for political ends did not undo the fact that, even within Ybor City and West Tampa, lives were very much segregated, although through de facto practice, after independence.

93. Nicholas Foulkes, *Cigars: A Guide* (London: Penguin Random House, 2017), 60, 63, 76.

94. Ingalls, *Urban Vigilantes*, 150; *CMOJ*, January 1932. I thank Robert P. Ingalls for all his work on violence and vigilantism in Tampa, research that has been central to my understanding of Ybor City.

95. Ingalls, *Urban Vigilantes*, 150.

96. *Tampa Morning Tribune*, November 8, 1931.

97. *Tampa Morning Tribune*, November 8, 1931; *La Gaceta*, November 8, 1931; *La Gaceta*, November 9, 1931.

98. *Tampa Morning Tribune*, November 4, 1931; see also *La Gaceta*, November 4, 1931.

99. Ingalls, *Urban Vigilantes*, 152.

100. Ingalls, *Urban Vigilantes*, 152.

101. Ingalls, *Urban Vigilantes*, 152.

102. Ingalls, *Urban Vigilantes*, 152.

103. *Tampa Morning Tribune*, December 15, 1931; Ingalls, *Urban Vigilantes*, 152.

104. José Vega Díaz, oral history interview by Gary R. Mormino, 1980, SCUSF; Gary R. Mormino and George E. Pozzetta, "The Reader and the Worker: *Los Lectores* and the Culture of Cigarmaking in Cuba and Florida," *International and Working-Class History*, no. 54 (Fall 1998): 1–18.

105. Díaz, interview by Mormino; Mormino and Pozzetta, "The Reader and the Worker"; Pérez, "Reminiscences of a *Lector*."

106. Gonzalez-Llanes, *Cigar City Stories*, 53.

107. Gonzalez-Llanes, *Cigar City Stories*, 53.

108. Mormino and Pozzetta, *Immigrant World*, 182–83.

109. Manuel González, "Letter to R. E. Van Horn," October 28, 1936, HMAMD.

110. Ingalls, *Urban Vigilantes*, 155.

111. Ingalls, *Urban Vigilantes*, 155, 155–58; *La Gaceta*, November–December 15, 1931.

112. Studs Terkel, interview with Jose Yglesias, in *Hard Times: An Oral History of the Great Depression* (New York: New Press, 2011), 109–12; "Jose Yglesias Talks with Studs

Terkel," Studs Terkel Radio Archive, 1967, https://studsterkel.wfmt.com/programs/jose-yglesias-talks-studs-terkel.

113. Ingalls, *Urban Vigilantes*, 150–52.

114. Ingalls, *Urban Vigilantes*, 158–59.

115. Ingalls, *Urban Vigilantes*.

116. Barbara Habenstreit, *Eternal Vigilance: The American Civil Liberties Union in Action* (New York: J. Messner, 1971), 13; Ingalls, *Urban Vigilantes*, 200; Nancy A. Hewitt, "Economic Crisis and Political Mobilization: Reshaping Cultures of Resistance in Tampa's Communities of Color, 1929–1939," in Harley, *Women's Labor in the Global Economy*, 70.

117. H. L. Mitchell, *Mean Things Happening in This Land: The Life and Times of H. L. Mitchell, Co-founder of the Southern Tenant Farmers Union* (Montclair, N.J.: Allanheld, Osmun, 1979).

118. Mormino and Pozzetta, *Immigrant World*, 117; Ybor and West Tampa Oral History Collection, SCUSF; Hillsborough County Oral History Collection, SPOHP.

119. Ingalls, *Urban Vigilantes*, 184.

120. Ingalls, *Urban Vigilantes*, 180–82.

121. Ingalls, *Urban Vigilantes*, 182.

122. Ingalls, *Urban Vigilantes*, 185.

123. The Tampa Police Department has no record of an investigation of the Shoemaker murder. While the case did eventually go to court following an order from the governor, after a nationwide letter-writing campaign compelled him to do so, neither a complaint nor an investigation was ever filed at the local level. "Tampa Police Department Files and Police Reports, 1930–1940," Tampa Police Department, Tampa, Fla. As a note, in order to access files from the Tampa Police Department, one must call the records department at the downtown office. An hourly fee is required to use the microfilm. There are no finding aids. These records are highly guarded and difficult to access. Furthermore, records are destroyed after eighty years. There is no policy within the city or state that requires they be preserved.

124. R. E. Van Horn, "Letter to Manuel Gonzalez," October 8, 1936, HMAMD; González, "Letter to R. E. Van Horn." These are among the documents that Ruiz and I have shared with each other.

125. Van Horn, "Letter to Manuel Gonzalez"; Gonzalez, "Letter to R.E. Van Horn."

126. Van Horn, "Letter to Manuel Gonzalez"; Gonzalez, "Letter to R.E. Van Horn."

127. Van Horn, "Letter to Manuel Gonzalez"; Gonzalez, "Letter to R.E. Van Horn."

128. Ruiz, "Of Poetics and Politics," 32; Ruiz, "Una Mujer sin Fronteras," 8; Ruiz, "Moreno and Latina Labor Activism," 180; Ruiz, "Class Acts," 9.

129. Campbell, *Cigar Industry of Tampa*, 66; Hewitt, "Economic Crisis," 71. See also Ingalls, *Urban Vigilantes*, 248n214. According to the WPA board, there were approximately 24,000 Latinas/os living in Ybor City in 1938. Of those 24,000, only 9,300 were employed by cigar factories. Most of these employees were women. This forced men to leave Ybor City and Tampa in search of work. Also, the number of cigar factories had dwindled from 122 at the industry's height to 31 in 1938. See FWP, "Ybor City General Description" (unpublished manuscript, 1941), 1, 60, 68, 76, SCUSF.

130. FWP, "Life History of John Cacciatore" (unpublished manuscript, 1941), SCUSF.

131. Campbell, *Cigar Industry of Tampa*, 12.

132. Campbell, *Cigar Industry of Tampa*, 66.

133. FWP, "Life History of John Cacciatore."

134. Campbell, *Cigar Industry of Tampa*, 10.

135. Dolores Patiño Río self-identified by using both of her last names; however, she did not use Spanish-language order conventions. Her married name was Río and her maiden name was Patiño. In Ybor City, such naming conventions can be generational but also according to preference. There is no consistency across the community on this matter.

136. Dolores Patiño Río, interview by Nancy A. Hewitt, September 4 and 10, 1985, interview in the author's possession. This oral history will become a part of the Nancy Hewitt Collection at SCUSF in the future. Nancy A. Hewitt, "Women in Ybor City: An Interview with a Woman Cigarworker," *Tampa Bay History* 7, no. 2 (Fall/Winter 1985): 164; Hewitt, *Southern Discomfort*.

137. Río, interview by Hewitt, 1986.

138. Ethel Lombard Best and Mary Viola Robinson, *Women in Florida Industries* (Washington, D.C.: Government Printing Office, 1930), 45.

139. Best and Robinson, *Women in Florida Industries*, 48.

140. Campbell, *Cigar Industry of Tampa*, 3.

141. FWP, "Life History of Gerardo Cortina Pinera" (unpublished manuscript, 1941), SCUSF.

142. Campbell, *Cigar Industry of Tampa*, 7.

143. Hewitt, "Economic Crisis"; Cybelle Fox, *Three Worlds of Relief: Race, Immigration, and the American Welfare State, from the Progressive Era to the New Deal* (Princeton, N.J.: Princeton University Press, 2012).

144. FWP, "Life History of John Cacciatore."

145. FWP, "Life History of Domenica Ginesta" (unpublished manuscript, 1941), SCUSF.

146. FWP, "Life History of Domenica Ginesta."

147. FWP, "Life History of Domenica Ginesta"; see also FWP, "The Círculo Cubano: Its Contribution to Society" (unpublished manuscript, 1941), 143, SCUSF.

148. *La Gaceta*, October 29, 1937.

149. Lambe, *No Barrier Can Contain It*; Ana Varela-Lago, "¡No Pasarán! The Spanish Civil War's Impact on Tampa's Latin Community, 1936–1939," *Tampa Bay History* 19, no. 2 (1997): 5–35. See also Ana Varela-Lago, "'We Had to Help': Remembering Tampa's Response to the Spanish Civil War," *Tampa Bay History* 19, no. 2 (1997): 36–56. Varela-Lago conducted an extensive oral history project in which women and men of Ybor were interviewed about their experiences of the Spanish Civil War. This collection is rich with detail and scope. It deserves to be digitized and made more publicly available.

150. Quoted in Varela-Lago, "¡No Pasarán!," 7; also see *La Gaceta*, August 3 and 4, 1936.

151. For an understanding of Spaniards and the reasons they immigrated, see Ybor City Oral History Project, SCUSF; Spanish Civil War Oral History Project,

SCUSF; FWP, "Ybor City and Tampa: A Sociological Study" (unpublished manuscript, 1941), SCUSF; Gary R. Mormino and George E. Pozzetta, "Spanish Anarchism in Tampa, Florida, 1886–1931," in *Hidden Out in the Open: Spanish Migration to the United States (1875–1930)*, ed. Phylis Cancilla Martinelli and Ana Varela-Lago (Louisville: University Press of Colorado, 2018), 91–128.

152. *La Gaceta*, November 17, 1936.

153. For an expert and succinct overview of the Spanish Republic, the Falange, and the history surrounding the Spanish Civil War, see Lambe, *No Barrier Can Contain It*, 4–8.

154. *La Gaceta*, November 17, 1936. Between August and November 1936, there were frequent meetings of the antifascist committee at the local Labor Temple. In some reports from *La Gaceta* Moreno was noted as being in attendance. Furthermore, Moreno sought to bring in speakers and leaders of the global antifascist movement to union meetings. She was intimately involved in this process—it is likely that she was a consistent antifascist coalition meeting attendee.

155. The date of Manteiga's immigration varies across records. Some documents, such as his Declaration of Intention for U.S. Citizenship, indicate 1912, while his reports to census officials vary between 1913 and 1915. The earliest record of Manteiga entering Florida through immigration is 1911, to Key West. "Declaration of Intention, Victoriano Manteiga y Rios," U.S. Naturalization Records, Tampa Petitions, District Court of Tampa, 1927, NARA; *Passenger Lists of Vessels Arriving at Key West, Florida, 1898–1963*, Records of the Immigration and Naturalization Service, 1787–2004, Record Group 85, NARA, accessed via Ancestry.com, *Florida, Passenger Lists, 1898–1963*; United States Census Office, *Fourteenth Census of the United States, 1920*; United States Census Office, *Fifteenth Census of the United States, 1930*; United States Census Office, *Sixteenth Census of the United States, 1940*. Today *La Gaceta* is a trilingual newspaper and the only one of its kind in the United States. It is still family owned and in production. Patrick Manteiga is the current owner and editor. I owe many thanks to him and his family for their efforts to keep the memory of Ybor City alive.

156. *Tampa Morning Tribune*, November 17, 1936; for more detail on the extent of the boycott in historiography, see Varela-Lago, "¡No Pasarán!"

157. *La Gaceta*, July 24, 1936.

158. *Tampa Morning Tribune*, November 12, 1936.

159. *Tampa Morning Tribune*, November 17, 1936.

160. *Tampa Morning Tribune*, November 17, 1936.

161. *Tampa Morning Tribune*, November 17, 1936.

162. *La Gaceta*, November 18, 1936; *Tampa Morning Tribune*, November 17, 1936.

163. *La Gaceta*, November 23, 1936.

164. Quoted in Varela-Lago, "¡No Pasarán!," 17.

165. Ruiz, field notes from interview with Moreno, July 1978.

166. *Tampa Morning Tribune*, November 17, 1936.

167. *La Gaceta*, December 10, 1936; Peter Parrado, interview by the author, March 2011, interview in the author's possession.

168. United States Census Office, *Twelfth Census of the United States, 1900*; United States Census Office, *Thirteenth Census of the United States, 1910*; United States Census

Office, *Fourteenth Census of the United States, 1920*; United States Census Office, *Fifteenth Census of the United States, 1930*; United States Census Office, *Sixteenth Census of the United States, 1940*. Aurelio Tuldela was the husband of Maria Luisa Pita, the younger sister of Margarita Pita, and he died in 1935 at the age of forty-two. For more, see Aurelio Tuldela, Florida Death Index, 1877–1998, accessed January 2022 from Ancestry.com; Aurelio Tuldela, grave site, Woodlawn Cemetery, Tampa, Fla.

169. Lambe, *No Barrier Can Contain It.*

170. Varela-Lago, "¡No Pasarán!," 7. The details of shipments to Spain are copiously recorded in *La Gaceta* from May to December 1937. Daily updates including fundraising information are available. See also Hewitt, "Economic Crisis," 75.

171. Varela-Lago, "¡No Pasarán!," 7.

172. Varela-Lago, "¡No Pasarán!," 10.

173. Varela-Lago, "¡No Pasarán!," 7. According to Varela-Lago, at least six of the those who joined the International Brigades were of Cuban descent.

174. Varela-Lago, "¡No Pasarán!," 7. Newspaper and union records do not illustrate Moreno's role in the march beyond that of organizer. Between the bombing of Guernica and the event, Moreno penned multiple opinion editorials that were published in the local Spanish-language newspaper, *La Gaceta*. However, beyond her work to politically mobilize women, her role in the event cannot be verified.

175. *La Gaceta*, May 4, 1937.

176. *La Gaceta*, May 3, 1937.

177. *La Gaceta*, May 3, 1937.

178. *La Gaceta*, May 3, 1937.

179. *La Gaceta*, May 7, 1937.

180. *La Gaceta*, May 7, 1937; *La Gaceta*, May 6, 1937; *Tampa Morning Tribune*, May 7, 1937. The May 6 *La Gaceta* report lists Latina leaders of the event and named Rosa Prado. The May 7 report states that "Señorita Prado" carried the U.S. flag. It is most likely that Rosa Prado is Señorita Prado. According to the May 6 report, Luisa Moreno led the first phase of the march, but the May 7 report lists her as a participant. Moreno was at the event and one of the thousands of women, but the prominance of her role cannot be confirmed. She did, however, take an active role in the planning of the protest.

181. *La Gaceta*, May 7, 1937; *Tampa Morning Tribune*, May 7, 1937. According to *La Gaceta*, more than 7,000 participated in this event. The *Tampa Morning Tribune* estimated that 5,000 women constituted the population of the marchers. According to these estimates, it is reasonable to conclude the number of non-Latina community supporters from Ybor City was roughly 2,000 people.

182. *La Gaceta*, May 7, 1937.

183. FWP, "Study of Tampa Cubans" (unpublished manuscript, 1941), 283–84, SCUSF.

184. Neither Spanish-language nor English-language newspapers reported on the identity of the woman who stepped forward to address the mayor, and her identity remains unknown.

185. *La Gaceta*, May 7, 1937.

186. *La Gaceta*, May 7, 1937.

187. Cigar Makers' International Union Records, "Correspondence," in "Local 336, Tampa, FL, 1926–1973," Series 2, Reel 19, Frame 1776, HMAMD.

188. *La Gaceta*, September 1, 1938; see also *La Gaceta*, 1938–39. All activity, including marches and parades, are under daily reports of activity in the community. There is reel-to-reel footage of the 1938 parade in SCUSF.

Chapter Three

1. Federal Writers' Project (hereafter cited as FWP), "Pedro and Estrella," folklore observation conducted in January 1939 by Stetson Kennedy, in American Guide, Tampa, Florida (hereafter cited as Tampa Report), 436–56, SCUSF. The FWP Tampa Report, which centers on Ybor City, was compiled circa 1942. This report includes sixty-one individual studies, interviews, and folklore reports. When possible, the date of the document/interview/report and the name of the author have been provided; however, most are not dated and do not include clear authorship notation. From evidence within the reports, it is clear that the FWP studied the community throughout the years of 1936 and 1941. Kennedy wrote "Pedro and Estrella" as an anthropological story through folklorist methodology while he worked as a writer for the Works Progress Administration (WPA). In the study, Kennedy noted that he did this work and did this story while off duty. Kennedy was not assigned to the Ybor City or Tampa study, but was on a trip to see his wife's family. Kennedy, however, did become famous from his work with the WPA in which he documented women and men who had been formerly enslaved and later infiltrated the Ku Klux Klan. For more on his work and writing, see, for example, Stetson Kennedy, *Palmetto Country* (Gainesville: University Press of Florida, 2009); Stetson Kennedy, *Southern Exposure: Making the South Safe for Democracy* (Tuscaloosa: University of Alabama Press, 1946); Stetson Kennedy, *I Rode with the Klan* (Tuscaloosa: University of Alabama Press, 2010).

2. "E. Regensburg and Sons cigar factory at 2701 16th Street in Ybor City, front and side facades," Burgert Brothers Photographic Collection, Digital Collections, John F. Germany Library, Hillsborough County Public Library System, Tampa, Fla.; FWP, "Pedro and Estrella."

3. FWP, "Pedro and Estrella."

4. FWP, "Pedro and Estrella"; Gary R. Mormino and George E. Pozzetta, *The Immigrant World of Ybor City: Italians and Their Latin Neighbors in Tampa, 1885–1985*, 2nd ed. (Gainesville: University Press of Florida, 1998), 105, 113; Dolores Patiño Río, oral history interview with Nancy A. Hewitt, 1980, interview in the author's possession. This oral history will become a part of the Nancy Hewitt Collection at SCUSF in the future.

5. FWP, "Pedro and Estrella." Those who owned chinchales rolled cigars anywhere they could. Some used their own homes and porches as their primary workspace. As labels became more popular, some were able to move into their own brick-and-mortar space. One famous brand that took this route is Arturo Fuente. Perhaps the most famous cigar brand from Ybor that survives today, Arturo Fuente was a chinchal during the late 1930s and did not expand until the 1960s. For more, see Paul Guzzo, "Cynthia Fuente: The First Lady of Cigars," *Cigar City Magazine*, August–September 2012, https://issuu.com/cigarcitymagazine/docs/cigarcity40.

6. FWP, "Pedro and Estrella," 6.

7. For more on the welfare state in Tampa, see Elna C. Green, "Relief from Relief: The Tampa Sewing Room Strike of 1937 and the Right to Welfare," *Journal of American History* 94, no. 5 (March 2009): 1012–37; James Francis Tidd, "Stitching and Striking: WPA Sewing Rooms and the 1937 Relief Strike in Ybor City," *Tampa Bay History* 11, no. 1 (June 1989): 5–21. For more on women and the early welfare state, see Linda Gordon, *Pitied but Not Entitled: Single Mothers and the History of Welfare, 1890–1935* (Cambridge, Mass.: Harvard University Press, 1998); Gwendolyn Mink, *The Wages of Motherhood: Inequality in the Welfare State, 1917–1942* (Ithaca, N.Y.: Cornell University Press, 1996); Cybelle Fox, *Three Worlds of Relief: Race, Immigration, and the American Welfare State, from the Progressive Era to the New Deal* (Princeton, N.J.: Princeton University Press, 2012); Alice Kessler Harris, *In Pursuit of Equity: Women, Men, and the Quest for Economic Citizenship in Twentieth-Century America* (New York: Oxford University Press, 2001); Michael K. Brown, *Race, Money, and the American Welfare State* (Ithaca, N.Y.: Cornell University Press, 1999).

8. The literature on this topic is extensive; see, for example, Mae M. Ngai, *Impossible Subjects: Illegal Aliens and the Making of Modern America* (Princeton, N.J.: Princeton University Press, 2004); Suzanne Oboler, ed., *Latinos and Citizenship: The Dilemma of Belonging* (New York: Palgrave Macmillan, 2006).

9. On ethnic Americanism and the Popular Front, see Michael Denning, *The Cultural Front: The Laboring of American Culture in the Twentieth Century* (New York: Verso, 1996).

10. Jennifer Guglielmo, *Living the Revolution: Italian Women's Resistance and Radicalism in New York City, 1880–1945* (Chapel Hill: University of North Carolina Press, 2010); David T. Beito, "'Practice of Thrift and Economy: Fraternal Societies and Social Capital, 1890–1920," *Journal of Interdisciplinary History* 29, no. 4 (Spring 1999): 585–612; David T. Beito, "'Thy Brother's Keeper': The Mutual Aid Tradition of American Fraternal Orders," *Policy Review* 70 (Fall 1994): 55–60.

11. FWP, "Study of the Círculo Cubano," in Tampa Report, 106–45; FWP, "Study of the Centro Asturiano," in Tampa Report, 313–37; FWP, "Study of the Centro Español," in Tampa Report, 338–91; Robert Kerstein, *Politics and Growth in Twentieth-Century Tampa* (Gainesville: University Press of Florida, 2001), 48; Robert P. Ingalls, *Urban Vigilantes in the New South: Tampa, 1882–1936* (Gainesville: University Press of Florida, 1988).

12. *Tampa Morning Tribune*, May 15 and 17, 1914, quoted in Nancy A. Hewitt, *Southern Discomfort: Women's Activism in Tampa, Florida, 1880s–1920s* (Urbana: University of Illinois Press, 2001), 201; Emanuel Leto, *Fraternidad: The Mutual Aid Societies of Ybor City* (Tampa, Fla.: Ybor City Museum Society, 2004), 13.

13. Hewitt, *Southern Discomfort*. In 2002, Hewitt noted that a copy of Luisa Capetillo's book, *Mi opinión sobre las libertades, derechos y deberes de la mujer*, signed by the author, sat in the Centro Asturiano library. As of 2022, the book is no longer there.

14. For more on mutual aid, see Mormino and Pozzetta, *Immigrant World*; Hewitt, *Southern Discomfort*; Susan D. Greenbaum, *More than Black: Afro-Cubans in Tampa* (Gainesville: University Press of Florida, 2002); Robert P. Ingalls and Louis A. Pérez Jr., *Tampa Cigar Workers: A Pictorial History* (Gainesville: University Press of Florida, 2003); Kenya C. Dworkin y Méndez, "Latin Place Making in the Late Nineteenth

and Early Twentieth Centuries: Cuban Émigrés and Their Transnational Impact in Tampa, Florida," *English Language Notes* 56, no. 2 (October 2018): 124–42; Ana Varela-Lago, "From Patriotism to Mutualism: The Early Years of the Centro Español," *Tampa Bay History* 15, no. 2 (Fall/Winter 1993): 5–23; Leto, *Fraternidad*.

15. Mormino and Pozzetta, *Immigrant World*, 180–81, 188–97; Leto, *Fraternidad*, 8.

16. For more on the conflicting and nebulous relationship with race in Cuba during the movement of independence, see Lillian Guerra, *The Myth of José Martí: Conflicting Nationalisms in Early Twentieth-Century Cuba* (Chapel Hill: University of North Carolina Press, 2005); see also chapter 2, "Resisting," in this book.

17. Nancy Raquel Mirabal, "De Aquí, de Allá: Race, Empire, and Nation in the Making of Cuban Migrant Communities in New York and Tampa, 1823–1924" (Ph.D. diss., University of Michigan, 2001), 199–202. As a note, there were two Black Cuban associations in Tampa, the Martí-Maceo Society for Free Thinkers and La Unión; in 1904 they united and created La Sociedad de la Unión Martí-Maceo.

18. Mirabal, "De Aquí, de Allá," 199–202; FWP, "The Life History of Ramón Sanfeliz," interview conducted in January 1939, in Tampa Report, 510–15. See also Greenbaum, *More than Black*.

19. Quoted in Mirabal, "De Aquí, de Allá," 201; José Rivero Muñiz, "Los cubanos en Tampa," *Revista Bimestre Cubana*, 1958, 128–29.

20. Greenbaum, *More than Black*, 126–27.

21. Sylvia Griñan, quoted in *Tampa Morning Tribune*, September 14, 1977; also in Ingalls and Pérez, *Tampa Cigar Workers*, 119.

22. The namesakes of the La Sociedad de la Unión Martí-Maceo (the Cuban writer and martyr José Martí and the Afro-Cuban general Antonio Maceo) fought in the Cuban War for Independence. Placing their names together sought to emphasize the centrality of anti-racism as a component of the promise of a free and independent Cuba as well as the principles leaders of this club wished for their organization to represent. For more on this topic, see Susan D. Greenbaum, "Afro-Cubans in Exile: Tampa Florida, 1886–1984," *Tampa Bay History* 7, no. 2 (1985): 82–84; Greenbaum, *More than Black*.

23. Leto, *Fraternidad*, 18; Greenbaum, *More than Black*.

24. Mormino and Pozzetta, *Immigrant World*, 187.

25. Quoted in Mormino and Pozzetta, *Immigrant World*, 187; Juan Maella, oral history interview, August 15, 1982, SCUSF.

26. FWP, "Study of the Círculo Cubano"; FWP, "Study of the Centro Asturiano"; FWP, "Study of the Centro Español"; Mormino and Pozzetta, *Immigrant World*, 175–205; Leto, *Fraternidad*. Additional information on the widening of mutual aid membership is available through SCUSF in the membership booklets located in collections for Centro Asturiano, Centro Español, Círculo Cubano, La Unión Martí-Maceo, and L'Unione Italiana. Each year mutual aid societies issued new membership booklets with updated information about benefits and the state of each institution.

27. FWP, "Study of the Círculo Cubano"; FWP, "Study of the Centro Asturiano"; FWP, "Study of the Centro Español," 342–41; Hewitt, *Southern Discomfort*, 202.

28. Tony Pizzo, "Tony Pizzo's Ybor City: An Interview with Tony Pizzo," *Tampa Bay History* 2 (Spring/Summer 1980): 22–39; Ingalls and Perez, *Tampa Cigar Workers*, 131.

29. FWP, "Life History of Dr. M. Santos," in Tampa Report, 516–28.

30. FWP, "Study of the Centro Español," 342–44; FWP, "Study of the Círculo Cubano"; FWP, "Study of the Centro Asturiano."

31. FWP, "Study of the Centro Español" 342–44; FWP, "Study of the Círculo Cubano"; FWP, "Study of the Centro Asturiano"; Guglielmo, *Living the Revolution*, 140–43.

32. FWP, "Study of the Centro Español" 342–44; FWP, "Study of the Círculo Cubano"; FWP, "Study of the Centro Asturiano"; Guglielmo, *Living the Revolution*, 140–43.

33. Mormino and Pozzetta, *Immigrant World*, 200.

34. *Tampa Morning Tribune*, February 11, 1973; Mormino and Pozzetta, *Immigrant World*, 201, 197–203; Leto, *Fraternidad*, 20; FWP, Tampa Report, 106–39, 313–37, 342–44.

35. FWP, Tampa Report, 358; Leto, *Fraternidad*, 19; Mormino and Pozzetta, *Immigrant World*. The exact amount of unemployment varied between centros. At the Centro Español the benefit was $6.00 a week for sixteen weeks, while La Unión Martí-Maceo supported members with $1.50 per day of unemployment.

36. FWP, "Ybor City, Medical and Welfare Aid," in Tampa Report, 355–58; FWP, "Welfare Aid," in Tampa Report, 385–87.

37. FWP, "Welfare Aid," 385–87.

38. FWP, "Welfare Aid," 385.

39. FWP, "Welfare Aid," 385. The timeline of dismissal from the sociedad varied between organizations. While the Centro Asturiano and Círculo Cubano permitted three months of delinquent payments, the Centro Español allowed only two. For more, see FWP, "Study of the Círculo Cubano"; FWP, "Study of the Centro Asturiano"; FWP, "Study of the Centro Español." See also Salatha Bagley, "The Latin Clubs of Tampa, Florida" (master's thesis, Duke University, January 1948).

40. Río, interview with Hewitt, 1980; Nancy A. Hewitt, "Women in Ybor City: An Interview with a Woman Cigarworker," *Tampa Bay History* 7, no. 2 (Fall/Winter 1985): 164–65 (for reference to children and labor), 161–65 (full context and discussion).

41. Río, interview with Hewitt, 1980; Hewitt, "Women in Ybor City," 164–65.

42. Río, interview with Hewitt, 1980; Kennedy, *Palmetto Country*.

43. Landon R. Y. Storrs, *Civilizing Capitalism: The National Consumers' League, Women's Activism, and Labor Standards in the New Deal Era* (Chapel Hill: University of North Carolina Press, 2000); Suzanne Mettler, *Dividing Citizens: Gender and Federalism in New Deal Policy* (Ithaca, N.Y.: Cornell University Press, 1998); Lizabeth Cohen, *Making a New Deal: Industrial Workers in Chicago, 1919–1930* (Cambridge, Mass.: Harvard University Press); Patricia Sullivan, *Days of Hope: Race and Democracy in the New Deal* (Chapel Hill: University of North Carolina Press, 1999).

44. Green, "Relief from Relief"; Tidd, "Stitching and Striking."

45. FWP, "The Cuban Family in Ybor City," in Tampa Report, 270.

46. FWP, "The Cuban Family," 271.

47. FWP, "The Cuban Family," 272 (quotation), 270–75 (full context and discussion).

48. FWP, "The Cuban Family," 272 (quotation), 270–75 (full context and discussion).

49. FWP, "The Cuban Family," 272 (quotation), 270–75 (full context and discussion).

50. FWP, "The Cuban Family," 272.

51. FWP, "The Cuban Family," 272.

52. FWP, "The Cuban Family," 273. Jose Yglesias remembers similar stereotypes of Cuban women in his testimonio *The Truth about Them* (1971; repr., Houston, Tex.: Arte Público Press, 1999), 83.

53. From accounts of the 1930s, there are references to sex work, but few that are direct. In the testimonio Stetson Kennedy recorded of his encounter with Estrella and Pedro, that conversation discusses one woman who labored as a sex worker. Given, however, the nature of the Depression and the catastrophic effect it had on the community, it is likely that this was more common than oral histories or written accounts relay. See FWP, "Pedro and Estrella," 392–411.

54. FWP, "The Cuban Family," 261–300.

55. FWP, "The Cuban Family," 261–300.

56. FWP, "The Cuban Family," 261–300.

57. FWP, "The Cuban Family," 261–300.

58. FWP, "The Study on Religion in Ybor City," in Tampa Report, 248–84.

59. *Tampa Morning Tribune*, July 30, 1944.

60. Frank Urso, oral history interview with Gary R. Mormino, SPOHP; Mormino and Pozzetta, *Immigrant World*, 24. For more on the use of this epithet, see Frank Urso, *A Stranger in the Barrio: Memoir of a Tampa Sicilian* (Lincoln, Nebr.: iUniverse, 2005); Yglesias, *The Truth about Them*. Many oral histories at SPOHP and SCUSF discuss this phrase.

61. Yglesias, *The Truth about Them*, 127.

62. Perla M. Guerrero, *Nuevo South: Latinas/os, Asians, and the Remaking of Place* (Austin: University of Texas Press, 2017); Natalia Molina, *How Race Is Made in America: Immigration, Citizenship, and the Historical Power of Racial Scripts* (Berkeley: University of California Press, 2014); Natalia Molina, *Relational Formations of Race: Theory, Method, and Practice* (Berkeley: University of California Press, 2019). For more on anti-Blackness in the U.S. South, see Cecilia Márquez, *Making the Latino South: A History of Racial Formation* (Chapel Hill: University of North Carolina Press, 2023).

63. *Tampa Morning Tribune*, March 8, 1940.

64. *Tampa Morning Tribune*, March 8, 1940.

65. "Carta de Fermin Soto a Embajada de España Washington, D.C.," June 2, 1937, Box 6, Folder Centro Español Correspondence, TPC. This folder details four years of correspondence between Tampa Latinas/os and the ambassadors of Spain and Cuba. For more on antifascist movement in Tampa, see chapter 2, "Resisting," in this book.

66. *Tampa Morning Tribune*, March 8, 1940.

67. *Tampa Morning Tribune*, March 8, 1940. For more on radicalism and anti-communism in the U.S. South, see Mark Fannin, *Labor's Promised Land: Radical Visions of Gender, Race, and Religion in the South* (Knoxville: University of Tennessee Press, 2003); Robin D. G. Kelley, *Hammer and Hoe: Alabama Communists during the Great Depression* (Chapel Hill: University of North Carolina Press, 1990); M. J. Heale, *American Anticommunism: Combating the Enemy Within* (Baltimore: Johns Hopkins University Press, 1990).

68. *Tampa Morning Tribune*, March 8, 1940.

69. Zaragosa Vargas, *Labor Rights Are Civil Rights: Mexican American Workers in Twentieth-Century America* (Princeton, N.J.: Princeton University Press, 2007), 168–69.

70. Letter from J. S. to Brown, October 28, 1935, Microfilm Reel 298, Folder 3990, 1, CPUSAR; *Tampa Morning Tribune*, October 1935. For more on anticommunism in Tampa, see *Tampa Morning Tribune*, *St. Petersburg Times*, and *Tampa Times*, from 1935 to 1945. See also Ingalls, *Urban Vigilantes*; Mormino and Pozzetta, *Immigrant World*; Hewitt, *Southern Discomfort*; Ingalls and Pérez, *Tampa Cigar Workers*.

71. Letter from J. S. to Brown, October 28, 1935; FWP, "Amanda and Enrique," folklore observation conducted in January 1939 by Stetson Kennedy, in Tampa Report, 412–35; "In the Matter of Cigar Manufacturers Association of Tampa, Florida and Cigarmakers International Union of America," U.S. Department of Labor Report, February 1, 1938, CMIUC; *Daily Worker*, October 13, 1938. See also Ingalls, *Urban Vigilantes*.

72. A. M. De Quesada, *Images of America: Ybor City* (Charleston, S.C.: Acadia Publishing, 1999); "1938 CIO March in Ybor City," video footage, SCUSF; *La Gaceta*, March–April, 1939; *Tampa Morning Tribune*, April 1, 1939. For more on the history of antifascism in Ybor City and Tampa and the Spanish Civil War, see chapter 2, "Resisting," in this book; Ana Varela-Lago, "¡No Pasarán! The Spanish Civil War's Impact on Tampa's Latin Community, 1936–1939," *Tampa Bay History* 19, no. 2 (1997): 5–35; Ana Varela-Lago, "'We Had to Help': Remembering Tampa's Response to the Spanish Civil War," *Tampa Bay History* 19, no. 2 (1997): 36–56; Spanish Civil War Oral History Project, interviews by Ana Varela-Lago, SCUSF.

73. FWP, "Amanda and Enrique," 12; Jacquelyn Dowd Hall, "The Long Civil Rights Movement and the Political Uses of the Past," *Journal of American History* 91, no. 4 (March 2005): 1233–63.

74. "Letter to Francis Perkins from Ybor City Cigar Workers," February 11, 1938, and "Letter to Eleanor Roosevelt from Ybor City Cigar Workers," February 11, 1938, Cigar Makers' International Union Papers, National Archives Microfilm Publication, DOL.

75. *Tampa Morning Tribune*, March 8, 1940.

76. Sylvia Vega, interview with Nancy A. Hewitt, January 27, 1989, interview in the author's possession. This oral history will become a part of the Nancy Hewitt Collection at SCUSF in the future.

77. *Tampa Morning Tribune*, May 26, 1944; Gary R. Mormino, "Ybor City Goes to War: The Evolution and Transformation of a 'Latin' Community in Florida, 1886–1950," in *Latina/os and World War II: Mobility, Agency, and Ideology*, ed. Maggie Rivas-Rodríguez and B. V. Olguín (Austin: University of Texas Press, 2014), 13–42; Steven F. Lawson, "Ybor City and Baseball: An Interview with Al López," *Tampa Bay History* 7, no. 2 (1985): 59–76.

78. Cesar Marcos Medina, oral history interview with Gary R. Mormino, May 22, 1984, SPOHP.

79. Medina, interview with Mormino; conversation between Andrea McNamara and Sarah McNamara, June 2021. Pedro Blanco is the great-grandfather of the author and the son of Amelia Alvarez; see introduction, "Searching," in this book.

80. Medina, interview with Mormino; see also Mormino, "Ybor City Goes to War"; Mormino and Pozzetta, *Immigrant World*.

81. Evelio Grillo, *Black Cuban, Black American: A Memoir* (Houston, Tex.: Arte Público Press, 2000), vii, 19, 39.

82. *Tampa Morning Tribune*, June 13, 1944.

83. *Tampa Morning Tribune*, July 30, 1944.

84. *Tampa Morning Tribune*, September 27, 1944; *La Gaceta*, September 27, 1944.

85. *Tampa Daily Times*, February 25, 1935; Emanuel Leto, "Viva La Verbena: Tampa's Original Cigar Festival," *Cigar City Magazine*, September–October 2007. See also Brad Massey, "Señoritas and Cigarmaking Women: Using 'Latin' Feminine Types to Rebrand and Market Ybor City, 1950–1962," *Sunland Tribune* 34 (2017): 54–82; Blain Roberts, "A New Cure for Brightleaf Tobacco: The Origins of the Tobacco Queen during the Great Depression," *Southern Cultures* 12, no. 2 (2006): 30–52.

86. *Tampa Morning Tribune*, January 6, 1941. For more on tobacco queens and promotional material in Tampa, see Burgert Brothers Photographic Collection, Digital Collections, University of South Florida; Burgert Brothers Photographic Collection, John F. Germany Library, Digital Collections, Hillsborough County Public Library System, Tampa, Florida.

87. "The National Registration of Aliens: Instructions for Registration and Specimen Form," August 27, 1940, Box 31, Folder: Immigration Administration, TPC.

88. "Alien Registration and the Spanish Speaking Non-Citizen," November 6, 1940, Library and Archive of the Centro Asturiano, Centro Asturiano de Tampa, Tampa, Fla.

89. "Alien Registration and the Spanish Speaking Non-Citizen."

90. United States Census Office, *Fourteenth Census of the United States*, 1920; United States Census Office, *Fifteenth Census of the United States*, 1930; United States Census Office, *Sixteenth Census of the United States*, 1940; United States Census Office, *Seventeenth Census of the United States*, 1950; Braulio Alonso Jr., conversation with Gary R. Mormino, Tampa, Fla., May 24, 2001. See also Braulio Alonso Jr. File, SCUSF. The file contains a series of essays Alonso wrote at the request of Mormino; Mormino, "Ybor City Goes to War," 20–21. I thank Gary R. Mormino for his work interviewing and writing about Ybor Latinas/os of the World War II generation, a topic few have documented. His work guided me through this section, and I am thankful for his scholarship, generosity, and kindness.

91. For more on the number of factories in business on the eve of World War II and detailed information on the state of the industry, see A. Stuart Campbell, *The Cigar Industry of Tampa, Florida*, with W. Porter McLendon (Gainesville: Bureau of Economic and Business Research, University of Florida, 1939), 90, 134, Digital Collections, Special Collections of George A. Smathers Libraries, University of Florida, Gainesville, Fla., accessed November 2020, http://ufdc.ufl.edu/UF00055151/0000; Abraham Scherr, "Tampa's MacDill Field during World War II," *Tampa Bay History* 17, no. 1 (Spring/Summer 1995): 5–15; Gary R. Mormino, *Hillsborough County Goes to War: The Home Front, 1940–1950* (Tampa, Fla.: Tampa Bay History Center, 2001); Lewis W. Wynne, "Shipbuilding in Tampa during World War II," *Sunland Tribune* 16 (1990): 35–42; Andrew T. Huse, *From Saloons to Steak Houses: A History of Tampa* (Gainesville: University Press of Florida, 2020), 188–89. For more on the experience of World War II throughout the Tampa area, see Susan O'Brien Culp, "For the Duration: Women's Roles in St. Petersburg and Tampa during World War II," *Tampa Bay History* 17, no. 1 (Spring/Summer 1995): 16–32; Ellen J. Babb, "A Community within a Community: African American Women in St. Petersburg during World War II," *Tampa Bay History* 17, no. 1

(Spring/Summer 1995): 34–47; "The Homefront on Florida's West Coast: A Photographic Essay," *Tampa Bay History* 17, no. 1 (Spring/Summer 1995): 48–64; Catherine Féré, "Crime and Racial Violence in Tampa during World War II," *Tampa Bay History* 17, no. 1 (Spring/Summer 1995): 65–82; "V-J Day Celebrations in Tampa Bay Area," *Tampa Bay History* 17, no. 1 (Spring/Summer 1995): 83–91.

92. Mormino, "Ybor City Goes to War," 27–28.

93. Jose Yglesias, *One German Dead* (Leeds, UK: Eremite Press, 1988), 6; Ingalls and Pérez, *Tampa Cigar Workers*, 204; Robert P. Ingalls, "Remembering Ybor City: The Life and Work of Jose Yglesias," *Tampa Bay History* 18, no. 1 (Spring/Summer 1996): 12; Mormino, "Ybor City Goes to War," 29.

94. *La Gaceta*, December 8, 1941; *La Gaceta*, June 19, 1944.

95. Mormino, "Ybor City Goes to War," 21. See also Braulio Alonso Jr. File, SCUSF.

96. Alonso, conversation with Mormino; Braulio Alonso Jr., "German Surrender in the Dolomite Alps," Braulio Alonso Jr. File, SCUSF; Mormino, "Ybor City Goes to War," 31.

97. Grillo, quoted in Greenbaum, *More than Black*, 260; Grillo, quoted in Mormino, "Ybor City Goes to War," 34. See also Grillo, *Black Cuban, Black American*.

98. Frank Andre Guridy, "Pvt. Evelio Grillo and Sgt. Norberto González: Afro-Latino Experiences of War and Segregation," in Rivas-Rodríguez and Olguín, *Latina/os and World War II*, 43–58.

99. Mormino, "Ybor City Goes to War," 37.

100. Providence Velasco, interview with Nancy A. Hewitt, January 16, 1989; *Tampa Morning Tribune*, December 19, 1941; *La Gaceta*, December 19, 1941; Vega, interview with Hewitt; *La Gaceta*, April 7, 1942.

101. Mormino, "Ybor City Goes to War," 26–27.

102. Jose Yglesias, "Buscando un Sueño de Tampa a Nueva York," *Mas*, July–August 1991, 60–61; also in Mormino, "Ybor City Goes to War," 37.

103. *La Gaceta*, June 5, 1944.

104. *Tampa Morning Tribune*, May 26–June 8, 1944.

105. *Tampa Morning Tribune*, June 2–8, 1944.

106. *Tampa Morning Tribune*, July 4, 2008; Mormino, "Ybor City Goes to War," 32.

107. Ingalls and Pérez, *Tampa Cigar Workers*, 201.

108. Mormino, "Ybor City Goes to War," 39.

109. Mormino and Pozzetta, *Immigrant World*, 300–301; Mormino, "Ybor City Goes to War," 39.

110. Mormino, "Ybor City Goes to War," 38–39. See also *Tampa Morning Tribune*, September 5, 1945; *Tampa Daily Times*, September 9, 1947; Mormino, *Hillsborough County Goes to War*, 131–32.

Chapter Four

Epigraph: Quoted in Robert P. Ingalls and Louis A. Pérez Jr., *Tampa Cigar Workers: A Pictorial History* (Gainesville: University Press of Florida, 2003), 13.

1. *Tampa Tribune*, June 3, 2012; *Tampa Tribune*, November 19, 1963; *Tampa Tribune*, November 17, 1963.

2. United States Census Office, *Fourteenth Census of the United States, 1920*. Julia Maseda was born in Cuba to a Spanish father and a Cuban mother. By nationality, both Julia and her mother were, indeed, Cuban.

3. The earliest records of José Maseda's career indicate that he began as a selector in 1899. By 1908, he was promoted to management and worked as a foreman in the factories and continued this through the 1920s. In 1930, he again worked as a selector; *Tampa City Directory*, 1899–1920, TBHC; United States Census Office, *Fourteenth Census of the United States, 1920*; United States Census Office, *Fifteenth Census of the United States, 1930*; "Maseda House at 3001 Chestnut and Gomez," Tampa Pix, March 15, 2014, www.tampapix.com/westtampawalk.htm. For more on the work of Maseda's cigar factory, see *Tampa City Directory*, 1934–36, TBHC. For a review of the entirety of Maseda's employment history, see Tampa City Directories at TBHC. For information on the details of labor-based terminology in the Cuban cigar industry, see chapter 1, "Building," in this book.

4. *Tampa Tribune*, June 3, 2012; *Tampa Tribune*, November 19, 1963; *Tampa Tribune*, November 17, 1963; *Tampa Tribune*, February 12, 2012; *La Gaceta*, March 2, 2012; United States Census Office, *Fifteenth Census of the United States, 1930*. For a more detailed history of Marcelo Maseda's employment history, see *Tampa City Directory*, 1940–60, TBHC; United States Census Office, *Sixteenth Census of the United States, 1940*; "Marcelo Maseda World War II Draft Registration Card," Records of the Selective Service System, National Archives at St. Louis, NARA; Mario Núñez, Steve Cannella, and Sally Núñez, "Tampa Natives Show: Marcelo Maseda-Alcalde," *Tampa Natives Show*, episode 86, accessed June 2022, https://digitalcommons.usf.edu/tampa _natives_show/86. For more on suburbs, see Becky Nicolaides, *My Blue Heaven: Life and Politics in the Working-Class Suburbs of Los Angeles, 1920–1965* (Chicago: University of Chicago Press, 2002); Lisa McGirr, *Suburban Warriors: The Origins of the New American Right* (Princeton, N.J.: Princeton University Press, 2001).

5. *La Gaceta*, March 12, 2022; *Tampa Tribune*, February 26, 2012.

6. Gustavo Jesus (Gus) Alfonso, conversation with the author, June 20, 2022, field notes in possession of the author; Emilio Gonzalez-Llanes, *Cigar City Stories: Tales of Old Ybor City* (Bloomington, Ind.: iUniverse, 2012); Gary R. Mormino, "Ybor City Goes to War: The Evolution and Transformation of a 'Latin' Community in Florida, 1886–1950," in *Latina/os and World War II: Mobility, Agency, and Ideology*, ed. Maggie Rivas-Rodríguez and B. V. Olguín (Austin: University of Texas Press, 2014), 13–42; Clarita Garcia, *Clarita's Cocina: Great Traditional Recipes from a Spanish Kitchen* (Gainesville, Fla.: Seaside Publishing, 1990).

7. *Tampa Tribune*, December 14, 1969; also in Ingalls and Pérez, *Tampa Cigar Workers*, 205; United States Census Office, *Seventeenth Census of the United States, 1950*; *Tampa City Directory*, 1945–50, TBHC and SCUSF.

8. Alfonso, conversation with the author; Mormino, "Ybor City Goes to War"; Ingalls and Pérez, *Tampa Cigar Workers*, 206–11; Federal Writers' Project (hereafter cited as FWP), "Life History of Fernando Lemos," interviewed in January 1939, in American Guide, Tampa, Florida (hereafter cited as Tampa Report), 491–95, SCUSF; FWP, "Life History of Enrique Pendas," in Tampa Report, 496–509; "Arturo Fuente Story," video, accessed June 2022, www.youtube.com/watch?v=9nUqDgIUXQ4; Paul Guzzo, "Cynthia

Fuente: The First Lady of Cigars," *Cigar City Magazine*, August–September 2012, https://issuu.com/cigarcitymagazine/docs/cigarcity40. For information on labor-based Cuban cigar industry terminology, see chapter 1, "Building," in this book.

9. Gustavo Jesus (Gus) Alfonso, conversation with the author, June 20, 2022, field notes in possession of the author; comparative analysis of the 1940 and 1950 censuses, as well as city directories during this period, illustrates this trend in noncigar industry employment in Ybor City and West Tampa. See United States Census Office, *Sixteenth Census of the United States, 1940*; United States Census Office, *Seventeenth Census of the United States, 1950*; *Tampa City Directory*, 1940–50, TBHC and SCUSF.

10. For more on postwar consumerism, see Lizabeth Cohen, *A Consumers' Republic: The Politics of Mass Consumption in Postwar America* (New York: Vintage Books, 2004); Charles F. McGovern, *Sold American: Consumption and Citizenship, 1890–1945* (Chapel Hill: University of North Carolina Press, 2006).

11. Gary R. Mormino and George E. Pozzetta, *The Immigrant World of Ybor City: Italians and Their Latin Neighbors in Tampa, 1885–1985*, 2nd ed. (Gainesville: University Press of Florida, 1998), 53–59, 147; Robert Kerstein, *Politics and Growth in Twentieth-Century Tampa* (Gainesville: University Press of Florida, 2001), 99, 103, 118–19; Robert P. Ingalls, *Urban Vigilantes in the New South: Tampa, 1882–1936* (Knoxville: University of Tennessee Press, 1988).

12. Thomas Devine, *Henry Wallace's 1948 Presidential Campaign and the Future of Postwar Liberalism* (Chapel Hill: University of North Carolina Press, 2013). I thank the excellent work of the historian Jared G. Toney, whose thesis illustrated the importance of the Henry Wallace campaign in Tampa and the direction it provided this examination. Jared G. Toney, "'Viva Wallace!' Tampa Latins, the Politics of Americanization, and the Progressive Campaign of 1948" (master's thesis, University of South Florida, 2002).

13. Zaragosa Vargas, *In the Cause of Freedom: Early Mexican American Political and Intellectual Activism and Transnational Struggle, 1946–1963* (New Haven, Conn.: Yale University Press, forthcoming), 13; Devine, *Henry Wallace's 1948 Presidential Campaign*. Throughout 1948, *La Gaceta* praised Wallace. For more accounts, see especially *La Gaceta*, February, October, and November 1948.

14. Vargas, *In the Cause of Freedom*, 16; Devine, *Henry Wallace's 1948 Presidential Campaign*.

15. "Manifesto," n.d., Reies López Tijerina Collection, 1888–1978, MSS 654BC, Box 54, Folder 1, CSR.

16. "Manifesto"; United States Census Office, *Seventeenth Census of the United States, 1950*.

17. Devine, *Henry Wallace's 1948 Presidential Campaign*, ix.

18. Devine, *Henry Wallace's 1948 Presidential Campaign*, ix–x.

19. Devine, *Henry Wallace's 1948 Presidential Campaign*, x, 69, 233–68; *New York Times*, September 11, 1948; *Tampa Morning Tribune*, October 5, 1948; Toney, "'Viva Wallace!,'" 57–59.

20. *Lakeland Ledger*, February 6, 1948. See the *Lakeland Ledger*, February–October 1948. Such advertisements are plentiful and frequent; also in Toney, "'Viva Wallace!,'" 40.

21. *Tampa Morning Tribune*, June 1, 1948; *Tampa Morning Tribune*, October 27, 1948; *Tampa Morning Tribune*, October 28, 1948; Toney, "'Viva Wallace!,'" 68–69.

22. *St. Petersburg Times*, February 17, 1948; see also, Devine, *Henry Wallace's 1948 Presidential Campaign*.

23. *St. Petersburg Times*, February 17, 1948; *Tampa Morning Tribune*, February 17, 1948; *Tampa Morning Tribune*, February 18, 1948; Toney, "'Viva Wallace!,'" 65.

24. Toney, "'Viva Wallace!,'" 64.

25. *Tampa Morning Tribune*, February 17, 1948; *La Gaceta*, February 17, 1948; Toney, "'Viva Wallace!,'" 62. During the rally at Plant Field, anti-Franco declarations were made. See the previous newspapers and Devine, *Henry Wallace's 1948 Presidential Campaign*.

26. *Tampa Tribune*, February 18, 1948; *St. Petersburg Times*, February 18, 1948; *Tampa Tribune*, February 25, 1948.

27. *Tampa Tribune*, February 18, 1948; *St. Petersburg Times*, February 18, 1948.

28. *Tampa Tribune*, February 18, 1948.

29. *Tampa Tribune*, February 18, 1948; *St. Petersburg Times*, February 18, 1948.

30. *Tampa Morning Tribune*, February 18, 1948; *Tampa Morning Tribune*, February 17, 1948; *St. Petersburg Times*, February 18, 1948; Toney, "'Viva Wallace!,'" 60–74; Devine, *Henry Wallace's 1948 Presidential Campaign*.

31. Toney, "'Viva Wallace!,'" 73; *La Gaceta*, November 3, 1948. For more election figures and precinct maps, see Toney, "'Viva Wallace!,'" 73–74, 78–80.

32. Toney, "'Viva Wallace!,'" 74. I agree with Toney's assertion of this fact and argue that efforts to join national political parties as avenues of political representation in years prior were also illustrations of this effort. See chapter 2, "Resisting," and chapter 3, "Surviving," in this book.

33. Mormino and Pozzetta, *Immigrant World*, 302; Mormino, "Ybor City Goes to War"; chapter 3, "Surviving," in this book.

34. Susan D. Greenbaum, *More than Black: Afro-Cubans in Tampa* (Gainesville: University Press of Florida, 2002), 271–72, 270–80; *La Gaceta*, November 11–December 2, 1955; *St. Petersburg Times*, November 27–28, 1955; *Tampa Morning Tribune*, November 27–28, 1955. For more on the Cuban Revolution in the United States, see Teishan A. Latner, *Cuban Revolution in America: Havana and the Making of a United States Left, 1968–1992* (Chapel Hill: University of North Carolina Press, 2018). Paul Guzzo, a journalist for the *Tampa Bay Times*, has published articles on the visit of Castro to Tampa and the work of the 26th of July Movement in the city. For more, see his writings in the *Tampa Bay Times* as well as *Cigar City Magazine*.

35. *Tampa Morning Tribune*, November 28, 1955; also in Ingalls and Pérez, *Tampa Cigar Workers*, 213; Greenbaum, *More than Black*, 270–71.

36. Ada Ferrer, *Cuba: An American History* (New York: Scribner, 2021), 289, 290–311; Tómas, oral history interview with Susan D. Greenbaum, n.d., quoted in *More than Black*, 271–72. In Greenbaum's study of Ybor City's Afro-Cuban community, she provides lengthy excerpts of transcripts with interviewees about the Cuban Revolution. These interviews have not been donated to a university archive, but the portions of the interviews published in Greenbaum's book offer essential insight into the community and its perspective toward Castro and the Cuban Revolution.

37. Tómas, oral history interview, quoted in Greenbaum, *More than Black*, 271–72.

38. *La Gaceta*, November 25, 1955. Ferrer explains that this story was central to the origin story Castro created as part of the revolution. He also told this story during his speech in Tampa. It is likely that his discussions with people would have centered on the same topic. See, Ferrer, *Cuba*, 273–312.

39. Quoted from Ferrer, *Cuba*, 279–80. See also Lillian Guerra, *Heroes, Martyrs, and Political Messiahs in Revolutionary Cuba, 1946–1958* (New Haven, Conn.: Yale University Press, 2018); Margaret Randall, *Haydée Santamaría, Cuban Revolutionary: She Led by Transgression* (Durham, N.C.: Duke University Press, 2015); Antonio Rafael de la Cova, *The Moncada Attack: Birth of the Cuban Revolution* (Columbia: University of South Carolina Press, 2007).

40. Ferrer, *Cuba*, 289.

41. Greenbaum, *More than Black*, 274.

42. Tómas, oral history interview, quoted in Greenbaum, *More than Black*, 271–72, 270–80; William Watson Jr., "Fidel Castro's Ybor City Underground" (master's thesis, University of South Florida, 1999).

43. *La Gaceta*, April 15, 1955; *La Gaceta*, April 29, 1955; *La Gaceta*, July 8, 1955. For an examination of the state of mutual aid societies in the late 1940s, see Salatha Bagley, "The Latin Clubs of Tampa, Florida" (master's thesis, Duke University, January 1948).

44. *Tampa Morning Tribune*, November 28, 1955; *Tampa Sunday Tribune*, November 27, 1955; Tómas, oral history interview, quoted in Greenbaum, *More than Black*, 272–73.

45. Círculo Cubano Records, SCUSF; La Unión Martí-Maceo Records, SCUSF. Within these two collections are the minutes of all meetings and the membership records. Both of these items document political talks and events held at the centros during the 1950s and illustrate that ethnicity of the membership was not solely Cuban.

46. *Tampa Sunday Tribune*, November 27, 1955; *La Gaceta*, November 27, 1955; *La Gaceta*, December 2, 1955. The risk of being perceived as supporting anti-American action was a real threat in 1955. The House Un-American Activities Committee held trials in Miami in 1954 and even called some members of the Ybor City community to testify for past actions. See United States Congress, "Investigation of Communist Activities in the State of Florida—Part 1," *Hearings Before the Committee on Un-American Activities* (Washington, D.C.: Government Printing Office, 1955); see also chapter 3, "Surviving," in this book.

47. *La Gaceta*, November 25, 1955.

48. *Tampa Sunday Tribune*, November 27, 1955.

49. Greenbaum, *More than Black*, 270–71, 274.

50. Greenbaum, *More than Black*, 274–75. For more on the history of José Martí Park, see Mark I. Scheinbaum, ed., *José Martí Park: The Story of Cuban Property in Tampa* (Tampa: University of South Florida, International Studies Program, 1976).

51. *St. Petersburg Times*, November 28, 1955; *Tampa Morning Tribune*, November 28, 1955; *La Gaceta*, December 2, 1955; *St. Petersburg Times*, January 29, 1959.

52. *St. Petersburg Times*, January 29, 1959; *St. Petersburg Times*, November 28, 1955; *Tampa Morning Tribune*, November 28, 1955; *La Gaceta*, December 2, 1955; "Castro, Fidel," n.d., TPC.

53. *St. Petersburg Times*, January 18, 1959; *La Gaceta*, June 14, 1957. For more on the role and tone of *La Gaceta* throughout the Cuban Revolution and in the aftermath, see *La Gaceta*, January 1955–January 1960; Watson, "Castro's Ybor City Underground," 34.

54. Raúl Villamia, oral history interview with Maura Barrios, November 2006, Oral History Program, SCUSF; United States Census Office, *Fourteenth Census of the United States, 1920*; United States Census Office, *Fifteenth Census of the United States, 1930*; United States Census Office, *Sixteenth Census of the United States, 1940*; United States Census Office, *Seventeenth Census of the United States, 1950*; "Raúl A. Villamia Obituary," *Tampa Times*, December 7, 2020; "Raúl A. Villamia Obituary," Dignity Memorial, December 2020, www.dignitymemorial.com/obituaries/tampa-fl/raul-villamia-9931002; Watson, "Castro's Ybor City Underground." The rate of migration to Ybor City from Cuba as well as other countries slowed after 1930 due to the decline of the Cuban cigar industry and the difficulty of accessing work, and many people relocated to New York or New Jersey. While there was a population that fled Cuba as a result of the Gerardo Machado regime, these numbers were in the minority when compared to the foreign-born of previous waves as well as the native-born Florida population that existed in Ybor City and throughout Tampa by the 1950s. See the cited censuses as well as chapter 2, "Resisting," in this book; Mormino and Pozzetta, *Immigrant World*; Greenbaum, *More than Black*.

55. *Tampa Morning Tribune*, January 2, 1959; *St. Petersburg Times*, January 2, 1959; *La Gaceta*, January 2, 1959; *St. Petersburg Times*, January 18, 1959; "Castro's Success in Tampa Fires Wild Celebrations in Tampa," *Tobacco Leaf*, January 10, 1959, TPC. For a landmark study of the experience of Cuban exiles in South Florida, see María Cristina García, *Havana USA: Cuban Exiles and Cuban Americans in South Florida, 1959–1994* (Berkeley: University of California Press, 1996).

56. *Tampa Tribune*, July 27, 1984; Phil LoCicero, "My Meeting with Fidel Castro," *La Gaceta*, May 28, 1993, TPC. This issue of the *Tampa Tribune* provides excellent insight into the varied experiences of Cubans and tampeñas/os in Tampa. There is an additional section in the essay that includes oral histories with members of both communities. According to available documents on the Fair Play for Cuba Committee, a minority of the members had Latina/o surnames. For more on this and information on the committee's activities in Tampa, see Committee on the Judiciary of the United State Senate, "Castro's Network in the United States (Fair Play for Cuba Committee)—Part 2," *Hearings Before the Subcommittee to Investigate the Administration of the Internal Security Act and Other Security Laws* (Washington, D.C.: Government Printing Office, 1961); Frank S. DeBenedictis, "The Cold War Comes to Ybor City: Tampa Bay's Chapter of the Fair Play for Cuba Committee" (master's thesis, Florida Atlantic University, 2002). Jose Yglesias, the author and poet born in Ybor City, was unapologetically supportive of the Cuban Revolution. During the 1960s, he traveled to Cuba to see the changes Castro's new government brought to the island. For more, see Jose Yglesias, *In the Fist of the Revolution: Life in a Cuban Country Town* (New York: Vintage Books, 1968).

57. *Tampa Tribune*, May 14, 1979; United States Census Office, *Seventeenth Census of the United States, 1950*; *Tampa City Directory*, 1920–60, TBHC and SCUSF. Prior to

building their home, the Vega family lived on Thirteenth Avenue. Not only had they lived in the same home for fifty years, but they had lived on the same street for more than sixty years. The May 14, 1979, article from the *Tampa Tribune* misidentifies José Vega Díaz as Díaz rather than Vega. In Spanish, the first of two family names is the surname of the father, while the second is the surname of the mother. It is the first surname that passes to married partners and children. In all census and official paperwork, José Vega Díaz is identified as José Vega, as he often dropped Díaz in U.S. documentation. Likewise, the name Vega is the name his wife took, as did his children—none used Díaz.

58. *Tampa Tribune*, May 14, 1979; United States Census Office, *Seventeenth Census of the United States*, 1950; United States Census Office, *Sixteenth Census of the United States*, 1940; United States Census Office, *Fifteenth Census of the United States*, 1930; United States Census Office, *Fourteenth Census of the United States*, 1920; United States Census Office, *Thirteenth Census of the United States*, 1910; United States Census Office, *Twelfth Census of the United States*, 1900; *Tampa City Directory*, 1900–1960, TBHC and SCUSF; José Vega Díaz, oral history interview with Gary R. Mormino, August 24, 1980; *Tampa Times*, May 11, 1966; *Tampa Times*, May 27, 1965; *Tampa Tribune*, February 27, 1991; "Silvio Vega," Beneficiary Identification Records Locator System Death File, 1850–2010, Department of Veterans Affairs, Washington, D.C.; *Tampa Tribune*, September 19, 1966; *Tampa Times*, September 19, 1966; *Tampa Tribune*, September 23, 1966; *Tampa Times*, September 19, 1966.

59. *Tampa Tribune*, May 14, 1979.

60. "Home Ownership Loan Corporation," ca. 1930s, Map of Hillsborough County, Urban Planning Authority, Tampa, Fla.; Kerstein, *Politics and Growth*, 99–136. See also N. D. B. Connolly, *A World More Concrete: Real Estate and the Remaking of Jim Crow South Florida* (Chicago: University of Chicago Press, 2016); Keeanga-Yamahtta Taylor, *Race for Profit: How Banks and the Real Estate Industry Undermined Black Homeownership* (Chapel Hill: University of North Carolina Press, 2019); Richard Rothstein, *The Color of Law: A Forgotten History of How Our Government Segregated America* (New York: Liveright, 2017); A. K. Sandoval-Strausz, *Barrio America: How Latino Immigrants Saved the American City* (New York: Basic Books, 2019).

61. FWP, "Amanda and Enrique," folklore observation by Stetson Kennedy, January 1939, in Tampa Report, 412–13; Kerstein, *Politics and Growth*, 99–136.

62. "Alderman Pacheco Petition, October 26, 1936 and NAACP Response," Petitions 1936, Hillsborough County Municipal Archive, Tampa, Fla. John Pacheco was the uncle of Ferdie Pacheco, who was the famed fight doctor of Muhammad Ali and became a painter in retirement. The paintings of Ferdie Pacheco chronicle Ybor City during the 1930s and beyond.

63. "Alderman Pacheco Petition, October 26, 1936 and NAACP Response."

64. "Flor de Tampa," TBHC. See also "Flor de Tampa Cigars," video, accessed August 2022, www.youtube.com/watch?v=Kw5oTouIYco; *Tampa Tribune*, May 28, 1962; *Miami Herald*, February 8, 1959; also in Ingalls and Pérez, *Tampa Cigar Workers*, 210, 211.

65. *La Gaceta*, April 15, 1955; *La Gaceta*, August 10, 1955; *La Gaceta*, June 30, 2017. The series "The Vanishing Latin Quarter" ran throughout 1955 and again in 1965. For more, see *La Gaceta*, SCUSF.

66. For more on the history of Afro-Cubans joining civil rights organizations and moving in and between Tampa's African American communities in the post-WWII era, see Greenbaum, *More than Black*.

67. Brad Massey, "Señoritas and Cigarmaking Women: Using 'Latin' Feminine Types to Rebrand and Market Ybor City, 1950–1962," *Sunland Tribune* 34 (2017): 54–82; Brad Massey, "Defying the Sunbelt: An Economic and Environmental History of Tampa" (Ph.D. diss., University of Florida, 2017).

68. *Tampa Sunday Tribune*, June 15, 1952; "Alcalde," n.d., TPC; "Pledge of Affection," n.d., personal archive of the author, also in TPC; Massey, "Senoritas and Cigarmaking Women."

69. "Flor de Tampa," Ybor City and Hillsborough County Boosters, TBHC. Also available digitally at www.youtube.com/watch?v=Kw50TouIYco; *Tampa Morning Tribune*, January 30, 1956; *Tampa Daily Times*, November 26, 1956; Ingalls and Pérez, *Tampa Cigar Workers*, 14, 216. There are countless examples of this form of branding in Tampa newspapers throughout the 1950s; see also Massey, "Señoritas and Cigarmaking Women."

70. *Tampa Tribune*, June 3, 2012; *Tampa Tribune*, November 19, 1963; *Tampa Tribune*, November 17, 1963.

71. United States Census Office, *Seventeenth Census of the United States, 1950*; United States Census Office, *Sixteenth Census of the United States, 1940*; United States Census Office, *Fifteenth Census of the United States, 1930*; United States Census Office, *Fourteenth Census of the United States, 1920*; Vega, oral history interview Mormino; "Girls Basketball," *The Hillsborean*, Hillsborough High School Yearbook, 1936, Hillsborough High School Library, Tampa, Fla.; *Tampa Morning Tribune*, November 12, 1954; *Tampa Tribune*, May 12, 2007; Salvatore Salerno, "*I Delitti della Razza Bianca* (Crimes of the White Race): Italian Anarchists' Racial Discourse as Crime," in *Are Italians White? How Race Is Made in America*, ed. Jennifer Guglielmo and Salvatore Salerno (New York: Routledge, 2003), 294n21.

72. *Tampa Tribune*, October 4, 1958; "Urban Renewal in Ybor City: What It Can Mean to People Living Here and Owning Property Here," n.d., TPC; "Urban Renewal Pictures," n.d., TPC; "Urban Renewal," n.d., TPC; Ingalls and Pérez, *Tampa Cigar Workers*, 14, 217–22. See also Massey, "Señoritas and Cigarmaking Women," 64; Mark H. Rose and Raymond A. Mohl, *Interstate: Highway Politics and Policy since 1939* (Knoxville: University of Tennessee Press, 2012).

73. *Tampa Tribune*, May 13, 1979; "Ybor City Barrio Latino, Alternative Revitalization Plan, 1981," TPC; "Images Ybor City after I-4 and Urban Renewal," ca. 1969, Digital Collections, Hillsborough County Municipal Archive, Tampa, Fla.; Ingalls and Pérez, *Tampa Cigar Workers*, 222; *La Gaceta*, June 30, 2017; Emanuel Leto, "Ybor City before and after Urban Renewal," *Cigar City Magazine*, May–June 2008. For more on the Cuban embargo and its effect on the Ybor City cigar industry, see Sam Gibbons Collection, SCUSF.

74. Ingalls and Pérez, *Tampa Cigar Workers*, 14.

Index

Page numbers in *italics* indicate illustrations.

efforts to speak at, 157–60; *comités de damas* (women's committees), 111; decline of, 107, 113–14; hospitals and medical care provided by, 109, 113, 114; in post-WWII period, 158–59; racial segregation of, 3, 111–13; significance of, 108–13, *110, 112*; Spanish Civil War and antifascist movement, 95, 96, 99, 104; stage performances sponsored by, 75–76; unemployment insurance provided by, 75, 113–14, 226n35; La Verbena festival, 128. *See also specific clubs by name*

Cervantes, Miguel, 108

Chancey, Robert E. Lee, 101–2, 122–24, 129

chavetas, 45, 82

Chávez, Dennis, 131

chinchales (buckeyes/small-scale cigar enterprises), 46, 94, 105–6, 140, 169, 223n5

Cigar City Stories (Gonzalez-Llanes), 77–78, 216n79

cigar industry, 1–2, 18–19, 37–47, 177; Anglo women, employment of, 91, *93*, 143; antifascist movement and, 100, 101; apprenticeship require- ments, 44, 45, 51, 70, 76, 215n59; Black Latinas/os and Afro-Cubans in, 3, 51, 81; cigar makers versus cigar workers in, 186n4, 193n5; cigar- making process, 43–46, 204n106, 206n140; Cuban Revolution and death knell of, 173; decline of (in 1930s/1940s), 6, 7, 58, 86, 91, 132, 138, 154, 219n129; establishment and rise of (from 1860s), 1, 2, 18–19, 21, 37–47; festivals and fairs, events at, 128–29, *130,* 132, *133,* 142; in Key West, 38–40, 70; *lectura,* tradition of, 71, *71*–73, 84–85, 96, 162; mechaniza- tion of, 69, 82, 91, *93,* 94, 123, 131, 132; in post-WWII period, 143–44, 151, 154, 157, 162–63, 168–69, 173;

racial implications of, 21; small-scale enterprises (*chinchales* or buckeyes), 46, 94, 105–6, 140, 169, 223n5; Tampa, establishment in, 40–47, *44*; Tampa Board of Trade and control of workers in, 54–56; urban renewal and, 168–69, 173; Henry Wallace campaign and, 151; women and gender roles in, *xii,* 7–8, *44, 45,* 51–52, 91–94, *93,* 143–44, 169, 219n129; workplace schedules and conditions in, 50–51, 92; younger- generation Latinas/os moving away from, 125, 126, 131–32, 138. *See also* leftist/labor activism

Cigar Makers' International Union (CMIU), 59, 65–66, 69, 74–77, 79, 82–83, 85–87, 90, 94, 97, 99, 103, 123, 151, 211n27, 212n31, 212n33, 214n53, 215n59

Círculo Cubano (for white Cubans), 3, 52, 98, 106, 108, 109, *110,* 135, 158–60, 164, 213n45, 226n39

citizens' committee, 13, 56, 58, 87–88, 90, 96, 122, 145, 177, 178

citizenship: Alien Registration Act (1940), 129–31; first-generation immigrants applying for naturaliza- tion, 154; first-generation immigrants failing to change, 4; Great Depres- sion, access to relief work in, 7, 92–93; in WWII era, 107

Civil Rights Act (1866), 31, 200–201n73

civil rights movement, 135, 168, 171, 179

Civil War, 28–30, 36–37

Club Cívico (Cubans fleeing Revolu- tion), 164

El Club Nacional Cubano (interracial club), 109–11

clubs. *See centros* and *sociedades*

Cohn, Fannia, 64

Columbia Restaurant, 142

Comité de Defensa del Frente Popular Español. *See* Popular Front movement communists, communism, and CPUSA (Communist Party USA): anticommunism, and Henry Wallace campaign, 149, 150, 154; anticommunism, of Truman, 146; anticommunist feeling. rhetoric, rise of, 83–84, 86, 89, 98–99, 121–24; antifascism and, 95–96; leaders visiting Ybor City, 3, 53; membership of Ybor City residents in, 5, 11, 53, 77, 78, 122; Miami/South Florida versus Tampa/Ybor City Latina/o communities on, 14; Moreno and, 62, 63, 83, 97; post-war political activism of, 145; Russian Revolution, 78, 83; Soviet Union, 63, 121, 123–24, 149; White Municipal Party and, 12

Congress of Industrial Organizations (CIO), 53, 98, 99, 103, 123, 160

Corral Wodiska cigar factory, 92

Cortina Pinera, Gerardo, 92

Courthouse Square and Hillsborough Co. courthouse, 18, 19, 20

crackers, 27, 36, 120, 202–3n95

Crawford, Frank, 83, 86, 100

croqueta, 142

Cuba: Black Floridians migrating to, 26; *centros*, funding for, 159–60; de facto segregation in, 2, 186n8; independence from Spain, struggle for, 1, 2, 38–40, 53, 80–81, 161, 204n114, 218n92; map of Florida and Cuba, *xi*; Miami/South Florida and Tampa/Ybor City Latina/o communities, different Cuban origins of, 13–15, 164; Miss Cuba in Tampa, 128–29; Pedroso boardinghouse and government of, 160; Ten Years' War, 38. *See also* migration from Cuba to Florida

Cuba libre, 40, 156, 160

Cuban, Anglo use of, in Tampa, 120

Cuban bread, 2, 68, 125–26, 142

"The Cuban Family in Ybor City" (WPA/FWP report, 1942), 116–21

Cuban Revolution (1953–1959), 13–14, 142, 155–65

Cuban sandwich, 2, 142, 187n11

Cuban War for Independence (1895–1898), 1, 85, 100, 157, 225n22

cubanidad, 80, 217n86

cucinas economicas (soup kitchens), 75

Cuesta Rey and Company cigar factory, *xii*

danzón, 3

Darling, John, 30

Davis, Jefferson, 29

de León, Miguel Angel, 62, 67

de León, Mytyl, 58, 62, 66–67, 103

de León, Rosa Rodríguez. *See* Moreno, Luisa

de Palencia, Isabel, 98–99

de Soto, Hernando, 22, 36, 202n93

Debs, Eugene V., 3

Democratic Party, 14, 28, 31, 33, 37, 139, 141, 145, 146, 147, 166, 170

despaldilladoras (strippers), 7, 43–44, 52, 70, 76, 78

Dewey, Thomas, 149

Díaz, Adelfa, 132

Dies, Martin, 121–22, 123, 124, 129

Dorta, Armando, 158, 159

Drew Field, 132

Dworkin y Méndez, Kenya C., 50

early Latina/o community in Florida and Ybor City, 1–6, 16, 18–57; cigar industry, establishment and rise of (from 1860s), 1, 2, 18–19, 21, 37–47, 44; Civil War, Reconstruction, and post-Reconstruction politics, 28–37; community of Ybor City, 47–57; creation and construction of Ybor City, 41–43, 49; incorporation of Ybor City into Tampa, 55–56; Labor Day parade (1899), 18–21, 56; lack of natural space for Latina/o peoples in, 35–36; leftist/labor activism in, 3, 53–56; migration from Cuba to Florida, 1–4, 18–21, 47–48, 52; slaves, slavery, and freed people, 22–30, 36, 196n32, 197n38; snowbirds and early tourism, 33–35, *35*, 37; Spanish settlement and landholding, 21–25, 196n30, 198n50; statehood, Floridian acquisition of, 28–29; Tampa Board of Trade and cigar manufacturers, agreement between, 55–56; as U.S. territory (1821–1845), 24–28; West Tampa, creation and incorporation of, 46–47; white homesteading in Florida, 27–28, 36, 202–3n95

education and schools, 9, 125–28, 138, 178

Emancipation Day, 30

emigration. *See specific entries at* migration

enchilado, 142

equal pay, AFL statement on (1884), 79

escogedores (pickers), 45

Fair Play for Cuba Committee, 14, 164, 235n56

Falange, 95, 124, 134, 177

Falcón, Margot (née Blanco), 4, 6, 175

family wage, 79

fascism. *See* antifascism

Federal Housing Act, 167

Federal Theatre Project, 85

Federal Works Project (FWP), 93–94, 213n44

Federal Writers' Project (FWP), 18, 105, 113, 114, 116–19, 167, 223n1

feminism, 71–72, 77, 78

feminismo americano, 61, 210n8

Fendas, Enrique, 18

Ferlita Bakery, 174

Fernández, Eneida, 135–36

Ferrer, Ada, 156

festivals and fairs, cigar industry and Latina/o events at, 128–29, *130*, 132, *133*, 142

Fifteenth Amendment, 31

Flagler, Henry, 34–35, 37

Florida Brewing Company, 46

Florida State Fair, 129, 132, *133*, 152

Floridian Hotel, 149

Flynn, Elizabeth Gurley, 3

food and foodways: armed forces in WWII, care boxes for, 136; *cafeteros* in cigar factories, 70; cantina culture, 4, 19, 53, 68, 81, 108, 109, 158, 213nn44–45; Cuban bread, 2, 68, 125–26, 142; Cuban sandwich, development of, 2, 142, 187n11; *cucinas economicas* (soup kitchens), 75; in Great Depression, 8; mojo, 2, 187n11; in wartime economy, 133. *See also specific dishes, e.g.* croqueta

Fort Brooke, Battle of (Civil War), 36–37

Fourteenth Amendment, 31

Franco, Francisco, 95, 104, 123, 151, 177, 233n25

Frank, Andrew K., 197–98n45

Freedmen's Bureau, 31, 200n70, 201n79

Frente Popular. *See* Popular Front movement

Fuente, Arturo, 143–44, 223n5

Fugitive Slave Acts, 196n32

La Gaceta, 58, 94, 96–98, 124, 134, 136, 151, 154, 159–61, 169, 191n37, 221nn154–55, 222n174, 222n180

Galarza, Vicente, 38

Gallinor, William, 152

Gannon, Michael, 194n9

García. Jorge, 138

García y Vega cigar factory, 100, 101

Gargol, Bernardino, 40–41

gender issues. *See* women and gender

generational difference, 5–6, 8–10, 176–79; American-ness and un-American-ness, concerns about, 9, 124–28, 131, 175; cigar industry, younger-generation Latinas/os moving away from, 125, 126, 131–32, 138; citizenship status, 4, 154; in leftist/labor activism, 5–6, 8, 10, 175, 179; in post-WWII period (1948–1970), 154, 156, 163, 171–73, 178–79; university, younger-generation Latinas/os attending, 131–32, 134, 138, 143, 172, 179; in World War II era (1937–1948), 9, 124–28, 131–38

1–6, 16, 18–57 (*See also* early Latina/o community in Florida and Ybor City); generational changes in, 5–6, 8–10, 176–79 (*See also* generational difference); in Great Depression, 6–9, 16 (*See also* Great Depression; leftist/labor activism); leftist/labor activism of, 16, 58–104 (*See also* leftist/labor activism); map of Florida and Cuba, xi; Miami/South Florida Latina/o community, differentiation from, 13–15, 164; new ethnic non-Black identity, creation of, 10, 13, 171–72, 179; politics and political strategies, 10–11 (*See also* politics and political strategies); in post-WWII period (1948–1970), 9–10, 16–17, 139–74 (*See also* post-WWII period); racial issues and segregation, 11–13 (*See also* racial issues); regional and national trends, relevance to, 191–92n38; terminological use of *Latina/o* versus *Latin*, 15–16, 191n37; transnationality of, 10–11; women and gender, 10–11 (*See also* women and gender); in WWII era (1937–1948), 9–10, 16, 105–38 (*See also* World War II era). *See also specific locations in Ybor City and Tampa*

latinidad, 10, 15–16, 21, 23, 76, 116, 120, 129, 136, 139, 141, 171–72, 178–79, 217n86

lectura, tradition of, 71, 71–73, 84–85, 96, 162

leftist/labor activism, 16, 58–104; AFL and CMIU efforts to organize Ybor cigar workers, 3, 58, 59, 65–69, 74–75; anticommunism, rise of, 83–84, 86, 89, 98–99, 121, 122; changes induced by 1931 strike and 1933 agreement, 82–87; distinctive labor culture of Cuban immigrant cigar workers, 69–73, 71; early 20th century Ybor City as center of, 3, 53–56; of first versus younger generations of Latinas/os, 5–6, 8, 10, 175, 179; Great

Depression, changes wrought by, 90–94; of Key West cigar workers, 39, 40, 41; *lectura* in cigar factories, tradition of, 71, 71–73, 84–85; LGBTQ+ community and, 77–78; Martí and support for Cuban independence, 80–81, 218n92; Miami/ South Florida versus Tampa/Ybor City Latina/o communities on, 14; neighborhood solidarity behind, 75–76, 84, 100; political and vigilante efforts to suppress, 54–56, 58–59, 83–84, 86–90, 96, 100, 101; Popular Front movement, 59–60, 95–102, 121, 134, 151, 153, 177; racial politics of, 5, 11–12, 79–82, 218n92; racial segregation/integration of workers, 69, 74, 79–80, 81; relief programs, Latinas/os in, 120–21; La Sociedad de Torcedores de Tampa/La Resistencia, legacy of, 73–75; strikes and striking, 53–54, 73–78, 123, 215n57; Henry Wallace campaign and, 146–47, 149, 151, 153, 154; women's involvement in, 5–6, 6, 59–61, 64–65, 68–69, 76–79; in WWII era, 120–21, 123, 134. *See also* antifascism; Moreno, Luisa; *specific unions by name*

Lemlich, Clara, 64

Lemos, Fernando, 42

Les Misérables (Hugo), 72

Lesley, John T., 41

Lewis, John L., 98, 99

LGBTQ+ community, 77–78, 174, 216–17n80

La Liga de Costureras, 62–65, 66, 76

La Liga de Trabajadores de Cuba (League of Cuban Workers), 74

limit system, 92

Lincoln, Abraham, 29, 33

Long Seminole War, 26, 197–98n45

López, Al, 125

López, Marina (later Maseda), 141

Lowry, Sumter L., 150

lynchings, 13, 32, 56, 60, 88–89

MacDill Air Force Base, 129, 132, 164
Maceo, Antonio, 111, 225n22
MacFarlane, Hugh, 46
Machado, Gerardo, 235n54
Maella, Juan, 111
Maniscalco, Joseph, 159
Manrara, Eduardo, 41, 42
Manteiga, Roland, 169–70
Manteiga, Victoriano, 96–97, 159, 160, 163, 169, 221n155
Manufacturers Trust, 87, 91, 97
Marshall Plan, 146
Martí, José, 2, 53, 80–81, 111, 156, 157, 159–61, 163, 164, 225n22
Martínez, Bob, 155
Martínez Ybor, Vicente, 37–43, 46, 47, 49, 54–55, 137, 174
Maseda, José, 140, 231n3
Maseda, Julia, 140
Maseda, Marcelo (mayor of Ybor City), 139–41, 172
Maseda, Marina (née López), 141
Maseda, Marlene, 139–40, 141, 172
Maseda, Modesto, 140
Massey, Brad, 173
McGehee, John G., 28–29
McKay, Donald Brenham, 55
McNamara, Andrea Alfonso, 126
medical care, *centros* providing, 109, 113, 114
Medina, César Marcos, 125–26
Mexican-Americans, 147, 148
Mexico, 23, 24, 26, 62, 68, 161
Mi opinión sobre las libertades, derechos y deberes de la mujer (Capetillo), 72
Miami/South Florida and Tampa/Ybor City Latina/o communities, differentiation of, 13–15, 164
migration: from Florida to Northern states, during Depression, 6–7, 93–94; from Italy to Tampa/Ybor City, 2, 48, 49, 51, 52; Mexico, Cuba, and Haiti, Black Floridians migrating to, 26; of Moreno to New York City from Guatemala, 62; from Spain to

Tampa/Ybor City, 47–48, 49, 52, 220–21n151
migration from Cuba to Florida: after Cuban Revolution (1959), 13–14, 164–65; cigar workers, effects of immigrant status of, 69–70, 86; first wave of (1886-early 20th century), 1–4, 18–21, 47–48, 163; Key West, cigar industry in, 38–40; waves of, 163, 191n36, 235n54
Mirabal, Nancy Raquel, 109
Miranda (*croqueta* seller), 142
Modern Democrats, 88
mojadores (moisteners), 43
mojo, 2, 187n11
Molina, Natalia, 11
Moncada Barracks, Cuba, storming of (1953), 156–57, 161
Moreno, Luisa (Rosa Rodríguez de León): as AFL/CMIU organizer in Tampa, 3, 58, 59, 65–69, 90–91, 212n30; antifascist movement and, 59, 95–103, 221n154, 222n174, 222n180; background and biographical information, 58, 61–62; change of name by, 72, 209n2; collaborative leftist/labor culture of Ybor City and, 59, 61, 76, 96, 100; CPUSA and, 62, 63, 83, 97; *feminismo* and connection to women workers, 71–72, 76–77, 210n8; as labor organizer in New York City, 62–65; *latinidad* embraced by, 76; *lectores* hired by, 85; Manteiga and, 97; marriage, daughter, and household arrangements of, 58, 62, 65, 66–68; migration to/working in New York City, 62; Shoemaker lynching and, 89–90; split with AFL and CMIU, 59, 97–103; UCAPAWA, as founding member of, 103
Mormino, Gary R., 37, 136, 215n63, 229n90
Mussolini, Benito, 59
mutual aid societies. *See centros* and *sociedades*

Printed in the USA
CPSIA information can be obtained
at www.ICGtesting.com
CBHW031701120724
11514CB00005B/232